At-Risk Youth

SOURCE BOOKS ON EDUCATION
VOLUME 49
GARLAND REFERENCE LIBRARY OF SOCIAL SCIENCE
VOLUME 1021

AT-RISK YOUTH
THEORY, PRACTICE, REFORM

EDITED BY
ROBERT F. KRONICK

GARLAND PUBLISHING, INC.
NEW YORK AND LONDON
1997

Library of Congress Cataloging-in-Publication Data

At-risk youth : theory, practice, reform / edited by Robert F. Kronick
      p.   cm. — (Garland reference library of social science ;
v. 1021. Source books on education ; v. 49)
  Includes bibliographic references and index.
  ISBN 0-8153-1980-0 (alk. paper)
  1. Socially handicapped youth—Education—United States.
2. Socially handicapped youth—United States—Social conditions.
I. Kronick, Robert F. II. Series: Garland reference library of
social science ; v. 1021. III. Series: Garland reference library of
social science. Source books on education ; v. 49.
LC4091.A927 1997
371.93'08694-dc21   97-1480
                                            CIP

Printed on acid-free, 250-year-life paper
Manufactured in the United States of America

Contents

FOREWORD

How we define risk, how we think about risk, and what we do about risk are all social constructions. Unfortunately, we often define and study risk in a narrow manner, focusing on the individual who is at risk (or takes risk) rather than on the broader context that generates and sustains the risk or supports high-risk behavior. This narrow and mechanical approach is socially invidious and intellectually problematic. For example, by ignoring the ecological factors that contribute to students' leaving school, we confound dropping out with being pushed out. Dropping out is an individual phenomenon that can be aggregated into group statistics—a dropout rate—while being pushed out is a social phenomenon that is played out in individual actions. Similarly, when we ignore the social factors that contribute to a problem such as youth homicide, we end up focusing on the proximate cause (such as gangs) and ignoring such underlying factors as the number of guns in a society and the role of the media in promoting violence.

These narrow approaches ignore what sociologist Hans Spier (1969) defined as the "risk structure of a society":

> For an understanding of risk it is important to note that many risks are imposed upon man. They are suffered passively. This holds true of the derived economic risk of unemployment as well as the risk civilians and soldiers incur of being killed or maimed in war. . . . Imposed risk can lurk . . . in the form of illness, the danger of drowning, and most of the other chances of death. . . . Imposed risks may reside in the human organization of society. (Spier, p. 116)

If we are to reduce the number of dropouts and youth homicides and otherwise change social outcomes for children and youth who are placed at risk, we must address socially imposed risk factors and reconceptualize how we talk and think about "risk."

CONCEPTUALIZING BEING "AT RISK"

The constructs that we use to describe social phenomena act as lenses; they can sharpen or obscure our understanding of such phenomena. For example, we frame pushouts as dropouts (Fine, 1990). In so doing we ignore the factors that drive students out of school—the experiences of failure, boredom, cultural insult, peer rejection, and teacher hostility—and we ignore points where we can intervene successfully to prevent students from leaving school (Rumberger and Larson, 1994).

The term "at risk" is such a construction. Sometimes the term serves as a surrogate for poverty, race, or cultural group. In so doing it tends to sanitize, and paradoxically impersonalize, the historic forces of injustice and oppression that place people at risk. At other times this language suggests the intrapsychic or intrapersonal nature of risk factors, applying the logic that Ryan (1971) aptly called "savage discovery" and "blaming the victim"— focusing on the victims' differences and explaining victimization in terms of those differences rather than focusing on the social causes of victimization, be they dysfunctional public institutions or social injustice. Both formulations often lack the necessary specificity that will help target explanations and interventions—what is an individual at risk of and in what contexts?

Just as the language of risk obscures underlying factors, so studies of risk factors frequently ignore the risk structure of our society. Most studies examine risk in a narrow and mechanistic manner. These studies focus on those who are placed at risk, not the factors that place them at risk or how those factors are part of a broader historical and social context. This conceptualization, which frequently targets intrapersonal factors, focuses on the victim or proximate causes rather than on the underlying factors that contribute to sustained victimization. For example, we focus on "the poor" or "the homeless," not on the forces that contribute to and sustain poverty and homelessness. These studies, and the policies that are based on them, provide an intellectual justification for ignoring injustice whether that injustice be racial or cultural discrimination, regressive tax policies, or the maldistribution of social risks and services.

In addition, these studies lead to policies that confound remediation with prevention, and they confuse secondary prevention (intervening with a child who is already placed at risk) with primary prevention (removing the risk in the first place). Education is a case in point. We know what works for students—positive climates, clear and high performance expectations for all students, inclusionary values and practices throughout the school, relevant, engaging, and culturally and linguistically appropriate curricular instruction, and academic and social supports. We know, too, what does not work—overcrowding, insensitivity and poor accommodation of linguistic and cultural factors, poor teaching and irrelevant curriculum, a lack of academic and social supports, and a rejection of students who are at risk by teachers and peers. Yet studies of "at-risk students" frequently focus on the student who is in academic or behavioral trouble while ignoring the environment that contributes to that problem. Such approaches lead to solutions that attempt to fix (that is, remediate) the child, not to change the environment. Not surprisingly, such interventions, which often come too late, fail or fade over time, or they serve to justify the ritualistic exclusion of the "problem child" from the environment.

EDUCATION: ADDRESSING RISK FACTORS IN ONE AREA

The trajectory of behavioral and educational problems starts early for many young people. Although effective and cost beneficial success can be achieved by providing early identification and intervention, insufficient resources are devoted to this area. The structure of agencies, the lack of a continuum of available interventions, the lack of resources and support services, and a victim-blaming paradigm that minimizes the school's contribution to education and behavioral problems all contribute to the lack of successful early interventions.

Prevention ultimately depends upon addressing underlying problems such as racism, poverty, and the undermining of community support. Still, a variety of approaches will build on the strengths of young people and provide support for students and families who are placed at risk by social factors (Walker and Sylvester, 1991). For example, a comprehensive early childhood policy would help address barriers to learning at a more reachable point than later in a young person's development and before a cycle of failure, truancy, delinquency, and dropping-out has set in. Promising models exist for early interventions, including the First Steps Program in Eugene, Oregon, the Early Intervention Program in Cleveland, Ohio, and, nationally, the work of many Head Start programs.

As many of the chapters in this book reveal, schools can be transformed into supportive environments that respond to a multiplicity of student needs and strengths. The introduction of engaging and supportive learning environments that creatively incorporate learning supports, team teaching, and engaging instructional technologies can help students succeed in school. In addition, schools must focus on positive learning outcomes, valuing and addressing diversity among students, families, and staff, and reaching out to and collaborating with families in a respectful manner. Finally, attention must be paid to improving the capacity of schools and communities to address the needs of students and families though training, support, and assessment (Osher and Osher, 1995).

David Osher, Ph.D.
Senior Research Analyst
Chesapeake Foundation
Washington, DC

REFERENCES

Fine, M. (1990). *Framing dropouts: Notes on the politics of an urban public high school*. Albany: State University of New York Press.

Osher, D. M. and Osher, T. W. (1995). Comprehensive and collaborative systems that work: A national agenda. In C. M. Nelson, R. Rutherford, and B. I. Wolford (Eds.), *Developing a comprehensive system for troubled youth*. Richmond, KY: National Coalition for Juvenile Services.

Rumberger, R. and Larson, K. (1994). Keeping high-risk Chicano students in school: Lessons from a Los Angeles middle school drop out prevention program. In R. Rossi (Ed.), *Schools and Students at Risk* (141–162). New York: Teachers College Press.

Ryan, W. (1971). *Blaming the victim*. New York. Random House.

Spier, H. (1969). Social order and the risks of war: Papers in political sociology. Cambridge, MA: MIT Press.

U.S. Department of Education, Office of Research, Office of Education Research and Improvement (1993). *Educational reforms and students at risk: A review of the current state of the art*. Washington, DC: Author.

Walker, H. and Sylvester, R. (1991). Where is school along the path to prison? *Educational Leadership, 48*(1). 14–16.

Prefatory Note

In 1913 Helen Todd, a factory inspector in Chicago, systematically questioned 500 children of immigrants about working and going to school: Would they choose to continue working long hours in the sweat shops, or would they choose to go to school if they did not have to work? Four hundred and twelve children told her that they preferred factory labor to the monotony, humiliation, and even sheer cruelty that they experienced in school.* This book is an attempt to put an end to that line of thinking and to promote the concept of the school as a human service agency. We believe that it is no longer a question of whether the school will be a parent or not; the question is whether it will be a good parent.

The school as a human service agency can go a long way toward reducing our criminal and psychiatric populations, our welfare rolls, and our indigents in need of medical care.

All of us who participated in this book are committed not only to the acquisition of knowledge by students, but also to the prevention and remediation of problems for all those at-risk students whom we have yet to serve.

---

*Kliebard, H. (1986). *The struggle for the American curriculum: 1893–1958*. Boston: Routledge and Kegan Paul.

PART I
OVERVIEW

1 AT-RISK YOUTH

THE STATE OF THE ART

Robert F. Kronick

The National Center for Educational Statistics (NCES) has developed the following three methods of measuring dropouts. The *event rate* measures the proportion of students who drop out in a single year without completing high school. This tells us how many students are leaving school each year and allows year by year comparisons. The *status rate* measures the proportion of the total United States population who have not completed high school and who are not enrolled at a certain point in time regardless of when they dropped out. Status dropout rates reveal the extent of the dropout problem in the population. The status rate is an accumulative rate and thus is higher than the event dropout rate. The *cohort rate* measures what happens to a single group of students over a period of time. The cohort rate tells how many students in the ninth grade graduated four years later. It assumes equal in and out migration, and controls for early graduation and death. (NCES 1992)

Each of these measurements will lead to a different rate. Administrators and policy makers will be affected differently by each of these three methods. According to the NCES, the dropout rate is going down and has been doing so for the past 20 years. The Center for the Study of Social Policy, however, in 1993 came up with the opposite conclusion. According to this group, the percent of students graduating from high school from 1985 to 1990 decreased for whites, African Americans, and Hispanics. Yet the National Center for Educational Statistics claims that the dropout rate for blacks has decreased and that the gap between blacks and whites has lessened. These contradictory findings reflect the use of different definitions of "dropouts," different interpretations of the data, different data, or an ideological mandate of one type or another.

A recent study funded by the Rand Corporation casts yet another shadow on data about at-risk youth. This study claims that, in regard to at-risk youth, things are actually getting better. It finds that prior research, contrary to public opinion, has reported gains in student performance between 1970 and 1990 as measured by nationally representative test score data (Grissmer et al., 1994).

According to Grissmer et al., the largest gains were made by minority students, although a substantial gap still remains. The study attributes the rise in performance to changes in the family, especially to the parents' level of education. Other family characteristics cited were parents working or in the home, family size, income, and mother's age at child's birth. They also point out that public programs aimed at minorities must have had some positive effect.

One of the most telling statements from this study is the following:

> Research also indicates that mixed evidence—for example, evidence that N.A.E.P. scores are moving in an opposite direction from that of the S.A.T. scores—often results in stronger, not weaker, trust in the originally held belief (Nisbett & Ross, 1980). (Cited in Grissmer et al., 1994, p. 5)

It appears from this remark that we have a difficult time giving up old ideas about at-risk youth. Nonetheless, it is easy to see that, when it comes to data about at-risk youth, the information simply isn't there, or it is everywhere and we just can't make sense out of it. Grissmer et al. also relate that there is little agreement about what has caused the changes in national test scores in the last 25 years—and indeed, there are even differences in perception about what the direction of these scores has been. It may be that people tend to select and read information that agrees with their prior expectations. Hence it is extremely important that we begin to understand the extant data and that we be able to link test score information and dropout rates to prior independent variables so that interventions and policy decisions can be made.

The stakes are very high in this scenario, and this may account for the variation in reported findings in what is happening regarding America's school-age children. From a draconian perspective, school systems would like to see the dropout rate as low as possible. A high dropout rate reflects poorly on a school. Schools claim that researchers want to find a high dropout rate so that they can get grants to study the situation. It seems that, as so often is the case, the parts of the system are not working together. Thus we see emerging a problem of definition as well as a problem of teamwork.

Gordon and Yowell (1994) state that early usage of the term "at-risk" tended to focus on physical characteristics such as blindness, deafness, and mobility difficulties. They point out that health is highly correlated with school attendance and consequently with appropriate school behaviors, learning, and dropping out. Nonetheless, we have seen a move toward social circumstances such as race, gender, socio-economic status, and ethnicity in defining who is at-risk. Gordon and Yowell conclude that:

> At-risk status is a function of the inappropriateness of developmental environments to meet the needs of the person, and that a focus on these deficient environments may be more productive than a focus on the characteristics of the persons. We can then define at-risk as referring to a category of persons whose personal characteristics, conditions of life, situational circumstances, and interactions with each other make it likely that their development and/or education will be less than optimal. (1994, p. 53)

This definition is in strong concert with our emphasis on person-environment or person-context interaction. It is our contention that emphasis must be placed on the interaction of the person and the environment and that all parts of the system must be worked with together or there will be only failure for those who are most at risk.

It might move us along in getting past the problems of definition and teamwork if we were to take a systems look at the magnitude of the problem and try to put it into perspective with other social problems.

An entity is part of a system if a change in one brings about a change in another. Parts of the at-risk dropout system include, at a minimum, health, mental health, and corrections. Thus if a systems approach is applied a change in one must bring about a change in another or the parts do not constitute a system. A change in the education and treatment of children, beginning at the preschool level and when the school is a human service agency or part of the human service system, is a change in philosophy and practice that must be made. Emergence of a child's personality and capabilities results from an interplay between the common stages of development and the social institutions that form the child's environment. Children's development can be enhanced by changing the institutions with which they interact. As in any ecological system, change in one element precipitates change throughout the system to create meaningful change. Attention must be given to interactions among the multiple institutions that comprise the system. The developmental perspective suggests that initiatives target early periods in children's lives to prevent later problems so that gains can be sustained

(Weiner and Quaranta, 1992). Regardless of the number of at-risk students, it is too many. My inclination is that the NCES data is not accurate and that the number of at-risk children in America today is not only high but also costly to the individual at risk as well as to society at large. This cost can be expressed in terms both personal and monetary.

There is a need to intervene and reduce the number of dropouts because of some of the following reasons: (1) there aren't and won't be enough qualified workers to support those in retirement; (2) dropouts will be underemployed and not contribute much to the tax base; (3) being underemployed, they won't make enough money to keep themselves off welfare; and (4) there are enormous costs to support people who are over-represented on welfare rolls, prisons, and psychiatric hospitals and who are generally in poor health. Thus if intervention is not the right thing to do humanistically it is the right thing to do economically. By not focusing on and intervening with at-risk youth and their families we incur direct costs for care and incarceration as well as lose income opportunities because of unemployment. Rumberger (1987) has studied the economics of dropping out for the past decade and states: "In short dropouts are costly. One year's cohort of dropouts from Los Angeles city schools was estimated to cost 3.2 billion in lost earnings and more than 400 million dollars in social services." Stringfield (1994), in developing his notion of high-ability schools, makes this comment in regard to economics: "It would cost less to provide highly reliable schools for students at risk than to pay for continued expansion of welfare, police, and prison programs."

The cogency of need is also there because of the cyclical nature of this problem. Parents who did not graduate from high school are less likely to want their children to graduate than do those parents who did graduate from high school.

Let us return to our systems analysis. If we intervene at the schoolhouse, this intervention should bring about changes in welfare, corrections, health, and mental health, and they are all part of the same system. So let's see if this can be made into a system and if the systems approach can bring about necessary changes for the overall well-being of those targeted individuals and consequently for society as a whole.

I would like to put forth the argument that intervention with preschool children is prevention for prisons, psychiatric hospitals, and welfare rolls. If this philosophy were to be adopted and actions were to subsequently follow, other philosophical ideas would be forced to change and, subsequently, interventions would have to be recast to address the at-risk dropout population. This will have a tremendous ripple effect for those who are preparing the teachers and human service workers of tomorrow.

Before moving on let us return to the classic work of Abraham Maslow (1970). Every beginning human service worker, including teachers, should be familiar with Maslow's hierarchy of needs. The important point is that, following Maslow, the system must meet the child's lower needs before addressing the higher level needs. The child must come to school fed, clothed, rested, and unafraid before learning can be attempted. The school as a human service system must take responsibility to see that this is done.

The philosophy stated above will rankle some, especially those who believe that excellence is being passed by at the expense of equity. Nevertheless, it is a philosophy addressing realities that cannot be ignored if safety, security, and future well-being are going to be important to Americans in the 21st century.

It is critical that students in America be educated and socialized in the coming years by a school system that believes in working with the total person as well as valuing the acquisition of knowledge. It is not enough to focus on the learning needs of the child while ignoring his health, safety, and welfare needs. This does not mean that the school should cast out a net and catch all the deviants it can and refer them to corrections, mental health, welfare, or some other human service agency. It does mean that the school system should play a meaningful role in the holistic care of the children it refers for help, however help might be defined.

If the school is a human service agency, the necessary parts of the human service system will be on-site at the school. This will facilitate a quicker response to the problems and increase the probability of a team approach in addressing the child's needs. This type of systems approach will signify a proactive rather than a reactive approach. It would also fit into the philosophy of prevention that must be ever present, but rarely is, and lead to more humane and more effective delivery of service.

It should be pointed out that not only would human service workers be on site at the school, but also that the building would be open for extended hours during the week, perhaps from seven a.m. to ten p.m., for activities such as family conferences, counseling, or alcohol and drug meetings. The building would also be available on weekends for participatory athletics, arts and crafts, dance, etc. The school would be a reflection of the community. With a stake in what is going on within the school, students, parents, and teachers are more likely to take a positive role in the school's activities and, at the very least, not destroy what is going on in the community-based school system (Weiner and Quaranta, 1992).

Teamwork is an important concept for human service workers and teachers alike. Brill (1976) pointed out the importance of this process 20 years ago. Yet the academy needs to spend more time articulating this concept to student human services workers and teachers and facilitating their practicing teamwork. Students in the human services and teaching appear to have little knowledge of or experience with teamwork. We must pay more attention to this important, but often overlooked or taken for granted, process. As any sports fan knows, a team spends many more hours in practice than it does in games. The point is not to copy athletics but only to stipulate that practice in human service work, especially work in teams, is needed. Working in teams will help to cut down on turfism and reduce the number of clients that fall through the cracks due to system ineffectiveness.

A study by Meares in 1986, assessing the status of social work practice in the schools, shows that although practice was in transition away from a clinical casework approach to a systems change model, the collaboration and teamwork necessary to achieve these goals was not being practiced.

Teams could be made up of physicians, nurses, social workers, psychologists, and rehabilitation counselors, along with human service workers. In using a team model there may be a dominant profession involved—medicine, for instance—and this creates its own set of problems. It would then behoove educators within the academy to help students to practice group process and teamwork while they are in school. Obviously this is being done in some academic settings, possibly in Counseling Psychology, but it likely is not done enough. Let it not go unsaid that teamwork is only one approach to reach clients and is not to be used in all situations. Human services will find methods to fit the problems and not force problems into existing methods.

Teamwork can be viewed at the levels of the individual and the agency. At the level of the agency what is needed is interagency collaboration; what we advocate here is school-human service agency collaboration. Individuals in this collaboration would be the family and other seemingly tangential aspects of the community, such as parks and recreational facilities. The school is a natural place in which to work with the family because "the family," regardless of its configuration, is going to be at the school.

The ideal arrangement for the school as a human service agency is one where there are self-actualizing people who can effectively deal with cognitive dissonance, working in an open climate. The people are neither too stiff nor too casual, and the organization is not overly rigid; a classic bureaucracy will not work here, nor will one work where things are so loose that boundaries get lost. The idea is that the school as a human service agency is at an organizational level of development where it has moved beyond the collection of individuals or a collaborative group to an interdependence of persons and organizational frameworks. Optimal permeability combined with the true team player who is excited about kids leads to optimal organization interaction. The end result is a new organizational configuration, where turfism and old allegiances go by the boards, and new allegiances to the school/human service agency are forged. The team is the school.

The school-agency collaboration and teamwork provide opportunities for the delivery of a wide variety of services while at the same time reaching the child and several constellations that interact with him or her, including siblings, parents, and even extended family who may need services but do not seek them out.

It can generally be assumed that people do not have one problem; they have multiple problems. Therefore what the helper may be seeing is the presenting but not the real problem. An important point to remember when working with at-risk students is that they have problems in living although they are not sick and in need of healing. A concomitant point to keep in mind is to refrain from using a deficit model, where the strengths of the client are not considered or used. As stated above, we are working with people who have problems in living, not people who are problems.[1] If we move away from the deficit model we will remove some of the following barriers that keep people, including at-risk children and their families, from coming for services.

Mandell and Schram list nine barriers that exist in delivery of human services. These barriers are especially true for at-risk children.

1. *The difficulty of knowing how serious the problem is.* The problem of definition of dropouts leads to the problem of not knowing how many dropout students there are. School districts that are defensive hold the dropout figures down, while the districts that might want grant funds push the figures up. In most instances, because of the problems of definition and data gathering, the school districts don't know what the dropout rate is.

2. *The need to deny the gravity of the problem.* As stated above, the school system may not want to report the dropout level for fear that it might reflect negatively on the system. This may lead to shakeups within the system and realignment of job positions.

3. *The fear of being judged, labeled, or punished.* School systems, being the political animals they are, certainly do not want to be labeled as failures in the schooling of our children.

4. *The suspicion or distrust of human service workers and agencies.* Given the fact that so many families have had experiences with human ser-

vice agencies, not all of which have been favorable, it is no surprise that they may be reluctant to come forward to ask help for their child who is not doing well or simply not going to school. Items 1, 2, and 3 also suggest why the client rather than the school might be reluctant to apply for help.

5. *The shame of not being able to solve one's own problems.* This feeling can also be attributed to the school system as well as to the family. In fact, this dichotomy between school and family may be artificial in trying to describe the problems of at-risk children where the child's problems in living are ecological.

6. *Fear of the unknown, of change, and of unpredictability.* Those of us who have been in human service work know that too often the system is where intervention is needed, but too seldom is this where it is actually done. Throughout this text we have seen that the school system is resistant to change.

7. *The inadequacy of services.* Many students and families have had an unfavorable experience with a human service agency and believe that this will generalize to future situations. Primers on how to be good consumers would be useful for clients who find the human service system mystifying. Human services may be inadequate due to lack of funding or may appear inadequate to the client because of his or her lack of experience with the system.

8. *The difficulties of choosing the appropriate program and helper.* As mentioned above, the human service system is mystifying to many people and choosing the appropriate program or helper is most difficult. The problem of whether the child has a learning disability or is emotionally disturbed is typical of the dilemma of which programs or helpers to choose. Many of these families have been going to human service providers with their myriad problems for years and see little if any progress being made.

9. *Public image of the program may keep many potential clients from seeking services.* The school, too, may have a negative image. Consequently, many parents express no disapproval of, and often support, their children in leaving school. (Mandell and Schram, 1985, pp. 17–18)

There is an array of human services for at-risk children and their families. The issue is how to get the services to those who need them.

PERSON-ENVIRONMENT INTERACTION: THE SCHOOL AND HUMAN SERVICES

In working with a slippery topic such as at-risk children, it may become all too easy to sink into reductionist thinking because the issue is so difficult. Focusing exclusively on the person, or possibly even victim-blaming, yields one set of responses, albeit an incomplete one. Focusing exclusively on the school leads to the same simplistic type of answers; only the content will differ.

McPartland (1994) has devised a nifty paradigm with which he examines and tests school and outside effects. The school effects are defined in terms of opportunity for success or human climate of caring and support. Outside effects are seen in terms of relevance of school, the student's community, future, and help with the student's personal problems. McPartland has also devised a scheme in which these variables can be operationalized, measured, and tested. McPartland's work is certainly the beginning of theory generation and testing in the area of at-risk, dropout, and pushout youth.

Some very interesting and useful information emerges from McPartland's work. He points out that grades need to be looked at in a new light. They need to be more than artificial devices to label students. Grades may be nothing more than a way to confine students in a situation that is neither beneficial or even benign to them. Hargis (1990) takes an even more radical position on grades than McPartland and recommends doing away with them. He recommends tailoring the curriculum to the student; he also avers that the lockstep curriculum pushes students out of school, and grades are a key factor in the lockstep curriculum.

McPartland, when he stresses the importance of a student's need to see opportunities for success, may not be going so far as Hargis, but both want students to perceive that there is an opportunity for success in school and that this is a school effect. The second dimension of school effects McPartland calls the human climate of caring and concern. He operationalizes this concept based on whether or not the school provides testing and counseling.

The concept of social climate has tremendous ramifications for at-risk students in that it is possible that a positive social climate, or one operationalized as open by Moos (1970), could overcome the negative characteristics that the at-risk child has. It must be remembered that it is the perception of these characteristics and the resulting self-fulfilling prophecies, rather than the characteristics themselves, that put the child at risk.

It might be imagined that a school with a positive or open climate, such as one where the building is a clean, well-lighted place where teachers empower students and where the student feels autonomous, could in a sense overcome at-risk factors of students, causing them to learn, be excited about learning, and stay in school. Kronick (1972) found that students who had perceived at-risk characteristics—male, low IQ scores, low SES, and were black, but saw the school as open on the Moos social climate scale—made higher grades than those students who were female, had high IQ scores, were middle or high SES, and were white, but who saw the school climate as closed. These findings came from eighth grade students in a mid-sized southern town. It must be noted that the subsample sizes were small. Nonetheless, there is a glimmer of hope that school effects can make a difference, and it is not money that is being talked about.

McPartland's outside effects are: 1) relevance of school to student's community and future operationalized as employment services; and 2) help with the student's personal problems operationalized as tutoring and counseling and social services. On this item McPartland found tutoring and counseling more highly loaded with personal problems than social services. This is an important finding and worthy of discussion. Earlier we allude to the school as a human service agency. It is now time to develop this notion more fully.

The surprising finding that social services is not the place where students and families look for help with their personal problems may result from the fact that they are not used to social or human services being provided via a school system. If these services were always provided via the schools, students and families would come to expect these services and would use them. The school might begin its role as a human service agency by doing outreach.

Dryfoos (1990) cites evidence that early school failure is the "single event that predicts insurmountable barriers to life's opportunities." Echoing some of the themes expressed by Schorr (1989), she offers a comprehensive, multicomponent framework for linking educational enrichment with social supports. Also, documenting research supporting the inability of fragmented programs to produce the necessary changes, Dryfoos states that the highest priority should be given to school reform. Dryfoos concludes that in a multidisciplinary, comprehensive, and community-wide approach encompassing educational services, health services, and the familial and cultural needs of high-risk children, the primary institution has to be the local school.

The school as a human service agency would do well to observe the following guidelines, delineated by Kronick and Hargis, in working with students and their families:

1. *People are perceived as having problems in living.* This is opposed to seeing people as problems themselves, or sick. It moves away from deviance and deficit models of understanding human behavior.

2. *People rarely have one problem.* Often the presenting problem is only that and must be dealt with first, even though there are more pressing problems in the person's life.

3. *The person should be worked with as a total person.* Too often

persons are compartmentalized and only one aspect of them is dealt with. This leaves many other parts of their lives unattended. It is these unattended parts that often are in need of service. If the total person is worked with, then real change may come about.

Lizbeth Schorr (1989) quoting David Rogers, President of the Robert Wood Johnson Foundation, points out that "human misery is generally the result of or accompanied by a great untidy basketful of intertwined and interconnected circumstances and happenings." Logically this statement suggests that solutions need to be similarly intertwined and interconnected. In her examination of the problem of adolescents with "rotten outcomes"—youth who have children during adolescence, leave school illiterate, commit crimes, and are unskilled—she concludes that "risk factors are multiplicative (they are not merely found together, but reinforce each other), and the earlier the intervention the more promise of positive outcomes."

4. *Prevention is to be strived for.* In creating the school as a human service agency the opportunity for prevention is right there. Not only could the school as a human service agency work with the individual student, it could also work with younger siblings who are probably at risk, older siblings who might want to return to school but don't know how, parents who may want help with parenting skills, and provide an array of other services that would meet the needs of people within this family. Prevention is cost effective and humane. It needs to be done. Better to pay for prenatal care than the needs of a handicapped child, especially if these handicapping conditions could have been prevented.

5. *Services to students and their families need to be coordinated.* Too often a student is being seen by a mental health counselor or probation counselor, and the family has a welfare counselor, and none of the three knows what any other is doing. Coordination could be done using the school human service agency as the pivotal player. By having human service personnel on site at the school an array of services that does prevention, intervention, and remediation may be offered to all members of the client system (Kronick and Hargis, 1990).

Schorr, analyzing programs that are successful in reaching and helping the most disadvantaged children and families, made several conclusions about the programs' essential characteristics: they offer a broad spectrum of services; they are flexible; they cross traditional bureaucratic boundaries; they see the child in the context of family and the family in the context of its surroundings; they offer services that are coherent and easy to use; they provide continuity and communicate a sense of respect and care in common;

they go beyond bureaucratic and traditional professional expectations if the needs of those they serve are at stake.

Human service professionals will be proactive persons whom the student will know. They will not be sitting in their offices at the school waiting for referrals. They will be team players who are seen as assets rather than liabilities by teachers and principals. If problem situations can be attacked at the schoolhouse through service coordination, services will be delivered in a timely and cost-effective fashion.

The human services school based on the above five principles will educate the child in a holistic fashion, meeting the more basic needs of safety and survival and then moving on to the higher level needs of learning that will occur once safety and security have been assured.

This philosophy of school and human services collaboration will add to the work of the school but at the same time it will illustrate very clearly that a child's school failure is not the result of the school alone. When teenage girls leave school because they are pregnant and boys leave to find jobs it is more than a school problem that is being faced.

IMPACT ON INSTITUTIONS OF HIGHER LEARNING

If the school as a human service agency philosophy is to emerge into the field, colleges of education are going to have to make some changes. These changes may be characterized as moves "back to the future" if we pay heed to the AACTE Human Services Education Commission (1990) and Nash and Ducharme (1976). The Commission argued that in the light of the emerging human services society the teaching profession should broaden its range of vision beyond mere classroom competence. The goal was to produce a new kind of professional called a human services educator. Nash and Ducharme (1976) defined the human services educator as, foremost, a teacher, able to help people discover and use more effective and satisfying means to improve themselves through organizations and other social institutions. Nash and Ducharme contend that the human service educator must be willing to take a strong public position against the massive human misery that exists in cities, towns, nursing homes, prisons, schools, and other social institutions. This is exactly the posture that the human service educator must take in dealing with dropouts or at-risk students. It is with this type of passion, concern, and knowledge that working with at-risk students can be seen as prevention for welfare, corrections, bad health, and mental illness.

The AACTE Human Services Education Commission foresaw the day when colleges of education would become colleges of education for human services. Corrigan (1990) states that teaching and teacher education should be reconceptualized as an interdisciplinary activity, and schools and colleges of education should be seen as part of the human service delivery system. Following from this philosophy would be the differentiation of roles both in schools and in a variety of human service settings that would characterize teaching. Support systems could be established in which teachers share their specific knowledge and skills with other human service professionals. It goes without saying that these changes in schools and colleges of education include political, economic, and social reforms as well as educational ones. The human services practitioner would be a broad-based professional, a humanistic generalist, who could respond to a variety of ad hoc needs wherever and whenever they arise in the community (Corrigan, 1990). A human services educator (or provider) must be able to work in a variety of situations to make immediate responses and interact directly with people. This direct interaction includes being an active listener, showing empathy, knowing what services are available and how to make referrals to them. Other roles that the human service worker can play are outreach worker, advocate, educator, teacher educator, behavior changer, mobilizer, consultant, care giver, data manager, and administrator. These roles were suggested by the Southern Regional Education Board (SREB) in 1969.

It is unlikely that the SREB and the AACTE knew of each other but what they have outlined is astonishingly similar, albeit 20 years apart. It appears now, more than at any other time in history, that human services and education must, should, and can forge an alliance to meet the ecological needs of children.

Emerging programs that reflect the above philosophy and show the efficacy of collaboration have been described by Corrigan (1993) and Weiner and Quaranta (1992). Corrigan (1993) states:

> Central to the position of interprofessional education as a means of reforming education, health, and human services is recognizing that Colleges of Education, schools, and community agencies are interacting components of one system. In this system schools are a locus of advocacy for all children, the poor, the deprived as well as the rich and powerful. Because the school is the only community institution that sees every child every day, school leaders must accept the responsibility for helping mobilize community resources. (p. 6)

Corrigan's emphasis on systems is in concert with what we have presented earlier in this chapter. There can be no substitute for a systemic approach to this set of problems surrounding at-risk children. Corrigan says, "More than ever it is time to get the guy throwing the bodies in the water rather than just fishing them out," and goes on to say, "Tomorrow's schools will be the hub of a community network for facilitating access to the human services. They will be full service interprofessional schools" (Corrigan, 1993, p. 6).

The interprofessional dimension being advocated by Corrigan should be built into schools at the front end where education, health, and human services will work together as a team, not merely co-exist. As mentioned earlier, teamwork could be practiced in colleges of education and implemented by school personnel as well as health and human services workers.

As Corrigan cogently states:

> When one steps into a school today it does not take long to realize that the persistent life situation of many of today's students needs a multiple agency, multiple professional response—drugs, suicide, AIDS, teenage pregnancy, crime, jobs, poverty, and so forth. (1993, p. 6)

This paragraph captures the essence of what we are up against and illustrates the fact that we can no longer ignore or fail to put in place holistic programs for children.

Weiner and Quaranta (1992) also support collaboration between education and human services. They view the services of the teacher and the social worker as complementary in addressing the learning and skill development needs of the student. They propose collaboration among and between professions as a strategy for meeting the educational and social needs of disadvantaged students. In their view this collaboration needs to be addressed by the graduate schools as they prepare future educators and social workers to meet these needs.

Weiner and Quaranta support what we are proposing in this chapter regarding collaboration between education and human services broadly conceived. They tend, however, to focus on social work rather than on the broader field of human service providers. We would not support the notion that the only human service providers to work with colleges of education and schools should be social workers. With this point made, let's see what Weiner and Quaranta have to say that we can agree with regarding school and human service collaboration as a method of keeping more students in school.

The government's role in education and human service collaboration is exemplified by the Family Support Act of 1988, which emphasized partnerships between the welfare community and education. The act sees education as a central element in helping families avoid long-term dependence on public assistance. It requires states to make services available to participants by forging critical connections between schools and support services, expanding the range and capacity of educational programs for learners at risk, reducing the number of at-risk learners by creating innovative and more effective early intervention and prevention approaches, and building a more comprehensive and effective system for all youth and adults at risk (Weiner and Quaranta, 1992).

SCHOOL-HUMAN SERVICE PROGRAMS

The following programs are in various phases of development and show various levels of success even as we write. The interested reader could check Weiner and Quaranta as well as Orr (1987) for a more detailed analysis of ongoing programs.

Professional Development Schools, a part of the educational reform movement of the mid-1980s, are designed to bring about change in the world of practice as well as in colleges and universities. According to Nystrand (1991), the literature regarding PDSs is characterized by a lack of research about, or even descriptions of, them.

The Holmes Group (1990, 1–2) states that PDSs should help the teaching profession by: (1) promoting much more ambitious conceptions of teaching and learning on the part of prospective teachers in universities and students in school; (2) insuring that intriguing, relevant, responsible research and development are done in schools; (3) creating incentives for faculties in public schools and in education schools to work mutually; and (4) strengthening the relationship between schools and the broader political, social, and economic communities in which they reside.

By focusing on point four above, we should see some broad-based change in education that will impact on the preparedness of teachers, teachers in the field, new teachers, and human services workers so that education, as we know it today, can be changed radically in order to meet the needs of the total student. Houston (1992) suggests nine standards for assessing Professional Development Schools. Only one is cited here, but it is of special relevance for at-risk learners. She suggests that:

> Students be provided new opportunities to demonstrate their knowledge and know-how in ways that are responsibly diverse, thus providing teachers, parents, policy makers, and students themselves with multiple and authentic indices of learning. (Houston, 1992, p. 7)

This approach is in strong agreement with Hargis's (1990) Curriculum Based Assessment, where the curriculum is tailored to the student rather than have the child fit into a lockstep curriculum.

An ongoing project based on this model using diverse forms of evaluation is discussed by Higginbotham in Chapter 10. At-risk students appear to do well where learning environments are flexible and forms of evaluation such as portfolios are used. Students who are truant begin coming to school and learning when the school meets them halfway by knowing them as persons, treating them with respect, giving them assignments the teachers know they won't fail, and presenting material in a non-stand-and-deliver fashion only. The material presented is relevant to students in their daily lives.

Another program that bears discussion along with Professional Development Schools is what Stringfield (1994) terms High Reliability Organizations (HROs). These organizations are characterized by:

1. *Clarity of goals.* Educators should not be reticent about what their problems are.

2. *Optimum operating procedures.* Teddlie and Stringfield (1993) found that a higher rate of teacher consistency was clearly related to principals' behavior and not to the income level of the communities being served.

3. *Staff recruitment and training.* We may have higher standards for our students than for our teachers. Teacher training programs are trying various program alliances to better prepare teachers. One of the most promising alliances is between colleges of education and colleges of arts and sciences.

4. *Correction of procedural problems.* Levels of trust between community, administrators, teachers, parents, and students have too often not been high and have got in the way of correcting problems. Some localities, of course, deny that problems of any nature exist at all.

5. *Attention to performance evaluation.* This would allow for changes to be made while the evaluation is ongoing. Indicators for measuring outcome evaluation should be established at the very beginning of the project.

6. *Mutual monitoring by administration and staff.* This would help to prevent gridlock in a top-down type of organization. Monitoring and evaluation should go on throughout the organization not just in isolated pockets, such as direct service staff only.

7. *Vigilance to system lapse.* A refining of the team concept discussed in this chapter would be immensely helpful in this area. Teamwork is not something that can be worked on too often when facing at-risk students.

8. *Reliance on staff competence.* In an effort at team building and teamwork, staff competence must be recognized, acknowledged, and utilized

regardless of the status position(s) of the person(s) involved. Nicholas Hobbs (1982), in his discussion of re-education, develops a thorough and well thought out model that utilizes the concept of teams and teamwork as well as staff competence. His description of the *educateur*, which he developed after World War II, is an example of staff competence and teamwork being elevated beyond credentials.

9. *Flexibility toward rules.* It appears throughout the literature that this is something that has been ignored at a variety of levels, and yet flexibility seems to be highly correlated with successes in working with at-risk students, if not all students. There needs to be some flexibility in our rules structure. This is covered in depth by Rumberger and Larson (1994) in their work with Latino students, but it appears that the notion of flexibility could certainly be carried over to other types of students.

10. *The interdependence of staff.* In looking at cross-classroom and cross-grade coordination, Stringfield (1994) found positive predictions of school effects in terms of the outcome for at-risk students. His work shows that, when cross-grade and cross-classroom coordination are carried out, students learn much better. This appears to be almost like a self-fulfilling prophecy and is reminiscent of Levin's (1988) concept of accelerated schools, where he likes to see at-risk students taught as if they were gifted.

Another program is what Fine (1994) terms Charter Schools. Fine, like so many other scholars writing today, sees children who are at risk of dropping out of school as victims of circumstance. She defines the problem as residing within the context of school. Fine places great emphasis on the concept of community in describing charters. Charter schools are concerned with the total person. This is reminiscent of what has already been said in this chapter. We must work with the whole person, "fix a leak rather than merely clean up the water." Schools too often demur by saying that the personal life of the student is more than they can or should contend with. Charter schools handle this dilemma by seeing themselves as both intellectual and emotional communities. Fine states that "charters are a compelling vehicle through which a sense of connection among teachers, students, and parents has evolved. Charters are a place where at-risk can transform into resilience in a community."

Charters bring about a sense of mind also. They attempt to bring forth the positive thought process of all those involved in the school, where the attitude moves from this-is-the-way-it-has-always-been to thinking about what can be. This ideology grows out of what we know about self-fulfilling prophecies. It is a breath of fresh air when we see organizations having positive influences, especially people-processing organizations. The work of

Rosenthal (1968), in what he termed the Pygmalion Effect, also applies here, and Erving Goffman's study of asylums (1961) is cogent with Fine's concept of charters.

There are six attributes that characterize Charter Schools, according to Fine. They are:

1. *Governance.* Administrative decisions are based on principles of shared decision making.

2. *School organization.* There is a move away from the bureaucratic handling of human needs. Decisions are made within the charters.

3. *Professional development.* Teachers develop curricula that actually engage students in multicultural collaboration and, in some instances, in accelerated learning.

4. *Community.* Parents are actively involved. Access to community services is implemented as part of the curriculum. The school is a human service agency!

5. *Assessment/Evaluation.* Assessment includes traditional and non-traditional methods. Performance-based assessment strategies are central here.

6. *Partnerships.* There is a focus on transitions. Charters are the locus for school-based partnerships with universities, social service agencies, and employers. Resources are diverted toward transitions into ninth grade and into high school. (Fine, 1994, pp. 164–165)

Fine has a cogent paragraph that sums up what dealing with dropouts entails:

> The emotional, social, and psychological challenges of young adolescents are played out in our schools, masked as attendance problems, acting out, discipline, or even learning problems. We now know in Charters that the problems of at-risk youth can often be unraveled to reflect homelessness, family or community violence, learning difficulties, or cultural differences—the kinds of issues public education has extensively stayed away from. We now know that young people import these issues into our schools. (Fine, 1994, p. 177)

In sum, charter schools play a prominent role in the development of the idea of the school as a human service agency in dealing with dropouts in a school setting as a form of prevention and intervention.

Rumberger and Larson (1994) describe a program for Latino students in Los Angeles that targets the fastest growing segment of the population in American schools today, a segment that has one of the highest dropout rates.

Achievement For Latinos Through Academic Success (ALAS) bears a strong resemblance to programs already described in this chapter. ALAS is designed to enhance the traditional urban, middle, and secondary school experiences of high-risk Hispanic students outside regular classroom activities. ALAS attends to the needs of the total child by being flexible and individualizing. Here again we see an urgency to meet the needs of the total child by focusing on both school and nonschool issues.

Cities In Schools, an organization in Alexandria, Virginia, states its mission as being

> . . . the need to address the critical issues of at-risk youths, such as school attendance; literacy; job preparedness; teenage pregnancy; drug and alcohol abuse; teen suicide; and school violence, by developing public/private partnerships designed to coordinate the delivery of appropriate existing health, social, and other support services at educational sites in a personable and accountable manner. (Cities In Schools Documents, 1994, p. 9)

This philosophy presupposes that there are existing services and focuses on the coordination of those services. The assumption that these services already exist may, in fact, not be true. However, if the assumption is accurate, then the emphasis on coordination is important and relevant. If the needed programs and services do not exist, coordination of insufficient services would be foolhardy.

Findings so far reveal that massive overhauls rather than add-on programs are needed. Nonetheless, presuppositions of Cities In Schools must be taken into account when considering the development of programs for at-risk students. The five presuppositions of Cities In Schools are:

1. *Students frequently leave school for reasons unrelated to school.* We have already covered this point in this chapter, but suffice it to say that out-of-school experiences may be more powerful than in-school experiences at putting students at risk. These would include alcohol, tobacco, drug abuse, violence, and divorce.

2. *Many services/resources already exist to deal with the reasons students leave school.* This is accurate, but what we are advocating here is a systems approach, which requires a different type of thinking than has usually been followed. Since this requires circular rather than linear thinking, coordination would be an important factor.

3. *What is needed is a process to coordinate our resources.* The human services field, including education, can expect a steady amount of dol-

lars, if not shrinking dollars, over the next decade. Hence, carefully marshaling our resources is critical, and coordination will help greatly in this process.

4. *Change must come from within and cannot be imposed from without.* The city of Charlotte, NC, has one of the most successful CIS programs in existence. Even though Charlotte has experienced a great deal of immigration from other parts of the country, it appears that native Charlottoneans were the driving force behind the program. The CIS program in Charlotte also revealed the importance of the support of business and community leaders. Nation's Bank has been a strong supporter of CIS in Charlotte, along with other major business and economic concerns. Charlotte has generated many new businesses and economic enterprises because of its schools; at the same time, CIS has served as a centrifugal force bringing new businesses into the Charlotte area. Change from within reflects that CIS understands ethical entry into systems.

5. *Relationships, not programs, change people.* William Glasser (1965) stresses this point strongly in his book called *Reality Therapy.* Many helping professionals note that the relationship they have with their clients accounts more than any other variable for the way in which these clients change. Relationships appear to be more important than theoretical approaches in bringing about change. Even though these findings relate to psychological behavior, the same should also hold true for school and academic behavior. The importance of relationships has also been reported by alternative school students when they state why they prefer alternative to "regular" schools (Kronick and Hargis, 1990).

A final set of programs has been reported by Orr (1987) and is discussed in Kronick and Hargis (1990). Among these are the Boston Compact, the Twelve Together Program in Detroit, the Secondary Exchange Program in Texas and Washington, the Murray Wright High School Day Care Center, the Adolescent Primary Health Care Clinic, the Job Readiness Program in Chicago, Project COFFEE in Oxford, MA, and Rich's Academy. These programs are grouped into three major categories by Orr. The categories are supplemental services, programs designed to remove barriers to continued education, and comprehensive school-affiliated programs. Supplemental services programs are those in which supportive counseling and job readiness preparation are provided to marginally performing students who are still in school. Barriers to continuing education programs are designed to discourage students from leaving school; they include programs such as those which provide education and social services to pregnant teenagers. The removal of barriers to continued education programs are designed for youth where economic, family, or personal responsibilities keep them out of school. Comprehensive school-affiliated programs are ones in which the business world and the school work closely together. Their focus on the relationship between education and future economic security is a strong one. The focus of these programs is on school attendance and basic skills, plus collaboration with business employers. These programs are described briefly because they are covered in detail both in Orr and in Kronick and Hargis.

Looking at the programs described in this section, one can easily see that there is a shift from focusing on the at-risk student to focusing on the school. Historically it may have been assumed that at-risk or dropout students were at the margin of society. However, writers such as Hess (1994), DeYoung (1994), and Kozol (1991) explode upon us with the central thesis that these children are at the very core of America's inner city, urban, and rural schools. Even though it makes little sense to run from one end of the spectrum to another by focusing on the school instead of the student, let us now take a look at some organizational ideas that could help facilitate the school's becoming more effective as a human service agency.

Contributions from Organizational Theory, or How to Work Within the System

Client laterality is one of the first concepts from organizational theory that we want to discuss in regard to its importance for schools, students, and communities. Laterality allows us to focus on interaction among these three components, as well as to operationalize policies and interventions between helpers and clients. Client laterality reflects an interest by the organization and its employees in the client's biographical space, ranging from focus on a limited aspect of the client to a broad interest in who the client is as a person. It prompts a consideration of clients as vital participants in service-oriented organizations. Most importantly, a fix on client laterality focuses attention by the organization on the client as a person (Rosengren and Lefton, 1970).

It might appear by now, 1996, that this type of statement need not be made. It would seem that human service organizations/schools would see their clients as persons and as a viable part of the helping process, but there is too much information to the contrary to support this idea. It would seem that merely treating students as persons would go a long way in keeping them from being at risk.

Research by Kronick and Hargis (1990) on alternative schools found that students reported a liking for alternative schools more than regular schools because teachers and counselors related to them as persons at the alternative school.

Organizational behavior has been studied from at least four theoretical perspectives: classical, human relations, contingency, and systems. Given the long history of the study of organizations, it is intriguing to read the following quote from Bolman and Deal (1991): "Organizational behavior is rational but only in the sense that organizations act first and then analyze what they did rather than the other way around." Bolman and Deal use the term "framing" when describing organizational behavior and posit that it is the ignored frames that will cause problems for the organization. They term their frames structural, human relations, political, and symbolic. The structural frame is concerned with alignment and clarity, human resource with needs and skills, political with scarcity and conflict, and symbolic with meaning.

In looking at these frames as they might apply to schools, at-risk children or communities, we must keep them all in focus when trying to bring about change. If we listen to Bolman and Deal in trying to reframe organizations, we must pay attention to structure, needs, conflict, and loss. By focusing on these four factors and four frames we may be able to facilitate some needed and necessary change.

The four frames put forward by Bolman and Deal are defined as follows:

1. The structural frame, drawing mainly on the discipline of sociology, emphasizes the importance of formal roles and relationships. The structural frame looks beyond individuals to examine context in which individuals and contexts work together. Understanding the complexity of organizational context in the variety of structural possibilities can help to create structures that work for, rather than against, both people and the purposes of organizations.

2. The human resource frame, based primarily on the ideas of organizational social psychology, starts with the fundamental premise that organizations are inhabited by individuals who have needs, feelings, and prejudices. The human resource frame posits the assumption that organizations create systems that force employees to be highly dependent on supervisors and give them little control over their work.

3. The political frame, invented and developed primarily by political scientists, views organizations as arenas in which different interest groups compete for power and scarce resources. The political frame asserts that, in the face of enduring differences and scarce resources, conflict among members of a coalition is inevitable and power inevitably becomes a key resource. The scarcity of resources, always present in education, suggests that poli-

tics will be more salient and intense in difficult times. Scarce resources and difficult times appear to be continuous when it comes to education and support for schools. The political frame is likely to view divergent interests and conflict over scarce resources as an enduring fact of organizational life and is less likely to be optimistic about distinguishing among the better and the worse solutions.

4. The symbolic frame, drawing on social and cultural anthropology, abandons the assumption of rationality that appears in the other frames. The symbolic frame assumes that organizations are full of questions that cannot be answered, problems that cannot be solved, and events that cannot be understood or managed. Whenever that is the case, humans will create new symbols to bring meaning out of chaos, clarity out of confusion, and predictability out of mystery (Bolman and Deal, 1991, p. 15).

In concert with these four frames proposed by Bolman and Deal are the concepts developed by McGregor (1960) of Theory X and Theory Y. Theory X and Theory Y are important in all organizations but seem to be followed quite closely in schools and are vital to our understanding of the school as an important social organization. According to Theory X, subordinates are passive and lazy, have little ambition, prefer to be led, and resist change. Theory Y, on the other hand, claims that the essential task of management is to arrange organizational conditions so that people can achieve their own goals by directing their efforts toward organizational awards. One can only guess at the number of schools that are run on a Theory X rather than a Theory Y approach. The Theory X approach must certainly have a trickle-down effect. Bolman and Deal found that school principals spend an inordinate amount of time trying to handle a small percentage of abrasive or ineffectual teachers who are responsible for most of the discipline problems and almost all of the parental complaints. Kronick and Hargis found the same relationship between teachers, principals, and students. The teachers and principals claimed that 90 percent of their time was being spent on 10 percent of the students.

Earlier in this section client laterality, a concern for the client as a person, was discussed. Here are four points from Bolman and Deal designed to delimit the relationship between people and organizations.

1. *Organizations exist to serve human needs rather than the reverse.*

2. *Organizations and people need each other.* Organizations need people, energy, and talent. People need careers, salaries, and work opportunities.

3. *When the fit between the individual and the organization is poor, one or both will suffer.* Individuals will be exploited or will seek to exploit the organization, or both.

4. *A good fit between individuals and organizations benefits both.* Human beings find meaningful and satisfying work, and organizations get the human talent and energy they need. (Bolman and Deal, 1991, p. 121)

If the four points above are followed, an opportunity to avoid what Goffman (1961) describes as a total institution can possibly occur. The total institution is typified by the bureaucratic handling of human needs. Examples include prisons, psychiatric hospitals, convents, and monasteries. Depending on the level of totality present, schools can all too easily fall into the category of total institutions or, as Goffman titles his work, an asylum. We must do everything possible to see that people-processing institutions, if you will, including schools, do not take on the characteristics of asylums or total institutions. It would appear that in too many instances schools have taken on this posture, and the relationship between teachers and students is similar to the relationship between the keepers and the kept.

The following are characteristics that Goffman attributed to asylums. The reader is asked to think critically and insightfully about whether or not these factors describe accurately in any way what schools in America are like today.

1. Goffman claims that every institution captures something of the time and interest of its members and provides something of a world for them; every institution has encompassing tendencies.

2. The encompassing or total character is symbolized by the barrier to social intercourse with the outside and to departure that is often built into the physical plant, such as locked doors, high walls, barbed wires, cliffs, water, forests, or moors.

3. There is a breakdown of the barriers to sleep, play, and work. Goffman sees this as the central feature of the total institution.

4. There is a basic split between a large managed group conveniently called inmates and a small supervisory group called staff. How sad it is if the managed group and staff are students and teachers.

5. Social mobility between the two groups is grossly restricted. Social distance is typically great and often formally prescribed.

6. Goffman basically defines an asylum as the bureaucratic handling of human needs. This is, of course, something we would like to see avoided at all costs in America's schools today.

In developing methods in which schools can become more amicable places for students and parents, a look into the social organization literature reveals an interesting approach developed by Glisson (1981), in which he describes the Contingency Model of Social Welfare Administration. Much of what Glisson develops is applicable to schools. Psychosocial systems, which include informal power, social relationships, worker motivation, and job satisfaction, play a primary role in human service organizations and schools because the technology of service organizations involves humans attempting to process and/or change other humans.

Process and change are at the core of what schools are all about, with the former linking to the latter. If process is followed and an investment by faculty, students, and family occurs, then change has at least a moderate chance of occurring. Process and change are key elements in today's schools; both must occur for schools to keep pace with rapid social change in American society. Process is a necessary but not a sufficient facilitator of change. Change is more likely to come about if process has been a key factor involved in the change procedure. Change has also been found to be associated with empowerment and self-managed teams (Short, 1994). Empowerment, as discussed by Short, is supplied to persons as well as organizations.

Self-managed and empowered teams will be more than cognizant of Glisson's psychosocial sub-system with its emphasis on knowledge of informal power, social relationships, worker motivation, and job satisfaction. These four facets of the psychosocial sub-system place strong emphasis on the school as a human service agency.

Self-managed teams and charter schools, as well as other programs discussed in this chapter, rise and fall on how well people work together, in this case as teachers, students, staff, and families.

An effective team knows where informal power lies, and informal power is generally more effective in getting the important things done than formal power. To ignore informal power is to not realize where the important players are in the human relations sense. Informal leaders and their use of power, whether coming from in front or behind, are key facets in all social organizations. Knowledge of informal power is in concert with the human relations frame discussed earlier. Social relationships, whether within or between groups, are what make teaching groups successful or not. Social relationships may run from the very intense, such as described by Ouchi (1981) in Theory Z, to the more mundane that are found in day-to-day transactions that most of us experience. Social relationships in the work place are described by Herzberg (1975) as either motivation or hygiene factors. Motivational factors are directly related to what goes on in the work place.

Hygiene factors are extraneous to the work place but impact on the individual while they are in the work setting. Ouchi would like to see home and work lives integrated. He illustrates, via the Japanese system, how home and work lives are integrated with fellow employees taking their vacations together. Would this approach help classroom teachers? Would efficiency, morale, and other aspects of social relationships improve or increase under a Theory Z approach? Is it possible that parts of Theory Z and other theories could help make social relationships more productive within the schoolhouse? A key point to remember is that people are social animals. To be truly human we must interact with others. Studies of the types of relationships and interactions that go on between and among teachers, students, families, and staff that could aid in theory construction would go a long way in providing information that could be used to keep at-risk children in school.

Worker motivation, as mentioned above, has been looked upon from the perspective of motivation and hygiene factors. Motivation may also be looked upon from the perspective of Maslow's (1970) hierarchy of human needs. Low level needs of the worker must be met before the higher level needs can be attempted. The importance of meeting employee needs is too often overlooked. It seems strange that human service managers would be so remiss in not acknowledging the needs of direct service providers. Workers are more likely to be motivated when their needs as well as their efforts are being acknowledged.

Motivation has also been studied from the perspective of whether it is intrinsically or extrinsically caused. In human services education it would be hoped that care givers would be internally motivated, but of course it is naive to believe this in all cases.

The final facet of the psychosocial system is job satisfaction. This, in a sense, is an outcome of the relationships between informal power, social relationships, and worker motivation.

Could it be that efforts focusing on the needs of teachers could lead to a reduction of at-risk students and an increase in the retention of students as well as in learning? Healthy teachers would most certainly be more prepared and more likely to help produce healthy learners. It may be assumed that there are unhealthy teachers in America's schools today. A reduction in this number would serve a dual purpose of removing them as individuals but also removing their unhealthy influence on healthy and neophyte teachers. This removal might be on a short-term basis, but the teacher's need of rejuvenation, renewed vigor, and excitement might be brought about by taking a leave of absence, going to graduate school, or even swimming in the Bahamas.

The rigor of teaching school cannot be ignored. It is a demanding job physically and mentally. There must be avenues provided for teachers and human service workers to find new life so that they can give to their students and avoid permanent burnout. Burnout at its worst is eloquently described by Kozol (1991); certain Chicago teachers tell him they work only three days a week, and nothing can be done to them because the city cannot or will not spend money for their substitute replacements. These teachers are probably beyond anything which we have discussed, but some of our approaches might have prevented them from getting there in the first place. These teachers probably hold this position because of organizational as well as personal factors. There is no question that efforts focusing on job satisfaction could have helped prevent the above from happening. Programs geared toward job satisfaction would most certainly produce healthy teachers.

The following four dimensions of structure, hierarchy of authority, participation in decision making, procedural specification, and division of labor are developed by management to support the technology of the organization. The structure of an organization, in short, reveals the organization's philosophy of intervention and the goals and values within which it is attempting to function (Perrow, 1961). The structure of the school is operationalized along these four variables, and, depending on how these variables are acted out, the school may be seen as either open or closed (Rokeach, 1960; Kronick, 1972). The more open the school the more likely the various constituencies will be involved in decision making and the more likely these groups will feel empowered and that they have a stake in what is going on. At the same time, if this is the case, the less likely it is that the organization will be hierarchial in nature. The less hierarchial and centralized the organization the less need there is for informal power. Schools appear to be making more decisions at the school and fewer at the central office. This would seem to make sense, since the schoolhouse is where the action is and not at the central office. Schools appear to be good candidates for decentralization and places for authority to be based on competence rather than on a simple top-down model.

Agencies like schools that work with persons cannot have rigid organizational structures because people are too unpredictable. Their responses to interventions from the school or a human service agency are not going to fit into a nice, neat formula. Hence a school structure that is open should be more responsive to the needs of its clients, the students.

Procedural specifications and a traditional division of labor go along with a bureaucratic type of organization. Schools cannot exist without any procedural specifications, but to go too far in the opposite direction is not healthy either. A healthy balance is always preferable to chaos and/or rigidity. The technology of the school can be operationalized along the lines of what Alan Keith-Lucas (1972) termed art, science, and values in human services.

In our school the clients are more than students since we are advocating for the school as a human service agency. Clients in this model may include parents, siblings, and extended family. The school as a human service agency would educate the total person. The school, hence, is the easiest place to do outreach and to treat the entire family system regardless of its configuration. Parents, siblings, or extended family will all come into contact with the school in some form or fashion, and this is how the school as a human service agency could do some real helping. This will require changes in the professional training of teachers and human service workers and must be the wave of new college teaching for the year 2000. The knowledge base of these new professionals will have to be changed to a multidisiplinary one because of the complexity of the problems that are being addressed. The problems confronting today's school as a human service agency are that solutions proposed from one line of thought are doomed to fail. The knowledge base that is multidisiplinary, drawing from fields such as biology, anthropology, psychology, and sociology, is surely superior to an intervention based on a theoretical approach that draws on only one of these fields. A counseling approach with clients that is knowledgeable of Levay's (1991) work in genetics,[2] as it relates, for example, to sexual orientation; Spindler and Spindler's (1994) work on cultural therapy; Glasser's (1965) concept of involvement; and Cooley's (1922) concept of the looking glass self, is a giant step in the right direction. Teachers and human service workers cannot be knowledgeable in all fields, but they can study and learn from several. What is needed is a cadre of professionals who are more than dilettantes and who have continued to study and want to learn about the human condition as they try to meet the needs of their clients.

As is implied above, the professional training of teachers and human service workers must change in order to meet the challenge of the year 2000. The professional training that exists now is archaic and woefully inadequate for the many and complex needs of today's students. Colleges of education must make drastic changes in how and what they deliver to teacher education students and human service students. Sadly, there isn't much time to do this. These changes, which must come about quickly, could include a commitment to social justice; collaborative partnerships among faculty, students, and practitioners; excellence in scholarship; and innovative instructional excellence (UTK College of Education Document, 1993). Under these headings the professional training of the new professional would include more than perfunctory attention to multiculturalism. They would entail but not be limited to innovative field placements for student teachers and human service interns where they could work together in the same placement in learning how to do teamwork; the creation of useful scholarship by faculty, students, and practitioners; the use of technology where information is delivered to those who need it and will use it. The emphasis should not only be on the medium—Internet, Ethernet, etc.—but on the message as well. We must be getting out better and more useful information, not just something that is cutely packaged.

ATTITUDES, SKILLS, AND KNOWLEDGE, OR ART, SCIENCE, AND VALUE

In our schema the targets of intervention are not the students in the classroom but the students in their total environment. The focus is on curricular as well as noncurricular causes of the student's problems as well as the problems of the significant others of these students. As stated throughout this book, our emphasis is on the total person, which includes family in whatever form it may take.

Interventions based on this approach will use the school, a place where others in the student's life will receive help along with the student. This approach should be more cost effective than what is presently being done because the problem may actually be fixed. The presenting as well as the real problems will be dealt with under this systemic approach. A commitment to social justice could be operationalized into ethics, theology, and social traditions (Glisson, 1981). Commitment to social justice would use immersion experiences into multiculturalism as one of its cornerstones. The white child will be the minority child in the public school in the early part of the 21st century. Our teachers and human service workers are too often white and female. The human service professions must actively recruit on an honest basis, not a superficial one, more people of color. Ethically, the helping professions must attempt to reach the impacted clients of our society. The creaming of clients, where many do not need help but are served, must stop. Bureaucratic arbitrary ruling, such as when a certain level of income makes one ineligible for services, must end because what those rules do is teach people not to work so that they can receive benefits.

The ideology of the helping professions should focus on prevention, empowerment, and systems. Prevention, in regard to the Federal Crime Bill, has been cast in a bad light. As one wag put it, midnight basketball is nothing more than a paycheck for a social worker. Empowerment takes the Chinese proverb of "Give a man a fish and he eats today; give a man a fishing pole and he eats forever," and puts it into practice. Empowerment of clients allows them to take control of their lives and not become dependent on the system. The ideology of focusing on the system is a holistic view of social problems. This holistic approach should lead to problem solving rather than merely amelioration.

Part and parcel of all of this is the question of what are the social traditions in which these changes come about in meeting the needs of the total person, our student? If a conservative Darwinistic philosophy prevails, all of what we have so far discussed gets thrown into the proverbial file 13. What will occur will be situations where students with problems will make it or they won't, and the group response will be so what; who cares; they deserve it; let them disappear.

An ideology based on people who have problems in living and the holistic view of the person, based on problem solution, will lead to people getting to where they want to be in making contributions to society. These two ideological positions are mutually exclusive and only one will come to the fore by the beginning of the next century. From our perspective, to prevent "the fire next time from landing in our lap," we had better hope that the latter ideology is the one of choice.

The political frame mentioned earlier illustrates that scarce resources and conflict over them go hand in hand. None of these dramas will be played out in a vacuum, and a political frame is of utmost significance. Thus no matter how pristine the goals and values of our system the influence of the political frame will be felt. All involved in this process must be aware of these factors and use them so as not to be thwarted in implementing necessary programs for at-risk students and their families.

Illustrating the relevance and immediacy of our topic is the fact that *Time* magazine, on October 31, 1994, ran as its cover story *New Hope For Public Schools* (Wallis, 1994). At the same time one of the hottest selling books in America was *The Bell Curve* by Herrnstein and Murray. The *Time* article focused on parents and teachers seizing control of education in what *Time* called a grass roots revolt. These strong words illustrate the enormity of the problem and the frustration people across the country are feeling regarding public education. Topics that we have focused on so far in this chapter and that are discussed in further chapters are also highlighted by *Time*. They include school organization, especially bureaucracy. "Schools must break free of bureaucracy. Fifty years of top-down reform have not done the trick. The answer to this bureaucratic handling of human needs is to place the authority in the individual school, freeing it of the bureaucracy." W. E.

Deming's (1982) notion of pushing responsibility down the line to those who know the customer best is adhered to. In education those who know the customer best are in the neighborhood school, not in the central office.

The use of for-profit companies to run schools is a topic covered by *Time*. "The Edison Project" of Whittle Communications, presently headed by Benno Schmidt, former president of Yale University, and staffed by Chester Finn, John Chubb, and other conservative educators, is an example of companies running schools. Only time will tell the outcome of such a venture. Obviously there are other institutions, such as Boston College, that are running schools or school systems at the present time. This type of program will have various ripple effects going back to the preparation of teachers by colleges of education. It may be that the time for doing business as usual has come and gone.

In regard to Charter Schools, discussed earlier in this chapter, *Time* has this to say:

> But for all their diversity, it is interesting to note that many seem to be embracing a very similar set of pedagogical principles. First reduce class size. Make sure parents are heavily involved. Just as important keep school size small, particularly in the inner city where kids desperately need a sense of family and personal commitment from adults. Encourage active hands-on learning. Impart the intelligent use of technology. For older kids who opted for the traditional switching of gears in classrooms from math to social studies to biology every forty-five minutes substitute lengthier classes that teach across disciplines. (*Time*, October 31, 1994, p. 58)

In regard to curriculum, another point made in our text is that parents want to design a curriculum that is challenging, flexible, and tailored to their particular child. We have called this Curriculum Based Assessment; it is discussed briefly in this chapter and more fully by Hargis in Chapter 15. Curriculum Based Assessment fits the curriculum to the child rather than forcing the child to fit the curriculum, which leads to curriculum casualties in some instances. Herrnstein and Murray, in *The Bell Curve*, give us another exegesis on the correlation between race and intelligence, as expounded by Jensen, Shockley, and Herrnstein 30 years ago. *The Bell Curve* arrived on the scene after educators had become acutely aware that the white child is rapidly becoming the minority child in the public school and will definitely be so by the year 2010. But if Herrnstein and Murray are correct that blacks are not going to have IQ scores that rival those of Asians and whites, what are we going to do about it? Our only course of action is an ecological one in which the environment of poverty, crime, and racism is attacked by interventions aimed at preventing people of color from scoring badly in achievement tests. It will take environmental interventions to combat a biological force. So it may be a moot point at best if race determines intelligence. Those of us involved in the fight for children must and will rely on other theories for our paradigms and sources of information. These theories and approaches are discussed throughout this book. Let us briefly peruse some thoughts that are at loggerheads with the premise of *The Bell Curve*.

Kronick and Hargis (1990) take a holistic approach, focusing on curricular and noncurricular causes that are associated with school failure. The lockstep curriculum pushes students out. It requires failure because it forces the child to fit the curriculum, rather than fitting the curriculum to the child. This failure, coupled with no hope, leads to dropping out. It should be remembered that students drop out from learning long before they drop out of school. Dropping out itself might be better viewed as a process of disengagement from school, caused by social or academic factors (Rumberger, 1987). Dropouts thus become characterized by failure and retention. Failure and retention lead to frustration, which may be expressed through violence. Dropouts are generally identified by their overt behavior.

Students who must endure chronic failure will experience frustration, anxiety, and fear (Glasser, 1971; Simon and Bellonca, 1976; and Hargis, 1987). In the face of such experience some children will withdraw and avoid instructional activity. Some more naturally assertive and aggressive students will act out in more aggressive and disruptive ways (Kronick and Hargis, 1990).

Interestingly enough, it has been found that withdrawn students have even lower achievement levels than destructive ones. Thus we must use behavioral interventions with those who are at risk regardless of the cause of the problem, whether it be race or any other demographic variable. Attending school, arriving at class on time, paying attention to a teacher, completing assigned work (Finn, 1993) are behavioral variables that may be amenable to intervention regardless of their causes. These variables would lead to academic success and could be coached or taught to students. It is clear that the more the students behave in useful ways, the higher their academic achievement will be. It might be that these variables are correlated more strongly with certain races than others, but it is evident that if these variables are correlated with early school leaving and academic achievement there will be some intrinsic motivation on the part of the student to want to learn these skills which will lead to greater success in the classroom. These skills can be taught in a more indirect method to those who are not so motivated.

In concluding this chapter we need to recognize that the political climate in this country tends increasingly to signal that at-risk children will fall even lower on the priority scale of America. Those of us who are working to insure that this cannot happen must work even harder. The notions of prevention, particularly as they relate to mental health, corrections, and welfare, cannot be forgotten even though prevention is seen in a horrible light by some people at this time. Nonetheless, working with at-risk kids in school and keeping them there, plus giving them a relevant education that they can use, will certainly save us money in the long run and provide us with a healthier, happier, and less crime-ridden society.

NOTES

1. For discussion of this concept of people with problems vs problem people, see Cornel West (1993), *Race Matters*.
2. See Gorman, C. (1991). Are gay men born that way? *Time*, September 9, pp. 60–61.

REFERENCES

American Association of Colleges of Teacher Education Human Service Education Committee (1990). Washington, DC: Author.

Bolman, L. and Deal, T. (1991). *Reframing organizations: Artistry, choice, and leadership*. San Francisco: Jossey-Bass.

Brill, N. (1976). *Teamwork: Working together in the human services*. Philadelphia: J.B. Lippincott.

Center for the Study of Social Policy (1993). *Kids count*. Washington, DC: United States Department of Education.

Cities in Schools (1994). *Turning kids around*. Alexandria, VA: Author.

Cooley, C. (1922). *Human nature and social order*. New York: Charles Scribner's Sons.

Corrigan, D. (1990). *Context for the discussion of the collaborative development of integrated services for children and families: The education side*. A resource paper prepared for the National Symposium on Integrated Services for Children and Families, March 1990, Alexandria, VA.

———. (1993). An idea whose time has come—again. *ATE Newsletter*, September/October, p. 6.

Deming, W. (1982). *Quality, productivity, and competitive position or out of the crisis*. Boston: MIT Center for Advanced Engineering Study.

DeYoung, A. (1994). Children at risk in rural schools. In R. Rossi (Ed.), *Schools and students at risk* (pp. 229–251). New York: Teachers College Press.

Dryfoos, J. (1990). *Adolescents at risk: Prevalence and prevention*. New York: Oxford University Press.

Fine, M. (1994). *Chartering urban school reform*. New York: Teachers College Press.

Finn, J. (1993). *School engagement and students at risk*. Washington, DC: National Center for Education Statistics.

Glasser, W. (1965). *Reality therapy*. New York: Harper and Row.

———. (1971). *The effect of school failure on the life of a child*. Washington, DC: National Association of Elementary School Principals.

Glisson, C. (1981). A contingency model of social welfare. *Administration in Social Work, 5*(1), 15–28.

Goffman, E. (1961). *Asylums.* Garden City, NY: Anchor Books.

Gordon, E. and Yowell, C. (1994). Cultural dissonance as a risk factor in the development of students. In R. Rossi (Ed.), *Schools and students at risk* (pp. 51–69). New York: Teachers College Press.

Gorman, C. (1991). Are gay men born that way? *Time,* September 9, pp. 60–61.

Grissmer, D., Kirby, S., Berends, M., and Williamson, S. (1994). *Student achievement and the changing American family.* Santa Monica, CA: Rand Corporation.

Hargis, C. (1987). *Curriculum based assessment.* Springfield, IL: Charles C. Thomas.

———. (1990). *Grades and grading practices.* Springfield, IL: Charles C. Thomas.

Herrnstein, R. and Murray, C. (1994). *The bell curve.* New York: Free Press.

Herzberg, F. (1975). One more time: How do you motivate employees? In *Harvard Business Review* (Ed.), *Harvard business review—On management* (pp. 361–376). New York: Harper and Row.

Hess, G. (1994). Chicago school reform: A response to the unmet needs of students at risk. In R. Rossi (Ed.), *Schools and students at risk* (pp. 207–228). New York: Teachers College Press.

Hobbs, N. (1982). *The troubled and troubling child.* San Francisco: Jossey-Bass.

The Holmes Group (1990). *Tomorrow's schools: Principles for the design of professional development schools.* East Lansing, MI: Author.

Houston, H. (1992). Professional practice schools: How would we know one if we saw one? A guide to assessment. In Marsha Levine (Ed.), *Professional practice schools* (pp. 133–167). New York: Teachers College Press.

Keith-Lucas, A. (1975). Art, science, and value in human services. In R. Kronick and F. Spicuzza (Eds.), *Perspectives on human services: Theoretical and applied essays* (pp. 7–15). Lexington, MA: Xerox Individualized Publishing.

Kozol, J. (1991). *Savage inequalities.* New York: Crown.

Kronick, R. (1972). The impact of perceived organizational climate on academic performance. *The Southern Journal of Educational Research, 6*(3), 169–188.

Kronick, R. and Hargis, C. (1990). *Dropouts: Who drops out and why and the recommended action.* Springfield, IL: Charles C. Thomas.

Levin, H. (1988). *Accelerated schools for at-risk students.* Rutgers, NJ: Center for Policy Research in Education.

Mandell, B. and Schram, B. (1985). *Human services: Introduction and interventions.* New York: Macmillan.

Maslow, A. (1970). *Motivation and personality* (rev. ed.). New York: Harper and Row.

McGregor, D. (1960). *The human side of enterprise.* New York: McGraw-Hill.

McPartland, J. (1994). Dropout prevention in theory and practice. In R. Rossi (Ed.), *Schools and students at risk* (pp. 255–276). New York: Teachers College Press.

Meares, P. (1986). *Social work services in schools.* Englewood Cliffs, NJ: Prentice Hall.

Moos, R. (1970). Differential effects of the social climate of correctional institutions. *Journal of Research in Crime and Delinquency, 7,* 71–82.

Nash, R. and Ducharme, E. (1976). A future perspective on preparing educators for the human service society: How to restore a sense of social purpose to teacher education. *Teachers College Record, 77*(4), 441–471.

National Center for Education Statistics (1992). *National dropout statistics field test evaluation.* Washington, DC: United States Department of Education.

Nisbett, R. and Ross, L. (1980). *Human inference: Strategies and shortcomings of social judgment.* Englewood Cliffs, NJ: Prentice Hall.

Nystrand, R. (1991). *Professional development schools: Toward a new relationship for schools and universities.* Trends and Issues, Paper #3 S.E.R.I.C. Clearinghouse on Teacher Education. Washington, DC.

Orr, M. (1987). *Keeping students in schools.* San Francisco: Jossey-Bass.

Ouchi, W. (1981). *Theory Z*. New York: Avon Books.

Perrow, C. (1961). The analysis of goals in complex organization. *American Sociological Review, 2*(26), 856–866.

Rokeach, M. (1960). *The open and closed mind*. New York: Basic Books.

Rosengren, W. and Lefton, M. (1970). *Organizations and clients*. Columbus, OH: Charles E. Merrill Company.

Rosenthal, R. (1968). *Pygmalion in the classroom*. New York: Holt, Rinehart and Winston.

Rumberger, R. (1987). High school dropouts: A review of issues and evidence. *Review of Educational Research, 57*(2), 101–121.

Rumberger, R. and Larson, K. (1994). Keeping high risk Chicano students in school: Lessons from a Los Angeles middle school dropout prevention program. In R. Rossi (Ed.), *Schools and students at risk* (pp. 141–162). New York: Teachers College Press.

Schorr, L. (1989). *Within our reach: Breaking the cycle of disadvantage*. New York: Doubleday.

Short, P. (1994). School empowerment through self-managing teams: Leader behavior in developing self-managing work groups in school. *Education, 114*(4), 493–502.

Simon, S. and Bellonca, J. (Eds.). (1976). *Degrading the grading myths: A primer of alternative to grades and marks*. Washington, DC: Association for Supervision and Curriculum Development.

Southern Regional Educational Board (SREB) (1969). *Roles and functions for different levels of mental health workers*. Atlanta, GA: SREB.

Spindler, G. and Spindler, L. (1994). The process of culture and person: Cultural therapy and culturally diverse schools. In P. Phelan and A. Davidson (Eds.), *Renegotiating cultural diversity in American schools* (pp. 27–51). New York: Teachers College Press.

Stringfield, S. (1994). Identifying and addressing organizational barriers to reform. In R. Rossi (Ed.), *Schools and students at risk* (pp. 277–295). New York: Teachers College Press.

Teddlie, C. and Stringfield, S. (1993). *Schools make a difference: Lessons learned from a ten-year study of school effects*. New York: Teachers College Press.

The University of Tennessee College of Education (1993). *Planning a new future*. Knoxville: Author.

Wallis, C. (1994). New hope for public schools. *Time*, October 31, pp. 53–63.

Weiner, M. and Quaranta, M. (1992). *Collaborations for social support of children and families at risk*. Unpublished manuscript, Fordham University, Graduate Schools of Education and Social Work.

West, C. (1993). *Race matters*. New York: Random House.

PART II
SOCIAL, POLITICAL, AND HEALTH
ASPECTS OF AT-RISK YOUTH

2   THE POLITICS OF AT-RISK YOUTH

Sung Roe Lee and Robert Cunningham

Learning to analyze and play the game of politics demands that one focus on who gets what, when, where, how, and why (Lasswell, 1950). At-risk youth usually lose in the political arena. How are these political games structured? Are some games better for those in our society who are at risk? What are reasonable goals and effective strategies for at-risk youth and their advocates?

The purpose of this chapter is to explore how at-risk youth fare in the various games of politics. Four political games (approaches to politics) are presented, along with the implications for at-risk youth. Supporters of at-risk youth programs are better armed to advocate for their desired policies when they understand the games of politics—the hidden assumptions which underpin the arguments of people discussing at-risk youth, or any other issue.

SUMMARIZING THE GAMES OF POLITICS

Among political scientists the most popular way to think about political questions is in terms of a transparent game. In the transparent game, called "pluralism," the plays are mostly aboveboard and visible to interested players. Individuals and groups try to convince others that their ideas are best. The team which convinces the most people wins, and the other teams lose. The winners have their value system reinforced and perhaps receive material benefit. Losers' values are rejected, and they usually forfeit the opportunity for material gain. "Politics as pluralism" is the name of the game, and the game is continuous, so today's winners may become tomorrow's losers, and vice versa.

A second perspective from which to think about the political game is in terms of "elitism"—the "haves" and the "have-nots." This game lacks transparency. Elites ("haves") keep the rules of the game a secret and try to keep the "have-nots" from learning how to play, and even to keep them from realizing that a game is being played.

The third game is "politics by economics." It is assumed that economic growth and social stability are ultimate values, priority goals that are consensually accepted. The forces of the economy dictate winners and losers. As a group, at-risk youth will always lose this game, because people at the margins of the economy are hired and fired according to aggregate economic measures. An individual may escape the cycle, but as a whole, for at-risk youth, "at risk" means exactly that.

The final game is "politics as bureaucracy." This game has different rules from those of "politics by economics," but gives the same result for at-risk populations. When at-risk clients are served well by an agency, demand for the services of that agency increase. However, since the resources of the agency are fixed, service quality is degraded by heavy demand. This creates the paradoxical situation in which quantity and quality of services for at-risk youth are at their best when they are least needed; and conversely, when services are in high demand, availability is diminished and/or quality is poor.

Most of the discussion here is about politics as pluralism. Some suggestions for political action are offered. In general, the outlook for at-risk youth serves to suggest that perhaps politics, as well as economics, is a dismal science.

POLITICS AS PLURALISM

Politics is most frequently taught by political scientists as the interplay of social forces exerting their power and influence in the making of public policy. According to this pluralist theory of public policy (Dahl, 1961), political power in the United States is fragmented and dispersed more or less equally among various racial, religious, professional, linguistic, and ethnic groups. Such groups possess variable amounts of money, votes, and expertise, which they can use to influence public policy. Dahl suggests that all the active and legitimate groups can make a difference at some crucial stage in the decision process. "Pluralism of institutions, conflict patterns, groupings, and interests makes for a lively, colorful, and creative scene of political conflict which provides an opportunity for success for every interest that is voiced" (Dahrendorf, 1959, p. 317). No single group controls policy outcomes. Public policies result from interaction and bargaining as groups seek government support for their policy preferences. Almost every social group, however small its resource base, has an opportunity to influence and benefit from political decisions if it is selective in its quest. Loose coalitions, generally describable as "liberal" and "conservative," have developed around at-risk youth issues.

The Liberal Coalition

The liberal coalition holds a political idealogy that may be characterized as an "entitlement" perspective. It consists primarily of Congressional Democrats and various religious and not-for-profit agencies that espouse programs offering direct benefits to society's less advantaged. Supporting issues appealing to racial and ethnic minorities, women, single parents, community organizations, and state and local administrators concerned with child welfare, these groups seek more government attention to and spending on social welfare, especially for children. Their primary emphasis and greatest strength at present lie at the national government level. These groups lobby Congress and federal agencies on behalf of the liberal agenda. Underlying their arguments is the assumption that disparities of income and opportunities are unfair, and redressing these inequalities constitutes not only fairness but is cost-saving, as children become productive, taxpaying citizens rather than ending up on welfare or in state institutions at taxpayer expense.

The National Black Child Development Institute (NBCDI), for example, states that "every child is entitled to an early childhood experience that is developmentally appropriate to the age of the child and which meets the social and economic needs of the family" (Moore, 1994, p. 2). NBCDI argues that every child and family has a set of total needs, which the society is obligated to provide through social programs. In the words of Evelyn Moore, the executive director of NBCDI, such programs must:

1. recognize stages of growth and development in children;
2. provide stimulating experiences designed to facilitate cognitive, social, physical, cultural, and emotional development;
3. attend to the health and nutrition needs of children;
4. promote nurturing and supportive emotional responses for children.

If a child is deprived of one of these components, the child runs the risk of anti-social behavior in later life.

The NBCDI presents statistics showing disparities in income, health insurance coverage, and poverty rates between black and white populations in the United States in 1993.

David S. Liederman, executive director of the Child Welfare League of America, states:

Most poor families need a helping hand, not moral guidelines. They need jobs that provide a living wage and affordable housing in safe neighborhoods. Like other children, poor children need playgrounds and community centers and high-quality, flexible day care arrangements . . . they need competent teachers and welcoming schools, not better-armed police and bigger prisons. If they get what they need early enough, in the first three years, we can avoid the heartbreak and the expense that come from waiting until the damage is done.

Let's be bold enough to suggest that our efforts to date have failed, where they failed, because we haven't helped enough, not because helping breeds dependency. We may just have to spend more, as well as spend smarter. (Liederman, 1994, p. 2)

The National Committee to Prevent Child Abuse (NCPCA) reported that a 50-state Child Abuse Survey showed that in 1993 three children died every day as a result of abuse or neglect (Child Welfare League of America, 1994). A recent Carnegie Corporation report suggests that lack of stimulation in the early months of life diminishes the capacity for learning (Child Welfare League of America, 1994). Both reports plead for structuring so-

TABLE 2.1 Facts for Child Advocates

	Black	White
1989 Median household income	$21,232	35,329
1993 Median household income (income in 1993 dollars)	$19,532	32,960
Married couple families, median income (1993)	$35,218	43,675
Female householder, median income (1993)	$11,909	20,000
Percentage of all persons not covered by health insurance during 1993	20.5%	14.2%
Poverty rate in 1993	33.1%	12.2%

Sources: US Bureau of the Census, Current Population Reports, Series P60–188. Income, Poverty, and Valuation of Noncash Benefits: 1993, Excerpt. US Department of Commerce, Washington DC, pp. x, 8, 9. US Bureau of the Census, Statistical Brief. Health Insurance Coverage—1993. US Department of Commerce, Washington, DC. Taken from *The Black Child Advocate*, Winter 1994, p. 9.

cial arrangements to keep mothers and fathers close to their children during the vital early months. Liederman (1994) argues that good parenting is hard work. He proposes to help these mothers complete their education, increase their job skills, and gain work experience.

African-American and Hispanic groups, prominent in the liberal coalition, are suspicious of mainstream American society. Raul Yzaguirre, former executive director of the National Council of La Raza (NCLR), the national umbrella organization working for civil rights and economic opportunities for Hispanics, chairs the National Neighborhood Coalition. He states that the Reagan administration's cutting of federal programs on employment, education, and neighborhood improvements had negative consequences for the Hispanic community (Yzaguirre 1987). Actions to reduce government spending, such as the Gramm-Rudman Deficit Reduction Law, brought devastating consequences for youth by cutting programs in education, community development, and health care. Community leaders argue that since many of the racial minorities are concentrated in inner cities, and most inner-city youth suffer from very high school dropout and unemployment rates, inner-city problems such as drug abuse and crime will worsen with a decline in federal spending on social service programs.

But the liberal coalition does not always speak with unanimity, and there is competition as well as cooperation within its ranks. The nation's largest agencies serving youth are uniting behind a Youth Development Block Grant bill (YDBG) introduced in Congress in 1995 (H.R. 4086 and S. 1746). The $400 million fund would go primarily to nonprofit community-based agencies engaged in youth development activities. These groups argue that federally funded programs have lost support in Congress, and so rather than losing in this battle they are opting for fighting at the local level for a share of the block grant pie.

David Liederman, executive director of the Child Welfare League of America and chair of the National Collaboration for Youth, seeks to preserve existing categorical programs in which agencies such as the Department of Health and Human Services' Center for Substance Abuse Prevention and the Labor Department's Employment and Training Administration or the Department of Education's Drug-Free Schools Program play a major role (Nichols, 1994). The National Assembly of Health and Social Welfare Agencies, a 15–member National Collaboration for Youth, argues that the federal government must go beyond small demonstration programs and must make a major investment in strengthening community-based youth development programs. However, the National Assembly has discord within its ranks.

Many youth agencies are engaged in a struggle for survival. WAVE, a national youth development agency that has worked with high school dropouts since 1969, faces termination. The Department of Labor refused to renew an annual grant of $1.3 million in 1993. WAVE has enjoyed abundant funding since its founding. In the 1970's the open-handed Comprehensive Employment and Training Act gave billions to DOL's Employment and Training Administration, and in turn to ETA's Office of Youth. Programs pumped out $10 million grants "to anyone who walked in the door," said one staffer. One observer says that the Clinton administration waited for 12 years to take revenge on WAVE because it had strong links to Republicans during the Reagan-Bush years (Vanneman, 1995).

Realizing that financial support from governments will be insufficient to maintain traditional levels of support, all groups are seeking funding from foundations and from the general public, which puts these groups in competition with each other for the charity dollar. For example, YouthBuild USA finds itself competing with a splinter group, LEEO (Leadership, Education, Employment, and Opportunities), for funding.

The liberal coalition has traditionally had its greatest impact on politics at the federal government level. As political emphasis appears to be shifting from the federal to the state and local levels, to be successful these organizations will likely shift their efforts to build their strength in these new arenas. Concentrating at the local level will require a revised strategy and new emphases.

The Conservative Coalition

The conservative coalition consists of Congressional Republicans, family advocacy groups, and business groups. These groups oppose allocating funds for the range of welfare programs, for three reasons:

1. philosophical—giving welfare discourages the will to work, so welfare begets more welfare;
2. financial—welfare strains the already out-of-control federal budget;
3. political—the people who benefit from such programs tend to vote Democratic, so why should Republicans subsidize the opposition?

The at-risk youth population shares the characteristics of limited education, limited work experience, and being single. Republicans do not see spending money on these people as a solution for the at-risk youth problem. In 1996, the Republicans, who were a majority in both houses of Congress after the 1994 election, seek to overhaul the welfare system by expanding the role of the states. Their primary instrument is block grants. Under block grants the federal government will turn over responsibility for certain programs to the states, and the federal government will provide a stated sum of money that the states can allocate as they choose in meeting state-defined objectives within the program guidelines. Tommy Engler, Georgia's Republican governor, states, "We think by turning programs back to the states with freedom and flexibility, we are able to leave money on the table in Washington and we are able to curb costs out into the future." (Katz, 1995a, p. 162). The effort began with the search for programs that could be consolidated into block grants. Included in the block grant proposal are 336 federal programs totalling about $125 billion a year. However, the GOP proposals have several obstacles to overcome before they become public policy. In the Fall of 1995 there was dissension in the Republican ranks as geographic regions argued over who was being disadvantaged.

The conservative coalition views teenage parents and their children as most likely to be welfare recipients. The Congressional Budget Office reports that 77 percent of unmarried adolescent mothers become welfare recipients within five years of birth of their first child (Katz, 1995b). The GOP's proposal in the "Contract With America" sought to deny AFDC to unwed mothers under age 18. Their policy rationale was that at-risk youth are brought into the world by unmarried welfare mothers. The dependency cycle should be stopped by discouraging young, unmarried women from becoming pregnant. Republicans view teenage parents and their children as most likely to be welfare recipients. The money that would otherwise go to these young mothers would be provided to states in block grants to promote adoption and to operate orphanages for children and residential group homes for unwed mothers. The bill would require states to terminate AFDC payments to families who had received welfare benefits for five years. States would have the option to end the benefits after two years.

Pro-family groups point out that the United States has the highest divorce rate and the highest illegitimate birth rate in the world. The consequences of divorce and illegitimacy for children are significant. Girls raised in single-mother families are at much greater risk for early sexual activity, non-marital pregnancies, venereal diseases, and divorce than are girls in two-parent intact families. Boys in similar situations are at greater risk of dropping out of school, and also are more likely to exhibit aggressive behavior. Pro-family groups recommend that mothers spend more time with children in their most impressionable and value-forming years, viewing mother care as superior to any other type of child care.

The Family Research Council (FRC) is committed to ensuring that public policy considers the interest of the family and seeks to advance the overall pro-family agenda. To accomplish its goals the Council moves on several fronts. First, the FRC works to promote the pro-family agenda in both the legislative and executive branches of the federal government through lobbying and educational work. Second, it provides policymakers with credible research data to support traditional family values. FRC policy analysts draft proposals for key decision makers and present critical data in professional journals. When Congress or media call for expert testimony from a pro-family perspective, the FRC—in addition to recommending its own policy experts—refers them to professionals from an extensive research resource network. Third, the FRC seeks to educate citizens about issues that affect the family, enabling them to influence their community and country on behalf of Judeo-Christian principles. The national FRC serves as an adviser to state and local groups, supplying them with information and political expertise.

Conservatives take issue with sex education. They believe that premarital sex should be opposed on moral grounds. Only teens who are married or who have formally announced their intention to marry should receive information on sex. Abstinence is the only effective method of avoiding pregnancy and sexually transmitted diseases (STDs). Moderate conservatives would accept sex education, as long as it stresses the importance of abstinence, the emotional and health dangers of promiscuity, and the failure of contraceptive devices to offer 100 percent protection against either pregnancy or STDs. Conservatives, in general, believe that homosexuality should not be discussed in sex education. Providing information about sex may encourage younger teens to initiate sexual activities at an earlier age. Abstinence is the best protection (Dennison, 1994).

The Business View

Although individual members of the business community range across the ideological spectrum on the question of at-risk youth, the business sector perspective generally considers the issue of at-risk youth in terms of supply and demand economics. It acknowledges the critical role young people play in the labor market. William Kolberg (1987) states:

> I think it is safe to say that we were all struck by the critical role today's young people will be playing in tomorrow's economy. If our economy is to grow as it is capable of growing, we must be able to use the talents of virtually all our young people, because the number coming into the labor force is declining. Yet the percentage of those young people who are at-risk is increasing. (Kolberg, 1987, p. 95)

In addressing the problems of at-risk youth, the business sector calls for the combined efforts of public and private leaders, government, community organizations, and families. The problem is double-edged: insufficient labor supply on the one hand, and on the other hand people who could be productively working constituting a drain on the economy.

It is an issue that affects national security as well as economic competitiveness. At the present time, our military requires one in every nine young people in order to maintain its strength. In ten years the youth population will decline in numbers so drastically that the military will need one in three. *If current rates of illiteracy, unemployment, illegitimate pregnancies, and drug and alcohol abuse among our youth do not decline, there simply will not be enough qualified young people to go around.* (Kolberg, 1987, p. 97, emphasis added)

The business sector's concern was expressed by the president of the National Alliance of Business, which was established in 1968 "to enlist the services of business in a campaign to bring structurally unemployed Americans into our country's economic mainstream." He said, as reported by Kolberg,

Simply put, the structurally unemployed are people who, for lack of education or training, are in danger of being not just unemployed but unemployable, people who could be jobless even in times of an economic boom. (Kolberg, 1987, p. 95)

The National Alliance of Business proposed a public-private partnership in the field of job training, which resulted in the Job Training Partnership Act (JTPA), designed to provide job training for the structurally unemployed. According to the JTPA, more than 600 private industrial councils (PICs) set and oversee job training programs in partnership with local administrators. The business sector expects PICs to play a significant role in addressing the problem of at-risk youth.

The private sector needs to be involved in a broader range of human resource issues because the private sector is where the jobs are, and private employers have a growing interest and stake in the success of human resource development efforts. (Kolberg, 1987, p. 99)

In some cities the business community has expressed its concern for at-risk youth. In an effort to reduce the city's 16 percent annual dropout rate and to improve youth employment opportunities, Boston's business and educational leaders came together to lend resources and support to schools. In 1982 public schools and the business community formally launched the Boston Compact, a joint pledge to improve the quality of educational preparation and access to employment for Boston's public high school students. The business community promised to hire a specific number of public school graduates. The Boston Private Industry Council (PIC) set up a summer jobs program and a "Job Collaborative" program. The Job Collaborative program seeks after-school and summer work for high school students who complete several job-readiness workshops. These programs strengthened the link between Boston's education and business sectors during the early 1980s. However, the dropout rate has not been reduced (Orr, 1987).

From the business sector's perspective, the future of at-risk youth is not bright. Anyone who desires employment must have basic literacy skills. Brad Butler, former Chair of the Committee for Economic Development's Subcommittee on Business and the Schools, said, "Every job currently being done by an illiterate can and will be done better and cheaper by a machine" (cited in Kolberg, 1987, p. 99). The business sector is seriously concerned with the education of children. It stresses the need for pre-kindergarten programs that would establish effective learning behavior during a child's formative years.

However, most minority groups seem to be skeptical of the business sector. In their view, the Job Training Partnership Act (JTPA) program is not particularly helpful because it has done little for the hard-core unemployed—those most likely to be involved in crime. Under contract with the U.S. Department of Labor, the JTPA provides job training to participants through local private industry councils. The government reimburses the councils only to the extent that trainees are placed in full-time jobs. This encourages "creaming" of applicants by JTPA providers. They tend to accept only the best educated, the most motivated, and the brightest— "the cream of the crop." The incentive to place people in jobs motivates trainees to leave the JTPA program as quickly as possible. By paying the agencies for quick placements, those who need the most training and attitude adjustment—the most needy—are by-passed (Yzaguirre, 1987).

Looking across the Atlantic to learn from the British experience, some analysts argue that in Great Britain the Department of Employment's Youth Training and Employment Training programs do not prepare young or long-term unemployed people for work. Job placement rates of about 55 percent of those who completed the program were roughly comparable to those who had not participated in the programs (Ainley, 1988; Dean and Taylor-Gooby,

1992). Statistics on the Employment Training program for long-term unemployed people indicate that about half the 215,000 people offered placements left jobs in three months. The scope of the program is being reduced, as it is officially regarded as ineffective. There is no evidence that those who go on such schemes are any more likely to find jobs than those who do not (Dean and Taylor-Gooby, 1992). It is argued that "the primary function of the schemes is to be understood in terms of the subjection of those excluded from the labor-market proper to work-place discipline and the erosion of expectations among unemployed people" (Dean and Taylor-Gooby, 1992, p. 65). In other words, these programs force participants to obey rules, and participants develop a sense of hopelessness about finding a job—hardly the intended outcome.

At-risk youth may fall off society's economic wagon and end up not as productive, tax-paying members of society, but as a drain on society's resources by becoming a client of the correction, welfare, or mental health system. The business community sees this danger, and the JTPA program—despite its controversial record—was an attempt to channel at-risk youth into skill-building opportunities as a means for achieving productive employment.

The business sector approaches the issue of at-risk youth with ambiguity. On the one hand, the moral view of business people accords with that of Republicans, yet they understand that rational or ethical arguments carry little weight with at-risk youth. They fear that the conservative coalition's prescription will not be effective in addressing the problem. On the other hand, since most of the business people are among, and identify with, the financially well-off, their fundamental instinct is not sympathetic toward the problems of at-risk youth. A poll of *Nation's Business* readers showed a business view that dependency on welfare results from irresponsible behavior, and that if recipients do not modify that behavior their benefits should be reduced or eliminated (*Nation's Business*, 1992). There is ambivalence in the business community. If business leaders can be convinced that a program to lower the economic and social costs of at-risk youth can be successful, some would likely break with the conservative coalition and back the program. In the meantime, they see no reason to forego their ideological predispositions.

To summarize the conservative perspective: government aid to the poor creates a "dependency culture" (Dean and Taylor-Gooby, 1992; McGlone, 1990). "[C]ertain types of social security encourage people to become dependent on these benefits and lower their desire to find work or behave in a responsible manner" (McGlone, 1990, p. 17). Among the consequences of the conservative viewpoint is a tendency to isolate youth at risk, who would otherwise be able to work, from the workplace. Yet the conservative coalition is split on how to deal with families. Some conservatives would oppose ending welfare support to pregnant teens for fear that abortions will increase. Others would reward families that stay together. The conservatives, like the liberals, do not speak with one voice.

American Public Opinion

Interest groups singly, or in coalition with other groups, attempt to impress their policy positions on representatives from the executive and legislative branches at all governmental levels. According to E. E. Schattschneider, "The outcome of every conflict is determined by the extent to which the audience becomes involved in it" (1960, p. 2). Groups attentive to an issue seek to mobilize sufficient support among the general public to achieve their policy goals. A losing coalition of interests will seek to mobilize support, or to change the arena where the decision is being made, in order to obtain a favorable outcome.

> The scope of conflict is an aspect of the scale of political organiza-
> tion and the extent of political competition. The size of the constitu-
> encies being mobilized, the inclusiveness or exclusiveness of the
> conflicts people expect to develop have a bearing on all theories
> about how politics is or should be organized. (Schattschneider, 1960,
> p. 20)

To win the game, conservative and liberal coalitions vie for support from the undecided public, that amorphous mass of the American populace whose shifting views and intensities they seek to mobilize. Information from public opinion surveys will be presented to convey the status and trends on matters related to at-risk youth. No survey data directly tap policy options toward at-risk youth. However, the political map of at-risk youth may be approached through the socioeconomic and political issues of social welfare reform and crime control. Several measurements suggest significant changes in American public opinion over the past 20 years.

In the past, Americans were supportive of social welfare programs. A 1972 Gallup poll showed that 76 percent of the people were either supportive or silent about social welfare programs. Only 24 percent wanted to see welfare programs either cut or ended altogether. Americans are now less supportive of social welfare programs and, presumably, less likely to support programs for at-risk youth. A 1994 Gallup poll showed that 54 percent of the American public believed that welfare spending should be reduced or ended altogether (See Table 2.2 below).

TABLE 2.2 Change in Opinions of American People about Spending on Welfare Programs, 1972–1994

	1972	1994
Should be:	% of respondents	
Increased	31	10
Kept at present level	40	32
Reduced	18	44
Ended altogether	6	10
No opinion	5	4

Source: McAneny, Leslie and David W. Moore, "Public Supports New Programs To Get People Off Welfare," *The Gallup Poll Monthly*, May, 1994, p. 3.

Many analysts attribute the change in public attitudes toward the recipients of Aid to Families with Dependent Children to substantial increases in welfare-supported illegitimate children and the growing acceptance of working mothers (Kenneth, 1992). Perhaps the public backlash against the program is motivated by public perception that inner-city black families are the chief beneficiaries of AFDC (Kenneth, 1992). Many Americans tend to associate particular races with criminal behavior. Hispanic and African-American teenagers are perceived as more likely than white teenagers to commit crime; see Table 2.3 below.

Today, many Americans seem to believe that crime is the most important problem facing this country. On the policy question of whether enforcement should be strengthened or crime attacked as a social problem, the pattern is inconsistent, but the overall trend is clearly in the direction of favoring strengthened enforcement and a reduced level of support for addressing crime as a social problem; see Table 2.4 below.

American public opinion is taking a harder line against both adult and youth crime. Public opinion about the death penalty also has shifted radically. In 1957, 47 percent of Americans supported capital punishment for adults; today 80 percent do. Thirty-five years ago only about one in nine Americans (11 percent) advocated the death penalty for teenagers who commit murder. In 1994 the figure was 72 percent. Only 20 percent believed that a teenager should be spared because of his youth (see Table 2.5a).

In 1994, 40 percent of Americans were willing to treat first-time juvenile offenders less harshly than first-time adult offenders, while about half would treat both juveniles and adults the same. If a youthful offender had committed two or more crimes, 83 percent of those polled believed that juvenile and adult offenders should be treated the same, while only 12 percent were still willing to let juveniles off with less punishment (see Table 5b).

These various indicators suggest that over the past 40 years American public opinion has evolved toward a more punitive and less rehabilitative attitude toward at-risk youth. Public opinion has swung against welfare, against rehabilitation, toward harsher punishment, and in favor of treating youthful offenders no differently from adult offenders. According to the public, crime should be dealt with strictly, with little consideration for the age of the person charged.

The dominant public view has shifted away from the policy positions espoused by the liberal coalition and has taken on the views of the conservative coalition. At present, assuming Schattschneider's theory of decision-making, one short-run liberal strategy would strive to keep decisions on at-risk youth issues out of the public arena; a conservative strategy would

TABLE 2.3 Likelihood of Committing Crime

	More likely than others	Less likely than others	Same as others	No opinion
	% of respondents			
Male teenagers in general	58	6	34	2
Homeless people	40	20	36	4
Blacks	37	5	56	2
Hispanics	30	7	59	4
Whites	6	21	71	2

Source: *The Gallup Poll Monthly*, December, 1993, p. 38. Methodology: The Gallup Poll results are based on telephone interviews with a nationally representative sample of 1,244 adults, 18 years and older, conducted October 13–18, 1993. The sample included 870 whites and 313 blacks. To allow reporting of results by race, Gallup supplemented a nationally representative sample of telephone households by screening for 235 additional blacks in areas of the country where the black population is concentrated. A statistical weighting procedure was used to ensure that blacks and whites were included in their proper proportions for results based on total sample.

For results based on samples of this size, one can say with 95 percent confidence that the error due to sampling and other random effects on the opinions of whites and blacks is plus or minus 4 and plus or minus 6 percentage points, respectively; for the entire sample, the margin is plus or minus 3 percentage points. In addition to sampling error, question wording and the practical difficulties in conducting surveys can introduce error or bias into the findings of public opinion polls.

TABLE 2.4 American Public Opinion on How Crime Should Be
Controlled (1994)

	Should attack as social problem	Should strengthen enforcement	No opinion
		% of respondents	
1994	51	42	7
1992	67	25	8
1990	57	36	7
1989	61	32	7

Source: Adapted from *The Gallup Poll Monthly*, August, 1994, p. 12.

TABLE 2.5A Shift in Public Opinion about Death Penalty for Teenagers
Who Commit Murder, 1957–1994 (based on those who are pro-death
penalty for adults)[**]

	1957	1994
	% of respondents	
Death penalty	24	72
Be spared	56	20
No opinion	20	8
	100	100

[**]1957: 47 percent of total sample; 1994: 80 percent of total sample
Source: *The Gallup Poll Monthly*, September, 1994, p. 3.

TABLE 2.5B American Public Opinion Concerning Punishment of
Teenagers vs. Adults for Their Second and Third Crimes, 1994

Should be:	% of respondents
Treated the same	83
Less harshly	12
Depends	4
No opinion	1
	100

(N=515 respondents ± 5%)
Source: Moore, David W., "Majority Advocate Death Penalty for Teenage Killers," *The
Gallup Poll Monthly*, September, 1994, p. 3.

expand the scope of the conflict to give greater weight to the public view. Keeping at-risk youth issues out of the political arena is not an effective long-term strategy, and the public opinion data do not mean the liberal cause is lost. The liberals abandoned the local arenas in the 1950s as they devoted their attention to the national scene. If they re-orient their thinking, define problems locally, recruit supporters and advocates locally, and lobby locally, liberals have a humanitarian message that can resonate with the public and a pragmatic message that business can appreciate. Either the policies or the presentation must change in order to avoid a conflict with dominant public opinion, and the implementation strategy must accommodate the reality of a new political arena. The conservative coalition is presently winning because it has captured local attention with its simple, if inconsistent, message, which will be difficult to implement. The local arena is a battlefield on which the liberal coalition must join the issues if it is to fulfill its vision for at-risk youth.

Lobbying

Interest groups are organizations which seek to further particular causes. Toward that end, they adopt several strategies. First, interest groups seek to educate the public, government, and corporate leaders about an issue by conducting research and disseminating the findings by press release, press conference, or newspaper advertisements. They compile statistics and maintain extensive files of unpublished materials from member agencies. Second, interest groups can publicize the voting records of members of Congress. Americans for Constitutional Action (ACA) and Americans for Democratic Action (ADA) have created summary indicators of the degree to which each member of Congress has adhered to conservative and liberal positions, respectively, on legislation. Other groups publicize how members of Congress have voted on issues the group considers important. Third, interest groups can demonstrate by marching and carrying placards to draw public attention to their issue-position. Fourth, leaders of interest groups can attempt to influence legislation by asking their members to write letters or call their representatives (Berry, 1989). Even though the tactics are widely used, few interest groups use them all at once or only one of them exclusively. They select among these tactics as they see fit.

Family values have brought to the political arena intense ideological conflict.

> Most of this struggle has been about the American family: the role of women; the primacy of parental values over those introduced by the schools or television; and the perceived moral decay of America

that undermines religion and the traditional nuclear family. (Berry, 1989, p. 100)

Groups interested in youth policy cooperate with each other and with like-minded members of Congress. Both liberals and conservatives work with public interest groups which support their positions, and they employ public relations firms to lobby legislators. The Democratic Party controlled Congress regularly from the 1950s to the 1990s. Even Republican presidents (Eisenhower, Nixon, Ford, Bush) have been primarily oriented to a national constituency, or interested in conservative business values rather than conservative family values. Also, interest groups which favor the liberal position on issues of family values have adopted a strategy of working at the national level. Because they have been successful there, they have relied on nationally based public information campaigns to get out the message to the grass roots. Interest groups favoring a conservative position, because they found barren ground in Washington, turned to state and local levels. This is harder work, demanding more people and time. They found local Republicans receptive to their message because not only was the ideology compatible, but also the interest group activists constituted a group that could be mobilized for electoral campaigns. When the Congressional Republicans swept into Washington in the Fall of 1994, their conservative family values backers were quick to demand legislation supporting their position.

It is now the liberals who must regroup to mount a counter-attack at the local and state levels, organizing themselves at the grass roots and supporting like-minded Congressional candidates in order to triumph in the game of pluralistic politics.

The discussion above assumes that the significant decisions of public policy are made based upon the actions of interest groups and public opinion. Other political observers think that the important decisions are determined by the wishes of an elite, a game of politics dominated by a small group of rich people who work behind the scenes to benefit themselves at the expense of the majority.

ELITISM

In the aftermath of the Oklahoma City bombing of April, 1995, the publicity about various private militias carrying out para-military training on the weekends brought home one point clearly. An intense minority perceives that the American federal government, whether controlled by Republicans or Democrats, is an overwhelming, sinister force which seeks to strip citizens of their individual rights and to trample down the "little people." This intense minority thinks that an international conspiracy led by huge financial interests controls the lives of us all. The only effective way to protect our constitutionally guaranteed freedoms requires a willingness to use violence. Unless forcibly stopped, the federal government will wipe out alternative lifestyles that challenge federal authority, just as the federal Department of Alcohol, Tobacco, and Firearms harassed the Weaver family at Ruby Ridge, Idaho, and leveled the Branch Davidian compound near Waco, Texas, killing its inhabitants.

Such thinking represents an unsophisticated form of the elitist theory of rule, but able scholars do subscribe to the view that the major decisions are made by elites. In contrast to the pluralist theory of democracy, the elitist theory suggests that governments are run by a handful of wealthy and knowledgeable people (Mills, 1954). Michael Parenti (1977) argued that in America,

> Public policies, whether formulated by conservatives or liberals, Republicans or Democrats, consistently favor the large corporate interests at a substantial cost to many millions of workers, small farmers, small producers, indigent elderly and rural poor. (Parenti, 1977, p. 316)

Government policies are merely strategic and symbolic manipulation of economic resources to prevent social unrest. Frances F. Piven and Richard A. Cloward (1971) write:

> The key to an understanding of relief-giving is in the functions it serves for the larger economic and political order, for relief is a secondary and supportive institution. Historical evidence suggests that relief arrangements are initiated or expanded during the occasional outbreaks of civil disorder produced by mass unemployment, and are then abolished or contracted when political stability is restored. We argue that expansive relief policies are designed to mute civil disorder, and restrictive ones to reinforce work norms. (Piven and Cloward, 1971, p. xiii)

According to an elitist perspective, elites respond only to pressure. Blacks drew attention to their plight with riots in Detroit, Watts, and Washington, and were rewarded with "hush-money" in the form of federal grants, which had the result not of solving the problem but of providing financial support for those who could articulate the interests of those who participated in the disturbances. The elites will pay off, co-opt, or eliminate aggressive opposition. At-risk youth will have its interests addressed only if these people who are at risk constitute a personal threat to the lives or economic base of the economic and political elites.

The elitist argument cannot be supported or refuted by public opinion, because elites are suspected of communicating privately and leaving no documented evidence for scholars. However, the elite explanation for how decisions are made is attractive to people on both the left and right of the political spectrum. The action strategy for achieving the goals of at-risk youth suggests that violence, or the credible threat of violence, is the only means to gain attention and to have one's needs addressed. While violence may be attractive to some disadvantaged, it is unlikely to achieve lasting policies of benefit to at-risk youth.

POLITICS BY ECONOMICS

From the perspective of a mainstream economist, solving the problem of at-risk youth is highly unlikely, regardless of how many resources are thrown into the battle. A fundamental aspect of the problem is the inability of these people to find jobs. Eliminating unemployment among at-risk youth would create unacceptable inflationary pressures. It is an article of faith among most economists that when unemployment is low, there is competition among employers for workers, which, in a free market, bids up the price of labor. Because the price of labor increases, the cost of the product produced by that labor increases, which decreases the amount of aggregate products which will be bought, which leads to lower profit for the producer, higher unemployment, and a lower standard of living for all Americans.

To forestall this inflationary cycle, if the unemployment rate dips below a critical level, which seems to be around six percent, the Federal Reserve Bank raises the interest rate it charges to banks. This increases the cost of borrowing to the investor/producer, which reduces expansion in the economy, which means less investment, leading to fewer new jobs, or laying off employees from existing jobs.

By raising the cost of doing business through interest rate increases, unemployment will rise, and the threat of wage-based inflation will recede. Most people are unaffected by these small shifts in the economy. Their jobs continue, no matter what. However, heavily affected by counter-inflationary policies are those who are the last hired and first fired, those people at the margins of employment, who are "at risk." The strategy to contain inflation, which protects the majority in their social world, creates a permanent class of marginally employed workers, who are in or out of work depending on the condition of the economy.

Within this mind-set on economics and politics, there is no way to improve the lot of everyone. According to the system, there must be losers—those who will be thrown out of work when the economy has overheated and excludes its flotsam. Some individuals may escape from the revolving door of unemployment, but others must take their places. If one person gains permanent employment, another is put at risk. It is not possible for 98 or 100 percent of those seeking work to be employed. Hence fulfilled is the Biblical injunction, "The poor you have with you always." Within this game, there is no use trying to enhance employment. Hiring and firing will take place at the fringes, regardless of training. Advocates for at-risk populations may wish to seek better welfare and jobless benefits to ease the inevitable transition from work to unemployment, including psychological counselling so that people can understand the macro-economic forces at work which determine their situation. Efforts at job training will only raise expectations and result in disappointment as the pendulum swings away.

POLITICS AS BUREAUCRACY

The at-risk population is dependent on public or not-for-profit bureaucracies for a substantial proportion of their basic needs: welfare, education, job-training. As mentioned above, the job opportunities for populations at risk respond to market criteria; unfortunately, bureaucracies do not respond to these same forces. Their budgets do not rise counter-cyclically in order to meet needs of at-risk populations.

When dealing with at-risk populations, those who pay for the public services are not the same people who receive the services. The incentives for payers, recipients, and providers are conflicting. Those who receive the services want high quality and have no incentive to moderate their demands. Those who pay want the service delivered at the lowest possible cost, and they have less interest in quality.

In the vortex of these forces stand the street-level bureaucrats (SLBs), who want to deliver quality services to needy individuals but face often recalcitrant clients, a maze of rules that inhibit their ability to respond in the way dictated by their professional training, and a workload that prevents adequate individual attention to the client (Lipsky, 1980). This drama takes place against the backdrop of a fluctuating economy and rigid budgets, which ignore issues of quality while emphasizing accountability by means of paperwork. For self-protection the harried SLB sticks to the rules, minimizes personal risk, and for emotional protection (Hirschhorn, 1988) disregards the unique situation of individual clients.

Take a hypothetical example of how a quality program degenerates.

Jane Jones, located in Silver City, manages an education-jobs program for state government. During the first year she had remarkable success, finding jobs at a $7-per-hour wage or higher for 70 percent of the people who entered her program. Because the reputation of this program was widely publicized, during the second year the number of entrants into her program doubled, yet her budget remained the same. She is required under the terms of the grant to take all who qualify for her program. The instructors in her program now feel overworked and unable to provide the same one-on-one instruction and counselling that was possible last year. The economic boom of last year has receded, and employers are laying off workers; therefore placements from the program are down. Fewer placements mean a lower rating by the government and a risk of losing funds when the program comes up for renewal. Instructors are disheartened, which lowers the morale of the students, and the program drifts back to an operational mode in which instructors are more interested in credentialing than teaching, in processing the paperwork properly to insure that employees are paid and that students receive their stipends. Jane, a dynamic manager, moves on to a more interesting job where one need not spend so much time shuffling paper and fighting for the program against an uninformed public that sees only the discouraging numbers.

Michael Lipsky describes these dynamics in his book, *Street-Level Bureaucracy* (1980). A successful program attracts clients. The increased client load decreases the ability of the organization to be responsive, which decreases the effectiveness of the organization, which causes clients to satisfy their needs elsewhere. In the public sector, unlike the private sector, enhanced performance and effectiveness do not generate revenues which one can use to maintain and improve the level of services.

Users of the services are not paying for the services. These users have no reasonable alternative to accepting the services, and their sole interest is ensuring that quality services continue. However, those who deliver the services have little incentive to maintain service quality to the captive audience they serve, because they end up with more clients and more work. Responsiveness increases costs and demand for the services. Those who pay are not using them, and their concern is less with effectiveness than with cost. SLBs are squeezed between the people who want services delivered as promised and the people who are paying for the services.

This bureaucratic maze entangles at-risk youth. Politics occurs outside their system, and they can do little to affect it. SLBs and at-risk youth are both trapped in a wider system which neither can influence, yet these are the institutions to which at-risk youth are socialized. Is it any wonder that they see their world as random, unaffected by their own actions? The values they internalize do not connect to middle class practices of working and saving, deferring gratification, and learning by taking moderate risks. The world of at-risk youth is unpredictable, and in an unpredictable environment a random response is rational. In a bureaucratic world there is no rational strategy for the advocates of at-risk youth.

CONCLUSION

By understanding the games and the players, advocates for at-risk youth can avoid the cycle of expectation followed by disappointment and can plan a strategy to maximize self-interest. For example, the business community is a potential ally, but business people must be convinced that a proposed program will result in skilled, trained workers who have appropriate attitudes for the labor market. At-risk youth advocates must consider innovative ways to cooperate with business to achieve their common goals.

Emphasizing job training for at-risk youth is insufficient. Successful job-training programs cannot solve the at-risk youth problem. Constraints of the economic game throw people into the bureaucratic game. That vicious cycle cannot be exited without changing economic assumptions or building a stronger safety net. Washington in the foreseeable future will not furnish the safety net. The caps on block grants by Washington to the states mean that state or local authorities bear financial responsibility. Agencies that serve dependent and needy people must localize, decentralize, and speak a common language to gain the support of well-intentioned, politically active people at the local level.

In summary, advocates for at-risk youth must think both substantively and politically. They must rethink their principal goals and develop local strategies, building alliances and coalitions that will provide the political basis for achieving their goals. Perhaps they would be better served by scaling back their expectations for the success of any program and becoming aware of the likely long-term futility of their efforts, while at the same time pressing ahead with local programs.

REFERENCES

Ainley, P. (1988). *From school to YTS*. Milton Keynes, Great Britain: Open University Press.

Berry, J. M. (1989). *The Interest Group Society* (2nd ed.). Glenview, IL: Scott, Foresman/Little, Brown.

Child Welfare League of America. (1994). New studies document children's plight: Proposed solutions. *Children's Voice, 3*(4).

Dahl, R. (1961). *Who governs: Democracy and power in an American city*. New Haven, CT: Yale University Press.

Dahrendorf, R. (1959). *Class and class conflict in industrial society*. Stanford, CA: Stanford University Press.

Dean, H. and Taylor-Gooby, P. (1992). *Dependency culture*. New York: Harvester Wheatsheaf.

Dennison, M. (1994). Finding an answer for sex education and teen pregnancy. *Youth Today, 3*(2), 20–24.

The Gallup Poll Monthly. (1993, December), Racial overtones evident in Americans' attitudes about crime. (selected items).

———. (1994, May), Leslie McAnney and David W. Moore, Public supports new programs to get people off welfare.

———. (1994, August), David W. Moore, Public wants crime bill.

———. (1994, September), David W. Moore, Majority advocate death penalty for teenage killers.

Hirschhorn, L. (1988). *The workplace within: The psychodynamics of organizational life*. Cambridge, MA: MIT Press.

Katz, J. (1995a). House GOP welfare plan shifts focus from work to teen mothers. *Congressional Quarterly, 14*, 159–162.

———. (1995b). GOP rift delays action on welfare. *Congressional Quarterly, 14*, 159–162.

Kenneth, J. (1992). Welfare Reform. *CQ Researcher, 2*(14), 315–331.

Kolberg, W. (1987). Employment, the private sector, and at-risk youth. *Annals of the American Academy of Political and Social Science, 494*, 94–100.

Lasswell, H. D. (1950). *Politics: Who gets what, when, how*. New York: Peter Smith.

Liederman, D. (1994). Executive directions. *Children's Voice, 3*(4), 2.

Lipsky, M. (1980). *Street-level bureaucracy: Dilemmas of the individual in public service*. New York: Russell Sage Foundation.

McGlone, F. (1990). Away from the dependency culture. In S. Savage and L. Robins (Eds.), *Public policy under Thatcher* (pp. 159–170). London: Macmillan.

Mills, C. W. (1954). *The power elite*. New York: Oxford University Press.

Moore, E. (1994). From the executive director. *The Black Child Advocate, 21*(4), 2.

Nation's Business. (Nov. 1992). *80*(11), 81.

Readers' View On Welfare Reform. (1992). *Nation's Business, 80*(11), 76–83.

Nichols, M. (1994). Federal money may create rivals as well as opportunities. *Youth Today, 3*(3), 1–12.

Orr, M. T., ed. (1987). *Keeping students in school: A guide to effective dropout prevention programs and services* (pp. 176–189). San Francisco, CA: Jossey-Bass.

Parenti, M. (1977). *Democracy for the few* (2nd ed.). New York: St. Martin's Press.

Piven, F. and Cloward, R. (1971). *Regulating the poor: The functions of public welfare*. New York: Pantheon Books.

Schattschneider, E. E. (1960). *The semi-sovereign people: A realist view of democracy in America*. New York: Holt, Rinehart and Winston.

Yzaguirre, R. (1987). Public policy, crime, and the Hispanic community. *Annals of the American Academy of Political and Social Science, 494*, 101–104.

Vanneman, A. (1995). Once-mighty WAVE reduced to a ripple. *Youth Today, 4*(1), 10–12.

3 THE REAL WORLD

TEENAGE HIGH SCHOOL LEAVERS SPEAK OUT ABOUT ALCOHOL, OTHER DRUGS, AND LIFE PROBLEMS

Sandra L. Putnam, James E. Malia, and

Suzanne F. Streagle

INTRODUCTION

Based on 1990 United States Census data on selected labor force and community characteristics, Tennessee's population included about 300,000 youth between 16 and 19 years of age. Of these, 13 percent or about 40,000 were not enrolled in school and had not graduated from high school; only 38 percent of these high school leavers were employed or in the Armed Forces. The state's dropout rate was 18 percent of ninth graders dropping out of school before the end of 12th grade in 1992–1993, amounting to more than 15,000 students. The annual event rate was about five percent.

These teenage school leavers pose a serious problem for the State of Tennessee and for the United States as a whole. A population's educational level impacts and influences the quality of the work force and the economic opportunities of its citizens. Low educational attainment is associated with the need for public assistance and is a drain on the economy. It is estimated that less than 40 percent of AFDC adults have completed high school. Adult school leavers are found to be at higher risk of unemployment and poverty, have excess health and mental health problems, lack health insurance coverage, and suffer other adverse consequences (Community Health Research Group [CHRG], 1995). Such consequences are a detriment to the individual and, if widespread, impose an added burden on society.

Long before they drop out, at-risk students develop behavior patterns which further hinder their education. They may disrupt classes, skip school, work long hours on a job, abuse drugs or alcohol, or become pregnant. Dropping out is the last stage in a process which began long before the decision to leave school.

One of the ways in which it is believed that high school leavers are particularly vulnerable is in their use and abuse of alcohol and other drugs (AOD). Involvement with alcohol and other drugs may have been influential in many students' decisions to leave high school or their dismissal by school authorities. The continuing use and abuse of these substances is a major barrier for many youth as they try to become contributing members of society (Schmidt and Hankoff, 1979; Werch et al., 1987). However, previous research is sparse concerning the dynamic interrelationship between substance use and abuse and leaving high school without a diploma or GED certificate.

We recognize those who complete their educations by their successes—degrees obtained, good jobs secured, and contributions to society. We do not know much about those who leave high school early. High school leavers are a difficult population to study because they are hard to locate, and it is a very risky proposition to generalize to the total school leaver population based solely on the most accessible school leavers.

Yet knowing what happens to these former students once they leave high school can help school systems be more responsive to students' needs in helping them finish high school. Additionally, schools and other agencies can use such information to help students better cope once they have left school, if indeed it is their decision to leave before graduation. Services can be directed in an appropriate manner that will reduce society's costs and that will support these youth in becoming productive and successful adults.

This chapter is a glimpse at what happens to a group of Tennessee teenagers who left high school without graduating and struggle to make it in an adult world. Information in the chapter is drawn from a study conducted by the Community Health Research Group, The University of Tennessee, Knoxville, in the summer of 1994. The study, sponsored by the Tennessee Department of Health, Bureau of Alcohol and Drug Abuse Services, examined the health risks, the use and abuse of alcohol and other drugs, and the life problems experienced by this group.

The chapter profiles these young people according to sociodemographic characteristics, their use, abuse, and problems with alcohol and other drugs, and their exposure to treatment and prevention programs. Open-ended comments from the respondents tell of their reasons for leaving school and the role alcohol and other drugs have played in their lives, offer advice to other young people about leaving school, and provide suggestions to school officials to help students stay in school.

BACKGROUND

To better understand the dynamics of teenage high school leaving, it is helpful to examine the broader context of risk factors for leaving school early. There is a considerable literature on this phenomenon, especially from the viewpoint of school-based prevention. Studies in this body of research seek to describe the characteristics of those youth who leave school before graduating and elucidate the factors influencing early or premature school leaving behavior (Cairns et al., 1989; Evans and Matthews, 1992; Hawkins et al., 1992; Johnson et al., 1990). Once students have dropped out of school, however, research on them drastically diminishes, owing in large part to the difficulty of locating such youth (Kandel, 1975; Radford et al., 1989; Smart and Adlaf, 1991; Windle, 1989).

Mensch and Kandel (1988), in a review of the findings on the determinants of early high school leaving, identify the following correlates: poor high school grades and academic failure; negative attitudes about school and teachers; delinquent behavior (such as disciplinary problems in school, school suspension, and probation); the early assumption of adult roles (such as worker, spouse, or parent); strong attachment to peers, especially the lack of conventionality and attachment to social institutions; low religiosity; and dating. They point out that personality variables are not the most important predictors of early school leaving. Such personality predictors include low educational and professional aspirations; low commitment to conventional goals; and low psychological well-being reflected in high levels of anxiety, depression, resentfulness, and irritability. Self-esteem and sociability or social adjustment have not proved significant in some multivariate models. Further, Mensch and Kandel point to the background variables of parental education, income, and occupation as being significant predictors of early school leaving, even controlling for other factors. The implications of work during high school for the completion of education vary, but generally intensive employment (greater than 14 hours per week) or working full time have a negative impact upon high school completion.

DeRidder and Dietz (1988) report a list of identifiers that typically characterize the majority of school leavers. As they point out, these factors are interrelated, interactive, and cumulative. These identifiers include: low socioeconomic status; low family income; unemployed or unskilled parents; poorly educated parents; single parent (divorce, death, etc.) or unhappy homes; low value on schooling by parents and friends; large number of siblings; low reading or math skills (one or more years behind age or grade level); low self-esteem; retained one or more years; failing in one or more subjects; little or no participation in extracurricular activities; no interest in or dislike of school; bored, unhappy, isolated, or few friends; poor attendance or frequently tardy; pregnancy and/or marriage; two or more years older than classmates; educational program not meeting needs; member of a minority group; approaches to learning differ from norm; ill health, fatigues easily, or handicapping conditions; needs guidance; male gender; resents control of teachers or school; achieves below capacity; IQ below 90; employed full time while in school; low value on education by the student's community; teachers and counselors not interested in student; many school-to-school transfers; siblings dropped out; and needs more vocational education.

As noted earlier, it is frequently postulated that AOD use/abuse is associated with lower educational achievement and early school leaving (Centers for Disease Control, 1991), and that high school leavers are at high risk for AOD use, abuse, and problems (Bachman et al., 1991; Chen and Kandel, 1995; Eggert and Herting, 1993; Lorion et al., 1991; Windle, 1990). There is, however, a dearth of research that examines the interrelationship between leaving school early and substance use or abuse, and some of the research that is available is of dubious value. A 1991 report by the U.S. General Accounting Office (GAO) criticized the more recent research in this area because it relied on old data. As a result the GAO was "unable to present current findings from sound research on teen drug use and pregnancy and dropping out of school" (United States General Accounting Office [USGAO], 1991, p. 1). The GAO concluded that in reality various risky behaviors, including early sexual experimentation, drug abuse, and quitting school, can be viewed as manifestations of general difficulties that have earlier origins. Research on teen risk behaviors should attempt to answer questions about constellations of problem behavior rather than one or two behaviors in isolation. For example, "research may find spurious relationships between drug use and pregnancy or dropping out of school because they stem from the same underlying factors rather than because drug use causes the others" (USGAO, 1991, p. 1).

A recent publication relying on earlier data used the High School and Beyond (HS and B) database to investigate the experiences of high school leavers and high school graduates in 1986, four years after the projected date of graduation. The original study compared high school leavers and graduates with no post-secondary education in regard to the personal, social, and economic consequences of leaving school early. One of the variables examined was alcohol use (McCaul et al., 1992). This study found that high school leavers scored significantly higher in their alcohol consumption. Differences in alcohol consumption were confined to males, however. In two separate analyses—one controlling for background factors and one not—only male school leavers were significantly different from male high school graduates in their use of alcohol. No significant differences were found between female school leavers and female graduates (McCaul et al., 1992).

The authors note that the HS and B data set does contain some limitations. The HS and B survey's base year sampling involved high school sophomores. Young men and women leaving school before the tenth grade may represent a "hard core" group of youth whose post-school experiences are considerably more negative than those of the group of school leavers studied. As a result, some differences between school leavers and graduates may be underestimated. Care must be taken, therefore, in generalizing study results to the total population of school leavers. Further, the alcohol-use composite measure in this study yielded an approximate measure of leavers' and graduates' alcohol consumption, not the actual effects of alcohol consumption and the problems associated with it. Also, alcohol was the only drug studied.

One of the only studies that looks at the interrelationship between early high school leaving and drug use is reported by Mensch and Kandel (1988). This is also one of the few studies that examines potential differences between terminal leavers and young people who leave school but subsequently obtain a high school equivalency certificate (GED). The study addresses three major issues: First, are the use of drugs and quitting school related to each other? Second, does drug use have a unique effect on, and is it a predisposing factor for, leaving school early? Finally, do high school leavers who eventually acquire a GED have different histories of drug use than those with no high school diploma? The data are from a nationally representative sample of young Americans from the National Longitudinal Survey of Youth (NLSY), an ongoing survey of over 12,000 youth who were aged 14 to 21 when first interviewed in 1979 and who have been interviewed annually since then.

Event-history analysis was used to determine to what extent drug use contributes to early school leaving, over and above the fact that both behaviors appear to share similar determinants. The authors found that for both sexes, lifetime and annual prevalence of the use of various legal and illegal substances and the intensity of use were higher, with the exception of alcohol, among those who left high school than among those who did not. Furthermore, differences between the groups were stronger with respect to the degree of involvement than with respect to any lifetime use of the drugs. Substance use among non-leavers, whether cigarettes, marijuana, cocaine, or other illicit substances, was more likely to be experimental than it was among leavers (Mensch and Kandel, 1988).

In general, the earlier the involvement in drug use, the higher the rates of leaving school early. The more socially unacceptable the substance, the stronger the association with school leaving (Merrill et al., 1994). Mensch

and Kandel conclude that "prior use of cigarettes, marijuana, and other illicit drugs at any age increases the propensity of both sexes to drop out. In
addition, the younger the initiation into alcohol, marijuana, and other illicit
drugs for men, and cigarettes and marijuana for women, the greater the likelihood of leaving school without a diploma" (1988, p. 111).

That high school leavers are at greater risk for health-related problems, especially with regard to substance use, is shown in results of a Youth
Risk Behavior Survey (YRBS) conducted as part of the 1992 National Health
Interview Survey (NHIS). The Centers for Disease Control (1994) analyzed
self-reported data from this survey and found that out-of-school adolescents
(not attending school and who had not graduated from high school or attained General Educational Development credentials) were significantly more
likely than in-school adolescents to report smoking cigarettes during the 30
days preceding the survey and to report ever having smoked cigarettes or
ever using alcohol, marijuana, or cocaine (see also Pirie et al, 1988). As the
report further states, alcohol and other drug use may have preceded and
contributed to the decision of some adolescents to quit school, and these risk
behaviors may increase after adolescents quit school.

Chavez et al. (1989) report significant differences between school
leavers and at-risk students and control groups for the use of several drugs.
High school leavers were found to have the highest rates of alcohol and
drug use, followed by at-risk students. The relative rates of use were about
the same for nearly all drugs, with the largest differences found for drinking to intoxication and use of marijuana, uppers, and cocaine. Females,
especially leavers, had higher rates of tobacco smoking than males. Rates
of cigarette smoking among leavers were significantly greater than among
controls only for males, however. Finally, school leavers were more likely
to have had serious illness within the preceding year than members of the
control group.

In sum, there is limited research which specifically examines the relationship between AOD use/abuse and early high school leaving. Studies
are non-comparable because of definitional differences—early school leaving encompasses a broad spectrum of behavior, the definition of which seems
to vary from study to study. Most of the studies are cross-sectional in design, which prohibits making inferences as to the temporal relationships
among AOD use/abuse and early school leaving. Sampling strategies and
sample sizes vary across studies as well, which further inhibits comparisons.
It is to profile teenage high school leavers that the Tennessee High School
Leavers Study was commissioned by the Tennessee Department of Health,
Bureau of Alcohol and Drug Abuse Services.

Respondents for the Tennessee High School Leavers Study (n=338) were drawn from three metropolitan regions of Tennessee—Knox County (40 percent), Davidson County (25 percent), and Shelby County (12 percent)—and from some surrounding rural regions (23 percent). The data were obtained mainly by face-to-face interviews with recent school leavers. Telephone interviews were conducted in 15 percent of the cases. Twenty-five percent of the respondents were interviewed in a youth detention facility in East Tennessee.

This non-probability sample of youth was selected using eligibility screening and soliciting volunteer subjects from recreational areas, housing developments, malls, waiting rooms of job service and unemployment offices, social service agencies, juvenile court and juvenile detention facilities, on street corners, at video arcades and pool halls, and in various GED programs. Many of the early respondents helped locate other youth in their neighborhood who had dropped out of school so that they too could participate in the study.

For the purposes of this study, an early high school leaver was defined as a youth between the ages of 16 and 19 who left school without receiving a high school diploma or GED certificate and who was not currently enrolled full-time in a public, private, alternative, technical, or vocational school or GED program. Eligible respondents could be working toward a GED as long as they were not enrolled in a program full-time. Usable data for the study were collected from 338 youth who met these criteria.

The questionnaire took approximately 15 minutes to administer. Questions included items on age, sex, race, employment, and other sociodemographic variables; health status and disability; reasons for leaving high school and future educational plans; lifetime, recent and current alcohol, tobacco, and other drug use and abuse as well as associated life problems; and some open-ended opinion and attitude questions. Where possible, incentives or tokens of appreciation were given to respondents after interviews were completed.

While the Tennessee High School Leavers Study is not longitudinal, much useful scientific data about AOD use among high school leavers can be obtained for exploratory purposes through the use of such a purposive cross-sectional sample design. A unique aspect of the study is the inclusion of a series of open-ended questions on reasons for leaving school, current employment, future plans, regrets, and advice to other youth. Sometimes poignant quotations included here provide an intimate look at the real position in which recent school leavers find themselves. These quotations from respondents record their unique perspectives and lend a human voice to quantitative study results. The following is a combination of quantitative survey results illustrated by answers to open-ended questions to flesh out the predicament in which many of these youth find themselves.

STUDY RESULTS

The Respondents

The majority of the respondents in the study (64 percent) were male. The respondents' average age was 17.6 years. Fifteen percent were aged 16; 28 percent were 17; 34 percent were aged 18; and 23 percent were 19. Fifty-five percent were African American. A third lived in female-headed households, and 20 percent lived in two-parent households. The largest proportion (40 percent) of these youth left school around age 16, after completing the tenth grade. Fifty-three percent had been in school within the past year, and 88 percent within the past two years. Sixty-nine percent were unemployed, and of the 31 percent employed, only 60 percent were employed full-time.

Most of the respondents were bright and courteous. They were comfortable talking about themselves, and they gave thoughtful and considered responses. There were very few outright refusals to participate in the study. The young people seemed to appreciate the fact that an adult was willing to spend time with them and take their opinions seriously.

WHY DID THESE YOUTH LEAVE HIGH SCHOOL?

These high school leavers describe a variety of reasons for leaving school. No one reason dominates, although disliking school is the most common reason given for leaving school early. A number of factors seem to build on one another until at some point leaving school seems to be the only available alternative. For some students the actual choice to leave school was not theirs. Because of behavioral or academic problems, pregnancy, or their own or family illness or need for employment, a number of students were encouraged to seek alternatives outside school or were dismissed outright.

The phenomenon of "dropping out," which we are calling "school leaving," is complex and multicausal. As a result many of the respondents had more than a single reason for leaving high school, and reasons were sometimes difficult to classify. More than one-quarter expressed a general dislike of school. This reason, however, was frequently combined with other reasons such as pregnancy, disciplinary problems, trouble with teachers or administrators, academic problems, economic pressures, and legal problems.

After general dislike of school, the most frequent reasons given for leaving high school early were pregnancy, marriage, or child care problems; disciplinary problems; academic problems; economic pressures; and legal problems (Figure 3.1). Other reasons were trouble with teachers or administrators; own or family members' illness or injury; and moving or changing schools and having trouble with transferring. Only a few mentioned violence-related reasons for leaving school, but many had been involved in violent incidents both at school and outside.

Reasons for school leaving differed somewhat by sex—in particular, leaving school for pregnancy, marriage, or child care problems. Thus 86 percent of those who left school because of child care problems were female and 14 percent were male. On the other hand, those who reported disciplinary problems, economic pressures, and legal problems were significantly more likely to be males, who were represented at 80 percent, 85 percent and 94 percent, respectively, of those reporting such problems.

The fact that fully 15 percent of respondents explicitly attributed their school leaving to use of and problems with alcohol and other drugs underscores the role that alcohol and other drugs played in their decision to leave school and the continuing impact these substances have on their lives (Figure 3.1).

Use of Alcohol and Other Drugs

Reported alcohol and other drug problems ranged from direct violation of school drug policies to more subtle effects of AOD on concentration, judgment, and lifestyles. Selling and using drugs caused a number of former students to be dismissed. As simply stated by one respondent: "I got locked up because I was selling drugs at school." Others were using drugs at school. They got caught and were dismissed. A number were caught smoking marijuana. "I was smoking weed, and I got caught in the bathroom smoking it." Others were caught possessing an illegal substance. "Possessing cocaine. Got caught with it at school."

Another used the opportunity to sell drugs as a way to make good money. School could not compete with that opportunity. "I started making money—fast money—didn't want to go to school then." Some left school so that they could sell drugs. "I left so I could sell drugs." And some wound up going to jail. "I am going to jail. I got caught selling drugs."

Some students spent all their time selling drugs and partying. They became too busy to go to school; the lure of money and a good time was too great. One young man was more interested in a good time that he was in school. "I wanted to have fun and school was not fun! I was selling drugs at the time."

CHAPTER 3, FIGURE 1. REASONS FOR LEAVING SCHOOL AMONG TENNESSEE HIGH SCHOOL LEAVERS, 1994

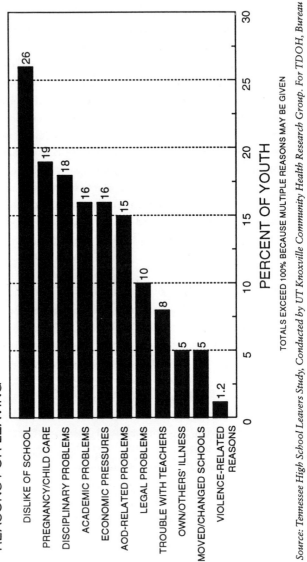

REASONS FOR LEAVING

DISLIKE OF SCHOOL	26
PREGNANCY/CHILD CARE	19
DISCIPLINARY PROBLEMS	18
ACADEMIC PROBLEMS	16
ECONOMIC PRESSURES	16
AOD-RELATED PROBLEMS	15
LEGAL PROBLEMS	10
TROUBLE WITH TEACHERS	8
OWN/OTHERS' ILLNESS	5
MOVED/CHANGED SCHOOLS	5
VIOLENCE-RELATED REASONS	1.2

PERCENT OF YOUTH

TOTALS EXCEED 100% BECAUSE MULTIPLE REASONS MAY BE GIVEN

Source: Tennessee High School Leavers Study, Conducted by UT Knoxville Community Health Research Group. For TDOH, Bureau of Alcohol and Drug Abuse Services, 1994.

Lack of Interest

As some high school leavers describe it, they just did not want to be in school. "I didn't want to get up in the morning . I didn't want to do my school work," is how one person described the feeling. For many the interest just was not there: "I didn't like it, so I quit." Other youth were tired of school and were looking for something more exciting. As stated by one young man: "I got tired of it; I wanted to hustle and make some money."

Absence of Help and Support

Some school leavers perceived that they did not get the help and support they needed to stay in school. Many girls who were pregnant left because they were unable to get assistance with homebound study or other kinds of assistance that would have made it possible to continue their education and deal with their pregnancy. "I dropped out of school when I was pregnant with my first child, then I tried to finish my education by returning. I couldn't make it work because I have no sitter for my children to return to school." In some schools, it was unacceptable to stay in school once a girl was pregnant. In others, ridicule from students made it uncomfortable to stay, and in other cases complications with the pregnancy became paramount and other concerns, such as school, were secondary. So the girls left. Several school leavers indicated that they were put out of school when they reached age 17 or 18. Teachers did not want them in their classes, and they were told to leave.

Some who had difficulty with academic work did not receive the assistance they needed and left school. In the words of one: "I have a difficult problem with reading and spelling, and in the schools I went to, the teachers didn't have time to stop and help one kid. I got tired of all the bull crap."

One youth moved and then had trouble enrolling in school. He was very bitter: "Twelve years and you don't get anything but a piece of paper—twelve years for nothing, they don't get you a job, or nothing."

Problems with Authority

A number of youth interviewed had difficulty dealing with authority either at home or at school. They would respond by fighting, arguing, or in other ways making it difficult to control them. The school's attempt to discipline them only aggravated the situation, and students left because they did not want to be disciplined, or the school would dismiss them. The dilemma for both students and administrators is aptly expressed by one respondent: "They got smart with me; I got smart with them back."

Several students had difficulty in getting along with parents. Some would leave home and go to live with friends who were out of their school district. Then they would have difficulty getting into another school, or the disruption of moving and trying to settle into another family took them away from school. In these situations it was easy at some point just not to go to school.

One young man claimed his independence: "I had problems with my parents. We argued a lot. This was my main problem with them. They wanted to force me to obey them. They wanted to whip me with a belt, and I would not let that happen to me."

Fighting and Other Forms of Violence

Fighting caused several former students to be dismissed. As described by several of them: "I lost control of my temper, that got me into trouble. I had no problems learning and no conflict with students. I had trouble with teachers and my parents." "I caused lots of trouble. . . . I argued with teachers and physically fought with students." Racial issues were the cause of some problems. "I got suspended for fighting. Rich white kid called me a 'nigger' and I hit him."

Some students were victims of violence which resulted in their leaving school. "I got shot in the stomach with a pistol and it continues to give me problems but it gave me so much trouble I was unable to return to school." "I received a stab wound to the head while engaged in a fight. When I returned to school, my concentration was poor. I couldn't complete any assignments; therefore I dropped out of school." Others were unable to deal with the intimidation and threat of violence that permeates some schools and for this reason left school. "Too much violence and gang people fuckin' with you; school itself sucked—too many drugs and guns."

One young women left school because she refused to be a victim of violence. "I got kicked out. I wouldn't let the principal paddle me because I was six months pregnant."

Demands at Home

For many girls, and for some boys, lack of dependable child care and the need to support a family kept them away from school. "I had to take care of a child I fathered," said one young man, who in taking responsibility for his actions had to leave school. Much more typically, girls assumed responsibility for child care. "I had twins and didn't have anyone to keep them." "It was hard for me to work and take care of my child, so I dropped out of school." For these girls and many others, being a mother was incompatible with being a high school student.

A number of respondents said they had to take care of parents or grandparents. "I was in trouble a lot; we had bills, and I needed to help my mother with the bills. . . . I quit school because I had to help my mother." One young woman was burdened with too many demands to stay in school. "My mom was very sick with cancer—paralyzed. When I was 15, I was going to school, working, and taking care of mom and the house all at the same time. Because I wasn't getting along with the kids and some of the teachers, the school board let me quit and get a GED."

Academic Problems

Poor academic records beset a number of students who could see no way of improving themselves or of ever gaining enough credits to graduate. At some point the academic hole they had dug themselves into was too great to climb out of, and it was easiest to just give up. "I was not pleased with my grades. I was making Ds and Fs when I reached the ninth grade. My problem with grades continued through the tenth grade."

Some of the former students needed a relatively few credits, but they were not willing to earn them. "I had 9 ½ credits, needed 9 ½ more credits. I decided to try for a GED and get a job, but it has been very hard."

One young man felt out of place in school. "I was stupid. I couldn't wait to start working so I could make some money and get a car." And another had other things to do. "I didn't like school, and I was working on the farm. Also, I was so far behind in school."

How Do These Youth Use and Abuse Alcohol and Other Drugs?

Alcohol Use

Alcohol has indeed played a large part in most of these young peoples' lives, as study results attest. Ninety percent of the respondents have drunk alcoholic beverages at some time in their life. The average age when they first took a drink of alcohol was 14. Seventy-five percent were drinking alcohol by age 16. Sixty percent had drunk alcoholic beverages within the past 12 months, while 31 percent had done so in the past 30 days.

Among current drinkers, those who had drunk alcohol within the past 30 days, 11 percent drank alcohol daily. Nearly half (44 percent) of current drinkers were heavy or binge drinkers, that is, had drunk five or more alcoholic drinks on an occasion within the past 30 days; 55 percent reported at least one episode of intoxication, and a similar proportion reported one or more episodes of driving after drinking alcohol during the 30-day period (Figure 3.2).

ALCOHOL USE AND ABUSE

CHAPTER 3, FIGURE 2. ALCOHOL USE AND ABUSE BY CURRENT DRINKERS AMONG HIGH SCHOOL LEAVERS, TENNESSEE, 1994

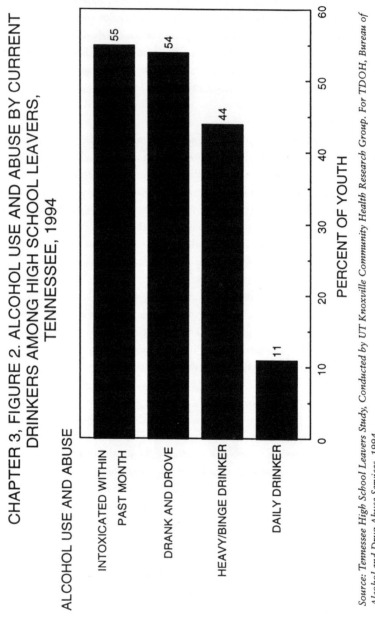

PERCENT OF YOUTH

Source: Tennessee High School Leavers Study, Conducted by UT Knoxville Community Health Research Group. For TDOH, Bureau of Alcohol and Drug Abuse Services, 1994.

Tobacco Use

Next to alcohol, tobacco was the drug of choice for these youth. Sixty-five percent had smoked cigarettes in their lifetimes, 59 percent in the past 12 months, and 48 percent in the past 30 days. Twenty percent had used smokeless tobacco at some time and seven percent had done so within the past 30 days. It is important to note that nearly three-quarters of all youth who have ever tried cigarettes have continued to smoke them, underlining the addictivity of tobacco products and cigarettes in particular.

Other/Illegal Drug Use

Experimentation with other drugs is also common. While many of the respondents have used illegal drugs at some time in their lives, few are current users, defined as having used the drug in the 30 days prior to the interview. Marijuana was the most frequently used illegal drug other than alcohol. Sixty-three percent of school leavers have used marijuana in their lifetime, 47 percent in the past 12 months, and 20 percent are current users. A smaller proportion of these youth have used other illegal drugs: 15 percent had used cocaine or crack, and five percent are current users; 11 percent have used hallucinogens, and one percent are current users; two percent have used heroin, and less than one percent are current users; 2.5 percent have used steroids but no one currently uses them. Psychoactive prescription drugs were used by nearly one-quarter of these youth at some time in their lives, although only four percent are current users; and 16 percent have used inhalants but only one percent are current users. Three percent of the sample had mainlined or injected drugs.

Alcohol- and Other Drug-Related Problems

Many serious life problems experienced by these young people are related to their use of alcohol and other drugs. Arrests and other illegal activity caused problems for many. Nineteen percent have been arrested for alcohol-related offenses and 23 percent for drug-related offenses. Nearly half (48 percent) have been arrested for other offenses, including assaults, burglary, stolen vehicles, weapons charges, runaway, and driving without a license. Of this group, 31 percent reported using alcohol or other drugs at the time of the incident. Between 60 and 75 percent of these arrests occurred in the 12 months prior to the interview. Thirty percent of the respondents have sold illegal drugs, and 19 percent have worked for someone who was selling drugs.

Personal or family problems were frequently exacerbated by alcohol or other drug use. Problems included having arguments or fights, difficulty with money, drinking and driving and being asked not to do so, ruined friendships, and job losses. Most of these incidents occurred within the 12 months prior to the interview (Figures 3.3 and 3.4).

The abuse of alcohol and other drugs is clearly a concern for a large number of the respondents. Fifty percent of the respondents have tried to cut down on their alcohol or drug use or have felt the need to stop. Forty-three percent have had hangover or withdrawal symptoms, and a like percentage are worried or concerned because of their use of alcohol and other drugs. From 62 to 69 percent of respondents with dependence problems had experienced them within the past 12 months. Experience of these symptoms and problems within the 30 days prior to the interview was also fairly frequent. Forty-two percent of those reporting worry or concern because of alcohol and other drug use, 36 percent of those with feelings of guilt and dissatisfaction associated with alcohol and other drug use, 36 percent of respondents with attempts to cut down or stop drinking or using other drugs, and 16 percent of those with hangovers and withdrawal symptoms were reported within the prior 30-day period (Figure 3.4).

Need for and History of AOD Treatment

The use and abuse of alcohol and drugs can, and often does, lead to dependence/addiction and the need for AOD treatment. Twenty-three percent of these young people said they had been addicted to a drug or substance in their lives. Fourteen percent of all respondents felt they were currently addicted to a drug or substance. Eleven percent did indicate that they were concerned about their use of alcohol, and ten percent reported that they were concerned about their use of other drugs. Those who believe they are addicted to a substance and those who are concerned about their use of alcohol or other drugs are prime candidates for treatment.

Many respondents had already been exposed to both formal and informal treatment programs, the latter consisting of self-help and 12-step group attendance. Twenty-five percent had received formal alcohol or drug treatment, 69 percent of these in the prior 12 months and 36 percent in the prior 30 days. Twenty-eight percent had attended a self-help or 12-step group, 69 percent in the past 12 months, 38 percent in the past 30 days (Figure 3.5). The fact that fully 60 percent of those who reported ever having been addicted to a drug or substance reported current addiction suggests that treatment effectiveness was limited and/or that relapse potential for this group is high.

In thinking about their lives many of the respondents regretted their involvement with alcohol and other drugs. Most understood the connection between their alcohol and drug use and other problems they were having in their lives. They would have liked to change that aspect of their lives and somehow start over. Typical comments were the following:

"I wish I had never started drinking or tried any kind of drugs in my life. It was the biggest mistake I ever made." "I would never have taken drugs—that would have kept me out of trouble and in school." "I wouldn't drink so much." "I wouldn't be addicted to coke—I would start all over again—I wouldn't live in the projects." "I wouldn't have sold drugs. I sold drugs and dropped out of school and got caught and put in here. I'd finish school."

Several of the former students knew that they could not relive their lives. Rather than wish that their lives could be different, these young people had actually made the commitment to stop using alcohol and other drugs and had sought appropriate treatment. Each expressed pride in the decision:

"I haven't touched alcohol or drugs in over two years and I hope I never will."

"I just got out of rehab. I know it's going to be hard because I know what it is like. I'll be an addict for the rest of my life. All I can do is take one day at a time and don't worry about yesterday or tomorrow."

Not all the respondents had made that decision or taken that much control of their lives. Many were content as they were or saw no future for themselves and hence had nothing for which to strive. Some were selling drugs as a way to make money. Other lived off their parents or friends so money was not an issue. They described their lives in the following ways:

"I'm doing what I gotta do, you know. I'm posted on this corner, selling weed and coke." "I'm just hanging out, dealing drugs."

A number of the respondents spent their time "just hanging out." A typical description was: "I'm outside drinking beer and stuff, riding around, hanging out with friends."

Other Comments from Teenage High School Leavers

The former high school students described in this chapter were able to tell us much about why they left high school and what it is like for them now as they try to make it without a high school diploma. A number have advice that they would like to pass along to current students who might be thinking about leaving school. Finally, many of these former students have suggestions that schools might consider to help students like themselves stay in school and graduate.

CHAPTER 3, FIGURE 3. LIFETIME PREVALENCE OF ALCOHOL AND OTHER DRUG-RELATED LEGAL PROBLEMS AMONG HIGH SCHOOL LEAVERS, TENNESSEE, 1994

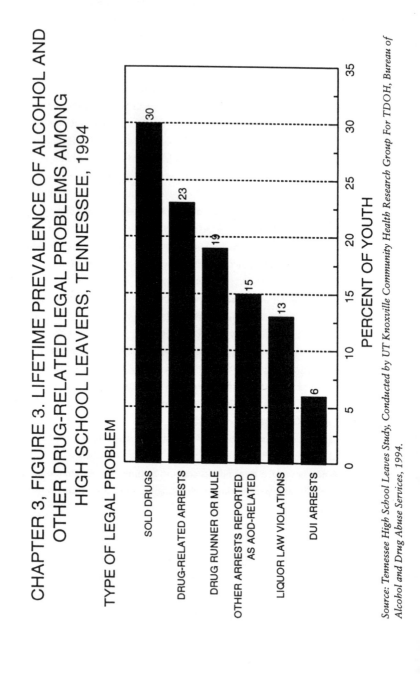

TYPE OF LEGAL PROBLEM

PERCENT OF YOUTH

Source: Tennessee High School Leaves Study, Conducted by UT Knoxville Community Health Research Group For TDOH, Bureau of Alcohol and Drug Abuse Services, 1994.

CHAPTER 3, FIGURE 4. LIFETIME PREVALENCE OF AOD-RELATED PROBLEMS AMONG HIGH SCHOOL LEAVERS, TENNESSEE

1994

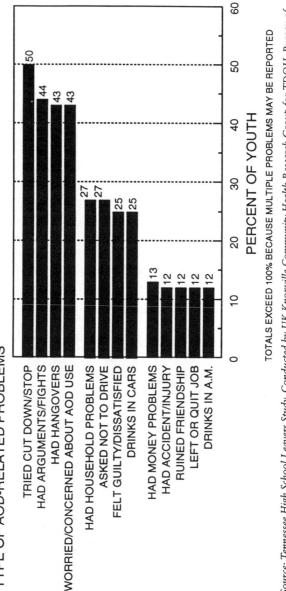

TYPE OF AOD-RELATED PROBLEMS

Type	Percent
TRIED CUT DOWN/STOP	50
HAD ARGUMENTS/FIGHTS	44
HAD HANGOVERS	43
WORRIED/CONCERNED ABOUT AOD USE	43
HAD HOUSEHOLD PROBLEMS	27
ASKED NOT TO DRIVE	27
FELT GUILTY/DISSATISFIED	25
DRINKS IN CARS	25
HAD MONEY PROBLEMS	13
HAD ACCIDENT/INJURY	12
RUINED FRIENDSHIP	12
LEFT OR QUIT JOB	12
DRINKS IN A.M.	12

PERCENT OF YOUTH

TOTALS EXCEED 100% BECAUSE MULTIPLE PROBLEMS MAY BE REPORTED

Source: Tennessee High School Leavers Study, Conducted by UK Knoxville Community Health Research Group for TDOH, Bureau of Alcohol and Drug Abuse Services, 1994.

CHAPTER 3, FIGURE 5. TREATMENT EXPOSURE AND TREATMENT NEED AMONG HIGH SCHOOL LEAVERS IN TENNESSEE, 1994

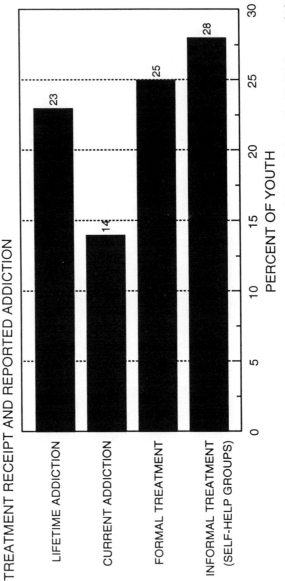

TREATMENT RECEIPT AND REPORTED ADDICTION

PERCENT OF YOUTH

LIFETIME ADDICTION — 23
CURRENT ADDICTION — 14
FORMAL TREATMENT — 25
INFORMAL TREATMENT (SELF-HELP GROUPS) — 28

Tennessee High School Leavers Study, Conducted by UT Knoxville Community Health Research Group for TDOH, Bureau of Alcohol and Drug Abuse Services, 1994.

Early high school leavers have limited options. Some of the respondents in this study recognized this and took steps to increase their options. "I'm working on my GED and expect to obtain employment when I complete my course of study. I also have a part-time job and my money is used to share responsibilities of the apartment that I share. I want to someday earn more money and help my brother and sisters financially." "I'm working toward my GED and feel pretty good about my situation because I want to open my business in the future. My time is divided between working on my GED and working part-time. I don't have much free time but I usually spend it with my two-year-old son. I want to become financially independent and have good health for the rest of my life, and I want peace on earth."

Others of the respondents, however, are seemingly making no effort to prepare themselves for something better than what they are doing. They are content, or they see no future for themselves and hence have nothing to work for. "I'm doing good. I feel okay because I can hang out with my friends much of the day. I usually get money from my mom and dad and I usually gamble a lot, and when I win, I buy clothing with the money. I like the freedom of not being in school."

The streets are a mean place for someone who is young and naive. "There is no life in the streets." "You see kids, babies really, 12 and 13, on the street trying to make money. They need something else to do. They don't know what they're getting into. They need to be home with their mommas."

"It's not easy being out here out of school. Some jobs you just can't get without a diploma." Those who do work are primarily in unskilled, marginal, low-paying jobs. The list of jobs following is a good description of what is available to someone without a high school diploma:

Farm work - manual labor at produce wholesaler - restaurant work - taking orders, ringing cash register - busboy at restaurant - server at restaurant - kitchen, work as a cook, prep mate - landscape work - cashier at grocery store - Kroger's as a stocker - courtesy clerk at grocery - bus tables - part-time at fast food restaurant - dry cleaning work - sell plasma - animal caretaker at a vet clinic - construction work - waitress - janitorial services - load trucks - telemarketing and customer service and clerical work - answer phone, secretarial work - machinist, inspect pencils and pens in a pencil-pen factory - work on cars, mechanic - trim trees - janitorial work at a business - industrial-type work, coat grills with enamel - make burners for water heaters - sawmill, forklift, turning logs - farm hand, work in the fields, drive tractor, clean stalls - sew clothes for people, clean houses - mow lawns.

For many of the young people in this study, trying to make it without a high school diploma has taught them many things about themselves and how the world works. Responses reflect a range of reactions from satisfaction with their decision to leave school to wishing that they had remained in school. Many comments acknowledge that respondents would like to have done some things differently and that there are things about themselves they would like to change. They have apt descriptions of what life is like without a high school diploma, and many have advice for students who are thinking about leaving school.

Satisfied with Their Decision and Current Life

Some school leavers are satisfied with their decision to leave high school early. From their perspective, leaving school was right for them. "I don't miss school at all, and I didn't like much about attending. It is the teachers I liked least. If there is something I would change it would be the teachers." One young woman expressed both contentment and regret. "I wouldn't change it now—except to take away the pain I caused my parents."

Wished They Had Stayed in School

While a few of the respondents were satisfied with their decision to leave school, a more common theme, expressed by most of the respondents, was the wish to have stayed in school. "I probably would have stayed in school, 'cause once you quit you wish you didn't." "I would like to turn back the clock and not get involved with the wrong crowd."

WHAT THEY WOULD DO DIFFERENTLY; HOW ARE THEY TRYING TO CHANGE?

Experience and hindsight are always great teachers. Some high school leavers profited by the insights gained and attempted to act on the lessons they have learned. Being out of high school without a diploma has been a profound learning experience for most of the respondents.

Wishing They Had Waited

Most of the girls who were sexually active and had children wished that they had waited. "I wouldn't have had a baby, and I would have stayed in school." A young man expressed a similar desire: "I would have waited until I was older to get married. I mean I love my wife and my son—I wouldn't trade them for the world. But I see how hard it is to support a family."

Starting Over

A number of respondents would like to go back in time and start over. "I would go back two years and change what happened in school. I got into a fight, a bad fight. That wouldn't have happened." "I'd go back to first grade and make myself go to school instead of my mom letting me lay out."

Being More Positive

Some respondents expressed a desire to adopt more positive behaviors and attitudes. "I would not have messed up. I would have stayed in school, and I wouldn't have given in to doing what my friends wanted me to." "I'd be good, be a nerd or something so I could stay in school." "I probably would start all over again, I wouldn't be the person I used to be. I would think more about what I did before I did it. I wouldn't be so quick to get mad." "I am trying to change my life now—doing good and not wrong. I want to make something out of myself instead of being a street thug."

Longing for Respect

One young man expressed a longing to be able to read and to be respected by his peers: "I would learn how to read. I never learned how to read while in school, so I would change that. The kids always made fun of me for not being able to read. I would change that."

SOME ADVICE FROM HIGH SCHOOL LEAVERS TO OTHER YOUTH ABOUT LEAVING SCHOOL

Respondents were free with their advice to students who might be thinking about leaving school. They hoped that others could learn from their experiences. They were adamant that students should stay in school. "Don't quit school. There ain't anything out here without an education. It's not worth it—you can't get the best out of leaving school, you need a diploma." Life is difficult without a degree. "If you're not in school it is a big mistake. You can't get a job—either have to sell drugs or rob, females go into prostitution; don't get in wrong crowd—stay out of gangs, teacher shouldn't put too much pressure on kids." Young people who become adults too quickly miss something. "I would tell youth to do their work and don't give up. It ain't fun in the real world."

A number of the respondents had learned from their experiences and wanted to pass along their insights to other young people. Their advice was very consistent. With respect to using alcohol and drugs—don't do it. With respect to staying in school—do it. Their suggestions are loud and clear; stay focused on what is important—school, the right friends, and parents. A sampling of their comments follows:

"Don't do any drugs; don't hang around with the wrong people."

"Tell them not to ever take the first drink. Don't even try it. It will change your life forever."

"Don't get in trouble. Stay out of trouble when you're young; don't let your friends influence you; stay out of drugs and alcohol."

"Don't use drugs. You can get hooked on them very easily, and they could kill you."

"Stay away from drugs and people who use or sell them. Stay away from alcohol and people who use it."

Several of the respondents had advice for adult decision makers urging them to better protect young people from alcohol and drugs. "Keep them away from illegal substances like drugs and alcohol. Make sure parents know what's going on in school—grades, attendance."

"People need to understand how drugs affect them."

What Suggestions Are Made for Schools to Help Students Stay in School?

Along with advice to students who might be thinking about leaving high school, respondents had a number of suggestions for how the schools could be more supportive of at-risk students and help them want to stay in school. Their suggestions focused on being more flexible, having greater respect for the students, making more effort to understand these students and to talk with them, reducing exposure to conflict, and providing a variety of classes, academic support, practical living skills and treatment opportunitites. A selection of their comments and the general themes they reflect is included below.

Increase Flexibility

The respondents perceived the school systems to be rigid and uncompromising in accommodating special needs and circumstances. There should be some accommodation for students who need to work. "I know some people who quit school because they needed to work and earn money. If they could go to school part-time and work part-time maybe more people would stay in school." "Help people who are having economic problems. The schools don't take family situations into consideration; work laws for minors are a problem."

Respect Us As Individuals

The respondents enjoyed talking with the interviewers because they were respected as individuals. These young people ask for the same sense of re-spect from teachers and school officials. Teachers drew the most criticism. "The teachers need to pay more attention to the needs of the class instead of having an attitude. They should explain questions you ask instead of dissing you." [putting you down] "Teachers don't believe in us. They don't think that we can make it or that we know nothing. They need to start be-lieving in us more." "Teacher's attitudes—kids have problems from home and teachers get on their back all the time. Teachers want to be big bosses. They're quick on the trigger, they don't talk things out."

Reach Out To Us, Try To Understand Us

Related to the issue of respect is the need to make an effort to reach out to at-risk students and to try to understand them. The former students suggested early intervention. "Talk with kids early when they first start high school, to see how they are doing." "Start counseling kids at an early age about stay-ing in school and getting an education." And not all the responsibility should be on the school. "Teachers and parents should get more involved with the kids in order to keep them in school." "Have better programs for the trouble makers in school, other than sports. We need more teachers that care. Need more parents that care." Simply talking to students can make a difference.

Reduce Conflict and Deviant Behavior

Reducing conflict and deviant behavior in the schools would make them much more attractive places to learn. "School is too hard nowadays. Kids take guns and drugs to school and they want to fight if you just look at them. I just couldn't stand it. It's just too much. If they get the kids that didn't want to be there out then they would get rid of the guns and the drugs." "Get rid of the drugs and violence." "Hire teachers who care."

Offer a Variety of Classes, Academic Support, and Practical Living Skills

At-risk students often have a number of special needs that many times are not met through the regular curriculum. Many of the respondents believed that if some of their academic and life skills needs had been met, they would have remained in school. Based on their experiences, they suggest the fol-lowing as a way to meet like needs in current students:

"School needs more classes about drugs and sex. Classes should be taught about what kids do to avoid having children. I was never taught about teen pregnancy."

"Prevent pregnancies. Educate women about birth control because men won't use protection if women won't make them. Have dropouts talk to students to tell them how hard it is."

"Make school more interesting." "Don't offer so many academic courses but offer more skills classes instead."

"Better teachers in the classrooms and classes where you can go at your own speed. The teachers need to explain things better if you don't understand them the first time." "Need to help everyone, not just the smart ones, to read."

"Take them out to some of the job sites where we work and let them see what they could end up doing." "Show them what happens to people who drop out of school. Show them that they won't make much money." "Have students envision themselves ten years after dropping out—would they be able to support themselves?"

Offer Incentives and Support for Abstinence, Early AOD Intervention, and Treatment

Some of the most important suggestions from these youth hinge on their personal experiences with alcohol and other drug use as a correlate of their school leaving. Programs like student assistance programs, peer counseling, and early intervention and treatment are essential for addressing the AOD-related needs of these youth. Many of their concerns and attitudes to alcohol and other drugs were revealed in their previous statements, and alcohol and other drug use and abuse are major risk factors for delinquency, teenage pregnancy, injury and violence, and dropping out.

CONCLUSIONS AND RECOMMENDATIONS

This study provides valuable insights into the lives, dreams, and problems of youth in Tennessee who left high school before graduating. Their lack of training leads to poorer occupational and economic prospects and is related to possible poorer life-coping skills. Lack of respect from others represents a major problem along with excess family and other responsibilities, resulting in loss of a sense of protection and time for development and innovation ordinarily offered by adolescence. While combined with other life problems, the use of alcohol and other drugs is high among these youth and seems to exacerbate other life problems. The addiction and dependence potential of at-risk youth is relatively high. Their rate of receipt of treatment suggests appropriate response from the system, particularly the criminal justice system. However, the fact that most youth who say they have ever been addicted to a drug or substance are still addicted poses a serious problem for treatment providers and educators alike.

Involvement with alcohol and other drugs has been debilitating for many interviewed for the study. Fifteen percent of the group reported drug use as a direct cause in leaving high school without a diploma. For many more it is a contributing cause. Many of the respondents continue to be plagued by alcohol and drug problems, although alcohol problems clearly predominate. Involvement with these substances has a direct negative influence on their lives as well as exacerbates other problems with friends, family, and the many social institutions that shape their lives.

It is difficult to draw firm conclusions from the limited research in this area. Perhaps the strongest insight is that there are a number of factors that account for high school leavers' decisions to leave school early and that impact their behavior once they are out of school. It can best be said that, for some, the abuse of alcohol and other drugs was a significant factor in their leaving school and continues to shape their behavior in socially unacceptable ways on into adulthood. For others, an increased lack of structure and additional free time once they had left school probably made them more vulnerable to use and abuse problems. And for still others, both during and after high school, the use and abuse of alcohol and other drugs exacerbated personal problems and vulnerabilities, making it much more difficult for these individuals to be productive members of society.

The former students live in a permissive environment where there is little support for not using alcohol or drugs. At the same time there are plenty of examples as to why it is a good idea not to misuse these substances. Many students have learned from their experiences and are taking the necessary steps to give themselves a better future. They are breaking their dependence on alcohol or drugs where that is needed, and they are getting the education and training they need. Their advice to other young people is to stay in school and not to become involved with alcohol and drugs. Others in the study appear not to have learned from their experiences and are content with their status quo.

Recommendations for solutions to the myriad problems of these youth include increased flexibility of systems to accommodate needs and demands that are not the norm, increased respect for these youth despite their troubled pasts, increased understanding of their individual and unique circumstances, improved communication, reduced conflict and deviant behavior, practical alternative schooling coupled with support and practical living skills, positive incentives and normative support for abstinence, and increased AOD prevention and treatment opportunities.

Other recommendations include addressing alcohol, tobacco, and other drug education in schools to the special needs of this group, including emphases on the role of alcohol and other drugs in unplanned sexual activity; violence and crime; depression and suicidal ideation; and fetal alcohol syndrome and other drug-related birth defects. Student assistance programs in schools as well as employee assistance programs (EAPs) in fast food chains and chain grocery and convenience stores should target the special needs of these youth in order to improve their school and job performance and maintain their commitment to the work force. Finally, youth detention centers should provide adequate alcohol and other drug treatment, including self-help and 12-step programs, and support from probation officers and others once youth are released from custody. In general, the results of this study provide valuable practical applications to an educational component and student assistance programs for schools, a youth-oriented EAP for work places, and alcohol and other drug treatment and prevention opportunities for these youth in the community.

REFERENCES

Bachman, J. G., Wallace, J. M., Jr., O'Malley, P. M., Johnston, L. D., Kurth, C. L., and Neighbors, H. W. (1991). Racial/ethnic differences in smoking, drinking, and illicit drug use among American high school seniors, 1976–89. *American Journal of Public Health*, *81*(3), 372–377.

Cairns, R. B., Cairns, B. D., and Neckerman, H. J. (1989). Early school dropout: Configurations and determinants. *Child Development*, *60*, 1437–1452.

Centers for Disease Control. (1991). Current tobacco, alcohol, marijuana, and cocaine use among high school students—United States, 1990. *Morbidity/Mortality Weekly Report*, *40*(38), 659–663.

———. (1994). Health risk behaviors among adolescents who do and do not attend school—United States, 1992. *Morbidity/Mortality Weekly Report*, *43*(8), 129–132.

Chavez, E. L., Edwards, R., and Oetting, E. R. (1989). Mexican American and white American school dropouts' drug use, health status, and involvement in violence. *Public Health Reports*, *104*, 594–604.

Chen, K. and Kandel, D. B. (1995). The natural history of drug use from adolescence to the mid-thirties in a general population survey. *American Journal of Public Health*, *85*(1), 41–47.

Community Health Research Group (CHRG). (1995). Comparison of young high school leavers and stayers in Tennessee: A population subgroup analysis from the Tennessee Alcohol and Other Drug Needs Assessment Survey of 1993. Knoxville, TN: CHRG at the University of Tennessee, 600 Henley St., Suite 309, Knoxville, TN 37996-4133.

DeRidder, L. M. and Dietz, S. C. (1988). The importance of identifying and retaining potential dropouts in Tennessee. *Tennessee Education*, *18*(1), 22–25.

Eggert, L. L. and Herting, J. R. (1993). Drug involvement among potential dropouts and "typical" youth. *Journal of Drug Education*, *23*, 31–55.

Evans, I. M. and Matthews, A. K. (1992). A behavioral approach to the prevention of school dropout: Conceptual and empirical strategies for children and youth. *Progress in Behavior Modification*, *28*, 220–249.

Hawkins, J. D., Catalano, R. F., and Miller, J. Y. (1992). Risk and protective factors for alcohol and other drug problems in adolescence and early adulthood: Implications for substance abuse prevention. *Psychological Bulletin*, *112*(1), 64–105.

Johnson, C. A., Pentz, M. A., Weber, M. D., Dwyer, J. H., Baer, N., MacKinnon, D. P., Hansen, W. B., and Flay, B. R. (1990). Relative effectiveness of comprehensive community programming for drug abuse prevention with high-risk and low-risk adolescents. *Journal of Consulting and Clinical Psychology, 58*(4), 447–456.

Kandel, D. (1975). Reaching the hard-to-reach: Illicit drug use among high school absentees. *Addictive Diseases: An International Journal, 1*(4), 465–480.

Lorion, R. P., Bussell, D., and Goldberg, R. (1991). Identification of youth at high risk for alcohol or other drug problems. Preventing adolescent drug use: From theory to practice. *OSAP Prevention Monograph, 8.* (91–1725).

McCaul, E. J., Donaldson, G. A., Jr., Colardarci, T., and Davis, W. E. (1992). Consequences of dropping out of school: Findings from high school and beyond. *Journal of Educational Research, 85*(3), 198–207.

Mensch, B. S. and Kandel, D. B. (1988). Dropping out of high school and drug involvement. *Sociology of Education, 61*, 95–113.

Merrill, J.C., Fox, K. S., Lewis, S. R., and Pulver, G. E. (1994). *Cigarettes, alcohol, marijuana: Gateways to illicit drug use.* New York: Center on Addiction and Substance Abuse at Columbia University.

Pirie, P. L., Murray, D. M., and Luepker, R. V. (1988). Smoking prevalence in a cohort of adolescents, including absentees, dropouts, and transfers. *American Journal of Public Health, 78*(2), 176–178.

Radford, J., et al. (1989). *Street Youth and AIDS.* Ottawa, Ontario: Runge Press.

Schmidt, M.T. and Hankoff, L. D. (1979). Adolescent alcohol abuse and its prevention. *Public Health Reviews, 8*(2), 107–53.

Smart, R. G. and Adlaf, E. M. (1991). Substance use and problems among Toronto street youth. *British Journal of Addiction, 86*, 999–1010.

United States General Accounting Office (USGAO). (1991). *Teenage drug use: Uncertain linkages with either pregnancy or school dropout.* Report to the Chairman, Select Committee on Narcotics Abuse and Control, House of Representatives. U.S. Government Printing Office, Washington, DC.

Werch, C.E., Gorman, D. R., and Marty, P. J. (1987). Relationship between alcohol consumption and alcohol problems in young adults. *Journal of Drug Education, 17*(3), 261–276.

Windle, M. (1989). Substance use and abuse among adolescent runaways: A four-year follow-up study. *Journal of Youth and Adolescence, 18*(4), 331–344.

———. (1990). A longitudinal study of antisocial behaviors in early adolescence as predictors of late adolescent substance use: Gender and ethnic group differences. *Journal of Abnormal Psychology, 99*(1), 86–91.

PART III
SOME INTRIGUING THEORIES
ON AT-RISK YOUTH

4 HOME AND SCHOOL CORRELATES OF EARLY AT-RISK STATUS

A TRANSACTIONAL PERSPECTIVE

Jean E. Dumas

Predictability is a major characteristic of human development. Under ordinary circumstances, physical, psychological, and social development follow an interrelated course that differs little in overall pattern from child to child, in spite of the active role played by each individual in the developmental process. At the psychosocial level in particular, all societies expose children to formative experiences through early affective and educational ties with close relatives and community members, followed by formal or informal schooling. Hand in hand with maturation, these experiences insure a high level of similarity in the manner in which children grow up to become full-fledged members of a particular social and cultural group.

The predictable unfolding of formative experiences at home and school characterizes both functional and dysfunctional development. When children develop into functional adolescents and adults, we assume generally that they were of average or better disposition and were exposed to mostly positive experiences; or, more simply, we take this positive outcome for granted. When the developmental outcome is dysfunctional, however, we have a host of potential risk factors to call upon to explain, often with hindsight accuracy, why a particular child grew up to become, say, a delinquent adolescent or a criminal adult. And when the outcome is functional in spite of the fact that the child was exposed throughout development to well-established statistical predictors of dysfunction (e.g., parental criminality or psychopathology), we can rely on several protective factors to explain this fortunate turn of events also.

This chapter opens with the outline of a coping-competence model of functional development, before illustrating key elements of the model with a clinical case study of a child at high risk for conduct disorder and related adverse outcomes. Model and case study are cast within a transactional perspective in which the course of development is assumed to be influenced not only by child characteristics and environmental variables, but by important transactional processes between the two. Within this perspective the chapter reviews the typical psychosocial "career" of children who present antisocial behavioral problems from an early age and who, consequently, are at high risk of adverse life outcomes in adolescence and adulthood—such as conduct disorder, delinquency, substance use, and criminality. The chapter concludes with a brief discussion of implications for prevention and intervention.

COPING-COMPETENCE: A MODEL

The coping-competence model presented here expands on an earlier formulation by Blechman et al. (1995), bringing together recent theoretical and empirical contributions from research on effective communication in children and adolescents (Blechman, 1990), attentional processes in dysfunctional family interactions (Dumas, 1990; Dumas and Wekerle, 1995; Wahler and Dumas, 1989), and automaticity in cognition and social interactions (Bargh, 1994; Smith, 1994).

Effective Communication

CHALLENGES

A child's day can be thought of as an obstacle course. Whether a child is attempting to walk for the first time, obtain the teacher's attention in preschool, or learn a new math concept in third grade, every day the child faces a series of challenges that require or prompt some kind of coping response (Lazarus and Folkman, 1984). In coping-competence theory, challenges—daily demands and difficulties, as well as developmental tasks and major life events—are features of the environment that tax or are beyond the child's current coping capacity, tend to evoke strong emotions, and are experienced as stressful. The theory assumes that challenges and the coping responses they elicit fall generally into three domains: *affective*, for challenges requiring solutions to predominantly emotional situations and demands; *social*, for challenges involving primarily interpersonal and social situations and demands; and *achievement*, for challenges pertaining foremost to goal-directed activities, such as self-care tasks and academic and work-related demands and responsibilities. These domains, which obviously overlap, often to a considerable extent, describe the predominant features of a challenge as well as the three major areas of coping-competence.

Like adults, children cope with challenges in prosocial, antisocial, or asocial ways. When coping prosocially, they respond by resolving, or attempting to resolve, the challenge in a constructive manner. When coping antisocially, they attempt to resolve the challenge in an aggressive or destructive manner, or deny any responsibility in seeking a solution to the challenge, often hurting others and themselves in the process. And when coping asocially, they respond by withdrawing from the situation and from others or by hurting themselves, in an attempt to minimize or dismiss the stressful impact of the challenge (Izard, 1984; Waters and Sroufe, 1983). Coping-competence theory assumes that all young children exhibit ways of coping that are precursors of antisocial and asocial conduct but serve an important role in survival and development. For example, crying signals the infant's need for affection, food, and protection; avoidance of unfamiliar persons and situations prevents the toddler from straying far from caregivers and getting into danger; angry outbursts are early expressions of affect that teach the child to express emotions in more suitable fashion in social situations; and impatient demands are early attempts to communicate assertively. In most cases, with repeated exposure to countless challenges coupled with consistent social support and guidance, older children and adults acquire predominantly prosocial ways of coping, even though they rely occasionally on antisocial and asocial strategies. Prosocial ways of coping depend to a considerable extent on effective communication skills, both with others and with one's self.

LANGUAGE DEVELOPMENT AND EFFECTIVE COMMUNICATION

Language plays a major role in the acquisition of prosocial ways of coping, as functional development requires that children make increasing use of effective communication to deal with affective, social, and achievement challenges and acquire coping-competence in all three areas (Luria, 1961; Pennebaker et al. 1990; Vygotsky, 1981). Coping-competence theory assumes that effective communication—at home and, later, at school—consists of three interrelated processes—information exchange, behavior influence, and problem solving—in which language skills are paramount (Blechman, 1990; Blechman et al., 1995).

In successful information exchange, two or more individuals use words and actions to disclose their feelings, thoughts, and experiences, and watch and listen to each other attentively and non-judgmentally in order to understand each other's perspectives and needs. Through information exchange, children learn to give and receive relevant and truthful information to/from others about challenges and to think and regulate their own behavior when faced with challenges through self-instructions. In families, children experiencing difficulties at school, for example, must learn to express their feelings and describe their frustrating experiences and to formulate potential coping strategies. If other family members listen carefully and convey acceptance and support of the child, problems dissipate often without overt behavior influence or problem solving.

In successful behavior influence, two or more individuals use words and actions to prompt each other to some specific action when faced with a challenge. Behavior influence can be present-oriented, for example when a family member makes a request for immediate action ("Please turn the TV down, I can't hear you.") to which another member complies, or future-oriented, for example when a teacher and child agree on a plan that will help the child complete assignments on time (Teacher: "If you agree to finish this assignment at home tonight, I will help you prepare it just after lunch." Child: "Good deal! Thanks."). Through behavior influence, children learn to exercise control over other people's behavior in prosocial fashion and, over time, to control their own actions (social influence and self-control are interdependent aspects of behavior influence).

In successful problem solving, two or more individuals use words and actions to recognize a common problem or challenge and devise mutually acceptable, often long-term, solutions that will require all persons involved to change their own behavior. As such, problem solving necessitates repeated use of effective information exchange and behavior influence. The incentive for problem solving lies in its impact on the enduring quality of the relationships people share rather than in any immediate reward.

Not surprisingly, empirical evidence indicates that at-risk youth, especially when they present antisocial behavioral problems from an early age, are likely to demonstrate a wide range of difficulties related to language and communication skills. Oppositional, noncompliant behavior is related to significant difficulties in language comprehension (Kaler and Kopp, 1990) and interpersonal problem solving (Spivack and Shure, 1974) in preschoolers; marked aggressive behavior covaries with communication difficulties with peers (Dumas et al., 1994) and reading difficulties (Stanton et al., 1990; Sturge, 1982) in children in elementary school; and delinquency is associated with complex verbal deficits (Moffitt, 1993) in adolescence. For example, Dumas et al. (1994) compared the communication skills of two groups of aggressive and nonaggressive elementary school children (selected on the basis of teacher ratings) in a structured peer communication task designed specifically to elicit cooperation. Analyses were based on direct observational measures of communication effectiveness and aggression, and on teacher, peer, and self-ratings of peer rejection and depressive symptoms. Results showed not only that aggressive children demonstrated less effective and more disruptive communication skills than their nonaggressive peers, but that these differences in communication effectiveness could not be accounted for by group differences in observed aggression and remained significant when differences in peer rejection and depressive symptoms were controlled for.

Attention

CONTEXTUAL EFFECTS

The coping-competence model identifies the language-based processes of information exchange, behavior influence, and problem solving as the actual means by which, over time, prosocial ways of coping supplant reliance on antisocial and asocial coping in children and adolescents within and across developmental contexts. As stated above, the model assumes that, to develop the effective communication skills without which they cannot cope with challenges in a prosocial manner, children must be repeatedly exposed to socializing agents (initially caregivers and siblings, followed by teachers and peers) who demonstrate such skills. It should be obvious that children who live in families in which members show little awareness of or interest in each other's points of view—apparent in minimal, ineffective information exchange, and in coercive attempts at behavior influence—and attend schools in which a comparable social climate prevails are likely to be inept at all forms of effective communication. However, the coping-competence model is not limited to the description of effective communication and of its role in the development of prosocial coping.

The coping-competence model recognizes that the extent to which children are exposed to effective communication at home, at school, and beyond depends to a large extent on contextual effects (Dumas, 1989; Wahler and Dumas, 1989). Wahler and Dumas (1989) showed in relation to dysfunctional parent-child interactions that one's ability to demonstrate prosocial ways of coping depends not only on whether one has acquired them but also on the presence of adverse contextual factors. For example, factors such as parental criminality and psychopathology (Dumas et al., 1989; Hops et al., 1987; Robins, 1981), parental alcohol and drug abuse (West and Prinz, 1987), marital discord (Fantuzzo et al., 1991; Reid and Crisafulli, 1990), and social isolation and socioeconomic disadvantage (Dumas, 1986; Dumas and Wahler, 1983, 1985; Wahler, 1980; Webster-Stratton, 1985) represent common sources of adverse experiences for at-risk youth that undermine the development of effective communication skills. In line with research findings relevant to different types of dysfunction (Dix, 1991; Hartlage et al., 1993), Wahler and Dumas (1989) assume that such skills are least likely to be demonstrated under conditions of chronic exposure to stress, because such exposure interferes with the key element of such skills, namely the ability to pay close attention to the messages, needs, and preferences of others.

STRESS: HIGH EMOTION, LOW ATTENTION

It is well established that exposure to stress is commonly accompanied by two closely related processes: a heightening of negative emotions (Frijda, 1986; Izard, 1984) and a narrowing of attention (Averill, 1973; Cohen, 1980; Kahneman, 1973). Subjects who experience stress report elevated levels of negative emotions and perform more poorly than control subjects on stimulus detection tasks, in part because they attend to information they consider central in a given situation at the expense of all others (e.g., Broadbent, 1971). Emotional arousal and narrowing of attention have affective, cognitive, and interactive correlates. For example, subjects who know that their performance will be evaluated experience subjective tension and related negative emotions, and often fail to display caution, proceed systematically, attend to details, or check their output (e.g., Hockey, 1973). Similarly, when asked to solve problems, they have greater difficulty in selecting alternatives likely to be successful and often misjudge probable outcomes or overlook the long-term consequences of their decisions (Jarvis, 1982; Mandler, 1982). Finally, studies of the aftereffects of stress on social behavior have shown that, following exposure to stress (especially if unpredictable or uncontrollable), subjects are prone to insensitivity: they are less likely to engage in helping behavior (Sherrod and Downs, 1974; Cohen and Spacapan, 1978), and more likely to display aggression and negative emotions (Frijda, 1986).

Not surprisingly, comparable effects have been reported in clinical studies such as studies of parents exposed to multiple stressors or to temporary laboratory analogues (e.g., Brody and Forehand, 1986; Passman and Mulhern, 1977). Passman and Mulhern placed mothers in an analogue teaching situation with their children, asking them to monitor the children's performance while simultaneously attending to increasing situational demands. These demands could be directly related to their children's behavior (child interruptions) or independent of it, and clearly specified or left unclear. Maternal punitiveness was a function of the children's frequency of interruptions and the level of certainty of the competing task. More frequent interruptions and unpredictable task requirements were associated with more intense punishment than less frequent interruptions and clearly specified task requirements. Similarly, under heightened emotional arousal parents tend to view their children negatively, to become more sensitive to aversive and less sensitive to positive child stimuli, to monitor child behavior poorly, and to act toward their children aversively (see Berscheid, 1986; Dix, 1991). For example, emotionally distressed or depressed mothers interpret their children's behavior as more maladjusted and aversive than nondistressed mothers, and tend to interact with them accordingly, even in the absence of measurable differences in the children's behavior (Dumas and Serketich, 1994; Panaccione and Wahler, 1986). In line with other findings in this area, these last two studies found that distressed mothers report higher levels of child maladjustment than nondistressed mothers, even though their children's behavior is comparable to that of comparison children—highlighting the fact that, under stress, mothers commonly fail to attend closely to what their children actually do.

STRESS AND NARRATIVE REPORTS
Clinical experience is consistent with the literature on stress, emotional arousal, and attention. For example, mothers who report child relationship problems are quick to respond aversively to whatever their children do and equally quick to describe their children's behavior as deviant, even in the absence of supportive evidence. In clinical settings their descriptions amount often to vague and inaccurate narrative reports of the children's behavior (Wahler and Dumas, 1989). Specifically, stressed mothers tend to describe their children in global terms, assigning blame or fault to them and accounting for their deviant behavior in terms of internal and stable characteristics (Wahler and Dumas, 1984). Ferreira and Winter (1968) were among the first to show that members of dysfunctional families, parents in particular, offered significantly less information when describing their interactions than did members of comparison families. This finding, which was replicated by Rodick et al. (1986), was also pursued by Wahler and Hann (1984), who analyzed conversations between mothers and their therapists and between the same mothers and their friends. Results showed that multi-stressed mothers said less about their problem children's actual deviant behavior than did comparison mothers. The former offered deviance-accentuating and blame-oriented narrative reports with little to substantiate them. Their narratives were usually global descriptions of how the mothers attempted to cope with their children's behavior problems. In these narratives, mothers made statements of helplessness, confusion, anger, or persecution, providing little detailed information about their and their child's actual behavior or sources of stress outside the immediate relationship (e.g., marital difficulties, financial worries).

Automaticity
To complete this brief description of the coping-competence model, *auto-*

maticity must be added as a third element complementing those of effective communication and attention. Considerable evidence confirms the common experience that skills improve with practice: "Practice makes perfect." The model assumes that this is true not only of complex motor and cognitive skills (Bargh, 1994; Kahneman, 1973; Smith, 1994) but also of relationship skills (Dumas and LaFrenière, 1993; Patterson et al., 1992).

People develop extremely complex, interdependent patterns of day-to-day interaction as a function of living together. In the case of children a major consequence of the unique asymmetry in role, power, and competence characterizing the young child's relationship with the primary caregiver (often the child's mother) is that the affective, cognitive, and interactive experiences taking place in the context of this relationship influence the child's social adaptation and behavioral consistency across time and settings (Maccoby, 1992). The coping-competence model assumes that regular practice of effective communication skills in this early developmental context leads both parent and child to acquire a high level of proficiency in the use of prosocial ways of exchanging information, influencing each other, and solving mutual problems. And, conversely, that repeated engagement in coercive interactions leads both members of the relationship to gain a high degree of skill in the use of short-term, aversive means of controlling each other (e.g., Milner, 1993; Patterson et al., 1992).

Specifically, the coping-competence model assumes that, with repeated practice under comparable learning conditions, patterns of day-to-day family interaction become integrated into *automatized transactional procedures* (ATPs) consisting of interrelated affective, cognitive, and interactive components that involve two or more family members (see Smith, 1994, for a discussion of procedural knowledge in the control of social behavior and the clinical case study below for an example). The distinctive feature of ATPs is their transactive nature. They cannot be considered simply as the sum of the individual characteristics of the family members who enter repeatedly into the same patterns of interaction. Rather they reflect the peculiar history of a relationship in which each member has acquired relationship-specific ways of feeling, attending, and behaving.

With time, ATPs can be performed with little or no conscious cognitive control or awareness. They become overlearned to such an extent that they give access to automatized emotions, cognitions, and actions that manifest themselves with little or no awareness and contribute directly to the maintenance of positive or aversive interactions, to their escalation over time, and to their generalization across settings. In particular, under conditions of stress characterized by high emotion and low attention, family members are most likely to rely on these overlearned patterns of interaction to manage each other's demands and, more generally, to respond to affective, social, or achievement challenges.

It is critical to recognize that the ATPs members of a family practice repeatedly in the course of living together are not only relationship-specific products of past interactions but essential guides to current and future interactions, both within the relationship and beyond. For example, the likelihood that a child will comply with a mother's command depends not only on the immediate stimuli that both of them exchange and on the presence of contextual events (e.g., child's involvement in a competing activity, maternal emotional distress). It depends also on the interactional history that child and mother have acquired over the years. Thus, even though the content of day-to-day interactions varies considerably across time and settings, ATPs provide a certain degree of continuity and stability in these interactions. When ATPs are dysfunctional, this continuity and stability tends to make relationship difficulties highly resistant to change, even though the protagonists—such as parents and children—may express a genuine desire to see their relationship improve. In addition, with the passage of time ATPs tend to generalize from the relationship in which they were acquired initially to other relationships, with each protagonist making use of skills that developed within a particular context (such as the disciplinary context of the parent-child relationship) in a variety of social settings. While this is a positive outcome in most circumstances, it is not for at-risk youths who have acquired coercive skills in early childhood. For such youths, coercive skills become increasingly "portable" with age so that, as they grow older and more skillful, these children are likely to display the antisocial ways of coping they have acquired at home in other relationships and settings.

JORDAN: CASE STUDY OF AN AT-RISK YOUTH

Jordan had just turned eight when I met him for the first time. With very short, straight hair, a prominent scar on his forehead, and a fairly large but short build, he looked more like an apprentice gang member than a carefree youngster. Beyond his physical appearance, Jordan's voice struck me immediately. It was deep and controlled, and sounded too old for his age. He spoke in rapid, short sentences that had a detached, almost business-like quality. Suspicious, he frowned more often than he smiled and seemed unable to relax. Even in the safety of the clinic, he looked tense, as if on guard against unpredictable dangers that might suddenly strike. It was only on the rare occasions when I heard him laugh that I was reminded of his age.

Jordan and his mother had been referred for psychological services by a local family support agency. The referral described chronic relationship difficulties, marked by severe child noncompliance and verbal and physical aggression, and by maternal inconsistency, harsh discipline, and possible isolated incidents of abuse. Mrs. S. had divorced Jordan's father when the child was five. However, she remained in almost daily contact with him and he played an important role in Jordan's upbringing and in that of his younger sister, Abbie. At the time of referral, Jordan's mother had been living for over two years with a male friend who was considerably younger. This friend was an alcoholic, who was often violent toward her but not to the children. Mrs. S. had a history of outpatient psychiatric care for anxiety and depression, and of short-term employment in poorly paid service sector jobs. She was unemployed at the time of referral and looking after her two children on governmental assistance.

Mrs. S. described Jordan as a temperamental, argumentative youngster who regularly opposed her authority, provoking her to lose her own temper and generally making life "hell" at home. Typically, she tried to cope with Jordan's disobedience, angry outbursts, and provocations by yelling and becoming angry herself, or by rejecting him and withdrawing into a state of almost total helplessness—all to no avail, as the situation had got worse over the years and had finally forced her to ask for help. This bleak picture was confirmed by Jordan himself. He did not hesitate to acknowledge that he had a "bad attitude" but, when asked for information about specific incidents, typically blamed others for his conduct or described it as justified retaliation against their unprovoked attacks or unreasonable demands.

After a few weeks of treatment—conducted by a therapist in training under my supervision—mother and child arrived for their appointment early one afternoon. Mrs. S. was visibly agitated. The therapist saw her first. Without taking time to sit down, she told him that Jordan had hit her earlier in the day, after she had disciplined him for swearing by slapping him on the face. She was crying as she showed her bruised arm, crying, she said, not so much because Jordan had hit her—it was not the first time—but because she feared that, instead of helping, treatment was making matters worse. In spite of slow, careful questioning, the therapist was unable to reconstruct the events that led to this physical confrontation.

"Do you remember what you were doing just before the incident started?"

After a short pause, "Nothing much."

"Nothing much?"

"No, nothing special. I was tired and so I was just lying down on the sofa. I was worrying about money because I was waiting for a cheque to come in today but I didn't get it and now I'll have no money for the long weekend that's coming up. I'll have to go to my mother and I hate it because when I ask her for money she uses it against me, always later on she does. The woman's mad and mean."

"I understand. But did something happen to make Jordan mad so that he would swear?"

"No, that's the thing. His sister wasn't even there. I can't really remember what happened. I don't know why I slapped him. I guess I just got tired of him cussing all the time. You know, he swears so much, I don't know if he could tell you himself why he was mad."

Later on, Jordan confirmed the incident but, like his mother, was unable to shed light on what happened. He did not deny but could not recall swearing.

"I don't know. She hit me and, like, the fist just came out of me" (stretches his arm, fist clenched, to demonstrate the blow).

Neither mother nor child appeared to be withholding information. Rather they seemed genuinely at a loss to account for the events leading to their physical confrontation.

Jordan's case illustrates some key features of the family background of many at-risk youths. First, Jordan and his mother lacked effective communication skills. They knew little about each other's feelings, needs, and preferences and, when faced with challenges in their day-to-day interactions, were ill-equipped to exchange information in a manner that was likely to address these challenges positively. Second, both were often preoccupied by chronically stressful contextual factors (such as the mother's financial worries and Jordan's vigilance against unpredictable dangers) that limited further their ability to attend to each other and communicate effectively. A correlate of this narrowing of attention was their inability to give detailed accounts of the events leading to their recurring, often violent disagreements. They were very poor observers, usually describing their own and each other's behavior in vague, uninformative terms. This was related to a third key feature of the families of at-risk youths, namely that Jordan and his mother had acquired so much practice at being verbally and physically abusive—they had become so "good" at using pain to exercise short-term control over each other—that they could fight with little clear awareness of what set them off or kept their dysfunctional interactions going.

In average families, a typical fight or argument between parents and children follows a highly predictable sequence of escalating events. The sequence can be started by either party. For example, the parent makes a simple request ("Please get ready for bed") or responds to the child's provocation or argument ("For goodness sake, leave your sister alone!"). The child reacts by ignoring the request or continuing to provoke or argue. The parent repeats the instruction, now speaking more loudly and criticizing the child ("How many times do I have to tell you to go to bed? Are you deaf or what?"). If the child continues to resist parental control, all elements are in place for a rapid escalation of the confrontation. Escalation takes place at three levels: *affective*, with parent and child becoming increasingly upset and showing more and more physical signs of anger (in facial expression, tone of voice, and body movements); *cognitive*, with each party interpreting the other's behavior in negative terms ("He does it just to annoy me." "Why does she always pick on me?"); and *interactive*, with both parties intensifying their use of negative behaviors such as yelling, criticizing, and becoming verbally and even physically abusive. In most families, this escalating sequence stops long before extremes are reached, when one party submits to the other by obeying, dropping the demand, or simply withdrawing, or when parent and child negotiate an acceptable solution to their disagreement.

However, in families in which the protagonists do not stop, practice essentially makes parent and child "perfect." So much so, in fact, that they can go through overlearned coercive sequences almost automatically, often cutting short or by-passing the early elements of the chain altogether and displaying only the more extreme, negative ones. In other words, over time, automaticity creeps in, consistently training the same family members to fight in the same manner, until they can do it with little attention or effort.

Experienced clinicians know that coercive family interactions rarely, if ever, involve all family members in the same manner and to the same extent, but are characteristic of specific relationships (e.g., mother and one child but not another; two siblings but not a third one). Coercive relationships are often striking by their well-rehearsed, almost choreographed nature. This is why they can be so terrifying and yet so difficult to change, even though most people who ask for help know how harmful they are and share a genuine desire to learn to get on better. Jordan and his mother shared that desire—at least in the clinic—and, yet, following a well-rehearsed script, for months into treatment they continued to come to blows almost automatically, usually unaware of what was actually happening until it was over.

Developmental Unfolding of Risk and Protective Factors

The developmental psychopathology literature on the home and school correlates of risk status for conduct disorder has grown so rapidly in recent years that a comprehensive review cannot be provided here. Rather, the remainder of the chapter presents the risk and protective factors that are generally considered most prominent and for which there is strong empirical support. In line with the coping-competence model, this presentation assumes that coping-competence in the affective, social, and achievement domains accounts in part for the linkages between the selected risk and protective factors and both aggressive behavior (a proximal outcome) and conduct disorder (a distal outcome) (Blechman et al., 1995; Prinz et al., 1994). Figure 1 depicts the hypothesized linkages between risk/protective factors and proximal/distal outcomes at three points in time: before school entry, by third grade, and by fifth grade. The proximal outcomes include the three coping-competence domains and aggressive behavior, whereas the distal outcomes include conduct disorder and early substance use. As the figure shows, risk and protective factors are hypothesized to lead to these proximal and distal outcomes both directly and via the three domains of affective, social, and achievement coping-competence.

Preschool Years

Parenting difficulties in a child's early life constitute the best-documented risk factor in the preschool years, predicting early oppositional-aggressive behavior and later conduct problems (Patterson, 1982; Patterson et al., 1992; Wahler and Dumas, 1987). Relevant parenting difficulties include primarily coercive processes of behavior influence (Patterson, 1982); inadequate discipline and monitoring (Farrington and West, 1981; McCord, 1988; Patterson et al., 1992); and insufficient teaching of prosocial skills (Loeber and Stouthamer-Loeber, 1986; Wadsworth, 1980). Specifically, parents of oppositional children appear to have particular difficulties in disciplinary encounters. At the interactive level, they are inconsistent. At times they scold, discipline harshly, and can even be abusive to their children. At other times they criticize and threaten but fail to follow through and even reinforce the child aversiveness. This inconsistency is evident at the affective and cognitive levels also, as parents oscillate often between an angry, power-assertive stance to control their children and a helpless, depressive stance through which they withdraw from the same children. Inconsistency is associated with inadequate monitoring; parents of oppositional children are poor observers of their children's actual behavior and do not supervise them adequately, often responding only when the children behave in a clearly aversive or disruptive manner (Dumas, 1992; Wahler and Dumas, 1989).

Children who present early temperamental difficulties may invite and be particularly prone to the adverse effects of parenting difficulties (Bates et al., 1991; Offord et al., 1991), with the two factors operating transactionally to aggravate family conflict and parental attentional problems and, over time, produce oppositional and aggressive behaviors of greater intensity than either factor could be expected to produce alone (Dumas, 1992; Moffitt, 1990).

A third set of risk factors in the preschool years (and beyond) centers around several contextual sources of family adversity already mentioned above, including parental criminality and psychopathology, parental alcohol and drug abuse, marital discord, and social isolation and socioeconomic disadvantage (Dumas, 1992). Not surprisingly, families affected by various sources of adversity often lack social support, thereby depriving at-risk children from the potentially protective benefits of such support (Dumas, 1986; Wahler, 1980). During the preschool years, family adversity factors, especially in the absence of social support, are likely to affect child behavior primarily by heightening any parenting and temperamental difficulties already present and limiting the child's exposure to effective family communication and teaching of prosocial skills. Over time, chronic family adversity contributes to an escalation in child oppositional and aggressive conduct, setting the stage for a difficult transition to first grade.

The coping-competence model assumes that the risk and protective factors just reviewed may be sufficient to account for lack of affective and social competence prior to first grade. By the end of first grade and beyond, factors such as negative classroom experiences, disturbed peer relations, school climate, and achievement coping-competence are predicted to contribute to the outcome.

Early School Years

Adding to parenting difficulties carried over from the preschool years, children who enter first grade exhibiting high rates of aggressive and oppositional behavior and poor affect regulation are at high risk for classroom behavior problems, such as ignoring teacher instructions and disrupting class, and developing conflictual relationships with peers (Prinz et al., 1981). These problems heighten risk for learning difficulties (Offord and Waters, 1983; Rutter and Giller, 1983), future conduct disorder and delinquency (Loeber, 1988, 1990), and adolescent substance use (Brook et al., 1990; Kellam et al., 1985). Specifically, the transition to first grade exposes children already at-risk to two new risk factors: negative classroom experiences and disturbed peer relations. For example, aggressive and disruptive child behaviors in the classroom provoke aversive responses from teachers (Campbell, 1991), while negative feedback from teacher to parent strains family-school relations and further taxes parents who are struggling with multiple sources of family adversity and lack of family social support in addition to parenting difficulties. Risk is increased significantly when, in addition to their affective and social problems, at-risk children develop learning difficulties, particularly in reading and language-related skills (Moffitt, 1993).

Aggressive and disruptive behavior at time of school entry leads often to peer rejection and social isolation around second or third grade, or even earlier (Bierman, 1986; Cantrell and Prinz, 1985; Dodge, 1989). Thus peer rejection further restricts the development of social coping-competence in children who are already significantly lacking in this domain.

Disruptions in affective and social coping-competence continue to play important roles in the early school years in the emergence of antisocial behavior (Asarnow, 1988; Dodge et al., 1986), with disruptions in achievement coping-competence in general, and in reading skills in particular, taking on increased significance by the middle of elementary school (Shinn et al., 1987; Sturge, 1982).

Middle School Years and Early Adolescence

When family, peer, and school-related risk factors continue to exercise their deleterious effect over time, often compounding their influences in a transactional manner, the affective, social, and achievement difficulties of at-risk youth escalate as they approach adolescent years. Typically, parenting difficulties—especially inadequate monitoring and supervision—tend to become magnified about the time of fourth and fifth grade, while disturbed peer relations—particularly peer rejection—worsen as children grow older (Dishion et al., 1991). In school, chronic classroom disruptive conduct, teacher rejection, and learning difficulties contribute to poor "bonding" to the school context, significantly increasing the likelihood of school failure and dropout or expulsion (Hawkins and Lishner, 1987; Hawkins and Weis, 1985).

Research indicates that two protective factors, family social support and positive school climate, may mitigate this bleak picture, raising the probability that some children will desist from this negative escalation over time. (These two factors are discussed in relation to late childhood and early adolescence because relevant research has focused predominantly on this period, but the coping-competence model assumes that they can exercise a protective effect at earlier stages of development.) Growing evidence points to family support as a critical variable for positive adjustment in childhood and adolescence (Rutter, 1978; Zelkowitz, 1987), and suggests that support may act as a protective factor for conduct disorder and adolescent substance use (Cauce et al., 1990; Rutter, 1979; Wills et al., 1992).

Finally, research suggests that a positive school climate may act as an important protective factor for at-risk youths. Although there is no agreed-upon definition of school climate (see Rutter, 1979), there is some evidence that schools that address interpersonal conflict and discipline problems in an effective manner—i.e., through peaceful conflict-resolution and fair but not overly punitive discipline—may experience fewer conduct problems, lower truancy and school dropout, and enhanced bonding to school (Hawkins and Lam, 1987).

IMPLICATIONS

Major disagreements persist about the most effective means of preventing or reducing conduct disorder in at-risk youths. However, there is widespread agreement among mental health professionals, educators, criminologists, policymakers, and the general public that conduct disorder inflicts untold psychological, social, and economic costs on children, families, victims, and communities, in such forms as physical and emotional harm to others, property destruction, outpatient and inpatient mental health services, remedial education, school dropout, teen parenthood, law enforcement, delinquency and adult criminality, and substance use and abuse. Although some youths do not present conduct problems until adolescence, those at highest risk typically display aggressive and oppositional behavior problems in the preschool or early school years that escalate to cross-situational conduct disorder by late childhood or early adolescence (Dumas, 1992; Loeber, 1988, 1990; Patterson et al., 1989).

The seriousness of conduct disorder and the fact that it becomes increasingly resistant to change as children grow older (Kazdin, 1987) point to the importance of early intervention or, better, prevention. The coping-competence model described in this chapter offers a theoretical framework for prevention and intervention. The model is predicated on the assumption that a reduction in the frequency and intensity of antisocial and, to a lesser extent, asocial coping (e.g., via a reduction of aggressive and oppositional behavior at home and school) will not lead by itself to an increase in prosocial ways of coping. If the model is incorrect, the affective, social, and achievement domains of coping-competence should not account for antisocial outcomes beyond what is explained directly by risk and protective factors. If the model is correct, they should account for these outcomes, and therefore prevention and intervention efforts should seek to maximize coping-competence as much as they target specific risk and protective factors. Preliminary research evidence supports the coping-competence model (Dumas et al., 1994; Prinz et al., 1994). However, the model still awaits the verdict of a comprehensive, longitudinal test.

ACKNOWLEDGMENTS

The author wishes to thank Jean-Luc Lambert, Ronald J. Prinz, Eliot Smith, and Noam Shpancer for their helpful comments on an earlier version of this chapter.

REFERENCES

Asarnow, J. R. (1988). Peer status and social competence in child psychiatric inpatients: A comparison of children with depressive, externalizing, and concurrent depressive and externalizing disorders. *Journal of Abnormal Child Psychology*, 16, 151–162.

Averill, J. R. (1973). Personal control over aversive stimuli and its relationship to stress. *Psychological Bulletin*, 80, 286–303.

Bargh, J. A. (1994). The four horsemen of automaticity: Awareness, intention, efficiency, and control in social cognition. In R. S. Wyer and T. K. Srull (Eds.), *Handbook of social cognition* (2nd. ed., vol. 1, pp. 1–40). Hillsdale, NJ: Lawrence Erlbaum Associates.

Bates, J. E., Bayles, K., Bennett, D. S., Ridge B., and Brown, M. M. (1991). Origins of externalizing behavior problems at eight years of age. In D. J. Pepler and K. H. Rubin (Eds.), *The development and treatment of childhood aggression* (pp. 93–120). Hillsdale: NJ: Lawrence Erlbaum Associates.

Berscheid, E. (1986). Emotional experience in close relationships: Some implications for child development. In W. W. Hartup and Z. Rubin (Eds.), *Relationships and development* (pp. 135–166). Hillsdale, NJ: Lawrence Erlbaum Associates.

Bierman, K. L. (1986). Process of change during social skills training with preadolescents and its relation to treatment outcome. *Child Development*, 57, 230–240.

Blechman, E.A. (1990). A new look at emotions and the family: A model of effective family communication. In E. A. Blechman (Ed.), *Emotions and the family: For better or for worse* (pp. 201–224). Hillsdale, NJ: Lawrence Erlbaum Associates.

Blechman, E. A., Prinz, R. J., and Dumas, J. E. (1995). Coping, competence, and aggression prevention. Part 1. Developmental model. *Applied and Preventive Psychology*, 4, 211–232.

Broadbent, D. E. (1971). *Decision and stress*. New York: Academic Press.

Brody, G. H. and Forehand, R. (1986). Maternal perceptions of child maladjustment as a function of the combined influence of child behavior and maternal depression. *Journal of Consulting and Clinical Psychology*, 54, 237–240.

Brook, J. S., Brook, D. W., Gordon, A. S., Whiteman, M., and Cohen, P. (1990). The psychosocial etiology of adolescent drug use: A family interactional approach. *Genetic, Social, and General Psychology Monographs*, 116, (Whole No. 2).

Campbell, S. B. (1991). Longitudinal studies of active and aggressive preschoolers: Individual differences in early behavior and outcome. In D. Cicchetti and S. L. Toth (Eds.), *Rochester Symposium on Developmental Psychopathology, Vol. 2: Internalizing and externalizing expressions of dysfunction* (pp. 57–90). Hillsdale, NJ: Lawrence Erlbaum Associates.

Cantrell, V. L. and Prinz, R. J. (1985). Multiple perspectives of rejected, neglected, and accepted children: Relationship between sociometric status and behavioral characteristics. *Journal of Consulting and Clinical Psychology*, 53, 884–889.

Cauce, A.M., Reid, M., Landesman, S., and Gonzales, N. (1990). Social support in young children: Measurement, structure, and behavioral impact. In B. R. Sarason, I. G. Sarason, and G. R. Pierce (Eds.), *Social support: An interactional view* (pp. 64–94). New York: John Wiley.

Cohen, S. (1980). Aftereffects of stress on human performance and social behavior: A review of research and theory. *Psychological Bulletin*, 88, 82–108.

Cohen, S. and Spacapan, S. (1978). The aftereffects of stress: An attentional interpretation. *Environmental Psychology and Nonverbal Behavior, 3,* 43–57.

Dishion, T. J., Patterson, G. R., Stoolmiller, M., and Skinner, M. L. (1991). Family, school, and behavioral antecedents to early adolescent involvement with antisocial peers. *Developmental Psychology, 27,* 172–180.

Dix, T. (1991). The affective organization of parenting: Adaptive and maladaptive processes. *Psychological Bulletin, 110,* 3–25.

Dodge, K. A. (1989). Enhancing social relationships. In E. J. Mash and R. J. Barkley (Eds.), *Behavioral treatment of childhood disorders* (pp. 222–244). New York: Guilford Press.

Dodge, K. A., Pettit, G. S., McClaskey, C. L., and Brown, M. M. (1986). Social competence in children. *Monographs of the Society for Research in Child Development, 51* (2, serial No. 213).

Dumas, J. E. (1986). Indirect influence of maternal social contacts on mother-child interactions in distressed families. *Journal of Abnormal Child Psychology, 14,* 205–216.

———. (1989). Let's not forget the context in behavioral assessment. *Behavioral Assessment, 11,* 231–247.

———. (1990). Contextual effects in mother-child interactions: Beyond an operant analysis. In E. A. Blechman (Ed.), *Emotions and the family: For better or for worse* (pp. 155–179). Hillsdale, NJ: Lawrence Erlbaum Associates.

———. (1992). Conduct disorder. In S. M. Turner, K. S. Calhoun, and H. E. Adams (Eds.), *Handbook of clinical behavior therapy* (2nd. ed., pp. 285–316). New York: John Wiley.

Dumas, J. E., Blechman, E. A., and Prinz, R. J. (1994). Aggressive children and effective communication. *Aggressive Behavior, 20,* 347–358.

Dumas, J. E., Gibson, J. A., and Albin, J. B. (1989). Behavioral correlates of maternal depressive symptomatology in conduct-disorder children. *Journal of Consulting and Clinical Psychology, 57,* 516–521.

Dumas, J. E. and LaFreniere, P. J. (1993). Mother-child relationships as sources of support or stress: A comparison of competent, average, aggressive, and anxious dyads. *Child Development, 64,* 1732–1754.

Dumas, J. E. and Serketich, W. J. (1994). Maternal depressive symptomatology and child maladjustment: A comparison of three process models. *Behavior Therapy, 25,* 161–181.

Dumas, J. E. and Wahler, R. G. (1983). Predictors of treatment outcome in parent training: Mother insularity and socioeconomic disadvantage. *Behavioral Assessment, 5,* 301–313.

———. (1985). Indiscriminate mothering as a contextual factor in aggressive-oppositional child behavior: "Damned if you do, damned if you don't." *Journal of Abnormal Child Psychology, 13,* 1–17.

Dumas, J. E. and Wekerle, C. (1995). Maternal reports of child behavior problems and personal distress as predictors of dysfunctional parenting. *Development and Psychopathology, 7,* 465–479.

Fantuzzo, J. W., DePaola, L. M., Lambert, L., Martino, T., Anderson, G., and Sutton, S. (1991). Effects of interparental violence on the psychological adjustment and competencies of young children. *Journal of Consulting and Clinical Psychology, 59,* 258–265.

Farrington, D. P. and West, D. J. (1981). The Cambridge study in delinquent development (United Kingdom). In S. A. Mednick and A. E. Baert (Eds.), *Prospective longitudinal research: An empirical basis for the primary prevention of psychosocial disorders.* New York: Oxford University Press.

Ferreira, A. J. and Winter, W. D. (1968). Information exchange and silence in normal and abnormal families. *Family Therapy, 5,* 415–419.

Frijda, N. H. (1986). *The emotions.* Cambridge, England: Cambridge University Press.

Hartlage, S., Alloy, L. B., Vazquez, C., and Dykman, B. (1993). Automatic and effortful processing in depression. *Psychological Bulletin, 113,* 247–278.

Hawkins, J. D. and Lam, T. (1987). Teacher practices, social development and delinquency. In J. D. Burchard and S. N. Burchard (Eds.), *Prevention of delinquent behavior* (pp. 241–274). Newbury Park, CA: Sage.

Hawkins, J. D. and Lishner, D. (1987). Etiology and prevention of antisocial behavior in children and adolescents. In D. H. Crowell, I. M. Evans, and C. R. O'Donnell (Eds.), *Childhood aggression and violence: Sources of influence, prevention, and control* (pp. 263–282). New York: Plenum Press.

Hawkins, J. D. and Weis, J. G. (1985). The social development model: An integrated approach to delinquency prevention. *Journal of Primary Prevention, 6,* 73–97.

Hockey, R. (1973). Changes in information selection patterns in multi-source monitoring as a function of induced arousal shifts. *Journal of Experimental Psychology, 88,* 277–281.

Hops, M., Biglan, A., Sherman, L., Arthur, J., Friedman, L., and Osteen, V. (1987). Home observations of family interactions of depressed women. *Journal of Consulting and Clinical Psychology, 55,* 341–346.

Izard, C. E. (1984). Emotion-cognition relationships and human development. In C. E. Izard, J. Kagan, and R. B. Zajonc (Eds.), *Emotions, cognition, and behavior* (pp. 17–37). Cambridge, England: Cambridge University Press.

Jarvis, I. L. (1982). Decision-making under stress. In L. Goldberger and S. Breznitz (Eds.), *Handbook of stress: Theoretical and clinical aspects* (pp. 69–87). New York: Free Press.

Kahneman, D. (1973). *Attention and effort.* Englewood Cliffs, NJ: Prentice Hall.

Kaler, S. R. and Kopp, C. B. (1990). Compliance and comprehension in very young toddlers. *Child Development, 61,* 328–347.

Kazdin, A. E. (1987). Treatment of antisocial behavior in children: Current status and future directions. *Psychological Bulletin, 102,* 187–203.

Kellam, S. G., Brown, C. H., and Fleming, J. P. (1985). Longitudinal community epidemiological studies of drug abuse: Early aggressiveness, shyness and learning problems. In L. N. Robins (Ed.), *Studying drug use and abuse.* New York: Neale Watson Academic Publishers.

Lazarus, R. S. and Folkman, S. (1984). *Stress, appraisal, and coping.* New York: Springer-Verlag.

Loeber, R. (1988). The natural histories of juvenile conduct problems, substance use, and delinquency: Evidence for developmental progressions. In B. B. Lahey and A. E. Kazdin (Eds.), *Advances in clinical child psychology,* Vol. 11 (pp. 73–124). New York: Plenum Press.

———. (1990). Development and risk factors of juvenile antisocial behavior and delinquency. *Clinical Psychology Review, 10,* 1–41.

Loeber, R. and Stouthamer-Loeber, M. (1986). Family factors as correlates and predictors of juvenile conduct problems and delinquency. In N. Morris and M. Tonry (Eds.), *Crime and justice: An annual review of research,* Vol. 7 (pp. 29–149). Chicago: University of Chicago Press.

Luria, A. R. (1961). *The role of speech in the regulation of normal and abnormal behavior.* New York: Basic Books.

Maccoby, E. E. (1992). The role of parents in the socialization of children: An historical overview. *Developmental Psychology, 28,* 1006–1017.

Mandler, G. (1982). Stress and thought processes. In L. Goldberger and S. Breznitz (Eds.), *Handbook of stress: Theoretical and clinical aspects* (pp. 88–104). New York: Free Press.

McCord, J. (1988). Parental behavior in the cycle of aggression. *Psychiatry, 51,* 14–23.

Milner, J. S. (1993). Social information processing and physical child abuse. *Clinical Psychology Review, 13,* 275–294.

Moffitt, T. E. (1990). Juvenile delinquency and attention deficit disorder: Developmental trajectories from age 3 to age 15. *Child Development, 61*, 893–910.

———. (1993). Adolescence-limited and life-course-persistent antisocial behavior: A developmental taxonomy. *Psychological Review, 100*, 674–701.

Offord, D. R., Boyle, M. C., and Racine, Y. A. (1991). The epidemiology of antisocial behavior in childhood and adolescence. In D. J. Pepler and K. H. Rubin (Eds.), *The development and treatment of childhood aggression* (pp. 31–54). Hillsdale, NJ: Lawrence Erlbaum Associates.

Offord, D. R. and Waters, B. G. (1983). Socialization and its failure. In M. D. Levine, W. B. Carey, A. C. Crocker, and R. T. Gross (Eds.), *Developmental-behavioral pediatrics*. Philadelphia: Saunders.

Panaccione, V. F. and Wahler, R. G. (1986). Child behavior, maternal depression and social coercion as factors in the quality of child care. *Journal of Abnormal Child Psychology,14*, 263–278.

Passman, R. H. and Mulhern, R. K. (1977). Maternal punitiveness as affected by situational stress: An experimental analogue of child abuse. *Journal of Abnormal Psychology, 86*, 565–569.

Patterson, G. R. (1982). *Coercive family processes*. Eugene, OR: Castalia Publishing Company.

Patterson, G. R., DeBaryshe, B. D., and Ramsey, E. (1989). A developmental perspective on antisocial behavior. *American Psychologist, 2*, 329–335.

Patterson, G. R., Reid, J. B., and Dishion, T. J. (1992). *Antisocial boys*. Eugene, OR: Castalia Publishing Company.

Pennebaker, J. W., Colder, M., and Sharp, L. K. (1990). Accelerating the coping process. *Journal of Personality and Social Psychology, 58*, 528–537.

Prinz, R. J., Blechman, E. A., and Dumas, J. E. (1994). An evaluation of peer coping-skills training for childhood aggression. *Journal of Clinical Child Psychology, 23*, 193–203.

Prinz, R. J., Connor, P., and Wilson, C. (1981). Hyperactive and aggressive behaviors in childhood: Intertwined dimensions. *Journal of Abnormal Child Psychology, 9*, 191–202.

Reid, W. J. and Crisafulli, A. (1990). Marital discord and child behavior problems: A meta-analysis. *Journal of Abnormal Child Psychology, 18*, 105–117.

Robins, L. N. (1981). Epidemiological approaches to natural history research: Antisocial disorders in children. *Journal of the American Academy of Child Psychiatry, 20*, 566–580.

Rodick, J. D., Hengeller, S. W., and Hanson, C. O. (1986). An evaluation of the family adaptability and cohesion evaluation scales and the circumplex model. *Journal of Abnormal Child Psychology, 14*, 77–87.

Rutter, M. (1978). Early sources of security and competence. In J. S. Bruner and A. Garton (Eds.), *Human growth and development* (pp. 33–61). Oxford, UK: Clarendon.

———. (1979). Protective factors in children's responses to stress and disadvantage. In M. W. Kent and J. E. Rolf (Eds.), *Primary prevention of psychopathology: Vol. 3, Social competence in children* (pp. 49–74). London: University Press of England.

Rutter, M. and Giller, H. (1983). *Juvenile delinquency: Trends and perspectives*. New York: Penguin Books.

Sherrod, D. R. and Downs, R. (1974). Environmental determinants of altruism: The effects of stimulus overload and perceived control on helping. *Journal of Experimental Social Psychology, 10*, 468–479.

Shinn, M. R., Ramsey, E., Walker, H. M., Stieber, H., and O'Neill, R. E. (1987). Antisocial behavior in school settings: Initial differences in an at-risk and normal population. *Journal of Special Education, 21*, 69–84.

Smith, E. R. (1994). Procedural knowledge and processing startegies in social cognition. In R. S. Wyer and T. K. Srull (Eds.), *Handbook of social cognition* (2nd ed., vol. 1) (pp. 99–151). Hillsdale, NJ: Lawrence Erlbaum Associates.

Spivack, G. and Shure, M. (1974). *Social adjustment of young children.* San Francisco: Jossey-Bass.

Stanton, W. R., Feehan, M., McGee, R., and Silva, P. A. (1990). The relative value of reading ability and IQ as predictors of teacher-reported behavior problems. *Journal of Learning Disabilities, 23,* 514–517.

Sturge, C. (1982). Reading retardation and antisocial behaviour. *Journal of Child Psychology and Psychiatry, 23,* 21–31.

Vygotsky, L. S. (1981). The genesis of higher mental functions. In J. V. Wertsch (Ed.), *The concept of activity in Soviet Psykchology* (pp. 144–148). Armonk, NY: Sharpe.

Wadsworth, M. E. J. (1980). Early life events and later behavioral outcomes in a British longitudinal study. In S. B. Sells, K. Crandell, M. Roff, J. S. Strauss, and W. Pollin (Eds.), *Human functioning in longitudinal perspective* (pp. 68–180). Baltimore: Williams and Wilkins.

Wahler, R. G. (1980). The insular mother: Her problems in parent-child treatment. *Journal of Applied Behavior Analysis, 13,* 207–219.

Wahler, R. G. and Dumas, J. E. (1984). Changing the observational coding styles of insular and noninsular mothers: A step toward maintenance of parent training effects. In R. F. Dangel and R. A. Polster (Eds.), *Parent training: Foundations of research and practice* (pp. 379–416). New York: Guilford Press.

——— (1987). Family factors in childhood psychopathology: A coercion-neglect model. In T. Jacob (Ed.), *Family interaction and psychopathology: Theories, methods, and findings* (pp. 581–627). New York: Plenum Press.

———. (1989). Attentional problems in dysfunctional mother-child interactions: An interbehavioral model. *Psychological Bulletin, 105,* 116–130.

Wahler, R. G. and Hann, D. M. (1984). The communication patterns of troubled mothers: In search of a keystone in the generalization of parenting skills. *Education and Treatment of Children, 7,* 335–350.

Waters, E. and Sroufe, L. A. (1983). Social competence as a developmental construct. *Developmental Review, 3,* 79–97.

Webster-Stratton, C. (1985). Predictors of treatment outcome in parent training for conduct-disordered children. *Behavior Therapy, 16,* 223–243.

West, M. O. and Prinz, R. J. (1987). Parental alcoholism and childhood psychopathology. *Psychological Bulletin, 102,* 204–218.

Wills, T. A., Vaccaro, D., and McNamara, G. (1992). The role of life events, family support, and competence in adolescent substance use: A test of vulnerability and protective factors. *American Journal of Community Psychology, 20,* 349–358.

Zelkowitz, P. (1987). Social support and aggressive behavior in young children. *Journal of Applied Family and Child Studies, 36,* 129–134.

New Learning and Agency in the At-Promise Student

Graham E. Higgs and Nancy L. Tarsi

The past 20 years have marked an ongoing discussion regarding children who do not succeed in school. The debate most often centers on children who drop out, because substantial evidence ties dropping out to a host of unfavorable circumstances that follow, such as high unemployment, health problems, welfare dependence, drug abuse, and high crime and delinquency rates (Catterall, 1986; Lanier, 1986). In this chapter we join the ongoing dialogue with a focus on the student at-promise, recognizing that the language we use affects our experiences and thereby recreates our social reality. The discourse that places children "at-risk" assigns them to the role of "persons-in-trouble," a one-down position. When we focus on people in trouble, our attention is naturally drawn to what's wrong. We forget to look at what's right. If we must label the children who face greater compromises, then let us at least give them hope. We choose the label "at-promise" because we believe we will be more likely to see their strengths and find the path that will lead away from disillusionment. This interpretation arises from poststructural theory, which recognizes the power in language to construct social reality.

Therefore we choose to frame our discussion of dropouts as students at-promise, individuals whose unique gifts are often untapped in formal school settings. This view is substantiated by current research on creative dropouts, whose learning styles have been found to differ markedly from those of other students, lending credibility to the claim that their school "failure" has less to do with aptitude than with the way learning is structured in traditional classrooms.

In this chapter we will explore concepts of personal agency and the phenomenon of new learning in students at-promise, for whom the constructs have special significance. The philosophic underpinnings of each concept will underscore the personal reflections that follow. We offer a review of theoretical models that promote agency in students, as well as describe structural and curricular obstacles to its development. We are more interested in giving language to new ideas and evoking questions than in offering pat solutions, believing strongly in the value (and fun) of adding to the public debate about students who are dropping out of school.

Finally, the entire discussion is framed in a postmodern perspective in which three points are strongly held: first, that science cannot lay claim to ultimate truth; second, that all knowledge is partial and limited by perspective; and last, that all knowledge comes from a person who holds a social location (Lincoln, 1994).

NEW LEARNING

New learning is created in the alchemy of change. When a person's current knowledge is contradicted by new observations, a temporary state of cognitive dissonance often occurs. But when, out of the confusion, an integration of the contradictory information occurs and a synthesis emerges, the change can be said to have brought about new learning. Knowing this, it seems reasonable that we would want to embrace change. Resistance to change, however, is one of the established culture's most dominant characteristics, and it is one of the most powerful barriers to new learning. We believe it is from within the paradox of change and resistance that the answers to issues in education for all students may be found.

TEACHERS AS CONVEYORS OF CULTURAL VALUES

The role of the teacher in any culture is to incite new learning while at the same time preserving and transmitting cultural values. Under ideal conditions this is a difficult job and one that requires some delicate balancing even if the curriculum reflects current population needs and is well designed. The job is made much more difficult for teachers in poor schools that have little money for new books and materials, have increased class size, cannot afford teacher-aides, and whose students increasingly come from diverse cultural backgrounds and from families under stress due to pressures brought on by poverty, underemployment, illiteracy, disability, and crime. Teachers are expected to transmit the culture, creating a neatly organized and well-informed student cohort with the acceptable skills and values needed to succeed in contemporary society. In order to do this, they must successfully integrate and synthesize the cultures of a body of students who hail from a range of backgrounds as diverse and chaotic as can possibly be imagined.

The task placed before teachers in most American public schools would be largely insurmountable without some practical tools. Yet the reality is that the tools provided by the teacher training colleges are often highly idealized at best and have not kept up with cultural realities. Much is left to the ingenuity of the teacher. While the task for teachers seems unreasonable at first glance, the understanding that education is by nature dynamic and that "order arises from chaos," as Nietzsche has said, gives the practice of teaching new hope. At base, education is about creating new learning opportunities and new learning is about effecting change. The fact of education's dynamism is of particular concern to the teachers of students who lack necessary esteem, self-concept, and academic self-efficacy. Employing practices that increase these antecedents of agency will increase students' willingness to embrace the change necessary for new learning.

CRITICAL PERSPECTIVES AND THE RELATIONSHIP TO THE CONSTRUCT OF AGENCY

The consideration of agency in students, of what inhibits and promotes intrinsic motivation, is best examined using a narrow lens in which the relationship between schooling and society is highlighted. Critical theorists feel that the power of the dominant over the subordinate class is reinforced in the form of imposition of cultural standards as regular school practice (Bennett-deMarrais, 1995). How does the existent power structure in schools affect students' emotional and intellectual development? Some observations follow.

In order to be effective in motivating change and thereby learning in alienated students, counselors and teachers must be able to move inside to the heart of the students' concern and while there, listen carefully and respectfully for the voices that will indicate the steps to be taken. With at-promise students, more is needed than the standard didactic approaches; a respect for the voice of "the other" is critical. A willingness of seasoned practitioners to trust their intuitions, use their imagination, and rely on practical improvisation is essential in the adventure that constitutes helping disenfranchised people change their lives and embrace the dynamic process of learning.

In this chapter we would like to explore a philosophical and theoretical basis for methods that teachers and counselors might use when working with students who are at-promise. New, collaborative, non-competitive approaches to education are needed for teachers who will be motivating this population to change (Higgs and Franklin, 1994; Higgs and Plummer, 1995). We will purposely narrow the discussion to concerns related to improving academic achievement in these populations. An at-promise student can generally be defined as any member of a traditional population of academic peers whose chances to meet personal goals of achievement or goals of achievement set by their school have, for whatever reason, not yet been realized. This chapter considers the potentials inherent in the K–12 student.

SOCIAL, ENVIRONMENTAL, AND PHYSIOLOGICAL ANTECEDENTS

In looking for causes that compromise students' potentials, we discover a plethora of studies pointing to social conditions and environmental problems as sources of personal disintegration: single-parent families, drug abuse, gangs, homelessness, mental illness, learning disabilities, poverty, hunger, crime, immigration stresses, and a host of factors resulting from the interplay between these and other social ills. The scientific community offers overwhelming evidence that external conditions are major antecedent settings for the condition of compromise. Children who are at-promise typically come from single-parent homes, from socioeconomically distressed environments, and from socially and culturally alienated populations (U.S. GAO/HRD-94–21, 1993; U.S. GAO/HRD-93–105BR, 1993).

In addition to this popular understanding, we will argue that the rise in student alienation from schools is incidental to prevailing social and environmental conditions, conditions that evolve from much broader decisions made in the political arena. The environments resulting from these political decisions, which sacrifice American cultures to market forces more than willing to forfeit moral and ethical values to improve their bottom lines, are the contexts within which students and educators must work.

MARKET VALUES

Cornel West (1993) describes the destructive social effects of market strategies, intensified to "stimulate consumption, especially strategies aimed at American youth that project sexual activity as instant fulfillment and violence as the locus of machismo identity. This market activity," West contends, "has contributed greatly to the disorientation and confusion of American youth, and those with less education and fewer opportunities bear the brunt of this cultural chaos" (p. 84).

Arguments linking social context with market economic forces abound. We quote Cornel West because he speaks to a broader issue, imploring that we transcend racial and economic bias and focus on becoming a truly multicultural society. His message is clear: we must continue to work in the face of the context mounted against us. Historically, educators have focused attention on the external, social, and environmental conditions surrounding student failure, for this is the direction toward which our discourse has pointed. "Single-parent families," "low socioeconomic status," and "crime-ridden neighborhoods" are phrases strongly associated with school failure. The glaring social and economic contexts of the majority of students susceptible to school failure present such a compelling picture that we are naturally drawn to these contexts in search of answers. But there are explanations for these problems from outside of social science.

PHYSIOLOGICAL ETIOLOGY

We have said that new learning requires change and that resistance to change is the main barrier to learning. Biological research draws conclusions regarding the etiology of resistance that are somewhat different from those provided by our social theories. Sociobiological theory suggests that not only do physical systems evolve, behavioral and social systems do as well (Degler, 1991; Wilson, 1975). If social systems evolve and are influenced heavily by genetics, as the sociobiologists believe, then there may be other places to look for solutions to resistance in the schools in conjunction with changing students' social conditions.

For example, in interpreting the causes for resistance to change in education, social theorists might point to resistance evolving through group defenses against external threats to the social unit. But resistance can also be interpreted as a product of physical structure and evolution of the brain. Recent studies in brain physiology document clear physical differences between the brains of socially stimulated and non-stimulated animals, suggesting physical clues to why cognitive growth is so difficult and resistance to change so pervasive. Learning appears to initiate physiological growth in the brain (Swerdlow, 1995). Researchers believe that new learning requires a change in brain physiology and that in older brains this physical change is more difficult. Like retraining a muscle in the body to do a different job, the brain must be reconditioned in order to assimilate the new knowledge of reality. Placing new information into the old picture means that the entire picture must change. This process, which first accommodates and then assimilates the new information, is called learning.

Animal research teams at McGill University and the University of Southern California have shown that socialization and nurturing play an important role in brain structure development. Brain structural patterns developed early seem to form a foundation for the building of future knowledge structures. Fetal brain tissue transplanted into the brains of old animals provides the animals with an enhanced ability to learn new information (Yourgrau, 1990). The established brain structure is difficult to change. This could explain why we experience discomfort when confronted with information that challenges our known patterns.

Clearly, students, teachers, and administrators alike labor under the influence of physiological resistance to change. As we can see, social and cultural explanations unveil only some of the possible causes for barriers in education. Follow us now as we take this discussion forward and explore some different avenues.

THEORETICAL AND CURRICULAR WAYS TO PROMOTE AGENCY AND NEW LEARNING

While the undeniable social and environmental contexts are crucial and over-arching dimensions of the problems associated with students at-promise, experience has shown that many students from within these contexts are resilient and are able to transcend the debilitating influences. This observation alone points to influences other than social interaction as primary. The literature pertaining to psychological differences between students at risk and their not-at-risk peers highlights intrinsic factors that influence students' attribution toward learning in spite of context. Whether these factors are socially determined or biologically set is an important question and one that could influence how teaching and counseling interventions are done in the future.

INTRINSIC MOTIVATION

Theories that support self-efficacy promote new learning. Individual efforts of educators to build and facilitate the development of intrinsic motivation in their students may have greater long-term effectiveness and more power to help students overcome their compromising status than attempting to change their external conditions. While the move toward more socially responsive, full-service schools (Dryfoos, 1994) is slowly gaining momentum, a better knowledge of the practices that support intrinsic motivation and ways to build them into school programs is needed in the interim. To the benefit of school systems, methods that use the intrinsic resources of students and parents in a collaborative and cooperative program will be more cost effective.

STUDENT-CENTERED VERSUS TEACHER-CENTERED CLASSROOMS

Teaching and learning approaches that strengthen academic self-efficacy, improve self-concept, and help students move toward a more internal locus of control provide a better platform for individuals to make lasting changes in their beliefs about learning. Moving some responsibility for learning to students allows them to gain control over their education and reinforces antecedents of personal agency. There is also a dire need to begin the move away from competitive discourses that prevent cooperation and begin to build a theory of learning that is founded on a philosophy of collaboration.

Teachers and counselors must stay informed about current conditions affecting the children they work with in order to mediate in the acquisition of social services. Frequently school system policies inhibit the extent to which teachers or counselors may engage in social interventions. It is necessary to develop a network with helping professionals outside of the system who can provide necessary services. Large school systems are characteristically ineffective in taking necessary action to meet the needs of children and families who are at-promise. In larger systems where social services are fragmented into a bureaucracy of specialized units serving specific target groups, it is easy to push responsibility for complex problems onto other units or agencies. Latane and Darley (1970) demonstrated how responsibility to take action is diffused when the number of bystanders to an emergency increases. It follows that the complex of independent social service providers constitutes a similar diffusing group. There is an actual emergency in our schools that reflects an epidemic of violence and alienation in our society. It should be no surprise that so many children who have multiple needs slip through the cracks between agencies that are competing instead of collaborating.

OBSTACLES TO AGENCY AND NEW LEARNING

Many teaching approaches in use today rely on authoritarian methods that treat students like passive, hollow vessels to be filled with a quantity of objective facts. Their didactic approaches fail to tap into the student whose mind possesses a unique potential to creatively transform knowledge through interaction with the content. Much of public education today has become a competition through which the "best" minds are identified using standardized instruments and rank is determined using win/lose grading schemes that undermine the self-efficacy, esteem, and basic identity of a large portion of the student population. School has been seen by many, for generations, as a punitive experience. These conditions are in stark contrast to what we understand to be necessary for optimal learning.

That education is a dynamic institution (the perfect oxymoron) points to its catalytic relationship with cultural evolution. Education is both informed by and teacher to the living culture. We might take a hint from this natural relationship to position the teacher as student and flatten the hierarchy that allows domination partly by reinforcing didactic approaches as part of a competitive discourse. The process of educational alienation and decline has taken generations. There is no reason to assume it can or will be turned around quickly. But if, as the sociobiological research suggests, genetic and biological predisposition can be influenced by learning over time, we must begin to work on a plan of action to structure education in ways that build intrinsic motivation to learn. If it is indeed possible to influence evolution with social policy, then we must begin to take steps in that direction.

The Framework of Learning Must Change

The question of whether objective explanations should dominate subjective realities is not a new debate. The early (circa 475 B.C.) Greek philosophers Parmenides and Heraclitus argued similar fundamental questions (Wheelwright, 1966). Are all objective meanings founded on the principle that nothing comes from nothing? Parmenides's logical assertion, that being cannot arise from not-being, set the stage for the quantitative study of existence, empiricism, and ultimately, 2400 years later, behavioral science. But Heraclitus, an early phenomenologist, argued that, in spite of the desire to hammer down a logical plank, individual realities are always changing. In fact, he asserted, the only constant is change.

This early confrontation between positivist logic and the undeniable reality of qualitative change mirrors the same paradox that situates education in critical relationship with a vital and dynamic society. When the balance is upset and either of these antithetical positions holds sway for too long, education loses integrity and vitality. When this kind of paralysis occurs in education, large numbers of potential learners become alienated from schools. The etiology of alienation, we believe, arises from the dualism created by the Cartesian model which divides mind and body. The separation that is inherent in the discourse of competitive education and reflects the larger social discourse creates a kind of existential dread and revulsion in the student who has an internalized sense of alienation of the body from the mind. Education's commitment to the science of division sanctions the institution of systematic doubt and creates the tension of existential angst and alienation. This dread is what paralyzes some students.

Multicultural Learning Theory

The need to keep education dynamic is supported by a multicultural learning theory which suggests that new learning occurs when the dynamic tension between conflicting ideas is resolved through the integration of the enduring characteristics of the previous ideas and the creation of a synthesis. As cultures evolve, so must the education that catalyzes the necessary change.

Cognitive dissonance created by challenges between what one believes to be fact and conflicting reality is a major source of learning motivation (Festinger, 1957). Active learning, therefore, does not occur in a totally secure environment, hence the challenge to teachers of some at-promise children, particularly those with serious emotional disturbances, victims of abuse, neglect, and extreme poverty, whose need for basic safety, nourishment, and continuity must be met before they can weather challenges to their beliefs.

But a larger group of so-called "at-risk students" are, by default, fostered by the school system's unwillingness to embrace the changing culture. The inability of the schools to invoke students' subjective meanings and to listen and respond to the community creates a population that chooses not to adapt and is therefore disconnected from school. In classrooms where the emphasis is entirely on objective meaning, students are not encouraged to relate their personal subjective understandings. As Foster and Grant (1984) contend,

> To strip subjective meaning away from lesson content is to fragment, fracture, and strip away essential parts of the reality of anything we teach. Given the frequency with which subjective meaning is ignored, is there any wonder that many students graduate from schools without really knowing or caring about science or history or art, or about anything taught in schools? (p. 302)

The culture of alienation has evolved through a history of punitive educational experiences where learning is forced upon the natural child like a muzzle on a rabid dog, to control the inherent beast, to make society safe from the imagination's evils.

Can we teach "facts" and still invoke student participation in a process of discovery? Of course we can, and good teachers do. Good education requires that we include ideas contrary to the status quo and conflicting with the norms. By reaching into the student experience, we will find these contradictions and they will become the inspiration for thoughtful consideration of the "facts." Students change and the culture of learning changes. If we are sensitive to this, as Heraclitus was, we might remain flexible and recognize the potential for students' subjective cultural experiences to contribute to the learning process.

An Intrinsic Focus

Shifting our attention several thousand years, from the pre-Socratic dialogue about meaning, to the present, we encounter the cognitive theorists who believe it is students' thoughts about their ability to learn that are most important. The cognitive theorists examine psychological constructs to discover students' relationships to learning. Cognitive scientists believe that students can be empowered to learn if you change the beliefs they have about their ability to learn.

The concept of intrinsic motivation has received a fair amount of attention in the scientific literature, but practical applications and classroom conditions that specifically build antecedents are not common today. If this were not true, there would be more evidence of student-driven learning. Maslow's (1968) work can provide a basis for curriculum in mental health education. His interest in students' self-esteem is central to the model. Since self-esteem is a learned construct, it can be changed through teacher facilitation (Neal, 1981). Self-concept, self-efficacy, responsibility, and intrinsic motivation are in danger of being undermined in students if the locus of meaning in education continues to mirror extrinsic purposes. Students are alienated from the classroom where they are told that the content and the product are more important than they are, where the test scores are what matter, and where the value of students is measured by standards to which they cannot relate.

Teacher Methods: From the Teacher to Student

If meaning in education relates only to the external arena, and the locus of all value in our culture is wealth and power, there is a subsequent undermining of intrinsic purpose and integrity. Students become bored and emotionally separate from education that holds little meaning for them. The meaning of the problem lies in the context of a culture that places emphasis on the external pursuit of capital and power. But the problem substance resides in the unwillingness of educators to recognize and stop repeating the "facts" perpetrated and perpetuated by externally oriented market forces adept at manipulating both objective and subjective meanings.

Process Versus Product

As educators, conditioned by quantitative methods to look at numbers for truth and meaning, we develop a habit of assuming that reinforcing stimuli are largely external and we build teaching and assessment models based on this belief. Consequently we drift away from what we know to be true, that students who prevail under conditions we predict will create failure, do so because they possess an inherent quality of self that allows them to transcend a belief that quantities determine the value of their actions. This inherent tendency, the same potentiality described by Aristotle (Wheelwright, 1966), is what Deci and Ryan (1991) call agency.

Agency is the inner voice of assurance, the stable parent who quietly says, yes you can do it. If you try you can accomplish anything. Agency is the knowledge that one has the ability to originate and control behavior, to understand and assimilate incidents, and to develop a feeling of personal competence and a sense of personal control. This view of people suggests that motivation is inherent and is a natural tendency that should be drawn from within students instead of taught to students. In spite of the fact that we all know students who possess this sense of personal agency and who survive conditions that predict failure, we have not put enough study into the characteristics that motivate them to prevail. If we pay more attention to this remarkable tendency of all humans, we might develop a general theoretical model for applications that builds on students' natural motivation instead of sanctioning a social environmental excuse and further undermining hope.

There are several modern theories that provide foundations for the concept of human agency and motivation. The cognitive perspective (Bandura, 1989; Dweck, 1986; Eccles, 1983; Harter, 1988; and Weiner, 1990) holds that students are motivated more by a tendency toward cognitive equilibrium and competence than by external reinforcements. White (1959) suggests that students explore, learn, and enjoy learning for its own sake, not contingent on external reinforcement. In the cognitive view, intrinsic factors are more important over time.

Weiner's (1976) attribution theory suggests that students' attributions of success and failure are more responsible for their actual successes and failures than their ability. That some students underachieve and others overachieve would seem to support this view. If these cognitive views hold true across populations, then how can these factors be addressed in the classroom? A brief look at some of the findings on differences in cognitive constructs that correlate to academic achievement may provide some answers.

Agency as Philosophic Orientation

The literature indicates that, as a group, at-promise students are likely to have a history of unexcused absences from school. Their academic performance is much below average, and they display behavior that often results in disciplinary action (Nunn and Parish, 1992). Students who meet one or more of the above conditions have a significantly higher external locus of control (Hahn, 1987; Mills, Dunham, and Alpert, 1988; Payne and Payne, 1989). That is, they have a tendency to believe that forces outside of themselves have a greater control over their life. Unlike their school-successful peers, they believe personal behavior has little to do with success or failure. If you asked typical underachieving students what enabled them to make an A on a test, they would say, "It was luck." If you asked the same question to a student who succeeds in a traditional school setting, he or she would say, "I studied."

We know that motivation to achieve is influenced by a number of factors both intrinsic in the learner and in the learner's environment. Various studies of characteristics of students with different levels of achievement motivation have isolated some psychological constructs that predict achievement with reasonable accuracy. The construct of locus of control measures a student's attribution of personal control in various dimensions, one of which is academic achievement. The construct of self-concept measures the quality of students' beliefs about themselves. At-promise students, in addition to higher external locus of control, also have a less resilient self-concept (McCombs and Whisler, 1989). Students who have a poor self-concept do not feel connected to their community. They are confused about their identity and feel powerless to change their conditions (Coopersmith, 1981). Finally, students who are at-promise do not respond to the traditional teaching methods that require substantial achievement motivation and a higher self-efficacy for learning (Carbo and Hodges, 1988). Students who do not possess the belief that they can succeed academically are much less likely to keep trying or to use new strategies when they fail.

As a result of these psychological differences, the at-promise student in a traditional classroom is more likely to be assailed by feelings of powerlessness and personal incompetence. The classroom is a place that is frightening and degrading to many students, who prefer more informal and nontraditional approaches to learning. Clearly students who drop out are undermined by a lack of agency. The challenge for teachers, therefore, is to structure teaching and learning environments that build agency in students.

ORIGINS OF AGENCY

What are the origins of agency? Studies of motivation in humans have described two major arenas, intrinsic and extrinsic. The primary focus of most traditional approaches to changing the behavior of disenfranchised students has been to change external conditions and use external forces to motivate students who are not achieving. These techniques arise from the antiquated models of schools as training grounds for industrialized functions. The mechanistic classroom with teacher as foreman conducting group instruction no longer has validity for the culture of the information age. Additionally, the use of fear to motivate students has always been and continues to be a widespread practice. That paddling of students is less acceptable in some communities is a move in the right direction, but the attitude that it is all right to administer physical punishment to a child who is not doing what the teacher expects still prevails in many homes and schools.

Many of the current approaches designed to deal with "problem" students rely on behavior management models. In our view this has evolved because unsuccessful students display a higher percentage of unacceptable behaviors in the school setting than their successful peers. If they are to be served, efforts to change or modify their behavior become a priority. Paradoxical to their intent, some of the behavior modification programs are in danger of reinforcing a dependent, externally oriented population of students who become further alienated wards of the state with no familiarity with intrinsic hope. Their lot is to be passed from one social service agency to another or onto the streets where they eventually enter a correctional institution with a revolving door. In addition, the school systems' unwillingness to risk treating root causes of the at-promise condition prevents development of effective programs. These rigid policies compound hardships for all concerned—teachers, parents, children, administrators, and support personnel—ultimately causing enormous expense to society.

Attempts to build models that work in controlling antisocial behavior and at the same time provide an environment suitable for learning for all children have presented a major challenge to teachers and administrators since the advent of the Individuals with Disabilities Education Act (PL 99–457), a law designed to force systems to comply with what research tells us about learning and motivation.

As suggested above, methods that rely on the use of external enforcement, while appearing to have immediate positive outcomes, have met with limited long-term success. The road that has led to the current crisis concerning meeting the needs of some students began, in our opinion, with the closing of the schools to subjective meaning and the loss of willingness to entertain and debate changes from a qualitative perspective. In a culture driven by external market forces, the erosion of schools by factors in harmony with these competitive forces creates a significant portion of the population that is disenfranchised from the mythical mainstream.

Teaching practices that recognize the integrity of the individual student are philosophically different from models holding that students are to be filled with facts and that learning is the ability to regurgitate what has been force fed. In our opinion, students are alienated from schools in which methods of teaching do not allow student participation and are not relevant to students' lives.

POSTSTRUCTURALISM AND REFRAMING THE DISCOURSE TO COLLABORATION

A rather large and still emerging body of literature exists to support our postmodern thesis. In a variety of scientific disciplines including psychology, anthropology, education, physics, and others, methods reflecting poststructuralist thinking are evolving. No longer is the standard Cartesian logic, or the goals of modernism founded on it, being accepted without question. The postmodern age is upon us in force, reflecting a network of creative approaches to scholarly research and practice that reach beyond conventional method.

Postmodernism rejects the claim that any theory or application has a lock on universal truth for providing the right way to think about anything. Postmodernism is wary of all such claims as being embedded in self-serving struggles for personal, cultural, or political gain. On the other hand, postmodernism does not reject standard ways of knowing but critiques all approaches in relation to their own discourse. Postmodernism opens the door to new forms of inquiry and expects these forms to have particular value relative to their own vantage points (Richardson, 1994).

Dissatisfaction with the inability of the modernist perspective to respond to the complex questions of an increasingly diverse population involved in academic discourse has created an ever-broadening avenue where creative ideas can be played out unhindered by the limiting constructs of positivistic linguistics. Michel Foucault (1988) speaks of "fracture areas" (p. 37), which emerge in organized systems and give rise to new freedoms and the potential for transformation.

The ever dominant, analytic authority of scientific reason has cracks. We believe that it is through those cracks that the at-risk student falls. It is through those cracks that the disenfranchised members of our community disappear. It is into those cracks that the unheard minorities dissolve. The voice of reason does not speak for the disenfranchised. Henry Giroux (1990) discusses the inability of the modernist discourse to address issues of social justice or to understand the meanings of racial or ethnic voices in the ever-evolving present.

> Race and ethnicity have been generally reduced to a discourse of the Other, a discourse that regardless of its emancipatory or reactionary intent, often essentialized and reproduced the distance between the center and margins of power. Within the discourse of modernity, the Other not only sometimes ceases to be a historical agent, but is often defined within totalizing and universalistic theories that create a transcendental rational white, male, Eurocentric, subject that both occupies the centers of power while simultaneously appearing to exist outside of time and space. (Giroux, 1990, p. 7)

Radical voices like Giroux's contend that it is not possible to discuss educational theory in the "value neutral" terms prescribed by positivist methods (Giroux, 1981). On the other hand, there are benefits to science of nonpositivist analyses. An example can be seen in Thomas Kuhn's (1970) history of scientific change and in the discourse that followed. Kuhn's paradigm was an imaginative construct similar to Pepper's (1942) "world hypothesis," which facilitated a description of scientific change in revolutionary terms. As such, these ideas served to open a lengthy discourse that has evolved into a variety of alternative theories of the history of change in science (Lakatos, 1970, 1978 and Laudan, 1977, 1981). Examples like these suggest that the nonpositivist discourse of philosophers can make valuable contributions to science's self-understanding.

But there are other voices—voices not concerned with supporting or arguing from within the positivist paradigm—voices whose discourse is situated in the needs of nonempowered populations. These critical voices observe that the feast prepared for the powerful will not feed those who are not permitted to join them at the table.

John Cage (1961, 1969) provides a consistent challenge to structuralist notions of how knowledge is obtained and represented. His purpose seems to be to fragment the staid conceptions of reality. By counterpositioning fragments of one world view against another, or over another, then repeating this with other impressions, a multidimensional, multiperspectival world view emerges.

Other critical voices against the backdrop of scientific psychology provide challenges to the ability of psychology to respond to the diversity of human nature. Sampson (1993) suggests that alternative discursive frameworks for psychological analysis might provide a means to include underrepresented members of the ever-widening collective movements comprising African Americans, Hispanics, Native Americans, third world populations, women, lesbians and gays, and others. Adopting Sampson's methods would require changing much about how knowledge of people is gained and how psychology is practiced.

LEARNING AS CONNECTION

Learning is emancipation. What we call learning in schools may not be learning at all but a diet of information to be swallowed whole and digested for later use. True learning is a process of bridging a gap between disciplines, leaving the comfort zone of the known culture and integrating anomalies to one's world view.

Thi Minh-Ha Trinh (1991) writes about the dissonance of the struggle of learning across disciplines. She talks of the threats felt by the defenders of the traditional paradigm and the language that supports its continuation.

To cut across boundaries and borderlines is to live aloud the malaise of categories and labels; it is to resist simplistic attempts at classifying, to resist the comfort of belonging to a classification, and of producing classifiable works. Interdisciplinary is, for example, not just a question of putting several fields together, so that individuals can share their specialized knowledge and converse with one another within their expertise. It is to create in sharing a field that belongs to no one, not even to those who create it. What is at stake, therefore, in this inter-creation is the very notion of specialization and of expertise, of discipline and professionalism. (Trinh, 1991, pp. 107–108)

Trinh is a critical artist who uses film as the medium of her scholarship. In her book, she discussed the productive role of her art in the discourse of scholarship:

To disrupt the existing systems of dominant values and to challenge the very foundation of a social and cultural order is not merely to destroy a few prejudices or to reverse power relations within the terms of an economy of the same. Rather, it is to see through the revolving door of all rationalizations and to meet head on the truth of that struggle between fictions. Art is a form of production. Aware that oppression can be located both in the story told and in the telling of the story, an art critical of social reality neither relies on mere consensus nor does it ask permission from ideology. Thus, the issue facing liberation movements is not that of liquidating art in its not-quite-correct, ungovernable dimension, but that of confronting the limits of centralized conscious knowledge, hence of demystifying while politicizing the artistic experience. (Trinh, 1991, p. 6)

Octavio Paz (1991), Nobel Laureate in poetry, is another scholar whose voice questions the modernist tradition. In his collection of essays he discusses the place of poetry in our day and its role in the future of human societies. Paz examines the capitalist system founded on modernist tradition and concludes that "The examination of conscience and the remorse that accompanies it . . . have been and are the most powerful remedy against the ills of our civilization" (p. 150). It is critical self-examination, self-reflexive practice, the ongoing critical discourse of free learning, that are the most powerful tools of scholarship. We must use them to prevent the failure of our institutions to transmit viable culture.

Examples of nonpositivist scholarship are abundant in the "hard sciences" as well. James Lovelock is a scientist who writes novels about his work. *Gaia: A New Look at Life on Earth* (1982) is an example of imaginative scholarship that raised questions and aroused debate among peers and in the nonscientific community, leading to major shifts in thinking about the meaning of life in the universe. James Watson's *The Double Helix* (1980) is another sort of narrative of scientific evolution. His work serves to introduce the average intelligent reader to the complex world of nuclear genetics in a way that makes it simple to understand and provides us with a view of the lives of scientists as they live through their discoveries. Both Lovelock and Watson provide views of science through different lenses. With one it is the creative and imaginative exploration of questions of meaning and content. With another it is the exploration of the self of the scientist engaged in a process of discovery. Each account gives us something. Each account is scholarship that serves to enhance the field if only by providing the uninitiated a window into their world. The fact that scholarship in the sciences and the arts can share a discourse of expression and self-reflexive inquiry points to the viability of postmodern means of knowing and supports our reframing with invaluable precedents.

In the poststructural view, meaning and truth are conceptualized as arising from discourses that create social reality. This differs from the modernist paradigms that conceptualize meaning structures and use reductionism to determine truth. There are many ways to explore concepts when using a poststructural stance. Do we teach our students that there are fixed truths, immutable facts? Just what is truth? How is truth known? If truth is constructed using scientific method, is its meaning different than if it is constructed using poetry? Of course it is. All truths have meanings relative to their own purposes as explanatory fictions. As assuredly as narrative reconstruction is fiction, so is science. It is reasonable, therefore, that the search for the meaning of truth can take on many forms.

The salient themes of meaning in education for all children converge in their experiences of learning to be human, in their play as little children, in their discourses as teenagers and adults, in the selves created by their personal and cultural languages. To view the human condition only through the lens of science is to miss that which science will not see. To teach or learn only through the frame presented by the standardized curriculum is to become blind to a world of imaginative possibilities.

We are choosing to rethink the use of standard language and method when working with students at-promise because they have proven to be essentially ineffectual in our ongoing work with individuals, either as students or as clients who are systematically oppressed in academic settings for reasons psychological, economic, social, racial, or related to gender.

Making a persuasive and thorough argument for writing as a method of research, Laurel Richardson (1994) outlines a particular style of postmodern thinking called poststructuralism described by Weedon (1987). In poststructuralism, language is responsible for producing meaning. Language is not merely a reflection of social reality, it is the creator of reality. In Richardson's words:

> Language is how social organization and power are defined and contested and the place where our sense of selves, our subjectivity, is constructed. Understanding language as competing discourses, competing ways of giving meaning and of organizing the world, makes language a site of exploration, struggle. (Richardson, 1994, p. 518)

Thus if a child in a classroom, submitting to punitive controls, sees the means of behavioral control as "normal," then she is unlikely to perceive the punishment as abusive. Her experience of the events differs from the broader social discourse that rejects punishment in the context of schooling. The meaning of her experience, therefore, can be interpreted variously depending on the particular lens through which one looks. The child, because she is involved with constantly changing discourses between peers, authorities, at home and at school and elsewhere, is constantly evolving a language of self-creation that is never stable, always fluid, resisting static definition. Richardson continues:

> Poststructuralism thus points to the continual cocreation of Self and social science; they are known through each other. Knowing the Self and knowing "about" the subject are intertwined, partial, historical, local knowledges. Poststructuralism, then, permits—nay, invites—no, incites us to reflect upon our method and explore new ways of knowing.
>
> Specifically, poststructuralism suggests two important things to qualitative writers: First, it directs us to understand ourselves reflexively as persons writing from particular positions at specific times; and second, it frees us from trying to write a single text in which everything is said to everyone. Nurturing our own voices releases the censorious hold of "science writing" on our consciousness, as well as the arrogance it fosters in our psyche. Writing is validated as a method of knowing. (Richardson, 1994, p. 518)

It is from the postmodern tradition, using a poststructural discourse to create a new reality in order to generate new learning and facilitate the necessary changes, that we suggest a direction. We are heartened by the examples set by a few of our role models at the local, national, and international levels.

LOCAL LEADERS

In Knoxville, Tennessee, a pioneer in the movement toward student-centered learning was Dr. Mildred Doyle. Her foresight in providing students who were in danger of dropping out prior to graduation with a meaningful and supportive environment demonstrated an understanding and commitment to a practice of culturally significant education.

A leader in the movement toward student-centered education, Dr. Jerome Morton, has put Dr. Doyle's ideas into practice. He directed a school set up by Dr. Doyle in which he first empowered the faculty and staff, who in turn empowered the students to wake up their intrinsic sense of honor and nobility, allowing them to form a healthy self-concept, an internal locus of control, and ultimately a positive self-efficacy for achievement. It was the affirmation of their subjective meanings that helped change the children's views of themselves, resulting in changed attitudes and ultimately demonstrated successes (Kronick and Hargis, 1990). The social and environmental conditions of the students, outside of the school, remained the same.

In many instances the public school system appears to resist these student-honoring approaches, but the effects of leaders like Doyle and Morton can be seen in the development of revolutionary practices carried out in new alternative settings across the country. Unless educational systems can reorient practices to respect the needs for participation and tolerance for subjective meanings of the learning population, they will continue to fail to meet the needs of all students.

NATIONAL LEADERS

Michelle Fine (1987) is one of the talented educational researchers directing their energies to listening to the voices of disenfranchised students tell about their experience of school. Through many interviews she found that dropouts had internalized the values of the dominant culture, taking responsibility for their school failure despite educational structures that routinely exile disproportionately high numbers of low-income African-American and Latino youths (Carnoy and Levin, 1985). In a similar vein, Jonathan Kozol (1991) has written of financial imbalance imbedded in the institutional structure in his powerful book, *Savage Inequities: Children in American Schools.*

Fine and Kozol are among the critical theorists whose work cries out for the necessity of institutional change in policy and practice in order that equal educational outcomes be available for all students.

Other internationally known teachers like Paulo Freire and Myles Horton suggest a similar, emically founded theoretical base for the empowerment of learners. Freire related his views in a discussion with Horton (1990): "I began to discover that one of the main reasons why the students could learn with me and liked my class was that I respected them, no matter their age. I respected their mistakes, their errors, and their knowledge" (p. 61). If we look at the way Freire says what he says here, we can see his motives are genuine. He feels that his students learn *with* him, not from him or because of him. Freire positions himself with the student, not above or apart.

The use of authoritative instead of authoritarian methods is well documented as being more effective (Jago and Vroom, 1982; Lewin et al., 1939), but in practice this seems to be difficult for a people indoctrinated to a view of oppression/oppressor relationships. Efforts to provide programs that build on and honor the intrinsic value of at-promise populations as humans will be achieved only by replacing the competitive discourses that construct our social reality with a language of collaboration.

CONCLUSION

When students are no longer alienated, they become co-creators of the learning environment, taking responsibility for their own growth and contributing to the learning of those around them. It has been the thesis of this chapter that improving conditions for students at-promise is linked to the intrinsic orientation of motivation. The benefits of this approach to learning are well documented using quantitative methods by the cognitive theorists. We also look to critical social theory to support the argument for learner empowerment and emancipation. Shifting the locus of agency from external to internal, we believe, will give power back to the learner and promote new learning.

We must not make the mistake, however, of assuming that agency alone can form the basis of a movement to rise above intolerable social and environmental conditions. As Cornel West (1993) has amply argued, the notion of agency has become a tool used by conservative constructionists to throw competition back in the face of the majority of students who do not have a chance to compete. The conception of agency intended here is not one that focuses all intrinsic forces against the competition, for the setting of one against the other is the genre of competition.

We promote the model that makes a connection between empowerment, identity, and the fabric of meaning. In contrast we must work to move the discourses used in education and society from competition to one of collaboration and cooperation.

In our view, the children who are at-promise in the schools are actually our saviors. Their alienation is symptomatic of a disease rampant in the society. Possessing a creative bent representative of what is most important in humanity, they do not compromise and so become martyrs, sacrificed by a repressive regime of boredom, force-fed a diet of objective content devoid of the spice of subjective meaning. The creative children, those least able to adapt to repressive policies, are the indicators of the systems' dysfunction. Student-centered thinking asks what the school can do to honor these students' vision, not what these students can do to adapt to the school structure.

With growing evidence that brain physiology is affected by social and cultural practices, we began to understand the necessity in beginning a dialogue that generates new theory, one that promises to tap into the intrinsic motivation of learners from all walks of life. We wanted to find the common factors that would motivate all students. We began to see the need to study students from diverse cultures to find the common antecedents, not just the quantitatively derived psychological constructs of locus of control, self-efficacy, self-concept, and esteem, but other ways of knowing from themes derived from narratives of successful learning across cultures. What is needed is a practical model for a new pedagogy, a way of inciting a revolution of status, from student to learner and from teacher to facilitator.

The paradox of America's crisis in the schools is that out of it comes an opportunity for new learning and growth. This chapter mandates that we change the broader social discourse from competitive to collaborative, seek out and rebuild the foundations of agency intrinsic to all learners and move forward, embracing change and new learning.

References

Bandura, A. (1989). Human agency in social cognitive theory. *American Psychologist, 44*(9), 1175–1184.

Bennett-deMarrais, K. and LeCompte, M. D. (1995). *The way schools work: A sociological analysis of education.* White Plains, NY: Longman Publishers.

Cage, J. (1961). *Silence: Lectures and writings.* Middletown, CT: Wesleyan University Press.

———. (1969). *A year from Monday: New lectures and writings.* Middletown, CT: Wesleyan University Press.

Carbo, M. and Hodges, H. (1988). Learning styles strategies can help students at-risk. *Teaching Exceptional Children, 20*(4), 55–58.

Carnoy, M. and Levine, H.M. (1985). *Schooling and work in the democratic state.* Stanford, CA: Stanford University Press.

Catterall, J.S. (1986). *School dropouts: Policy prospects*. Charleston, WV: Appalachian Educational Laboratory.

Coopersmith, S. (1981). *The antecedents of self esteem*. Palo Alto, CA: Consulting Psychologists Press.

Deci, E. L. and Ryan, R. M. (1991). *Intrinsic motivation and self determination in human behavior*. New York: Plenum Press.

Degler, C. N. (1991). *In search of human nature*. New York: Oxford University Press.

Dryfoos, J. G. (1994). *Full service schools*. San Francisco, CA: Jossey-Bass.

Dweck, C. S. (1986). Motivational processes affecting learning. *American Psychologist, 41*, 1040–1048.

Eccles, J. (1983). Expectancies, values, and academic behaviors. In J. Spence (Ed.), *Achievement and achievement motives: Psychological and sociological approaches* (pp. 75–146). San Francisco: Freeman.

Festinger, L. (1957). *A theory of cognitive dissonance*. Evanston, IL: Peterson Row.

Fine, M. (1987). Silencing in the public schools. *Language Arts, 64*(2), 157–174.

———. (1991). *Framing dropouts: Notes on the politics of an urban public high school*. Albany: State University of New York Press.

Foster, J. T. and Grant, S. R. (1984). Education and meaning. *Clearing-House, 57*(7), 302–303.

Foucault, M. (1988). *Technologies of the self: A seminar with Michel Foucault*. Amherst: University of Massachusetts Press.

Freire, P. (1993). *Pedagogy of the oppressed*. New York: Continuum Publishing.

Giroux, H. A. (1981). *Ideology, culture and the process of schooling*. Philadelphia: Temple University Press.

———. (1990). The politics of postmodernism: Rethinking the boundaries of race and ethnicity. *Journal of Urban and Cultural Studies, 1*(1), 5–38.

Hahn, A. (1987). Reaching out to America's dropouts: What to do? *Phi Delta Kappan, 69*(4), 256–263.

Harter, S. (1988). The construction and conservation of the self: James and Cooley revisited. In D. K. Lapsley and F. C. Power (Eds.), *Self, ego, and identity: Integrative approaches* (pp. 43–70). New York: Springer-Verlag.

Higgs, G. E. and Franklin, M. L. (1994). Building bridges for at-risk students. *Tennessee Education, 24*(2), 10–12.

Higgs, G. E. and Plummer, K. (1995). Emotions in teaching: The relationship between students and teachers and the effect on learning. *Tennessee Education, 25*(1), pp. 23–24.

Horton, M. and Freire, P. (1990). *We make the road by walking: Conversations on education and social change*. Philadelphia: Temple University Press.

Jago, A. G. and Vroom, V. H. (1982). Sex differences in the incidence and evaluation of participative leader behavior. *Journal of Applied Social Psychology, 67*, 776–783.

Kozol, J. (1991). *Savage inequalities: Children in American schools*. New York: Crown.

Kronick, R. F. and Hargis, C. H. (1990). *Dropouts: Who drops out and why*. Springfield, IL: Charles C. Thomas.

Kuhn, T.S. (1970). *The structure of scientific revolutions*. Chicago: University of Chicago Press.

Lakatos, I. (1970). *Criticism and the growth of knowledge*. Cambridge: Cambridge University Press.

———. (1978). *Mathematics, science, and epistemology*. Cambridge: Cambridge University Press.

Lanier, N.W. (1986). *Educational excellence and potential dropouts: Theory, research, and policy implications*. Charleston, WV: Appalachian Educational Laboratory.

Latane, B. and Darley, J. M. (1970). *The unresponsive bystander*. New York: Appleton-Century-Crofts.

Laudan, L. (1977). *Progress and its problems: Toward a theory of scientific growth.* Berkeley: University of California Press.

———. (1981). *Science and hypothesis: Historical essays on scientific methodology.* Hingham, MA: Kluwer Boston.

Lewin, K., Lippitt, R., and White, R. K. (1939). Patterns of aggressive behavior in experimentally created social climates. *Journal of Social Psychology, 10,* 271–299.

Lincoln, Y. (1994). Taped lecture. New Orleans, LA: American Educational Research Association (AERA). Annual conference.

Lovelock, J.E. (1982). *Gaia: A new look at life on earth.* New York: Oxford University Press.

McCombs, B. L. and Whisler, J. S. (1989). The role of affective variables in autonomous learning. *Educational Psychologist, 24*(3), 277–306.

Maslow, A.H. (1968). *Toward a psychology of being.* Princeton, NJ: Van Nostrand.

Mills, R. C., Dunham, R. G., and Alpert, G. P. (1988). Working with high-risk youth in prevention and early intervention programs: Toward a comprehensive wellness model. *Adolescence, 23*(91), 643–660.

Neal, R. B. (1981, November). Preparing health educators to teach mental health. *The Journal of School Health, 4,* pp. 597–600.

Nunn, G. D. and Parish, T. S. (1992). The psychosocial characteristics of at-risk high school students. *Adolescence, 27*(106), 435–440.

Payne, B. D. and Payne, D. A. (1989). Sex, race, and grade differences in the locus of control orientations of at-risk elementary students. *Psychology in the Schools, 26*(1), 84–88.

Paz, O. (1991). *The other voice.* (translated from the Spanish by Helen Lane) New York: Harcourt Brace Jovanovich.

Pepper, S. (1942). *World hypothesis.* Berkeley: University of California Press.

Richardson, L. (1994). Writing: A method of inquiry. In Norman Denzin and Yvonna Lincoln (Eds.), *Handbook of qualitative research.* London: Sage Publications.

Sampson, E. E. (1993). Identity politics: Challenges to psychology's understanding. *American Psychologist, 48*(12), 1219–1230.

Swerdlow, J. L. (1995). Quiet miracles of the brain. *National Geographic, 187*(6), 2–41.

Trinh, T. M. (1991). *When the moon waxes red: Representation, gender and culture politics.* New York: Routledge.

United States General Accounting Office. (1993, August). Briefing report to Congressional Requesters. *School age demographics: Recent trends pose new educational challenges.* GAO/HRD-93-105BR. U.S. Government Printing Office, Washington, DC.

United States General Accounting Office. (1993, December). Report to the Chairman, Committee on Labor and Human Resources, U.S. Senate. *School linked human services: A comprehensive strategy for aiding students at-promise of school failure.* GAO/HRD-94-21.

Watson, J.D. *The double helix: A personal account of the discovery of the structure of DNA.* New York: Norton.

Weedon, C. (1987). *Feminist practice and poststructural theory.* New York: Basil Blackwell.

Weiner, B. (1976). An attributional approach for educational psychology. *Review of Research in Education, 4,* 179–209.

Weiner, B. (1990). History of motivational research in education. *Journal of Educational Psychology, 82*(4), 616–622.

West, C. (1993). *Race matters.* New York: Random House.

Wheelwright, P. E. (1966). *The presocratics.* New York: Odyssey Press.

White, R. W. (1959). Motivation reconsidered: The concept of competence. *Psychological Review, 66,* 297–333.

Wilson, E. O. (1975). *Sociobiology: The new synthesis*. Cambridge, MA: Harvard University Press.

Yourgrau, T. (Producer) and Storey, K. (Director). (1990). *The responsive brain* [Video]. Boston: PBS Adult Learning Service.

6 EFFECTS OF ALTERNATIVE EDUCATIONAL PROGRAMMING ON INTRINSIC MOTIVATION AMONG ETHNIC MINORITY ADOLESCENTS

Cynthia Hudley

INTRODUCTION

Successfully educating poor and minority children has become an increasingly urgent concern facing American education today. Currently, many low-income, minority children achieve at suboptimal levels, as measured by traditional indices (e.g., standardized test scores, GPAs, college entrance and completion) (Irvine, 1990). Further, these children consistently fare poorly in the completion of higher level reasoning and complex problem-solving tasks (Mullis et al., 1990). The social and economic isolation, student and teacher alienation, and dilapidated school facilities that are so pervasive in our inner cities (Waxman, 1992), leave little doubt as to why these students are also especially likely to drop out of high school prior to the attainment of a diploma (Irvine, 1990). Thus educators now search for programs that will provide children of color attending our public schools in our inner cities with the skills necessary to become intellectually competent citizens in an economically competitive workforce. As our country faces the reality of global economic competition coupled with escalating urban decay, these young people represent a constituency whose fate will help shape the future of this country.

In response to this challenge, educational researchers and practitioners alike have typically implemented school-focused interventions to support the achievement and persistence of low income, minority children (Bempechat and Wells, 1989). One type of intervention can be loosely construed as a restructuring of the school climate—those structural features, organizational policies, and management practices that determine the schoolwide interpersonal context (Edmonds, 1986). Restructuring classroom curricula and instructional practices, however, has historically been the preferred strategy when implementing academic interventions for youth at risk for school failure and dropout (Stringfield and Yoder, 1992).

Compensatory education, such as Chapter 1 programs, provides supplemental curricula and materials, diagnostic/prescriptive services, and additional classroom staff to better support the achievement and persistence of economically disadvantaged students. Features which successful compensatory programs share include computer technology, remedial tutoring, and cooperative learning techniques (Slavin, 1987). However, among elementary school participants, achievement gains, as measured by standardized test scores, typically disappear within two years of exiting the program (Stringfield and Yoder, 1992). How successful these programs have been in preventing high school students from dropping out is difficult to gauge.

A much more recent instructional intervention which has been advocated for African-American male children is the creation of single-sex, single race, self-contained educational programs, as exemplified by the original vision of the Milwaukee immersion academies (Ascher, 1991). These programs, though highly diverse in their individual approaches, all share a set of common characteristics: African-American male instructors, a rigorous Afrocentric curriculum, and high expectations (Ascher, 1991). The full effects of these programs are as yet unknown, although preliminary research suggests that student participants benefit from enhanced academic self-concepts (Hudley, 1995). Single-sex, single race public schools have been surrounded by controversy, and legal challenges have forced most if not all of them to either undergo substantial alterations or cease operations (Narine, 1992). However, self-contained programs for at-risk adolescents, once the preferred educational alternative (Swanson and Reinert, 1979), have re-emerged as a viable intervention in areas as diverse as Baltimore, Miami, and Southern California. Individual classrooms on comprehensive secondary school campuses typically provide services to all at-risk students, while often targeting their curriculum and instruction to the African-American male (Hudley, 1995; Narine, 1992).

Both models of intervention, the compensatory supplement to the traditional school program and the self-contained classroom, continue to be present at inner-city schools. Often, both models can be found on a single campus. However, the question of effectiveness for either model remains an open one. In addition, effectiveness is often narrowly defined as an increase in standardized test scores (Slavin, 1987; Stringfield and Yoder, 1992).

Reliance on standardized assessments ignores important affective issues such as attitudes toward school and achievement motivation, which these tests are unable to measure. Thus increasing standardized achievement test scores is a somewhat limited objective, which lacks any consideration of students' motivation to remain in an academic environment. Students must feel motivated to persist with schooling if they are to achieve full participation in the political process and the global economy as adults. The alternative, high levels of school dropout, represents billions of dollars in lost earnings, unrealized tax revenue, welfare programs, and criminal justice expenses for this country's economy (Baptiste, 1992).

<small>ACHIEVEMENT MOTIVATION AND COGNITIVE EVALUATION THEORY</small>

The study of achievement motivation distinguishes between intrinsic and extrinsic motivation. The former refers to a generalized human tendency toward active exploration of the environment, which is based on a need for competence (Deci and Ryan, 1992). The latter describes a tendency to respond to socially prescribed limits and demands to achieve goals or rewards that are separable from the task or activity per se (Ryan et al., 1992). Intrinsically motivated learning has been linked to higher levels of conceptual learning (Grolnick and Ryan, 1987), cognitive flexibility (McGraw and McCullers, 1979), and self-esteem (Ryan and Grolnick, 1987).

Cognitive evaluation theory (Deci and Ryan, 1987) has specified that an individual's intrinsic motivation for a particular activity will be strongly influenced by how the individual perceives the context in which that activity is experienced. In addition, the more competent a person perceives him- or herself to be at an activity, the greater will be the intrinsic motivation for that activity (Deci and Ryan, 1985). Thus intrinsic motivation to engage in a given activity will more likely be displayed in interpersonal contexts, which are perceived as supporting autonomy and competence. Conversely, contexts experienced as controlling will tend to diminish intrinsic motivation (Deci and Ryan, 1992). Thus the process by which intrinsic motivation is channelled toward academic activities and is sustained by academic environments may be central to the development of successful academic intervention programs for at-risk adolescents.

Identification of educational settings as either controlling or supportive of autonomy is especially compelling as adolescents make the transition from elementary to junior high classrooms. Prior research on stage-environment fit has identified systematic differences between elementary and secondary classrooms, which may account for some of the declines in achievement motivation typically found among early adolescents (Eccles, Midgley et al., 1993). For example, one of the more robust differences is a greater emphasis on teacher control of behavior in junior high (Eccles and Midgley, 1989). Low achieving youth, those most at risk for school dropout, are most likely to experience extremely controlling environments (Sinclair and Ghory, 1992). Such an emphasis would be likely to decrease intrinsic motivation for the activities presented there (Deci and Ryan, 1992), possibly exacerbating the likelihood of dropout. This emphasis on control also represents a particularly maladaptive influence for the adolescent's development of a sense of autonomy (Eccles and Midgely, 1989).

This motivational analysis of educational programming for at-risk adolescents should yield knowledge of both practical and theoretical significance. Schools, particularly those with a range of intervention programs available, might incorporate motivational variables into their assessment and evaluation procedures. This additional information should greatly enhance the accuracy of placement decisions. More precisely targeted placements, in turn, should enhance both the treatment effectiveness and cost effectiveness of intervention programs.

Further, the teacher-student relationship and the classroom context are environments in which achievement motivation can be either developed, sustained, or diminished (Deci and Ryan, 1987). Thus relationships between characteristics of learners and environments, and how these relationships impact motivational outcomes, can be effectively explored in the context of academic interventions for at-risk students. The systematic study of various learning environments has much to tell us about relevant variables for the development of achievement motivation and persistence in schooling, as well as necessary elements of a generalizable theory of human motivation.

SIGNIFICANCE OF THE RESEARCH

The study reported in this chapter explored the relationship between specific features of educational programs provided to at-risk adolescents and those students' levels of intrinsic motivation. As stated above, I identified classroom and teacher characteristics of three distinctly different educational interventions in one junior high school: a self-contained classroom emphasizing African-American history and culture; a group counseling elective class for students enrolled in the mainstream academic program; and a mainstream, remedial math class that enrolled low-achieving students. The self-contained classroom provided instruction in English, math, science, and history during a four hour block of time each day. Each of the other classes met for a single hour each day, with enrolled students receiving instruction in core academic subjects in a departmentalized configuration.

I also directly assessed perceived competence and levels of intrinsic motivation for academic tasks among students enrolled in these educational programs by means of student self-reports. Based on the formulation of cognitive evaluation theory, I hypothesized that environments that facilitated student autonomy and perceptions of competence and minimized the salience of teacher control would best sustain intrinsic motivation for academic activities among this group of at-risk learners. Students enrolled in classrooms with more choices of academic activities available, with teachers who provided positive, noncontrolling feedback, and with a minimum of competition and public evaluation were expected to display high levels of self-reported academic intrinsic motivation. Conversely, students enrolled in classrooms with strong emphasis on behavior control, competition, and evaluative feedback were expected to report relatively lower levels of intrinsic motivation. Finally, I expected a positive relationship between self-reported perceived competence and intrinsic motivation for specific academic domains (e.g., reading, math).

METHOD

Participants and Settings

Subjects ($N=65$) were eighth grade students enrolled in one of three classrooms and their teachers ($N=3$) in a junior high school of approximately 780 students and 35 faculty in Southern California. Each of the three classrooms provided services to students who were at risk for school failure and/or dropout. Students in attendance were residents primarily of the economically depressed neighborhood surrounding the school. Approximately 41 percent of the student body was eligible for the free lunch program. African Americans comprised the great majority (80 percent) of the student body and 20 percent were Latino.

Students in the three classrooms did not differ significantly by age (m's were 13.1, 12.8, and 13.2 for the self-contained, guidance, and remedial classrooms respectively). All students were fully proficient in English, of average intelligence, and none were receiving special education services at the time of the study.

SELF-CONTAINED SETTING

One participating classroom ($n=18$ students) provided all academic instruction (i.e., English, math, social studies, science) each day within a self-contained setting, and students were enrolled in mainstream classes for their physical education instruction and an elective. This classroom emphasized African-American history and culture, was taught by two African-American males (a teacher and a teacher's aide), and at its inception had enrolled only African-American male students. For the 1992/93 school year, when this study was conducted, the program had been expanded to include both females and Hispanic students.

School counselors enrolled students based on a survey of school adjustment indicators from the previous academic year: number of days absent, number of times tardy, number of days' suspension, number of disciplinary referrals to the dean's office, teachers' recommendations, and grade point averages. At the time of the study, 18 eighth grade students were enrolled: 15 males, three of whom were Hispanic, and three African-American females. In all instances, parental consent was required for inclusion in this program.

COUNSELING ELECTIVE

The second classroom (*n*=24 students) provided group counseling and support, study skills instruction, and career awareness instruction taught by the students' guidance counselor. The guidance counselor, an Anglo male credentialed as both a math teacher and a school counselor, taught four classes per day, each of which enrolled a maximum of 25 students. These 100 students, who represented the counselor's full caseload, received counseling services as part of a pilot program funded by the California State Department of Education. Students were recommended to the pilot program by the regular counselors during the school year prior to their enrollment. Placement was based on students' academic grades and disciplinary history during the prior year.

Students enrolled in this class as their elective, rather than shop or art classes. During this elective class students learned about various career options, heard guest speakers, developed their skills in textbook reading, note taking, test taking, outlining, critical thinking, and written expression, and participated in group counseling sessions on such high-risk behaviors as substance abuse and gang activity. Students attending the period selected for inclusion were enrolled in the eighth grade. At the time of the study 23 students were enrolled in this classroom: 12 boys, including two Hispanics, and 11 girls, including two Hispanics.

REMEDIAL MATH CLASS

The third classroom (*n*=24 students) was a math class typical of the school's mainstream academic offerings. This school engaged in a modified tracking procedure in which students were clustered into relatively homogeneous ability groups. Faculty in the core academic departments (English, math, science, and social science) recommended that students in their classes be enrolled for the following year in either "regular" academic classes or remedial academic classes, based on their class grades and standardized test scores. Thus students might receive remedial instruction in any or all of their core academic subjects, based on their previous year's performance. The classroom selected for inclusion was a remedial, eighth grade math class taught by an African-American male. In an effort to hold gender of teacher constant, this class was randomly selected from among the remedial academic offerings taught by men. Students received instruction in basic operations with whole numbers, fractions, and decimal numbers. At the time of this study 24 students were enrolled: 14 males, including four Hispanics, and ten females, including three Hispanics.

Materials and Procedures

MEASURE OF INTRINSIC MOTIVATION

During the spring of 1993 each student completed the Children's Academic Intrinsic Motivation Inventory (CAIMI) (Gottfried, 1986). This is a self-report inventory designed for use with children in fourth through eighth grade that assesses intrinsic motivation for school learning. The instrument consists of 122 items grouped into five scales, four of which measure intrinsic motivation in the subject areas of reading, math, science, and social studies, and a fifth which measures a general orientation toward school learning (Gottfried, 1986).

Specific items measure enjoyment of learning, a preference for challenging tasks, and curiosity and persistence relative to academic tasks. Scores are measured with a five-point Likert scale ranging from "strongly agree" to "strongly disagree"; high scores represent high levels of intrinsic motivation. Sample items include "I enjoy learning new things in reading" and "When I get bored, I look for new things to learn in science." Items are similar for each of the four subject areas. Internal consistency of the CAIMI is substantial, with alphas ranging from .83 to .93 in two standardization samples (Gottfried, 1986). An acceptable level of test-retest reliability was established with coefficients ranging from .66 to .76 over a two-month interval (Gottfried, 1986).

MEASURE OF PERCEIVED COMPETENCE

All students also completed the Self-Perception Profile for Learning Disabled Students (Renick and Harter, 1988). This instrument, an adaptation of the Self-Perception Profile for Children (Harter, 1985), contains ten subscales which tap differentiated perceptions of competence: general intellectual ability, global self-worth, reading, spelling, writing, math, social acceptance, athletic ability, physical appearance, and behavioral conduct. This version of the Self-Perception Profile was selected because it provides multiple measures of perceived academic competence by assessing perceptions for specific academic domains.

The instrument has proven to be quite appropriate for use with normally achieving children. The sample on which this scale was standardized included normally achieving children, and the instrument has proven psychometrically sound. Using Chronbach's Alpha, subscale reliability estimates for normally achieving children ranged from .80 to .90 (Renick and Harter,

1988). Using factor analysis, the scores of normally achieving children also revealed factor patterns that were consistent with the designated subscales.

The protocol also contains a separate measure of the students' judgments of the importance of each of the nine domain-specific subscales. Building on a Jamesian model of self-esteem, a student's sense of self-worth may be inferred from the discrepancy between perceived competence and judgment of importance of a particular domain (Renick and Harter, 1988). Feelings of self-worth generally should be high if the child perceives herself/himself to be competent in those areas which she/he judges to be important. Correspondingly, self-worth should be low if competence is perceived to be low in those areas judged to be important. Self-esteem is believed to be unaffected by competence ratings in those areas judged to be relatively unimportant. This measure, entitled "How important are these things to how you feel about yourself as a person?" includes two items for each of the nine domains tapped in the "Self-Perception Profile," resulting in an 18-item scale.

TEACHER INTERVIEWS

During the spring semester each of the three classroom instructors participated in a semi-structured interview consisting of 18 open-ended questions. Interviews were conducted in two sessions and ranges from three to three-and-a-half hours in duration per teacher. The interviews were designed to assess the teachers' support of children's autonomy, emphasis on behavioral control, use of positive feedback, beliefs about classroom cooperation and competition, uses and types of classroom rewards, and typical evaluation practices. Previous research has demonstrated that these specific attitudes and practices are significantly related to intrinsic motivation (Deci and Ryan, 1992). Interviews were conducted in classrooms during teachers' planning periods and before and after the normal school day.

RESULTS

Intrinsic Motivation

Raw scores on the CAIMI were first converted to standard scores with a mean of 50 and a standard deviation of 10. These T-scores allow for comparison across the five scales. Standardized scores were then analyzed in a repeated measures multivariate analysis of variance (MANOVA) with classroom type and gender as grouping factors and subscale type as the repeated factor. A significant multivariate effect was detected for classroom type (F [10,90]=4.63, $p<.001$). Subsequent univariate analyses demonstrated that the three classrooms differed significantly on four of the five subscales: reading

($F[2,49]=3.88$, $p<.03$), math ($F[2,49]=4.54$, $p=.01$), social studies ($F[2,49]=13.85$, $p<.001$), and science ($F[2,49]=12.46$, $p<.001$). Post hoc comparisons indicated that students in the guidance and self-contained classrooms typically scored significantly higher than those in the remedial math class (see Table 6.1). A significant main effect was also found for subscale type ($F[10,90]=8.50$, $p<.001$). Post hoc analyses revealed that, overall, students reported their reading and social studies motivation to be higher than their math, science, and general motivation. No significant interactions were detected, nor were main effects of gender significant.

TABLE 6.1   Student Ratings of Intrinsic Motivation

	Self-Contained Classroom (n = 18)		Remedial Classroom (n = 24)		Guidance Classroom (n = 24)	
	mean	sd	mean	sd	mean	sd
Reading Motivation	48.71[a]	7.2	42.24[b]	8.3	50.90[a]	12.4
Math Motivation	43.00[a]	6.7	37.77[b]	6.9	45.17[a]	9.2
Science Motivation	45.08[a]	6.5	35.91[b]	7.2	49.15[a]	6.7
Social Studies Motivation	45.38[b]	6.2	41.41[b]	8.3	52.40[a]	8.1
General Motivation	39.75	9.4	41.20	8.9	45.79	11.6

Notes. Differences in superscripts for row means indicate significance at probability .05 or greater. Each of the subject area subscales contains 26 items. The general subscale contains 18 items.

Perceived Competence and Importance Ratings

Ratings for the "Self-Perception Profile" were also analyzed in repeated measures multivariate analyses of variance (MANOVA). Ratings of perceived competence and judgments of importance were analyzed separately, using classroom, gender, and subscale as grouping factors, with repeated measures on the third factor. Although the three-way interaction failed to reach statistical significance for perceived competence, a significant multivariate classroom by gender interaction was detected ($F[20,48]=2.01$, $p<.03$). Subsequent univariate analyses demonstrated that perceptions of general ability, math competence, and behavioral competence accounted for the multivariate interaction (see Table 6.1 for means).

Ratings of perceived general intellectual ability were highest for girls in the guidance classroom and lowest in the self-contained classroom, while ratings for boys were highest in the self-contained and lowest in the remedial classroom. Ratings of behavioral competence and math competence dis-

played the same patterns of means; however boys' ratings of math competence did not differ significantly as a function of classroom type. Overall,
girls' ratings of perceived competence were highest in the guidance classroom,
while boys' ratings were highest in the self-contained classroom.

TABLE 6.2 Selected Ratings of Perceived Competence

	Self-Contained Classroom (n = 18)		Remedial Classroom (n = 24)		Guidance Classroom (n = 24)	
	mean	sd	mean	sd	mean	sd
General Intellectual						
Female	2.75[b]	.9	3.08[a,b]	.3	3.31[a]	.7
Male	2.91[a]	.7	2.36[b]	.7	2.76[a,b]	.7
Behavior Conflict						
Female	2.35[b]	.9	2.84[a]	.4	3.07[a]	.8
Male	2.91[a]	.3	2.31[b]	.8	2.70[a]	.5
Math Competence						
Female	1.92[c]	9.4	2.40[b]	1.0	3.06[a]	1.0
Male	2.86	.8	2.67	.7	2.75	1.0

Notes. Differences in superscripts for row means indicate significance at probability
.05 or greater. Responses are measured on a scale of 1 to 4. Higher numbers equal
greater perceived competence.

Analysis of the nine importance ratings revealed a multivariate classroom X subscale interaction ($F[16,368]=1.74$, $p<.05$). Subsequent univariate
analyses demonstrated that students in the three classrooms differed significantly in their ratings of the importance of general intellectual ability and
behavioral conduct. The guidance classroom students rated the importance
of intellectual ability significantly higher than did students in either of the
other classroom types (see Table 6.3). The importance of behavioral conduct was rated significantly higher by students in both guidance and self-
contained classrooms in comparison to students in the remedial classroom.

TABLE 6.3 Importance Ratings for Selected Domains

	Self-Contained Classroom (n = 18)		Remedial Classroom (n = 24)		Guidance Classroom (n = 24)	
	mean	sd	mean	sd	mean	sd
General Intellectual	2.95[b]	1.0	3.07[b]	.7	3.42[a]	.7
Behavior Conduct	3.10[a]	.8	2.57[b]	.9	3.26[a]	.7

Notes. Differences in superscripts for row means indicate significance at probability
.05 or greater. Responses are measured on a scale of 1 to 4. Higher numbers equal
greater perceived importance.

Relationships between Intrinsic Motivation and Perceived Competence

I next analyzed the relationships between perceived competence and intrinsic motivation separately for each classroom using a Pearson's product-moment correlation. Cognitive evaluation theory would predict a strong relationship between intrinsic motivation scores and perceived competence scores for each of the academic domains. For students in the guidance classroom, reading competence related significantly to reading motivation (r=.65, p=.01), as did math competence and motivation (r=.75, p=.01) and general intellectual ability and general motivation (r=.45, p=.05). For students in the self-contained classroom, only math competence and motivation were marginally related (r=.35, p=.08). For students in the remedial class, who received math instruction, math competence related to general motivation (r=.80, p<.01) and marginally to math motivation (r=.37, p=.08).

Teacher Interviews

The interview data were analyzed using Strauss's (1987) grounded theory approach. The analysis employed a "concept-indicator model, which directs the conceptual coding of a set of empirical indicators" (p. 25). Using this model, I derived conceptual categories directly from the transcribed interview data. I first analyzed attributes around which specific responses clustered (e.g., conditions for sharing student assessment information, consequences for students of initiating conversation with peers). Each cluster thus becomes a category, or a set of indicators of a conceptual class of events, behaviors, etc. I next examined internal relationships among responses within each category (i.e., subcategories) as well as relationships across the conceptual categories. Once the data were coded and categorized, a random sample of six different questions per protocol was coded by an independent rater. Inter-rater agreement, calculated as the proportion of similarly categorized question responses to all responses classified, was 84 percent.

Recall that the interview questions focused on teachers' thoughts regarding student autonomy, behavioral control, use of feedback, cooperation and competition, classroom rewards, and evaluation practices. Responses clustered into two dominant themes which emerged repeatedly throughout the data: the importance and nature of controlling students' behavior and the relative merits of cooperative and competitive classroom assignments and rewards. These themes revealed consistent differences among the responses of the three teachers.

SELF-CONTAINED CLASSROOM

The teacher in this classroom, Mr. L, is an African-American male in his late twenties with seven years teaching experience. The school year in which the study was conducted was the third year of the program's existence and also the first year during which enrollment was opened to "at-risk" students of any gender or ethnicity. However, Mr. L continued to emphasize African-American history and direct instruction in appropriate social behavior in his curriculum as initially mandated for the single-sex, single-race classroom.

During the interview, Mr. L referred frequently to his responsibility as the classroom leader in an innovative academic intervention program. He regularly attended specialized in-service training institutes addressing the unique needs and learning styles of African-American male students. This training is available to all instructors in the county in this alternative educational program and funded by the county office of education. He expressed a "deep sense of responsibility to serve as a role model for young brothers" but feels that techniques he has learned will be equally appropriate for "Latino kids; and even girls should benefit, though having girls in here has really changed the way I talk to the young men."

He perceived his students as those who presented behavioral challenges to other teachers, "kids who try to jump through the windows, or throw others out." However, in his self-contained classroom, he stated that things were "calm; it's like it's really a class." These students were responding, he believed, to the adjustments in the curriculum and environment dictated by the goals of this particular program. He perceived his Afrocentric curriculum to be of greater interest than the regular offerings, and by "keeping them busy and involved with things they want to know anyway, I minimize behavior problems." He also stated that students had a voice in choosing the topics of study from a set of alternatives offered by the teacher. "I let the kids participate in the decisions, for their studies and for the rules of the classroom. I am always the final authority, though. One of the things these kids with behavior problems really need is to know what the limits are and who is in control. They really appreciate the structure, and they thrive on it."

Mr. L endorsed cooperative learning groups at some times and for some activities. "Students also need to take individual responsibility for their work, and get the rewards or disappointment from their own effort." His preferred types of group activities included team competitions in which students compete to display their knowledge (e.g., times "relay races" to solve multi-step math reasoning problems) and peer collaboration activities in which students are paired to complete an assignment together. He provided "a lot, maybe 50 percent" of the curriculum offerings as individualized instruction. Students worked on their own separate assignments at their own pace, particularly in reading and math instruction. He also strongly endorsed posting graded papers on the bulletin board as "both an incentive and a model for others. The trick is to make assignments so that everybody gets their paper on the board fairly regularly." Classroom rewards consisted of letter grades and "free time; a person can earn time to pursue a preferred activity by completing a certain amount of assigned classwork." Preferred activities available included reading sports magazines, listening to books on tape, doing word puzzles, and playing a math board game.

GUIDANCE CLASSROOM

This program was led by a school guidance counselor who met with each of the students on his caseload on a daily basis in a classroom format. The classroom also served as the counselor's office. The counselor, Mr. S, is a European-American male in his middle thirties who was previously a math teacher for three years at the same school. This was his first counseling assignment; he completed his advanced degree during the initial year of the program. He has been the counselor of record for this program since its inception, the year prior to the start of the study. This program, funded by the state Department of Education, was awarded to this particular school site through a competitive proposal process and was the only one of its type in the state at the time of the study. Mr. S collaborated with the principal in the writing of the school's application and was chiefly responsible for the selection of the curriculum materials and instructional activities that comprised the content of the daily lessons.

Mr. S strongly advocated firm disciplinary control in the classroom, with a minimum of clear, behaviorally stated rules. This orientation is, he believes, mandatory in a program such as his, with "25 at-risk students in the same room; there's going to be behavior problems. So that's been my focus this year, on their behavior and citizenship. I make sure they know that they are accountable for their actions." He saw an emphasis on discipline and self-control as necessary not only for the smooth functioning of his classroom but also as a central instructional focus of the intervention program. "It all starts with citizenship. The kids have to realize that citizenship has a direct effect on their grade in all their classes. If they can focus their energies on getting to class and co-operating with the teachers, then their grades are going to start improving as well."

He described his curriculum as devoting a good deal of time to group discussions and role-playing how to behave appropriately in both his and the students' other academic classrooms. "With being a good citizen comes doing homework, listening in class . . . and hopefully the goal is to get the grade up." For example, when quarterly progress reports were issued, he had all students write their citizenship grades on the board, and then discuss their knowledge and understanding of the class subject matter. By publicly highlighting this relationship, Mr. S was "trying to get them to be more aware of the connection between citizenship marks and grades."

Mr. S divided his teaching time equally between whole class instruction and co-operative learning activities. Typically, he provided career awareness, health education (e.g., substance abuse, traffic safety), and consumer awareness in cooperative group activities. Students selected topics of interest within such broad categories and developed group projects to be presented to the class. Mr. S supplemented these presentations with lectures and guest speakers. "Students are either uninformed or misinformed on issues that affect their daily lives and their futures. I try to correct that by giving them information and giving them some choices in what they really want to study. I want to give them hands-on activity to make it real for them. Then they have a higher interest. But they have to listen to all the presentations and speakers, so they get a balance that way."

Whole class instruction (lectures, discussions) typically focused on appropriate classroom behavior and learning and study skills. As mentioned earlier, Mr. S believed that his program's goals were primarily to enhance students' academic grades by helping them to become better classroom citizens and secondarily to prepare them to become productive adults. Students are both evaluated and rewarded with letter grades in Mr. S's class on their participation and productivity both in his class and their other classes. Students brought in daily "check-up" sheets from their other classes, and each student had a weekly conference with Mr. S regarding his/her progress. Names were posted on the board of those making good progress as both a "reward and a model for others. In this school, failing classes is definitely acceptable among your peers. I want them to encourage each other to succeed."

REMEDIAL MATH CLASS

This classroom teacher, Mr. H, is an African-American male in his late fifties with 20 years of teaching experience. Teaching is his second career; Mr. H spent ten years as a building contractor before obtaining a bachelor's degree and teaching certification. He began teaching in an opportunity program, a self-contained classroom for behavior problem children, in the district where this research was conducted. That program was phased out, and he began teaching math in the mainstream program.

Mr. H emphasized the importance of establishing classroom order and control. "The class is not conducive to teaching or learning if students don't follow the rules. I say 'It's not for me; it's to prevent chaos in the room, make it quiet and more conducive to learning for you.'" His methods for establishing order were highly individualized. "I try to talk to kids and win them over on a personal level, let them know they can trust me. Instead of punishing them I'll say 'Is there anything wrong? Can I help?' I think positive reinforcement, only positive, is so important." However, he lamented the removal of corporal punishment as a discipline option for its effect as a deterrent. "I'm of the old school. I don't believe in hitting people, but the fact that you had them in an undefined situation was very forceful. Now you can't touch a kid, not that you want to. But they know it, and they tell you that. And it's been quite a disservice to the schools."

Mr. H's preferred instructional strategies consist of lecture, individualized instruction, and peer tutoring. Typically he presented a math concept at the board, had students practice that concept during guided and independent practice, then assigned more practice for homework. Those students having more difficulty were paired with a more successful student to work on additional assignments. "First I stand at the board for explanation, then I tell them what they are supposed to do and give them the assignment pages. I circulate around the classroom to check to see what's going on. If you didn't get it, I try to use the stronger students to help the slower ones. And I give them immediate feedback where they can grade their own papers." Mr. H said he assigned homework on a daily basis, and had students check each other's papers as the opening activity for each class period.

Mr. H, though a strong advocate of peer tutoring in class, did not place students in larger groups for any kind of cooperative activity. He felt students were off task "there with just each other; they chat and play around mostly. I also don't know who's honest, who'll cheat, and so forth." The opportunities were present for "cheating" in a group but not a dyad, according to Mr. H, because students would want to just rush through the assignment, copy from each other, and use their time to socialize. In an assigned peer tutoring situation the stronger student knew his or her responsibility to "help the peer, not just copy down the correct answers."

Discussion

The school programs described here provide diverse educational environments for learners perceived to be at-risk for school failure. The diversity among programs results both from the structural characteristics dictated by the school's organization and the respective teachers' educational philosophies. Among the three programs, two dealt directly with academic instruction while one emphasized personal and social skills. In one of the academic programs students remained with the same teacher for four hours per day and received all of their academic instruction in that classroom. These structural features may partially account for the reported differences in students' intrinsic motivation. The data give clear indication that the guidance program, which emphasized social-emotional skills, provides motivational benefits for girls; conversely the remedial classroom is an especially amotivating environment for boys.

The differences in teacher styles and strategies may also account for the reported differences in levels of intrinsic motivation. However, these relationships are not entirely consistent with cognitive evaluation theory. Overall, the guidance classroom students had the highest reported intrinsic motivation, yet their teacher was the strongest advocate of strict discipline, public evaluation, and continuous teacher pressure on students to perform in specific ways. On the other hand, the remedial class teacher relied on a more interpersonal approach to maintain classroom order, yet these students were the least intrinsically motivated.

However, as predicted by cognitive evaluation theory, the remedial classroom teacher also reported the least amount of student choice in classroom activities while the guidance teacher provided the greatest amount of choice. Finally, the self-contained classroom teacher reported intermediate levels of choice and teacher control but the highest levels of competitive classroom activities.

Overall these data provide mixed support for the relationships between autonomy, control, competence, and intrinsic motivation as postulated by cognitive evaluation theory. Intrinsic motivation among these students seems to be facilitated by the provision of autonomy and choice in classroom activities, but it is not seriously undermined by strict discipline and teacher control of behavior. In fact the classroom with the lowest level of teacher control of behavior also had the lowest levels of intrinsic motivation.

The expected relationship between perceptions of competence and intrinsic motivation was strongest in the guidance classroom as well. Only guidance students displayed a consistent relationship between perceived domain-specific competence and intrinsic motivation. As might be expected, a clear relationship existed between perceived math competence and math motivation as well as general motivation for students in the remedial class, which provided mathematics instruction. Perceived competence in the self-contained classroom may have been reduced by the competitive nature of group activities, yet students' interest in the curriculum may have provided some support for intrinsic motivation.

The picture which emerges suggests that intrinsic motivation among this group of at-risk students is enhanced by maximal amounts of autonomy in the selection of classroom tasks from a range of activities which they find personally relevant. As children move into adolescence, they are simultaneously experiencing expanding capacities to reason and think critically and more complex understandings of individual identity and peer relationships (Eccles and Midgley, 1989). Thus personal autonomy in the selection of topics of study and co-operative learning activities may be a developmentally appropriate instructional technique for these early adolescent students. This stage-environment fit may facilitate intrinsic motivation. Yet these children also seem to be most motivated when teacher expectations concerning behavior are highly salient.

Effective schools research convincingly demonstrates that clearly presented and consistently enforced behavioral expectations are a hallmark of those schools that are most successful in educating children who are at-risk for school failure (Edmonds, 1986). Cast in the framework of cognitive evaluation theory, the programs evaluated here, and effective schools in general, may facilitate student motivation by providing an abundance of informational feedback. Feedback can be characterized as informational if it supports competence and autonomy, as controlling if it pressures recipients to think and behave by rote and without reflection, and as amotivating if it signifies incompetence (Deci and Ryan, 1992). Thus even high levels of teacher control of behavior may not undermine intrinsic motivation if the expectations are presented as guidelines for behavioral competence rather than as punitive, disciplinary directives to be followed without question.

Research specific to African-American children also suggests that motivation is fostered when children perceive behavioral expectations to be clearly defined and discipline to be fairly enforced (Irvine, 1990). Conversely, ability tracking may constitute amotivating feedback if one is in a low track or remedial class. Low track or remedial placement may logically serve as a strong message of incompetence. Thus intrinsic motivation would be expected to be depressed among lower track students. Black children may be particularly vulnerable to the incompetence feedback inherent in tracking, as they are much more likely to be placed in lower tracks.

This research has identified a range of indicators that differentiate the three types of programs as either more or less motivation enhancing. However, the limitations of the present study require that the results be interpreted with caution and that these results be expanded upon by future research incorporating more rigorous methodological controls. For example, the present design has confounded the effects of class type (self-contained vs. departmental) and curriculum type (Afrocentric vs. mainstream, vs. social-motivational). Future research should concentrate on the effects of these factors in a fully crossed design, ideally with random assignment of students. Further, with such a small number of girls in the self-contained program, the interpretation of any gender effects is extremely problematic. For example, the extent to which girls benefit from an Afrocentric, self-contained program remains unclear. Systematic longitudinal research is perhaps the only means of assessing the full impact of these programs on the school persistence and ultimate life chances of the participants.

REFERENCES

Ascher, C. (1991). *School programs for African American male students* (Trends and issues No. 15, Institute for Urban and Minority Education). New York: ERIC Clearinghouse on Urban Education.

Baptiste, H. P. (1992). Conceptual and theoretical issues. In H. Waxman, J. Walker de Felix, J. Anderson, and H. P. Baptiste (Eds.), *Students at risk in at-risk schools* (pp. 11–16). Newbury Park, CA: Corwin Press.

Bempechat, J. and Wells, A. (1989). *Promoting the achievement of at-risk students* (Trends and issues No. 13, Institute for Urban and Minority Education). New York: ERIC Clearinghouse on Urban Education.

Deci, E. and Ryan, R. (1985). *Intrinsic motivation and self-determination in human behavior.* New York: Plenum Press.

———. (1987). The support of autonomy and the control of behavior. *Journal of Personality and Social Psychology, 53,* 1024–1037.

———. (1992). The initiation and regulation of intrinsically motivated learning and achievement. In A. Boggiano and T. Pittman (Eds.), *Achievement and motivation: A social-developmental perspective* (pp. 9–36). Cambridge, UK: Cambridge University Press.

Eccles, J. and Midgley, C. (1989). Stage/environment fit: Developmentally appropriate classrooms for early adolescents. In R. Ames and C. Ames (Eds.), *Research on motivation in education* (Vol. 3, pp. 139–186). San Diego, CA: Academic Press.

Eccles, J., Midgley, C., Wigfield, A., Buchanan, C., Rueman, D., Flanagan, C., and MacIver, D. (1993). Development during adolescence: The impact of stage-environment fit on young adolescents' experiences in school and in families. *American Psychologist, 48,* 90–101.

Edmonds, R. (1986). Characteristics of effective schools. In U. Neisser (Ed.), *The school achievement of minority children* (pp. 93–104). Hillsdale, NJ: Erlbaum Associates.

Gottfried, A. (1986). *Manual for children's academic intrinsic motivation inventory.* Odessa, FL: Psychological Assessment Resources.

Grolnick, W. and Ryan, R. (1987). Autonomy in children's learning: An experimental and individual differences investigation. *Journal of Personality and Social Psychology, 52,* 890–898.

Harter, S. (1985). *Manual for the self perception profile for children.* Denver, CO: University of Denver.

Hudley, C. (1995). Assessing the impact of separate schooling for African-American male adolescents. *Journal of Early Adolescence, 15,* 38–57.

Irvine, J. J. (1990). *Black students and school failure: Policies, practices, and prescriptions.* New York: Praeger Publishers.

McGraw, K. and McCullers, J. (1979). Evidence of a detrimental effect of extrinsic incentives on breaking a mental set. *Journal of Experimental Social Psychology, 15,* 285–294.

Mullis, I., Owen, E., and Phillips, G. (1990). *Accelerating academic achievement: A summary of findings from 20 years of NAEP*. Princeton, NJ: National Assessment of Educational Progress.

Narine, M. (1992). *Single-sex, single race public schools: A solution to the problems plaguing the Black community?* Springfield, VA: ERIC Document Reproduction Service. (ERIC Document Reproduction Service No. ED 348 423)

Renick, M. J. and Harter, S. (1988). *Manual for the self-perception profile for learning disabled students*. Denver, CO: University of Denver.

Ryan, R., Connell, J., and Grolnick, W. (1992). When achievement is *not* intrinsically motivated: A theory of internalization and self-regulation in school. In A. Boggiano and T. Pittman (Eds.), *Achievement and motivation: A social-developmental perspective* (pp. 167–188). Cambridge, UK: Cambridge University Press.

Ryan R. and Grolnick, W. (1987). Origins and pawns in the classroom: Self-report and projective assessments of individual differences in children's perceptions. *Journal of Personality and Social Psychology, 50*, 550–558.

Sinclair, R. and Ghory, W. (1992). Marginality, community, and the responsibility of educators for students who do not succeed in school. In H. Waxman, J. Walker de Felix, J. Anderson, and H. P. Baptiste (Eds.), *Students at risk in at-risk schools* (pp. 33–42). Newbury Park, CA: Corwin Press.

Slavin, R. (1987). Making Chapter 1 make a difference. *Phi Delta Kappan, 69*, 110–119.

Strauss, A. (1987). *Qualitative analysis for social scientists*. New York: Cambridge University Press.

Stringfield, S. and Yoder, N. (1992). Toward a model of elementary grades Chapter 1 effectiveness. In H. Waxman, J. Walker de Felix, J. Anderson, and H. P. Baptiste (Eds.), *Students at risk in at-risk schools* (pp. 203–221). Newbury Park, CA: Corwin Press.

Swanson, H. L. and Reinert, H. (1979). *Teaching strategies for children in conflict*. St Louis, MO: C.V. Mosby.

Waxman, H. (1992). Reversing the cycle of educational failure for students in at-risk school environments. In H. Waxman, J. Walker de Felix, J. Anderson, and H. P. Baptiste (Eds.), *Students at risk in at-risk schools* (pp. 1–9). Newbury Park, CA: Corwin Press.

7 THE NEGLECTED FACTOR

TELEVISION AND AT-RISK YOUTH

W. Thomas Beckner

The notion that dropping out of school constituted a contemporary social problem perhaps emerged with the intense educational scrutiny precipitated by the launch of Sputnik. Prior to that, the termination of one's education short of high school graduation was a relatively common practice free of social stigmatism (Greene, 1966). A 1947 Department of Labor study of youth out of school and in the labor market found that, among 14–17-year-olds, progress beyond the eighth grade was the exception rather than the rule (Johnson and Legg, 1948). While there had been an emerging recognition that dropping out was limiting in terms of one's upward social mobility, it was the technological revolution—fueled by fears of America's potential educational inadequacies, ignited by the space race, and characterized by an increasing inability to absorb the dropout into the work force—that initiated a new view which identified dropouts as serious social risks.

In the four decades that have followed the Sputnik launch, a large volume of literature addressing the "problem" of dropout proneness has accumulated. It presents a curious paradox, for although the historical trend is towards great improvement, with larger percentages of students currently completing their high school education than ever before, there continues to be increasing concern that our rapidly evolving society cannot be content with even these improved statistics and must work ever harder to reduce the number of students failing to survive in our educational system. There is a strong sense that the dynamic of change acting upon all sectors of an increasingly global society can only intensify the pressure on educators to further decrease numbers of dropouts.

The literature on dropouts initially tended to focus on the personal deficiencies of individual students, but more recently it has centered around either of two precipitating factors in dropout activity: institutional delivery systems and systemic concerns within the educational structure itself, or environmental conditions in the lives of at-risk student populations. Characteristic of discussions about the educational system's culpability is that, most often, the phenomenon of dropping out is treated as the problem rather than as a symptom of preexisting circumstances. For instance, it has often been noted that two of the most important predictors of dropping out are poor classroom grades and being held back (Bachman et al., p. 172), which has led some researchers to suggest that if teachers refrained from giving poor grades or holding back students, dropout rates would decrease. Ignoring the fact that such an argument is tautological, this and most other literature suggesting that dropout solutions are to be found in modifications within the educational structure assume that there are no contributing factors outside schoolroom walls. Dropping out may be a response to the experience of academic failure; it may also be a product of other frustrations which are brought into the classroom rather than acquired there. The one thing clear is that poor performance is indicative of some unsuccessful relationship between the individual student and the school environment, if not in the area of ability, at least in the area of motivation.

A search for the source of this mismatch among critical environmental factors is movement in the right direction, but here, too, the literature often fails to probe deeply enough. Merely identifying family demographics, socioeconomic status (SES), and similar concerns as contributing contexts for school-related activities is not enough. To state, for instance, that single-parent homes or low SES are associated with dropping out only describes the problem without sufficiently explaining the nature of that association. What is missing from the literature assessing environments that impact dropout proneness is an adequate exploration of how these associative factors function as causative agents that affect either learning processes or the student's psychological framework essential for successfully negotiating those processes. What is also missing is any consideration of a singularly pervasive environmental element that dominates the out-of-school experiences of nearly every child in America: television. This chapter argues that heavy television viewing is an environmental factor that has a measurable negative impact on the learning process and creates psychological predispositions that mitigate against successful school performance. As such, it constitutes a mental health hazard which should be recognized as a significant at-risk factor in the lives of school-age youth. Furthermore, unless educators acknowledge this danger, efforts directed at other at-risk factors will produce only negligible results.

Specifically, I will advance four propositions to support the notion that heavy TV viewing is a disruptive influence to any successful student-classroom relationship: 1) the biases of visual information processing are cognitively contrary to those of the linear processing model, which is essential for educational accomplishment; 2) excessive viewing is causally associated with lowered reading abilities, which in turn impact school achievement; 3) aggressiveness, caused by heavy TV viewing, creates problem behaviors that increase dropout potential; and 4) long-term exposure to television cultivates distorted concepts of social reality that interfere with educational settings.

At this juncture, it is important to distinguish between a *technology* and a *medium*. The former is an apparatus employed to deliver a specific product; in the case of the television industry, it consists of the physical equipment that converts and processes electronic images from one point to another. The latter, on the other hand, is what Neil Postman calls a "social environment," the contextual framework in which those images are delivered (Postman, 1985, p. 84). American television is essentially commercial television, a delivery system completely intertwined with the advertising industry, whose sole purpose is to deliver large numbers of potential buyers to those advertisers. Both its forms and its program content are determined by that social environment. It is this delivery system which dominates the attention of our youth and which this chapter contends is harmful to them. Frequently, advocates of TV confuse the apparatus of television with the environment within which it operates, arguing the prosocial potentials of the technology while defending the specific offerings of the medium.

This is not to say that there is such a thing as a neutral technology, which some have tried to argue. Every technology has an inherent bias, something contained within its essence that predisposes the ways in which it can function. Thus not only is the medium of television biased via its interconnectedness with commercial delivery, but the technology itself is biased in the ways it can deliver information because of the specific ways in which visual data are communicated to and processed by the human brain. In the first place, television has its own distinct "language"—visual rather than verbal—and secondly, the formal features of that language are the result of editing techniques and special production effects superimposed on the program content and capable of being applied to any material independent of content. All of these visual and auditory characteristics are special conventions of television or motion pictures, which are learned by the viewer and around which that viewer develops an interpretive schemata that can then be reapplied to other similar material. Because television's language is predominantly visual, audio tracks are supplemental to the visual material and seldom are capable of delivering cohesive meaning by themselves. Conversely, however, the visual content does have the capacity to communicate a great deal of information in the absence of accompanying audio. (As an instructor of scriptwriting courses, I always insist my students storyboard their treatment first, and that this visual arrangement of planned camera shots—free of any audio cues—adequately communicates a traceable narrative line.)

With its visual bias, television is best at delivering images, instantaneously absorbed unified impressions that have content and meaning, but which are not comprehended verbally and thus are not actually "thought" about. They are ingested and stored, deep within the viewer's psyche, without being subject to conscious management, accepted as "real" without reflection and "truth" without verification. Television's power lies in this image-creation; its weakness is the fact that this non-verbal "grammar" subordinates abstract thinking (Postman, 1985).

Many researchers have discussed the dual coding system of the brain, and some have suggested that heavy TV viewing maximizes reliance on right-side processing (spatial, imagistic), creating habituation at the expense of left-brain thinking (verbal-linguistic). However, it isn't necessary to accept the habituation premise to recognize that heavy doses of visually-processed material can impinge upon the academic life of students; it is only essential to acknowledge that the two modes contradict one another, and that substantive immersion in the one cannot help but somewhat diminish facility for the other. Thus the findings of the Children's Media Project, which reported that when children are called upon to produce their own narratives, those who are heavy TV viewers create stories that are choppier, entail fewer words per sentence, and tend to deal with more superficial elements than do those who watch less TV. They also tend to leave out elements that would require inferential processing, not only when recreating television narratives, but also when producing real-life narratives (Watkins et al., 1981). The researchers for the project concluded that visual learning preconceptions may be transferred to other kinds of information. In an analogous finding by Meringoff (1980), comparisons of the recall of seven- and nine-year-olds of stories conveyed either by illustrated book or by television showed that television was associated with greater recall of action and greater reliance on visual imagery. The implication is that experience with television may retard the ability to process text or to read.

Similarly, the 1983 report, *A Nation at Risk: The Imperative for Educational Reform,* after documenting declining scores on standardized achievement tests, SATs, college board exams, science and math scores, and declaring American student populations inferior by international standards, commented:

> Many 17-year-olds do not possess the "higher order" intellectual skills we should expect of them. Nearly 40 percent cannot draw inferences from written material; only one-fifth can write a persuasive essay; and only one-third can solve a mathematics problem requiring several steps. (National Commission on Excellence in Education, 1983, p. 9)

Still, the authors concluded that declines in educational performances were the result, in large part, of "disturbing inadequacies in the way the educational process itself is often conducted" (p. 18). The bulk of the report then focused on diluted and diffused curricula, inadequate expectations on the part of educators, too little time spent engaged in the classroom or with school work, and deficiencies in the teacher delivery system. It is astonishing that the only environmental factor even touched on, be it ever so lightly, had to do with time considerations, and even the mention of this was couched in terms that implicated the school rather than the home. What is less surprising is the absence of any reference to the impact of television on school performance, a vacuity which I have already noted is characteristic of at-risk literature.

Yet shifting between visual and linear modes does seem to present problems for young people. Cognitive theorists emphasize that individuals bring to each environment preestablished schemata or scripts based on previous experience and fantasized anticipations concerning what they expect to encounter in the environment. One cognitivist concerned about the possible transference of visual interpretive strategies to other materials is Gavriel Salomon (1983), who has developed the concept of AIME—"the amount of invested mental effort in nonautomatic elaboration of material"—to explain the cognitive processing of varying types of material.

> AIME can be expected to increase when a unit of material cannot be easily fitted into existing schemata. When it can, one would expect AIME to decrease, as the individual feels, rightly or wrongly, that there is little in the encountered material that warrants the investment of his or her mental efforts. (Salomon, 1983, 185)

In the first of two experiments Salomon divided 124 sixth-graders into two groups, one of which saw a film while the other read the equivalent version in print. He found that television was perceived by the first group to be a much "easier" medium, "demanding far less effort for comprehension than printed material of the same content" (p. 189). Those who saw the film manifested lower comprehension and reported expending less AIME. Salomon reasoned that "the way children perceive a medium (and their own efficacy in handling it) is quite strongly related to their investment of mental effort in processing its material, which in turn is related to how much they actually learn from it. If indeed the children's perceptions would have reflected only the real demands of each medium, the television group, rather than the print group, should have demonstrated better learning" (p. 190). The experiment was repeated with 96 college freshmen and yielded identical results. Obviously, young people treat television as an easy source of information, investing little effort in it and extracting little knowledge from it.

If cognitive theories are correct, schemata stored in the brain are in part dependent on one's developmental stage. Thus, as Salomon notes, the larger problem is that children miss the opportunity to develop higher order skills while viewing TV—skills that are needed when processing more difficult information at elevated levels of learning. Devoid of these higher abilities, children may approach more complex sources similarly to the way they approach television material. Commercial television programming is effectively processed at a low level of involvement, devoid of conscious management or reflection, and simultaneously elicits low expectations while receiving low investments of mental effort on the part of the viewer. The notion that heavy involvement with such a medium will have a deleterious effect on academic encounters is more than merely plausible.

Reading ability, of course, is the agent through which this visual processing bias attacks school performance. Learning the visual and structural conventions of TV, where cuts, zooms, flashbacks, and commercial interruptions are the norm, conflicts with reading strategies that depend on a form which is linear, developmental, and highly verbal. Moreover, comprehending commercial TV fare, where the average shot length is 3–4 seconds (2–3 seconds for commercials) requires pattern recognition as opposed to analytical decoding. While the television viewer instantaneously ingests a composite image requiring little or no interpretive activity, a reader is faced with a series of abstract signs which must first be translated into some mental conceptualization of events, objects, or ideas which these signs represent. As Kubey and Csikszentmihalyi (1990) noted,

> Perception involves more than a simple sensory decoding. Interpreting a message can require a great deal of cognitive processing—match-

ing stimuli to memory contents, recognition, classification, evaluation, and judgment—and on that score reading requires more effort, activity, and involvement than watching television. (p. 99)

Simply put, words and pictures inhabit different universes of discourse. One is discursive, the other non-discursive; one is propositional, the other presentational; one is rationalistic, the other emotive (Postman, 1982, p. 73). A word is always a symbol representing an idea, while a picture is a concretization of some tangible presence. Thus the grammar of verbal language dwells in the realm of ideas, which always engender reflection, questioning, and argumentation in ways that pictures, living in undeniable visual reality, cannot. This distinction is at the heart of reading, and reading is (or has been) at the heart of American education. The fear that excessive television viewing disrupts this relationship has often been expressed by concerned critics of the medium.

Studies relating television viewing to reading achievement and/or scholastic performance have most often centered around the issue of *displacement*. Time spent viewing TV must be time that displaces another activity. Needless to say, young people watch a great deal of television. Recent Nielsen surveys report that children between the ages of two and 11 watch slightly more than 28 hours per week, while teenagers watch about 24 hours weekly. Timmer et al. (1985), who studied time-use diaries completed by young people between the ages of three to 17, reported that television occupies more time than any other out-of-school activity, accounting for more than half of all their leisure time. But is reading impacted by this time allocation? There are, of course, some activities that can share time with television—eating, socializing with friends or family, etc. Reading and doing homework, too, are examples of shared-time activities, and some research has attempted to measure the efficacy of those tasks while attending to television. We can ignore this area of concern, since the results of these studies verify the obvious—competing tasks are always distractive to one another and therefore decrease efficiency. The critical question for our purposes is whether or not displaced activities are related to academic functions; specifically, the question is whether or not a relationship exists between time allocation for television viewing and reading or school performance.

One major study was specifically designed to measure the causal effect of television on reading and a number of other behaviors (Williams, 1986). The study involved three Canadian towns, similar except for the availability of television. *Notel* had no prior exposure to television, *Unitel* had been receiving one channel for several years, and *Multitel* had the availability of multiple television sources. The communities were studied on two occasions, just before *Notel* obtained TV for the first time and again two years later. This provided a unique opportunity to isolate the effects of television viewing, specifically with regards to causality features. The initial analysis showed that children's reading scores correlated inversely with the amount of available TV: reading scores were highest in *Notel* and lowest in *Multitel*. Two years after the introduction of television to *Notel*, reading scores in that community had deteriorated for children in grades two and three, though not in grade eight. Thus in the critical years when mastery of the alphabet takes place and the foundation for reading fluency is laid, television viewing plays a crucial negative role. Once basic skills are gained, the impact is less harmful. The researchers argue that television viewing displaces time that could have been spent learning to read: "television provides a more attractive alternative for most children, but especially for those who have most difficulty learning to read and who need the practice most" (p. 397).

Medrich et al. (1982), in a study of how children use their time out of school, found that, in comparison with heavy viewers, almost twice as many of the children who were light TV viewers read at least five days a week. Similarly, Heyns's (1976) study of out-of-school summer activities found that the two activities with the largest inverse relationship in terms of time allocation were reading and watching television. Her conclusion was that reading and TV viewing, both relatively "quiescent and solitary activities," involved greater trade-offs of time (p. 301). At least two other experimental studies with children (Gadberry, 1980; Wolfe et al., 1984) have verified that time devoted to reading increased when time with television was reduced.

In another examination of the relationship between displacement and reading achievement, Neuman (1988) asked three other pertinent questions: Are certain kinds of reading more affected than others? Is the effect on students greater at certain age levels? Would children spend more time on leisure reading if it were not for television? Using data from eight statewide assessments and the 1984 National Assessment of Educational Progress, her findings are quite revealing. First of all, while Neuman found no evidence to suggest that TV viewing was displacing other media activities such as leisure reading, she did find a significant, though small, negative correlation between television viewing and homework. Thus while her data contradict the notion that TV may affect usage of time devoted to engagement with other media, it does indicate that television viewing impacts activities such as homework that share a similar space but don't provide similar satisfaction. Given the choice between watching television and doing homework, school-age children will select the easier of the two activities. The data also indicated that differences in achievement were larger for high school than for lower level students, but that in all cases excessive viewing was consistently related to lower reading proficiency. Though the differences between scores of those students reporting little and those reporting moderate viewing reflected little variation in reading achievement means, the extreme cases demonstrated substantial differences.

> Watching more than 4 hours of television per day appears to be strongly related to lower achievement scores in all statewide assessments. Regardless of the specific skill being measured, [these graphs] indicate a dramatic downward trend in achievement for students viewing excessive amounts of television at all grade levels. (Neuman, 1988, p. 423)

It is instructive to recall that Nielsen figures show this four-hour plateau to be the *average* amount of consumption for two- to 11-year-olds, with nearly that much being ingested by teens. Obviously, significant numbers of youth are watching even more than these amounts.

Not all investigations agree that viewing correlates with overall educational achievement. A meta-analysis encompassing about two dozen samples varying widely with respect to sizes, ages, and measures used produced a small average negative effect size for the relationship between viewing and scholastic achievement (Williams et al., 1982). Ball et al. (1986) review 13 studies, nine of which fail to find evidence of that relationship and four which show negative effects. Morgan and Gross (1982), a more extensive review, report on studies producing both positive and negative relationships before concluding that "there is no one effect on television achievement, nor is there even one relationship" (p. 83). The key to understanding the complexity of the reading-viewing debate lies in Morgan and Gross's (1982) use of the word *one*. Indeed, the problem with many investigations is that they examine only simple bivariate relations between two variables, seldom controlling for background variables. What makes the Neuman (1988) study so compelling is its careful consideration of possible third variables.

Comstock and Paik's (1991) exhaustive review of every aspect of television's interaction with American children concludes that the evidence documents an independent and causal contribution to lowered achievement by television viewing (pp. 120–25). They cite four major sources in addition to Neuman (1988) that measure the television-scholastic achievement relationship: the 1980 California Assessment Program (CAP), with follow-ups in 1982 and 1986; the 1980 High School and Beyond (HSB) data; the 1983–1984 NAEP data collected by the Educational Testing Service; and a study conducted by Gaddy of a sample drawn from the HSB data from whom data were again obtained two years later (pp. 86–94). The total data from these sources report on more than 800,000 students in more than 30 states and were controlled for three different grade levels, for SES, and for ethnicity as potential third variables. There was strong agreement among all the studies on a number of points: a negative association, not just in reading, but also between other categories of achievement and amount of TV viewing; a stronger inverse relationship between the two variables at the high school level than at lower levels; and a suggestion of curvilinearity, or at least a threshold where moderate use of television may be associated with a rise in achievement before falling off rapidly with heavy viewing.

More crucial to the theme of this chapter was Comstock and Paik's investigation of socioeconomic status as a third variable. SES subsumes a host of traditionally identified at-risk factors such as education level of parent(s), single parent homes, ethnicity, etc., which in turn often contribute to the centrality of the role television assumes within the individual home. As might be expected, family SES is inversely associated with achievement, and this relationship is much stronger than that of the negative one between achievement and amount of television viewed (p. 90). But more important is the fact that this inverse relationship increases as family SES rises; indeed, the strongest relationship occurs with pupils from the highest categories of status. Evidence such as this is supportive of a trend identified by Comstock and Paik (1991):

> A second major trend has been the increasing equalization of consumption across strata. In the case of households in general, the trend has been observable in the progressively lessening degree to which amount of viewing is inversely related to socioeconomic status and, in particular, the educational level of the head of the household. In the case of children and teenagers, inverse relationships between television consumption and mental ability appear to have become less pronounced. Although these long-documented inverse relationships have not disappeared, the historical trend has been toward their lessening, as the experiencing of popular culture through television has become increasingly frequent and accepted among all strata. (p. 63)

What is essential to recognize here is that this documentation identifies a group of students heretofore exempted from traditional at-risk categorizations—students from high SES. These are students who are normally regarded as capable of success without special interventions. By implication, then, television viewing should be considered a more pervasive risk factor than some others since it works across certain other environmental at-risk boundaries (note that heavy viewing affected *all* students, regardless of SES considerations). Moreover, a relationship between television viewing and achievement is capable of being addressed by educators, pedagogically, much more effectively than can the larger political and societal concerns connected with at-risk factors surrounding SES.

To this point, we have been concerned with the indirect effects of television viewing; these result simply from using the medium, irrespective of its content. Historically, however, it has been content issues that have inspired most of the criticism directed at TV. Indeed, concern arose soon after its intrusion into the American home, and by the early 1960s debate among social scientists had already centered around the potential of entertainment television to stimulate antisocial behavior among youthful viewers.

These concerns were mirrored in a series of federally sponsored inquiries during the decade of the 1960s Congressional hearings under the leadership of Senator Thomas Dodd between 1961 and 1964; a 1964 report of the Senate Subcommittee on Juvenile Delinquency; and a published study by The National Commission on the Causes and Prevention of Violence (1968)—each of which strongly implicated commercial television as contributing to violent or aggressive behavior among viewers. Initially, network executives responded that current research was inconclusive and promised to conduct their own independent studies. When called to task over their repeated failure to deliver on these promises, media spokespersons eventually suggested that such research was impossible due to a lack of adequate research designs. By the end of the decade a groundswell of public concern over increasing societal violence culminated in a governmental mandate to the Surgeon General to initiate an investigation of the effects of TV violence on children and youth.

From their beginnings, those proceedings were shrouded in controversy. The television industry had been secretly allowed to exclude certain potential committee members and place its own representatives in five of the 12 committee positions. Later, at the insistence of its chair, Dr. Eli A. Rubenstein, the committee prepared a unanimous report interpreting the individual studies, but the report was so ambiguous and so full of deliberately neutralized evaluations that the publicly reported results seem to exonerate television as a factor in children's aggression. The incredible scenario of collusion and subterfuge on the part of the television networks was worthy of one of the soap operas the industry so effectively produces (see Lazar, 1994; Liebert and Sprafkin, 1988; Rothenberg, 1975; Wartella, 1988).

A review of the events surrounding the early public debates about television's effects on behavior serves to remind us that the forces which drive a commercial broadcast system determine that the programming transmitted by that system has one primary purpose, to gather and deliver as large an audience as possible for the purposes of selling that audience to an advertiser. Any other considerations are subordinate to this. As one researcher comments on this fundamental principle:

> There is nothing inherently right or wrong with this, but it is a fact that is important to keep in mind. Among other things, it helps to explain much of what people in the television industry do, by underlining what gods they serve and what outcomes they value. (Condry, 1989, p. 3)

The gods served by commercial television are financial, and the outcomes the networks value revolve around the most efficient and economical ways to gather their audience without regard to the well-being of the viewer. Thus an axiom emerges: society can never depend on the television industry to responsibly regulate itself. Whatever modifications take place to mitigate the adverse effects of media will have to be imposed from outside the industry.

In 1974, however, Congress settled for a self-regulatory effort—the Family Viewing Hour—which was subsequently declared illegal by a federal judge in 1976. Gradually the impetus of the collective movement to force programming changes subsided, and even a 1982 follow-up study (Pearl et al., 1982), which reaffirmed the conclusions of the earlier report in clearer and more forceful language, did little to inspire any combined effort against violent television content. Meanwhile the average number of viewing hours per child has steadily risen, program content has become increasingly more violent, and research continues to consistently demonstrate the relationship between heavy viewing and aggressive behavior. Thorough reviews of the research literature can be found in Pearl et al. (1982), Huesmann and Malmuth (1986), Liebert and Sprafkin (1988), and Comstock and Paik (1991). While a small but persistent minority of researchers resist the weight of the cumulative evidence, citing methodological faults in previous studies, questioning the size of effect, or arguing that correlational studies don't prove causal relationships (e.g. Freedman, 1984; Milavsky et al., 1982, 1988), nearly all researchers now accept the fact that excessive viewing of violent television programming can cause aggressive behavior. The question is no longer does such a relationship exist, but rather, how and under what conditions does it operate?

The first public disclosure of the Surgeon General's Report on the impact of televised violence (1972) appeared in the January 11, 1972, *New York Times* and initiated the most conspicuous misunderstanding of the report's contents, a misunderstanding that has continued to the present day. Reading only an 11–page summary, which was itself a summary of many separate technical reports, reporter Jack Gould declared that "violence in television programming does not have an adverse effect on the majority of the nation's youth but may influence small groups of youngsters predisposed by many factors to aggressive behavior" (as quoted by Liebert and Sprafkin, p. 111). Many of the researchers associated with the project felt their work had been seriously misrepresented and rebutted the story, as well as the summary itself. But Gould's use of the term *predisposition* gave birth to the myth that only those young people who had a predisposed proclivity towards aggressiveness might be affected by violent television programming. In fact, the technical reports to the Surgeon General pointed out the lack of uniform effect of viewing on children and discussed the nature of these differing influences on the basis of several factors. In the summary report all of these factors associated with increased aggressiveness were lumped together as *predispositions* (Surgeon General's Scientific Advisory Committee, 1972, p. 11). However, the predispositions included such factors as age, gender, and social and economic background of the child viewer. Thus, to be "predisposed" to aggressive behavior does not mean that one has some sort of aberrant trait; rather it is to belong to what many educators have traditionally identified as at-risk categories. Indeed, the available evidence from field studies suggests that a positive relation between exposure to media violence and aggression occurs among children at all levels of aggression (Huesmann et al., 1984). Furthermore, the literature repeatedly demonstrates that children most susceptible to violent programming are the same as those who are similarly prone to dropping out.

One argument sometimes directed at the research linking TV violence viewing with increased aggressive behavior in children is that the studies measure relatively minor aggressive acts (e.g. Cook et al., 1983). Ironically, these are precisely the type of actions that present discipline problems in the educational setting—hyperactivity, boisterousness, incivility, maliciousness—and that are often precursors to dropping out of school. While such behaviors are of less concern to some aggression researchers, since they present what the investigators feel are minimal societal risks, they are of great importance to educators seeking to understand at-risk factors. Huesmann and Eron's (1986) cross-national comparison of aggressive behavior used peer evaluations which asked students to rate their classmates by such criteria as: Who often says, "Give me that!"?; Who starts a fight over nothing?; Who pushes or shoves children?; or Who says mean things? (p. 32). Positive correlations were found between overall television violence and peer-nominated aggression. Comstock and Paik (1991) offer analyses of several surveys that found positive associations between both seriously delinquent and less serious behaviors (pp. 242–54). Once again, interpersonal aggressions such as hitting, name-calling, and fighting are identified and, according to the authors, are the factors most convincingly associated with exposure to violent TV viewing.

However, antisocial and aggressive behaviors do not invariably occur; they depend upon characteristics of both the viewers and the situation. Laboratory experiments strongly suggest that the viewing of violence has the ability to cause aggression in normal populations, but the impact will probably be greater on some groups or individuals than on others. Crucial to the development of aggression are home environment and parental reinforcement. In a set of now classical experiments in the early 1960s, researcher Albert Bandura (1963) established that children will imitate what they have watched on screen. But imitative aggression requires not only an occasion for learning, but also a sufficient incentive to carry out the learned behavior. The home environment, as structured and maintained by parents or guardians, "may provide incentives to the child to act out aggressive responses previously learned through observation, or it may threaten disapproval and thereby suppress such acting out" (Geen and Thomas, 1986, p. 11).

Many studies lend support to the cruciality of reinforcing factors that interact with the excessive viewing of violent programming. One longitudinal study, designed specifically to determine both the boundary conditions under which the violence-aggression relation occurs and to determine the relevant intervening variables, presents an interesting paradigm that is descriptive of many at-risk homes (Huesmann et al., 1984). The authors found a number of variables that were correlates of aggression and violence viewing. They found that, in addition to heavy viewing, the child most likely to be aggressive would be one who (a) has a more aggressive mother, (b) has parents with lower education and social status, (c) is performing poorly in school, and (d) is unpopular with his or her peers. They infer a model where violence viewing and aggression are enhanced by these related variables (p. 773). Others have reported that poor and minority children, with their limited access to diverse educational opportunities, rely heavily on television, not only for entertainment, but as a prime source for social learning (e.g. Greenberg, 1986; Huston et al., 1989), and that television commands more of the time, attention, and confidence of low income families (Comstock and Cobbey, 1982).

It seems evident that aggressiveness is to a great extent learned. In most cases it is also what is referred to as an overdetermined behavior, one that emerges at the point of intersection with a number of interrelated factors. "For most children, aggressiveness seems to be determined mostly by the extent to which their environment reinforces aggression, provides aggressive models, frustrates and victimizes the child, and instigates aggression" (Huesmann and Eron, 1986, p. 4). Obviously, these environments are most conducive to learning violent behaviors with which to respond to the social situations a child encounters. Where appropriate parental guidance, effective social control, and an adequate variety of alternative responsive strategies are available, viewing of television violence will be less dominant in the child's repertoire of behavioral choices. In the absence of these controlling factors, television's steady barrage of aggressive scenarios provides models to be tested in social situations. Often, a reciprocal process evolves where children, deprived of adequate modeling, turn to television for cues to solve interpersonal difficulties. Finding aggressive models there, they implement them in their own lives and, if they find reinforcement, the behavior is repeated and eventually habituated, creating school discipline problems and academic frustrations.

What much of the research implies, and what some investigators have stated directly, is that adult involvement is an essential component in the viewing activities of children. With the help of older, more sophisticated viewers to help discern problem areas of program content and interact with child viewers, the waters of commercial television can be successfully navigated. This argument, of course, is offered as a defensive strategy, and acknowledges the potential disasters in the river of program content. It also suggests the depth of the problem: in order for children to avoid the dangers of TV content, they will need a mediator to mediate the already mediated reality television proffers.

The argument about the relationship between television viewing and aggression is essentially an argument about the direct consequences of program content. Research has tended to focus on individual messages or program types and their ability to produce changes in viewer attitudes or behaviors, either immediately or at some point in the future. Cultivation theorists such as George Gerbner, however, are more concerned with the

generalized and far more pervasive consequences of heavy media exposure—
the cumulative effect of viewing on individual beliefs, perceptions and
wordviews. Cultivation theory "assumes dynamic, reciprocal relationships
between television messages and people's beliefs about them" (Morgan,
1989, p. 431).

In the past people have always learned about the real world from
observing it and living in it. Prior to the establishment of television in nearly
every American home there was seldom any question whether the world one
encountered was "real." Now, however, every person finds a large reposi-
tory of dramatic and fictional information about the world to which he is
exposed. Commercial television, rooted in entertainment values, has no
mandate to present a "real" world. Indeed, it offers for viewing pleasure a
highly dramatized world that is deliberately crafted to attract, intrigue, and
maintain the attention of the audience rather than to render any accurate
portrayal of reality. But for heavy viewers the distinction between fictional
and real may become blurred.

> In its simplest form, cultivation analysis has been utilized to deter-
> mine whether people who spend more time watching television are
> more likely to perceive the *real* world in ways that reflect the most
> common messages and "lessons" of the television world than people
> who watch less television but are otherwise comparable in terms of,
> for example, important demographic characteristics. (Morgan, 1989,
> p. 430)

According to Gerbner, "mainstreaming" occurs when heavy viewers
assimilate TV "facts" and premises as components of their own beliefs and
value systems. He further argues that heavy viewers, regardless of demographic groupings, develop a relatively homogeneous outlook with viewers
of other groups (Gerbner et al., 1980). The issue of homogeneity evokes considerable debate, as some recent investigators maintain that selective viewing by particular content-type may be more crucial to the cultivation process (Hawkins and Pingree, 1981; Comstock and Paik, 1991). No
researchers, however, appear to question the fact that the process itself takes
place.

Television programming, designed for entertainment purposes, is filled
with images, experiences, and situational constructs that are not within the
realm of immediate experience for most of its viewers. Crucial to viewing is
the possession of a complex cognitive view which has the ability to distinguish what is "real," or appropriate, and what is not. Adult viewers, with a

much more vast repertoire of life experiences and a more mature cognitive apparatus, are better equipped than young persons to sort out the inconsistencies and unrealities the media present. But the young, for the most part devoid of this crucial power and highly susceptible to suggestions of reality, attempt to form perceptions about the very experiences and situations television presents—things about which adults have already determined behavioral responses. Too often, when confronting the confusing complexity of the real world, the young rely on televised versions of reality.

It is precisely those areas about which viewers have the least knowledge that one would expect to be most susceptible to cultural cultivation. Though cultivation research has demonstrated associations between TV viewing and a variety of cultural perceptions—sex-and-age-role stereotypes, conceptions of occupations, minorities, to name a few—the focus has been overwhelmingly on issues of violence and interpersonal mistrust. In fact this cultivated worldview, where violence-laden television generates an exaggerated sense of danger and mistrust in the perception of the viewer, has been labeled the "mean world syndrome" (Gerbner and Gross, 1980). This emphasis on violence is, as we have seen, an important one, but similar cultivation paradigms can develop with regards to sexual attitudes, interaction with controlled substances, and other lifestyle choices where youth are searching for experiential examples or themes on topics about which they know relatively little (e.g. Roberts, 1982).

Consider television's portrayal of alcohol usage. Content analysis shows that alcohol is an extremely common cultivational context in television programming. Alcohol is mentioned in 80 percent of prime time programs, with the places where it is consumed frequently centerpieces of dramatic action. One study revealed that 40 percent of 233 scenes with alcohol involved "heavy drinking" and 18 percent more concerned "chronic" drinkers. Characters very rarely decline a drink or express disapproval of drinking, and any disapproval of their behavior expressed by others is usually mild or ineffective (Breed and DeFoe, 1981). Another content analysis focusing on violence on television points out that aggression is most often portrayed as a successful solution to conflict, that it seldom produces negative consequences for the aggressor, and is often depicted as humorous (Williams et al., 1982).

What do the children or adolescent viewers, exposed to enormous amounts of television filled with characters and contexts that model such behavior, learn from their viewing? To use Gerbner's terminology, what attitudes or values are cultivated in the mind of the young viewer as he or she formulates notions of social reality—notions that will become foundational for all his or her future behaviors? To name a few: verbal aggressiveness, particularly in the form of the perfect put-down, is a desirable trait rewarded by the admiration of peers; physical attractiveness and sexuality are crucial to one's acceptance by others; power in the form of position and wealth is to be coveted above all else; authority figures are seldom to be trusted; there are few lessons to be learned from the past; delaying gratification is an archaic notion. These are not always the overt messages of a television script, which sometimes offers a closing moralistic twist, but these are the messages of television's images and narrative frames which are most important to long-term acculturation. In the television world bad guys lose, but the good guys use force to overcome them; characters talk about the importance of virtue rather than beauty, but only attractive people populate the landscape; and a staggering number of commercials subtly communicate that inner satisfactions can only be obtained through commodities. A significant number of children and teens will come to accept the television "facts" about the world around them, absorbing them as part of their beliefs and value systems.

The preponderance of values and beliefs offered by commercial television interferes with the educational process in two distinct ways. First of all, the cultivated worldview is in direct opposition to that which the educational process attempts to nurture. The notion that human worth is based on internal and eternal values rather than on outward postures, that a sense of community is attained and maintained through cooperative efforts and not coercive force, that learning from the past is a necessary prerequisite for addressing the future—these are a few of the concepts that lie at the heart of the democratic ideals our educational system encourages. Secondly, television's worldview encourages behavior which is disruptive to successful engagement in the classroom. Learning is a slow and deliberate process requiring reflection and analysis, and its rewards are not always immediately perceived; it also requires that the student submit to and trust in the authority of both teacher and system. The student who accepts television's "facts" is at risk. Television has often been referred to as a window to the world (e.g. Liebert and Sprafkin, 1988), but if it distorts that world, if it offers false information about that world, or if it models defective strategies for functioning in the world, then it is a window opening upon a dark and fog-shrouded landscape.

Given the potential impact of heavy television viewing on the educational prospects of our youth, it is curious that most of the debate over possible negative consequences of television viewing has been initiated by social scientists and communication theorists rather than educators. For the most part academicians have attempted to forge some sort of marriage with a technology they perceive as potentially useful. There are even those who continue to deny that television is best suited to transmitting emotions or that it is a poor communicator of ideas, citing, for instance, introductory college lectures, video courses, and other educational programming as successful communicators of ideas. But these courses, and nearly every other example of prosocial television programming, presuppose a non-commercial format with longer individual shots, an abundance of narration to carry the thread of ideas, and content deliberately prepared to meet instructional rather than economic goals. Furthermore, even in these specially designed educational programs, one can easily identify an acquiescence to visual elements. First of all, the very selection of course material is prejudiced towards content that is easily transferrable to visual imagery or graphic elements. Planets and whales make for good TV, so there are a considerable number of educational programs with such visually attractive subject matter; on the other hand, mathematics and literature, for instance, are harder to represent visually and less likely to maintain student attention, so there is a dearth of programs about these subjects. This program distribution has nothing to do with the educational importance of the subjects depicted but everything to do with the visual bias of television technology, which mitigates against certain types of material dependent on different cognitive processes. Even the most brilliantly conceived educational TV program, such as the recent documentary about the Civil War, will be confined to presenting only that information that has a visual corollary to present on screen.

This visual dominance has even imposed itself on the ways in which our society engages with printed materials. Newspapers now rely heavily on pictures and graphic elements to coax the public to "read" them, and they're sold on the sidewalks from boxes that look like television sets. Successful magazines are dominated by pictures and contain short, quickly-read articles that encourage readers to absorb the content in one sitting rather than engaging in more time-consuming reflective thinking. And any educator can attest to the recent revolution in textbooks, which now often contain less text than picture, graphics, and white space. Our society is rapidly abandoning linear print forms and lengthier texts, which demand discursive reasoning, and embracing a graphic revolution that is biased towards the instantaneously perceived image with its limited content potential. Too many educators fail to see any dangers of this trend.

Nor have significant numbers of educational leaders been inclined to identify heavy television viewing as a contributor to reading difficulties and poor classroom performance. Despite the research evidence, the preponderance of at-risk literature has ignored this potential hazard, focusing instead either on systemic changes from within or political answers from without to provide solutions to the dropout problem. While environmental factors have been implicated in paradigms of student failure, the influence of television on that environment hasn't. At least part of the problem is that self-serving agents of the television industry have done an excellent job of convincing most Americans, educators included, that the medium is an important source of information about the world around us. This argument is framed in a context that is appealing to educators who are, by definition, great believers in the transmission of knowledge. However, the argument is patently false. Surely it is ludicrous to argue that television programming, with its plethora of sex-and-violence series offerings, exploitative talk shows, and soap operas, offers much in the way of useful information; or that the multitude of sports programs ranging from football to curling are more than simply entertainment; or that the repetitious lineup of made-for-TV movies hastily extracted from last month's sensationalized headline offers realistic help for dealing with life problems. In limited quantities the substance of these programs may not be hazardous and may serve as legitimate amusements; in excessive dosages, commercial program fare can be lethal when it interferes with academic success.

Even television news—the one category of programming considered most sacred by TV's critics—provides very little knowledge but lots of useless data. First of all, consistent with its technological bias, news programming centers on what is highly visual at the expense of any other consideration. Then that information is compressed into a collection of 30-second soundbites that the viewer is told will fully explain a series of complex events. Viewers are offered random bits and pieces of information from around the world, each one isolated from its context, and few of which have any real bearing on the daily lives of those watching. All of it is delivered with a great sense of urgency (although none of it so urgent that it can't be interrupted by a commercial break). Steady viewers have a Jeopardy-knowledge of the world; they possess all sorts of diverse facts, very few of which empower them in any way. Television's unique information-processing style contradicts the notion of careful analysis and thoughtful discourse essential to an educated public.

Only a handful of studies credit television viewing with initiating even small increases in school performance, and then only within very restrictive circumstances; low to moderate amounts of viewing can produce some vocabulary gains within households of lower SES non-English speakers in the lower elementary grades, and for hearing children of deaf parents. However, as reported above, significant numbers of well-designed investigations demonstrate TV's negative impact on the schooling process of at-risk youth. What some educators appear to be suggesting, however, is not that we develop strategies to neutralize or reverse that impact but that we shift the paradigm for learning. Kozma and Croninger (1992), for instance, arguing for the restructuring of schools to increase the effective use of technology, review two "promising" projects that incorporate their view. The first is "The Jasper Series," a videodisc-based mathematics program that uses stories as contexts for problem-solving. The authors commend the series because:

> First, the video-based stories provide students with rich mental models of situations, mental models that they would otherwise need to construct on their own with text. Text would also place more demands on reading ability and prior knowledge. With these demands preempted, the students can use their cognitive resources for problem-solving strategies. Second, the visual nature of the story is more likely to activate the situation-based prior knowledge that students have and connect their new learning to it. (Kozma and Croninger, 1992, p. 448)

So, this visual technology is effective, say the authors, because it disrupts the processes of problem solving that education has historically relied upon. It lessens demands on the student to either have a repertoire of information which he brings to a learning situation or to know how to read well. Furthermore, since the student need not get information from texts, one must assume that "situation-based prior knowledge" will be that which is gathered from some other narrative visual source. This sort of learning paradigm will only exacerbate the gap between at-risk students and their higher achieving counterparts.

Another project this study applauds is "HOTS," a computer-based project which downplays content. The teacher using this package "often wears costumes, tells jokes, and uses other dramatic techniques to arouse motivation and curiosity and promote emotional engagement" (p. 449). In other words, the teacher becomes a performer, and the classroom becomes another entertainment format. Strategies such as these, conforming to television-based learning models which students have been conditioned to learn from, may engage students emotionally, but all the evidence points to the fact that it will be at the expense of their intellectual growth.

Concerning the development of aggression, only the smallest minded of critics continue to strain at methodological gnats while denying the connection between this behavior and heavy viewing of television. In recent years some concerned groups have lobbied to change the content of the medium, stimulating a 1990 Congressional mandate that gave the television industry three years to formulate a policy to curb violent content. In a scenario reminiscent of the 1970s, the television networks have taken little action to address the situation, and public pressure has continued to mount. As this chapter is being prepared (1996), a bill has passed both the U.S. Senate and House of Representatives that would require television makers to install a special "V-chip" in TV receivers; the chip would allow parents to block any programs with excessive violence, sexually explicit content, or even verbal obscenities. It would also force TV and cable operators to establish a new rating system that would rank programs with respect to violent content.

The bill took nearly three years to pass and received the support of an impressive coalition of citizen and professional groups, including the PTA, National Education Association, National Association of Elementary School Principals, and National Association of Secondary School Principals. However, discussions surrounding the bill did nothing to underscore the validity of any educational issue, focusing instead on the morally objectionable content of TV programming and the effect of violent viewing on the social behavior of young people.

For cultivational theorists, of course, the emphasis on the violence debate is misplaced. The important thing is whether television viewing produces perceptions that have violent consequences in the long run. Perceptions of a mean world, TV-induced fear, and an atmosphere of insecurity and vulnerability may already have begun to produce a self-fulfilling violent reality. To the degree that the educational community fails to confront the cultural perceptions of its students, it fails to prepare them for meaningful engagement with the world of reality. If school is to be a place where our youth are equipped to solve real problems, it must be a place which confronts distortions in the schema of the social reality accepted by its participants. Educational environments, pedagogy, and course content should not reinforce the metaphors nor assimilate the postures of a commercially driven television system. Instead public education must frame the questions and channel perceptions, most particularly of those students having the least amount of success at deciphering the input they are receiving from media.

This chapter has argued that heavy television viewing is a significant environmental hazard in the lives of American young people and has presented a case for including this behavior within the matrix of at-risk factors affecting dropout proneness. Part of television's influence on school-age children is indirect. While there is much yet to be discovered about the precise mechanisms the brain employs in processing information, there is ample evidence that visual images are absorbed differently from texts and thus compete with predominantly linear educational paradigms. It is also clear that excessive exposure to this competing medium can impact reading abilities, and by extension, school performance, since reading is foundational to all educational success. But there are also measurable direct effects of television. Though television executives have consistently denied that there are any negative effects from TV viewing, they operate within a commercial system that is predicated on a corollary of the very premise they deny. Advertisers pay hundreds of thousands of dollars for each commercial minute because they are convinced that people respond to their message, either immediately or as the result of continual reinforcement. A solid body of research demonstrates that television viewing is causally related to both aggression and distorted perceptions of social reality, factors which seriously impair the relationship between students and the school environment.

This chapter has also underscored the ambivalence of educators to reach a consensus about television's detrimental effects, at least to the point of establishing any united assault in opposition to it. Perhaps part of that ambivalence is due to the fact that, even for adults, commercial TV has become so much a part of our surroundings that we accept it as natural rather than intrusive. Unable to conceptualize a world without it, we are quickly losing our ability to examine it objectively. But the fate of a great many students may depend on our ability to refocus our vision on the factors discussed above, which demand attention while we are still able to identify them.

Cries for courses that teach "visual literacy" are misdirected. Educators should not accept the position that the current commercial television system is immutable, and that we should therefore cut our educational losses by helping young people develop some sort of damage control strategies for operating in a world dominated by hazardous visual media. We do not need to equip young people to better decipher the wasteland of commercial television offerings; we need to encourage them to reject those offerings and then guide them on a journey of discovery of alternate messages that will provide constructive models for their individual lives and the society to which they belong. Those who are at risk are most susceptible to the damaging influence of commercial television. Until educators respond to their vulnerability, at-risk students will continue to fail in the classrooms and in the arenas of life for which those classrooms were to have prepared them.

REFERENCES

Bachman, J. G., Green, S., and Wirtanen, I. D. (1971). *Youth in transition: Volume III. Dropping out—problem or symptom?* Ann Arbor, MI: University of Michigan, Institute for Social Research.

Ball, S., Palmer, P., and Millward, E. (1986). Television and its educational impact: A reconsideration. In J. Bryant and D. Zillman (Eds.), *Perspectives on Media Effects* (pp. 129–142). Hillsdale, NJ: L. Erlbaum Associates.

Bandura, A., Ross, D., and Ross, S. A. (1963). Imitation of film-mediated aggressive models. *Journal of Abnormal and Social Psychology, 66*(1), 3–11.

Breed, W. and DeFoe, J. R. (1981). The portrayal of the drinking process on prime-time television. *Journal of Communication, 31*(1), 58–67.

Comstock, G. and Cobbey, R. E. (1982). Television and the children of ethnic minorities: Perspectives from research. In G. Berry and C. Mitchell-Kernan (Eds.), *Television and the socialization of the minority child* (pp. 245–259). New York: Academic Press.

Comstock, G. with Paik, H. (1991). *Television and the American child.* New York: Academic Press.

Condry, J. C. (1989). *The psychology of television.* Hillsdale, NJ: L. Erlbaum Associates.

Cook, T. D., Kendzierski, D. A., and Thomas, S. V. (1983). The implicit assumptions of television research: An analysis of the 1982 NIMH Report on *Television and behavior. Public Opinion Quarterly, 47*(2), 161–201.

Ekstrom, R. B., Goertz, M. E., Pollack, J. M., and Rock, D. A. (1986,1987). Who drops out and why? Findings from a national study. In G. Natriello (Ed.), *School dropouts: Patterns and policies* (pp. 52–69). New York: Teachers College Press.

Freedman, J. L. (1984) Effect of television violence on aggressiveness. *Psychological Bulletin, 96*(2), 227–246.

Gadberry, S. (1980). Effects of restricting first graders' TV viewing on leisure time use, I.Q. change, and cognitive style. *Journal of Applied Developmental Psychology, 1*, 161–176.

Geen, R. G. and Thomas, S. L. (1986). The immediate effects of media violence and behavior. *Journal of Social Issues, 42*(3), 7–27.

Gerbner, G. and Gross L. (1980). The violent face of television and its lessons. In E. L. Palmer and A. Dorr (Eds.), *Children and the faces of television: Teaching, violence, selling* (pp. 149–162). New York: Academic Press.

Gerbner, G., Gross L., Morgan M., and Signorielli, N. (1980). The "mainstreaming" of America: Violence profile no. 11. *Journal of Communication, 30*(3), 10–29.

Greenberg, B. S. (1986). Minorities and the mass media. In J. Bryant and D. Zillman (Eds.), *Perspectives on Media Effects* (pp. 165–188). Hillsdale, NJ: L. Erlbaum Associates.

Greene, Bert I. (1966). *Preventing school dropouts.* Englewood Cliffs, NJ: Prentice Hall.

Hawkins, R. P. and Pingree, S. (1981). Uniform messages and habitual viewing: Unnecessary assumptions in social reality effects. *Human Communication Research, 7*(4), 291–301.

Heyns, B. (1976). *Exposure and the effects of schooling.* Washington, DC: National Institute of Education.

Huesmann, L. R. and Eron, L. D. (Eds.) (1986). *Television and the aggressive child: A cross-national comparison.* Hillsdale, NJ: L. Erlbaum Associates.

Huesmann, L. R., Lagerspetz, K., and Eron, L. D. (1984). Intervening variables in the TV violence-aggression relation: Evidence from two countries. *Developmental Psychology, 20*(5), 746–775.

Huesmann, L. R. and Malamuth, N. M. (1986). Media violence and antisocial behavior: An overview. *Journal of Social Issues, 42*(3), 1–6.

Huston, A. C., Watkins, B. A., and Kunkel, D. (1989). Public policy and children's television. *American Psychologist, 44*(2), 424–433.

Johnson, E. and Legg, C. (1948). Why young people leave school. *National Association of Secondary School Principals Bulletin, 32*, 14–24.

Kozma, R. B. and Croninger, R. G. (1992). Technology and the fate of at-risk students. *Education and Urban Society, 24*(4), 440–453.

Kubey, R. and Csikszentmihalyi, M. (1990). *Television and the quality of life: How viewing shapes everyday experience.* Hillsdale, NJ: L. Erlbaum Associates.

Lazar, B. A. (1994). Why social work should care: Television violence and children. *Child and Adolescent Social Work Journal, 11*(1), 3–19.

Liebert, R. M. and Sprafkin, J. (1988). *The early window: Effects of television on children and youth* (3rd ed). New York: Pergamon Press.

Medrich, E. A., Roizen, J., Rubin, V., and Buckley, S. (1982). *The serious business of growing up: A study of children's lives outside school.* Berkeley, CA: University of California Press.

Meringoff, L. K. (1980). Influence of the medium on children's story apprehension. *Journal of Educational Psychology, 72*(2) 240–249.

Milavsky, J. R., Kessler, R., Stipp, H., and Rubens, S. (1982). *Television and aggression: A panel study.* New York: Academic Press.

———. (1988). Television and aggression once again. In S. Oskamp (Ed.), *Television as a social issue* (pp. 163–170). Newbury Park, CA: Sage Publications.

Morgan, M. (1980). Television viewing and reading: Does more equal better? *Journal of Communication, 30*, 159–165.

———. (1989). Cultivation analysis. In E. Barnouw (Ed.), *International Encyclopedia of Communications* (Vol. 1) (pp. 430–433). New York: Oxford University Press.

Morgan, M. and Gross, L. (1982). Television and educational achievement and aspiration. In D. Pearl, L. Bouthilet, and J. Lazar (Eds.), *Television and behavior: Ten years of scientific progress and implications for the eighties: Vol. 2. Technical reviews* (pp. 78–90). Rockville, MD: National Institute of Mental Health.

National Commission on the Causes and Prevention of Violence (1969). *To establish justice, to insure domestic tranquility: Final report.* Washington, DC: U.S. Government Printing Office.

National Commission on Excellence in Education (1983). *A nation at risk: The imperative for educational reform.* Washington, DC: U.S. Government Printing Office.

Neuman, S.B. (1988). The displacement effect: Assessing the relation between television viewing and reading performance. *Reading Research Quarterly, 23*(4), 414–440.

Pearl, D., Bouthilet, L. and Lazar, J. (Eds.). (1982). *Television and behavior: Ten years of scientific progress and implications for the eighties: Vol. 1. Summary report.* Rockville, MD: National Institute of Mental Health.

Postman, N. (1982). *The disappearance of childhood.* New York: Delacorte Press.

———. (1985). *Amusing ourselves to death: Public discourse in the age of show business.* New York: Penguin Books.

Roberts, E. (1982). Television and sexual learning in childhood. In D. Pearl, L. Bouthilet, and J. Lazar (Eds.), *Television and behavior: Ten years of scientific progress and implications for the eighties. Vol. 2. Technical reviews* (pp. 209–223). Rockville, MD: National Institute of Mental Health.

Rothenberg, M. B. (1975). Effect of television violence on children and youth. *Journal of the American Medical Association, 234*, 1043–1046.

Salomon, G. (1983). Television watching and mental effort: A social psychological view. In J. Bryant and D. R. Anderson (Eds.), *Children's understanding of television: Research on attention and comprehension* (pp. 181–198). New York: Academic Press.

Surgeon General's Scientific Advisory Committee on Television and Social Behavior. (1972). *Television and growing up: The impact of televised violence.* Washington, DC: U.S. Government Printing Office.

Timmer, S. G., Eccles, J., and O'Brien, K. (1985). How children use time. In F. T. Juster and F. P. Stafford (Eds.), *Time, goods, and well-being* (pp. 353–382). Ann Arbor, MI: University of Michigan, Institute for Social Research.

Wartella, E. (1988). The public context of debates about television and children. In S. Oskamp (Ed.), *Television as a social issue: Applied social psychology annual 8* (pp. 59–68). Newbury Park, CA: Sage Publications.

Watkins, D., Cojuk, J. R., Mills, S., Kwaitek, K., and Tan, Z. (1981). Children's use of TV and real life story structure and content as a function of age and prime-time television viewing. *First annual report to the Spencer Foundation: Children's media project.* Ann Arbor, MI: University of Michigan [as reported in Salomon, p. 195].

Williams, P. A., Haertel, E. H., Haertel, G. D., and Walberg, H. J. (1982). The impact of leisure-time television on school learning: A research synthesis. *American Educational Research Journal, 19*(1), 19–50.

Williams, T. M. (Ed.). (1986). *The impact of television: A natural experiment in three communities.* Orlando, FL: Academic Press.

Williams, T. M., Zabrick, M., and Joy, L. (1982). The portrayal of aggression on North American television. *Journal of Applied Social Psychology, 12*(5), 360–380.

Wolfe, D., Mendes, M., and Factor, D. (1984). A parent administered program to reduce children's television viewing. *Journal of Applied Behavior Analysis, 17,* 267–272.

PART IV
STUDENTS AND MOTHERS SPEAK OUT IN THEIR OWN VOICES

8 AN AFRICAN-AMERICAN FEMALE AND SCHOOL

Rosa Kennedy

I obtained the data in this chapter during a research project about students who were at risk of dropping out of school. The original study stated this question: "How do students who are pushed out of regular education classrooms describe key events in their retrospective life histories?" In this chapter I present data from one African-American female (Iesha), whose meaning perspective of school changed from "I like school" to "School is not for me." I link descriptions of her key life events to her later in-school performance and to relevant theory in the field.

Two theories support this paper: Mead's Theory of Symbolic Interactionism (1934) and Schur's Labeling Theory (1971). Mead's theory states that a person acquires meaning through social interaction with others. Because Iesha's mother is white and her father is black, her meaning through social interaction with others was unique. Iesha also grew up in the "projects," which she perceives is an experience unknown to most classroom teachers. Schur's Labeling Theory takes the following symbolic interactionist point of view: "At the heart of the labeling approach is an emphasis on process; deviance is viewed not as a static entity but rather as a continuously shared and reshaped *outcome* of dynamic processes of social interaction" (Blumer, 1969, pp. 62, 65, 66 as quoted by Schur, p. 8). The emphasis in Schur's theory is on the "audience," defined as society at large, a person's peers, and official organizational agents of control. The issues become those within the social context: the labeling of an individual and its consequences in interpersonal relations, stereotyping, self-concept, and role engulfment. The results of this study are tied to Labeling Theory in the Conclusions section.

Assumptions of the Original Study

In this study, the researcher made four assumptions:

1. A naturalistic approach using repeated, in-depth conversational type interviews was a sound research method for determining the student's "truth."
2. Iesha's truth was her perceived reality.
3. The findings of this study were not generalizable to a wider population but provided rich description from one student's perspective.
4. This student from the Alternative Center for Learning (A.C.L.), Knoxville, Tennessee, was a "pushout" rather than a dropout since she had been expelled or had received long-term suspension from the regular education classroom.

Symbolic Interactionism

The symbolic interactionist concentrates on the following questions:

1. How do people define themselves, others, their settings, and their activities?
2. How do people's definitions and perspectives develop and change?
3. What is the fit between different perspectives held by different people?
4. What is the fit between people's perspectives and their activities? (Taylor and Bogdan, 1984, p. 136).

I theorized that this "pushout" had a personal distorting lens that allowed her to interpret her school experience in a very different manner than would a teacher, a school administrator, or a parent. By being allowed to tell a personal story of "What's going on here?" Iesha interprets in-school interaction, which reveals how she derives meaning about herself and school. I am not interested in the absolute truth of the situation. Rather I focus on determining the subject's view of the truth as a means to understanding her meaning perspective. I determined that the way in which this student interpreted a social action and stored that action in memory was the result of interactive experience.

A step-by-step description of the methodology can be found in my dissertation completed at the University of Tennessee, Knoxville, 1993, entitled, *A Study of Four Student Pushouts from the Perspective of Four Sociological Theories* (Kennedy, 1993). The data used for this paper came from one-on-one private interviews conducted at the A.C.L. The interviews were taped and transcribed word for word. During the interview process the student became the authority in her own retrospective educational life history, and the interviewer took the role of listener. Howard Becker (1986) described the role of researcher in sociological life histories in the following excerpt:

> The sociologist who gathers a live history takes steps to ensure that it covers everything we want to know, that no important fact or event is slighted, that what purports to be factual squares with available evidence and that the subject oriented to the questions sociology is interested in, asks him about events that require amplification, tries to make the story told jibe with matters of official record and with material furnished by others familiar with the person, event, or place being described. He keeps the game honest for us. (Becker, 1986, 15)

Because the alternative school had been identified in an earlier study by Kronick and Hargis (1990), The Human Subjects Committee at the university would not allow taped interviews of teachers, counselors, or principals. I was allowed to ask yes or no questions of the above staff in order to verify information given in the private interviews. The student's records verified the extreme numbers of expulsions during her attendance at Madison School.

PARTICIPANT DESCRIPTION

Iesha (pseudonym) was a 14-year-old student attending an alternative school in Tennessee. She had jet black hair, nicely styled, sparkling black eyes, light brown skin, and a small gold leaf in her left nostril. She was of average height and size. She was highly verbal, telling her stories with the visual details of an artist. Self-descriptive statements, giving insight into Iesha's meaning and perspective representing her school experience from kindergarten through six months of eighth grade, can be found in the original study (Kennedy, 1993).

She had attended school only 54 days during the previous school year due to expulsions based on her behavior, which was characterized as violent and unruly. She had been passed to the next grade and court-ordered to attend the alternative school for the next academic year (1991–92). She lived in a housing project with her mother, who is white. Her father is African-American and was living in Ohio. They were now divorced. During the first five years of her educational life, Iesha spent the fall of each year in Ohio schools and the spring of each year in Tennessee schools. Since that time she had attended school in Tennessee.

IESHA'S MEANING PERSPECTIVE

Iesha's early meaning perspective concerning her social identity was similar to any person growing up in a housing project rather than that of an African-American. (Even though African-American is acknowledged as the descriptor of choice, I will use Iesha's term "black" throughout the paper.)

R (researcher): Can you tell me about your fifth grade teacher and why you like her? Why was she different from other teachers?

I (Iesha): Well, she, you know, (was) trusting and honest and helped us out because she was once from the projects too. And she understood what we was going through and all the pressure we had on us in the projects. And she used to keep our courage up high and tell us we could do it. You know, she did not think low of us because she was from the projects and she was about to get her master's degree. You know, everybody listen to her when other people who were not from the projects, they would say, "Well, I understand," but they don't understand because they haven't been there. You know, she had been there. We listened to her 'cause we could relate to her, but all the other teachers could not do that. I mean, she use to keep our hopes up high and tell us everyone had special needs in some areas. So everybody in her class did not feel like a failure. So you know, it was really good for all of us.

R: How many were in your class then?

I: About 23 in that class. And you know, didn't no whites get treated better than blacks. It was all equal because we all came from the same place. We all lived in the projects. We all grew up together and everybody know everybody in the whole school. More than likely the whole school knew every, each one, 'cause we all grew up in that area together.

Iesha identified her teachers as black or white only in response to specific questions about race. Her early school experience was positive except for the fact that for five years, kindergarten through fourth grade, she spent the fall of each year until Christmas with her father in Ohio and the remaining school year in Tennessee. She compared her favorite teacher from the projects to one she identified as "Mrs. Rich Preppy." In Iesha's words, "How could [she] relate to someone who doesn't even in their whole life get what [her] kids get in a couple of years?" Iesha described this teacher as having a father who was a plastic surgeon and a husband who was a "real big lawyer." "Nobody wanted to hear that, I mean, someone who has been there from the projects could relate better with what you are saying than someone who has come from a very rich family."

Except for occasional hassles at school, Iesha blended with those from the neighborhood. She was not labeled a troublemaker, nor was she perceived to be either unruly or violent. Then the neighborhood school was closed, and in school year 1990–91 Iesha was bussed to a school that was predominantly white middle class in population. Iesha was in seventh grade. She was quickly labeled unruly and violent and threatened with 24-hour mental health treatment, which to Iesha meant forced separation from her family. During an entire school year at her new school, Iesha was expelled for all but 54 days. In asking her to describe how the fights began, she said about herself, "I just cannot stand nobody talking about the color somebody is. And they just kept on . . . and they knew that I, it was my quick point." In Iesha's words, "(T)he school was full of racial."

She spoke of students coming close to her to "make black people jokes." One teacher was reported as having said, "You blacks don't get on my bad side, 'cause I don't like niggers." After Iesha reacted and was taken to the principal's office, the principal was informed that Iesha had started the trouble. "When I told the principal what she (the teacher) said, they did not want to believe me. The whole class heard it and they said they heard it, but they (school administrators) did not want to believe us."

As an example of her experience, she answered my question in the following way:

R: Tell me what somebody would say to you that triggered the "fight" on your part.

I: Okay, there was this boy, we were in science and it was the last period of the day. And this boy said, "Iesha." I said, "What?" He said, "How come you are black and your mom is white?" It just stunned me for a minute and I didn't pay no attention to him. I said, "Cause my dad is black." He said, "Your mom is a nigger lover?" and I just seen a chair that looked handy, and so I just picked it up and started throwing them at him. And the teacher tried to grab me and I smacked him with a book . . . I just cannot stand nobody talking about the color somebody is.

I: I mean, I, just when somebody say something about me I don't like . . . at first I just look at them and start laughing. And then I start getting real mad. And the next thing I know I be yelling and then I end up hitting them.

R: Do you make a decision to hit them or . . . how does that happen?

I: I don't think. I mean, I have no control over myself. It is like it is not me in my body. I have no control of myself.

IESHA'S BEHAVIORAL PATTERNS

Iesha described three patterns of behavior that she felt worked against her:

1. The other students, once they discovered her "quick point," would set her up for suspension or expulsion from school by making racial remarks and then reporting that Iesha started an incident.

2. The school authorities were not interested in her side of a story. They would first assign her the number of days of expulsion and then ask her if she had anything to say.

3. The school refused to assign her placement in the alternative setting even though both she and her mother requested such placement.

I: I mean they just would not let me out. It was like, well, if we let someone go, it will get us a bad rep [reputation]. So they just kept me there and using me like an experiment, talking about they was putting in all this counseling stuff. They going to see if this counseling can work with me. And then they use it on other students. I said, "I am not an experiment." And they just use to make me mad. Have me running around and then finally at the end of the year, they was like, "Well, I hope you come back with a better attitude next year." I said, "I am not coming back next year." And then my probation officer, she said that she did not want me back at Madison. And a court ordered me and only reason I was allowed back in Madison was to go get my referral sheet and all my suspension records. And I had to carry it to my probation officer and then bring them over here (to the alternative school). They said it would be the best place for me.

The alternative school staff and principal reported that Iesha had not had one incident requiring discipline in the alternative school setting since arriving there six months earlier. They described Iesha as a model student. Furthermore, the alternative school principal was the same one from Iesha's neighborhood school before the bussing took place. This principal had been placed at the alternative school after Iesha's neighborhood school closed. The principal stated that she would vouch for everything Iesha had described to me. She believed sincerely that Iesha told the truth.

Iesha's teacher, school counselor, and principal believed that Iesha's representation was honest.

During another interview session, Iesha described the following:

R: Was fifth grade the last grade that you liked?

I: No, sixth grade was.

R: And why did you stop liking school between sixth and seventh?

I: Well, because when I went to Madison it was just . . .

R: That was the difference?

I: Yeah.

R: You left (your neighborhood) school in the sixth grade and tried to do seventh at Madison? And seventh was where you had 54 days in school and the rest of them outside of school? And then this fall you started at the alternative school?

I: Yeah.

R: So that is your educational life history?

I: Yeah.

RESULTS

Iesha's statements included several recurrent themes:

1. Her seventh grade school was "racial."
2. Students set her up with black remarks once they discovered her "quick point."
3. Teachers at Madison were prejudiced against blacks.
4. Madison ignored her referral requests, fearing a "bad rep" for dealing with racial issues.

I asked Iesha to pretend she was principal of Madison and asked her what she would do differently. Her responses were as follows, taken as excerpts from the transcript:

1. I would use conflict resolution to sort out conflicts.
2. I would talk with all teachers and tell them that they would have to treat all students fairly, no matter what color, race, wealth or (unclear on tape).
3. I would expect white students to welcome the blacks with open arms.
4. I would have a talk with the black students and tell them they need to treat the whites fairly and give them a chance.
5. If kids need help on their work, I would have time set aside each day where the teacher would be there to help them.
6. If a teacher didn't treat the kids fairly, I would investigate and see really what happened.
7. I would cut the cost on school activities; cheerleaders would not be $500.
8. I would give everybody a fair chance.

CONCLUSIONS

This chapter supports Schur's (1971) Labelling Theory in that the way in which a students is labeled, violent and unruly in this case, was dependent upon the social context of the student. In analyzing Iesha's life history in regard to school interaction, an important finding was that while Iesha attended a neighborhood school close to the projects she was not considered to be a troublemaker. Her neighborhood school was closed and she was forced to attend Madison, which she considered the rich kids' school. Her behavior was rebellious, unruly, uncontrollable, and she was expelled many more days than she attended school that year. After the court ordered her to the Alternative Learning Center, she once again became a model student.

Iesha's identity and self-concept appear to be affected by the reactions of others. As long as Iesha was accepted as an insider, she was not forced to respond in a rebellious way. Once Iesha was perceived or labeled by others as an outsider, poor and black, Iesha's behavior changed dramatically. It appeared that Iesha's positive image of self demanded that she rise up using violent behavior in an effort to defend the black culture against racial slurs by whites.

Iesha was labeled a "black" in a white, rich kids' school. This stereotyping, called "pictures in our minds," was explained by Walter Lippmann in 1922 and quoted by Schur (1971) as follows:

> "We do not first see, then define, we define first and then see . . . We are told about the world before we see it. We imagine most things before we experience them and those preconceptions, *unless educa-*

tion has made us acutely aware [emphasis mine], govern deeply the whole process of perception. They mark out certain objects as familiar or strange, emphasizing the difference, so that the slightly familiar is seen as very familiar, and the somewhat strange as sharply alien." (p. 40)

Iesha's perception as she entered Madison, and the perception on the part of Madison students of an "outsider," especially a black, low socio-economic status outsider, appears to be the crux of the negative social interaction that took place. Iesha, in reporting the prejudicial comments by the one teacher and the racial slurs perpetuated by fellow students, learned that a person can be stereotyped merely by the color of one's skin. This kind of stereotyping, based upon one personal characteristic of being either white or black, places the other on the defensive in social interaction.

Labeling Theory also describes role engulfment in the form of immersion in a deviant subculture as a possible condition of the individual's developing a strong deviant self-concept (Schur, 1971). Iesha's identity with gangs and gang culture in the projects appears to place her in the adversarial position of defending African Americans and/or low socio-economic meaning systems. Those systems were contrasted by Iesha herself to the white middle-class standards evidenced at Madison, standards that Iesha found offensive. Again, what came into play was the "looking glass self." Iesha very quickly became aware that she was perceived as the "outsider" by others at Madison, and the prejudice she experienced did not make her feel good about herself. The prejudice Iesha perceived to be present was real in its consequences for her.

DISCUSSION

In reading Iesha's description of her varied school experiences, of her early love of school and her later meaning perspective change to that of "School is not for me," several questions arise as a result of the data collected: Why were there no methods of conflict resolution utilized by school authorities whereby both sides of a story could be heard? Iesha, in subsequent interviews, made comparisons as follows:

I: (Speaking about the alternative school) Well, for one thing there is less people. And everybody knows everybody because there is not so many people. If you have something wrong with someone, you have someone right there you can go and talk to. You all can get together and settle it. In regular school, you can't do that. And I mean, can work things out easier because there are less people.

R: Would teachers listen to you at Madison if you went to them? Do you think people hear what you say?

I: Yeah, you know, they understand (at the alternative school). The kids here . . . are here because they have problems and I think they (the teachers) understand that—that is when they listen to what we say and try to help us. But at Madison, they just looked over us.

Why was a student retained in a situation even after many requests for a different placement were made by the student, the parent, and the counselor? It took a court order to get Iesha a school placement such as the alternative school, where individual and group counseling is conducted on a regular basis for students with similar problems.

I: It did not start until last year at Madison and when I went to the mental health center. They were recommending me (to the alternative school) but Madison wouldn't accept. They (the school administrators) said that they thought I—they could help me better than the alternative school would; they could work it out with me. And it kept on continuing and continuing. I kept getting into fights and arguing with the teachers and . . .

How can school administrators ignore complaints about racial remarks and racial prejudice when ongoing incidents occur in certain classrooms? Iesha reported that at the beginning of the school year in one class, the teacher announced, "You blacks don't get on my bad side, 'cause I don't like niggers." Iesha reported the following:

R: Was there any reason for her to make a statement like that?

I: They said she also made it the year before.

R: At the very beginning of the school year, that was the announcement that she made in front of the class?

I: They said she made it (the announcement) last year and there was a big thing about it and the principal still didn't believe the kids. So they said there was nothing that was did about it.

RECOMMENDATIONS

After reviewing the data collected from one biracial student's perceived meaning change derived from her experience of school, I make the following recommendations:

1. It is imperative that colleges of education teach teachers entering the field about sensitivity to cultural diversity in the classroom.

2. It is imperative that teaching interns experience cultural diversity, especially that of low socio-economic communities, before they become certified professionals.

3. It is imperative that school authorities keep a watchful vigilance for outright prejudice in the classrooms. Principals and teachers must understand that once a student is labeled, others will initiate means to make the label come true. The student "wearing" the label has nothing to lose by "acting out" in behavior that is expected by others.

4. Conflict resolution can be utilized to deal with issues between two students (or between a student and a teacher) in an effort to "hear" all sides of a story before an expulsion decision is made.

5. It is imperative that teachers and school authorities be taught how to deal with cultural diversity issues, which often involve issues of poverty, divorce, abuse and unemployment.

All of these issues place a student at risk of dropping out of school and at risk of becoming an economic burden to society through social welfare costs, or worse, through incarceration. It is past time to act. Teachers can make a difference!

REFERENCES

Becker, H. S. (1986). Whose side are we on? *Social Problems, 14,* 239–247.
Blumer, H. (1969). *Symbolic interactionism.* Englewood Cliffs, NJ: Prentice Hall.
Kennedy, R. K. (1993). *A study of four student pushouts from the perspective of four sociological theories.* Unpublished dissertation, University of Tennessee, Knoxville.
Kronick, R. and Hargis, C. (1990). *Dropouts: Who drops out and why and the recommended action.* Springfield, IL: Charles C. Thomas.
Lippman, W. (1922). *Public opinion.* New York: Macmillan.
Mead, G. H. (1934). *Mind, self, and society: From the standpoint of a social behaviorist.* Chicago: University of Chicago Press.
Schur, E. W. (1971). *Labeling deviant behavior.* New York: Harper and Row.
Taylor, S. J. and Bogdan, R. (1984). *Introduction to qualitative research: The search for meaning* (2nd ed.). New York: John Wiley.

9 AFRICAN-AMERICAN MOTHERS' ROLES IN THEIR CHILDREN'S EDUCATION

Rhoda Barnes

The roles of African-American mothers in their children's education is the focus of this chapter. Parents' participation in their children's education is essential to the children's academic, social, and emotional success. Many parents are involved in the schools, usually in ways designed by schools. Parents today are faced with many problems, and coming to the school may not be a high priority. There is a need to understand these parents' involvement in their children's schooling, as well as a need to understand how this involvement aids students who may be at risk of school failure.

In the 1954 Supreme Court ruling on *Brown* v. *Topeka Board of Education*, the Reverend Brown objected to his daughter having to be bussed outside their neighborhood so she could attend an all-black school rather than the all-white school nearest her home. Kenneth Clark's (1977) research identified districts that were illegally practicing discrimination toward African-American children. From this major court case came the term "separate but equal" schools. Parents, like the Reverend Brown, began to challenge the American educational system, and thus other African-American parents became more involved with the schooling process. Parents assumed a new role, becoming the "first" teachers, and as a result, states enacted laws to establish parents as members of the school's governance council. This revolutionary development became a new trend in American schools, where communities, schools, and parents joined forces to make a commitment to children's futures. Unfortunately, this new commitment has somehow failed to include many children from the African-American communities.

BENEFITS OF PARENT INVOLVEMENT

Parent participation with schools, homes, and community has proven to be beneficial to students, teachers, and parents. Research has shown that when parents participate in the schooling process, either at the school or at home, their expectations for their children tend to be more realistic (Epstein, 1986; Herman and Yeh, 1983; Leler, 1983).

Herman and Yeh (1983) studied the effectiveness of parent involvement on school outcomes. They found that parent involvement is positively related to the child's academic achievement and success in school.

Students' Benefits from Parent Involvement

Students' academic achievement is usually higher when parents are involved with schooling (Irvine, 1990), and students are more likely to attend classes regularly when parents are involved at the schools (Becker, 1982; Haynes, Comer, and Hamilton-Lee, 1989). Other studies show a relationship between students' completed homework and parents' involvement (Rich, 1988), and that parent involvement affects children's behavior; fewer behavioral problems are reported among students who have had behavior problems before (Becker, 1982; Henderson et al., 1986; Leler, 1983).

Parents' Benefits from Parent Involvement

Parents also benefit from their involvement with schools and the educational process. When parents are actively involved with the schooling of their children they become aware of what takes place in the classroom (Comer, 1980; Epstein, 1984; Irvine 1990; Taylor, 1991), and thus they can more effectively serve as home tutors. Parents also benefit by meeting other parents; learning how the schools are operated; helping set rules, goals, and expectations in order to support the child and the teacher; and learning how to help educate their own children (Clark, 1983; Henderson et al., 1986; Leler, 1983).

Taylor (1991) discusses the importance of involvement of parents in the schools in order to develop a certain cohesiveness between school and home. She feels parents' knowledge about their children helps the school better serve the needs of children because parents share experiences from the home and the interactions they have with the child.

AFRICAN-AMERICAN PARENT INVOLVEMENT IN THE SCHOOLING PROCESS

African-American Parents in the Schools

In American education, students, their parents, and teachers all benefit when schools and families work together. Some studies have shown that African-American parents' involvement in the public schools is limited or nonexistent compared to white parents (Lightfoot, 1978, 1981). The aim of this research is to investigate, by means of interviews with three African-American mothers, how and to what extent these mothers are involved with their children's schooling.

This chapter presents the voices of three African-American mothers as they discuss their children's schooling. The questions asked of the mothers allow them opportunities to describe their feelings about parent involvement and the effects that involvement has had on their lives and the lives of their children. The discussion between the researcher and the mothers clarifies how these mothers perceive their involvement with schools.

Some research discusses the effects of African-American parents' involvement on their children's schooling (Clark, 1983; Comer, 1986; Hale-Benson, 1986; Taylor, 1991). One research aim of these earlier studies was to investigate the influence of African-American parents' involvement on their children's academic achievement. Other studies of home and school relations focus more on the practices that teachers use to involve parents in their classrooms. These studies indicate that African-American parents are either not involved or have limited involvement in the schooling process.

Usually, when African-American parents' involvement with school is researched, the parents' values are being compared with those of mainstream America. Often these studies use low-income African-American families as the comparison group with middle-class white families (Irvine, 1990; Liontos, 1992).

Other studies have explored issues such as African-American parents' participation in their children's education (Clark, 1983; Comer, 1984; Hoover-Dempsey, Bassler, and Brissie, 1987; Lightfoot, 1978; Ogbu, 1990; Taylor, 1991). These studies present families who struggle to find ways of dealing with an educational institution that is not willing to tolerate or nurture children from different ethnic backgrounds. For example, much of Ogbu's (1974) research on home and school relations has shown African-American children struggling to accept the middle-class values of their schooling. Ogbu states that African-American children must give up their culture and take on mainstream values to succeed in school. Given all this, Ogbu claims they still do not achieve the idealized "American Dream." African-American children's peer culture and attitudes combined with certain family practices and teacher attitudes toward these students cause conflicts between parents and school personnel. Lightfoot (1978) presents the struggle that parents have in communicating and interacting with school officials, especially teachers. This research shows that African-American parents who have difficulty communicating and interacting with school personnel have children who tend not to do well academically. Consequently, these children are required by the schools to attend vocational or general education classes.

Irvine (1990) discusses the lack of diversity affecting parental participation in most public schools and believes this lack of diversity is due to the small number of inner-city, predominantly African-American schools with programs designed to encourage effective participation of parents and student success.

The infrequency of African-American parents' participation, however, should not be interpreted as a sign of disinterest, according to Irvine. Rather, these parents are dealing with economic issues, but they are still committed to the quality of their children's education. These parents regard education as being the way for black children to escape poverty.

CONCERNS OF THE STUDIES

There is growing concern about the educational risks of African-American children in the schools (Irvine, 1990). In many instances these students are unable to fulfill the academic and cultural expectations of the teacher and the behavioral requirements of the classroom (Hale-Benson, 1986; Irvine, 1990). Taylor (1991) suggests that African-American parent involvement may enhance the child's ability to adapt to the school, as well as help the teacher adapt the classroom to accommodate the African-American child. Success for these children seems to depend to a degree on parent involvement in their schooling (Epstein, 1987; Hale-Benson, 1986; Irvine, 1990; Lightfoot, 1981; Taylor, 1991). Research on school and family connections indicates that schools need to become more like families and communities in order to improve African-American students' achievement (Comer, 1986).

ROLES OF AFRICAN-AMERICAN PARENTS

There is a need to understand the roles that African-American parents play in the schooling of their children. Irvine states that location of schools has a great impact on some levels of involvement (e.g., schools out of their neighborhoods may cause some parents not to become involved). African-American parents find it difficult to attend meetings, volunteer at schools, or communicate with teachers, especially during regular school hours.

Because African Americans tend to be speakers of nonstandard English, they are less likely to attend conferences with teachers, attend Parent-Teacher Association (PTA) meetings, respond to teachers in writing, and volunteer in the classrooms (Irvine, 1990). If they do become involved, it is usually on a limited and restricted basis. These findings are attributed not only to low-income African-American families but to middle-class families as well. Some teachers assume that all African-American students come from low-income communities with disinterested parents. Their interactions with these families, with both children and parents, tends to be stereotypical in nature (Boutte, 1992).

Reynolds (1989) finds that African-American parent involvement in children's early schooling proves worthwhile and provides positive outcomes for African-American children. This may help maintain parent involvement as children move through the grades.

Many parents want their level of involvement to increase for their children who are failing in school. Some African-American children experience difficulties with schooling, which leave them feeling alienated from their peers, lacking a connection with the school's activities and programs, and unable to do well academically.

Thomas and Chess (1977) in their "goodness of fit" theory state that teachers' and students' cultures are mismatched. Their "goodness of fit" theory provides the theoretical frame from which the term "cultural fit" will be used to explain one possible reason black children experience failure in the classroom. The relationship between "goodness of fit" and "cultural fit" relate to behaviors that children bring from their homes to the classroom. Children are to change their behaviors to match those desired by the teacher, but in many instances, students are unable to meet these expectations.

Angela Taylor (1991) identified four reasons why African-American children have problems with formal schooling: children's entry characteristics that may differ from those expected at schools, children's cognitive and behavioral skills, parent participation with schools, and peer relations.

African-American children display characteristics that conflict with those set by the teachers (lack of fit), especially if the teacher is a member of another race. Studies show that some of these characteristics are problematic, often requiring that these children be removed from these classrooms because teachers perceive these behaviors negatively (Boykin, 1986; Brice-Heath, 1989; Hale-Benson, 1986; Irvine, 1990; Lightfoot, 1981; Clark, M., 1976; Clark, R., 1983). Teachers establish appropriate classroom behavior (Taylor, 1991) and decide who is welcome (Lightfoot, 1981). However, if African-American children do not adjust to these preset rules, what can be done to overcome this mismatch?

Parents can express their feelings and those of their children to the schools (Hester, 1989), which helps the child adjust to the academic, social, cognitive, and emotional requirements of the teacher. These parents can also help teachers appreciate the culture that their children bring to the classroom.

Evidence presented in this study will identify the actual involvement of some parents with their children's schooling. School officials need to understand the relationships that African-American parents have with the local schools and educational programs. Because children are always at the mercy of adults in schools, in communities, and in the homes, their advocate must be their parents. Parents need to know when the school is unable to teach their children or when the school needs the parents' help in the schooling process.

Shared experiences of parents may provide ways of understanding their children's current school experiences. These experiences may in some ways affect parents' perceptions of their relationships with their child's school and may be helpful in identifying the "actual" parent-school relationship. Therefore, parents are the identifiers of what schools can do to encourage and increase the participation of African-American parents in the schools.

The children of the mothers addressed by this study attend schools where they may be the only black child in the class or at the school. They are not doing well academically and feel isolated socially. There is obviously a need to learn why schools are unable to teach children from diverse cultures.

METHODS AND PROCEDURES

The goal of this study is to present the voices of African-American parents as they describe their levels of involvement in their children's schooling. The study examined the presence of parent involvement issues that surfaced through a review of the literature on parent involvement, specifically focusing on African-American mothers' perceptions of their involvement with their children's schooling. Three African-American mothers with children in elementary and secondary schools participated in this study; open-ended, in-depth, structured interviews were used to solicit their perceptions of parent involvement and the issues related to this participation. This study was conducted over the course of one academic year in a Southern California community.

Sample Selection

The participants were three African-American mothers who had children in the local public schools in Southern California (Barnes, 1994). The three mothers were selected because they represented a middle-class standard of values and beliefs about schools similar to the mothers most often presented in the literature on white parents' involvement. They had completed high school and had some college education. They were either working or had worked on a job that required a college education.

African-American students represent less than three percent of the districts' enrollment equally divided between Latino and white students. Quite often there is only one African-American student in every classroom, and in some cases none.

Characteristics of the Sample

All names have been changed for confidentiality.

Case 1. Mrs. Dunn is a recently divorced African-American mother with three daughters (17, six, and three years). The oldest daughter is in the 11th grade, and the two younger girls are presently attending kindergarten and preschool. The mother has lived in this school district in Southern California for 14 years. This parent has a degree in business economics and is employed at a local university. She also serves as an ordained minister. Her oldest daughter is attending a high school in this community, which provides an excellent college preparatory curriculum. During the interview the oldest daughter was experiencing academic, social, and emotional problems at her local school. Her younger daughters were experiencing rejection from their peers.

Case 2. Mrs. Ashly has two children, one of whom is in school. She is separated from her children's father. This mother has lived in the area for 18 years. Her oldest son attended the local public school but dropped out before completing his senior year, and her youngest son is now in the third grade. Mrs. Ashly stated that she did not want her younger son to drop out of school as a result of her failure to be involved in his schooling.

Case 3. Mrs. Richy is the mother of four children, the youngest of whom is enrolled in a local school in the first grade. Two of the older children have completed high school, and another dropped out of school after being placed in special education. Mrs. Richy has lived in the area for 17 years.

Design of Interview Protocol

The protocol was developed from theories found in the literature on parent involvement. Questions were designed with the intent that each one would focus on parent involvement, "test" the paradigm researched, and reflect on the theories in the literature on home-school relations. This structured interview consisted of more than 100 questions, ranging from general demographics to specific parental involvement issues. The protocol consisted of questions to stimulate an ongoing conversation with the parent about her perceptions of parents' participation in her children's schooling.

Procedures

All interviews were tape-recorded and were conducted by the researcher. Each interview lasted two to four hours and was conducted over two or three sessions. After taping, the interviews were transcribed by the researcher.

First interview. The initial interview asked for the responses to 102 questions, covering the five major areas of investigation (Barnes, 1994). The participants were briefed about the nature of the study and advised about the confidentiality of the study. The first interviews were audio-taped and then transcribed. Whenever the need arose, the researcher also took field notes on the protocol, for later use when transcribing the data.

Follow-up interview. Once the interview was transcribed, the mothers checked the document for errors or misrepresentations that may have occurred during transcribing. The mothers made corrections to the document and returned it to the researcher. A general conversation between the family and the researcher was held to ensure accuracy.

Second follow-up interview. The researcher administered a third interview to some of the mothers in order to obtain clarity on incomplete data—that is, either to provide clarity on the information gathered or to get mothers to respond to specific questions that had not been addressed during the second interview. These interviews lasted 30 minutes to one hour. The final analysis of the data was again given to the participant for feedback on whether the researcher presented the perceptions intended by the participants.

Data Analysis

GROUNDED THEORY

The data were analyzed using Strauss and Corbin's (1990) Grounded Theory method of analysis. Grounded Theory not only tests and verifies theories, but also generates them. This methodological process requires the researcher to have some background knowledge, either experiential or theoretical, and not to be constrained by prior knowledge or existing theory.

Once the concepts of parental involvement were identified, they were grouped into categories by placing similar codes under a more abstract concept. If several concepts pertained to a similar phenomenon, the researcher placed them into a separate category or theme. For example, when a response identified what a parent is doing to become involved, the response was categorized under the theme "actual" involvement.

During the third step, the data were regrouped using axial coding, a procedure that allows the researcher to explore new ways of connecting the data, using conditions, actions, and behaviors. The purpose of this step is to take several main categories and, if possible, develop systematic sets of interrelated phenomena. This coding process allows the researcher to form categories based on causal relationships.

The next step in analyzing the data is selective coding, whereby the researcher validates systematic relationships and selects core categories. Selective coding investigates how these data come together to develop a story line, which helps the researcher conceptualize what the data are actually validating. This step also helps uncover patterns in the data, systematize properties identified in the data, and interpret these stories.

Because multiple data sets were used, a conditional matrix was employed to trace the conditions and consequences within each phenomenon through their impact on the general themes. Formal theories emerged from the data that were grouped under different themes and headings across the three data sets. Each parent had somewhat different stories to tell about her involvement in her children's schooling.

COMPARATIVE ANALYSIS

During the comparative analysis, the researcher looked for commonalties and differences in the three interviews. Using the core categories, the researcher organized the data by connecting similar responses into broader, more abstract headings. The next step was to look for differences throughout the data sets. Whenever a mother's response differed from that of the other participants, the researcher placed her response into the "difference" category.

The next section will present the evidence on the involvement of three middle-class African-American mothers and their participation in their children's schooling. Analyses identify similarities and differences in the three mothers' involvement.

DATA

Actual Parent Involvement

All mothers described their actual involvement in their children's schooling. Several questions were posed to all mothers to solicit their responses. This section provides the actual voices of the mothers as they describe their involvement with the schooling process.

Case 1: Mrs. Dunn

Mrs. Dunn describes her situation as follows:

> I joined the PTA by paying, but I never was able to really go and attend any meetings because of the time restraints and as well as a need for child care.
>
> When I had my last two [children] . . . I had a hard time having to leave them. So I spent a lot of time finding a place that I felt safe and I felt they [my children] were going to be well taken care of. I can't work wondering about what is happening to them.
>
> And when my daughter tells me she didn't want to be black anymore I would address it right then and there. And I would tell her

teacher about it. Her self-esteem has improved so much, and I know it had a lot to do with the fact that they were willing to work with me. And one little girl had told her she was ugly because she was black and we addressed that and [the teacher] talked with the little girl. . . .

I have to do my own share of educating people, this is true. I was forever over at the school, calling the teachers, jamming somebody up, and having them deny that they have treated my daughter unfairly. They [teachers, principals, school staff] would always deny it.

I hadn't been [to any meetings] but I definitely plan on going. I even told the principal that I would be on the PTA [committee], . . . since they [school and parent groups] were producing racist children. I wanted him to expect to see me [at the school and school meetings].

Well, I am involved more now because when my younger children were born my involvement was limited. I wasn't involved always before. But again, I was never overly active in the PTA because I've been a single parent for so long. And when I wasn't a single parent I was raising little ones and now they are getting older. Now I am a single parent again, but I have always been willing to help as much as I could and definitely played a major part in my children's education.

I have talked to them [my children] about classroom requirements. . . . . She [Nyk] understands that I am constantly questioning her actions in the classes and trying to make sure she is performing up to her potential. She knows that if her grades are not up to par that she will be grounded. We have even developed contracts and she has to sign them. She has been required to take a progress sheet around to her teachers and they have to give me a weekly report on her actions in class. This has caused her problems because she has asked me, "What difference does it make to you whether or not I do well in my school work?" . . . We have had our ups and downs in these schools. We talk about school and she knows that I expect her to do well.

Oh, yes and I went and spoke to Nyk's classes a couple of times.

Well, with Danyel's new school there's one meeting I have been asked to attend and that one was the parent tea, and there has not been anything else at the elementary schools. I went to the school's orientations. I have talked to a lot of teachers over the phone.

SUMMARY

The roles that Mrs. Dunn actually takes in her children's schooling include selecting their educational institutions, going to the schools to talk with teachers when she has concerns about what is happening to her children there, helping her daughters deal with racial issues, and socializing her children to what is required of them by the schools they attend. Often she has come to the schools to deal with racial issues and to help the teachers and peers understand her children and their needs.

While much of Mrs. Dunn's involvement in her children's education is outside of the school, she supports the schools' programs, and she communicates her feelings to the schools regarding issues that arise concerning her children. She expects the schools to be responsible in their expectations for her children and in educating all children to become responsible citizens and respect people of all cultures.

Case 2: Mrs. Ashly

Overall, Mrs. Ashly describes her situation as follows:

> It's my job as my son's advocate to see that he is in a place where he is able to learn, where he is comfortable, and he is treated well. So I am more like, maybe, a bird dog. I'm watching to see how the other children relate and react to him. I am watching to see how the teachers relate, react, and respond to him. How do they feel about him, and to see how the administration [relates and responds to him]. I am visible, and I can't help being visible. You walk on the campus and there are not many black people around; they see me.
>
> It is my job's description to keep informed; to have that conversation daily with my son. It is not a generic conversation—how was your day at school today? That it's not just a generic term. [When you ask this question] you are searching for a complete report on what happened. What happened at school today? And I expect to hear what happened, not just in the classroom, but on the school yard, on the way to and from school.
>
> My son knows that I support him, and he also knows that if he's wrong I will be on him like nobody's business. But he also knows that if he has a question about something, he can ask me and I can go to the school and find out [more about] it. So in that sense, he knows that I am not going to leave him hanging out there and he knows that he has my support. He knows that I have a good relationship with the people in the office, so he is comfortable and that is a part of my

whole game plan—that he is comfortable.

I have to give him his spelling tests. He is a good reader. If your reading and spelling skills are down [learned] then the school experiences are going to be more positive. He likes math.

I think it is imperative that I send to school a well-rested child, that I send to school a child who has been fed. I should send to school a child who is appropriately dressed so that if it is raining outside he is prepared; if it is freezing outside, he is prepared and that he is not sitting up there in thongs, shorts, and a tank top. That he is being sent to school with a mind to the purpose as to why he is there. He understands that he is to respect the people around him, as well as understand that the teacher is in charge. I am supposed to prepare him to go to school and do what he is suppose to do.

One, if he experiences failure we find out why it happened. Was it because we were goofing off? Was it because we weren't prepared? Was it because we did not get to bed on time the night before? Was it because you procrastinated? Was it because I kept you somewhere or were you somewhere you weren't suppose to be? Did you fail to inform me about something that needed to be done? Was the assignment unreasonable, and that has happened before. But if I don't think this is a reasonable expectation, in which case, we have to talk about it.

Well, I found out that my plans have been given to me by the school during Back-to-School Night. They have planned a two-day field trip to [town] and I found out that this trip will be paid for by the children, i.e., parents selling candy, unless they have the money to fork over for this trip. Then I also found out that in the sixth grade there is a three-day trip to [the islands]. Money is to be saved up for this trip. I then asked if there was any way we could start now raising money for that sixth-grade trip now. They say, "Oh, we have not thought about that." Then I go back into the fifth grade class and ask, "Where all this money is suppose to come from?" I have a real problem with this. It is like, if these kids are doing these kinds of trips now, what will it be like when they get older.

The second thing, the financial aspect of this; well, now is not the time [for me to worry about getting money together to finance a trip].

They [school] invite parents every week to come do something or another. I have never done those things. I just can't; I work for a living.

They are always soliciting people to come in the classroom and that is not something I am able to do. There are parents who are able to do that and I am very grateful for their participation. I think that is wonderful that you are able to do that and I am grateful that you are doing it. But at the same time, I got my hands full. I am trying to stay on top of my son's schooling.

Last year they asked me to come in to help teach the class during Black History Month or Christmas and give a little presentation. I declined to do that because it was a decision that I had to make because I realistically did not have the time to do it, even though I thought it was important because they were giving some attention to diversity. But I would have been cutting myself very short if I had gone.

I think that one thing that makes a big difference is when parents communicate with each other. What happens there is you typically have to start out at the beginning of a new year or when the children are young. You start out [then] maybe not knowing who the other parents are, [but] when your child gets up to fourth and fifth grade, you start [meeting some of the same parents], especially if you are in the same school. [Then] you start having relationships with other parents from the class and you can even start to compare notes. [Finding out] how so-so is doing here, and some of these other parents have older siblings and you can even compare students' reactions to various instructors.

SUMMARY

Mrs. Ashly's actual involvement in her son's schooling entails coming to the school and talking with school officials, monitoring her son's progress, and questioning him about his school day. She feels her role in her child's education is to make sure the schools are educating him well and providing a safe school environment. She also ensures that her son knows his role and responsibilities as a student.

She receives invitations to help in the classroom and teach culturally related lessons, but she feels she is not able to, nor does she really want to work in the classroom. Mrs. Ashly feels communication with other parents and their shared experiences is an important factor in her ability to work with the school and teachers. These conversations help her decide who will teach her son and what to expect from his new instructor.

Case 3: Mrs. Richy:

Mrs. Richy describes her actual involvement with her child's school as follows:

I seek them out, I look at the neighborhoods and the school's rating. I want to make sure the school is a good school for my child. I realize that it is not the total responsibility of the school to teach my child, and I want to help not only my child but all the children at the school. I visit my daughter's school at least four times a week. I am very involved. I watch what happens in the class.

I have attended all meetings. All the formal meetings I go to, and the PTA meetings once a month. I see my child's teacher at least twice a week. We have some sort of exchange even if it is not about my daughter. And she has asked me to do the art in the class.

I go and talk to her about what my child is doing with her and I observe my own child, and if I see she is having some difficulties, then I go back to the teacher and ask her why she thinks this child is having this difficulty. We need to find a way to resolve these difficulties that we are having. I do that for the first six weeks, the second six weeks, and if we do not have any more problems I don't feel as I need to waste her time. I let her have that time with people who need the time.

I sit in the class and work with the children in small groups. They ask that we [parents] assist in the classroom. I am doing art classes once a month . . . we are making a quilt. This quilt will be used in our fundraising efforts.

. . . When a teacher has more than 15 kids, she had too many kids to teach. For example, one teacher that I work with has 21 [students]. When I go into that class to help there is always some child not getting it [the instruction]. I say that every four or five kids need a person. . . . When kids need you, they really need you at that particular time.

In this school, I work with the principal, I work with the secretary, I work with the teachers, and I work with the PTA. My daughter is involved with the Brownies and I work with the Brownies as a co-person. They have the book fair at the school. I worked one day last week.

I have been asked to help by making sure she gets her work done, that she gets rest at home, ready to learn in the school environment.

I have tried to teach her about the classroom requirements by telling Laura that she can be anything she wants to be if she learns everything she needs to learn. If she questions why she has to do some assignment, I am there offering her some logical [reasons] why the assignment is necessary. For example, when she asks why she has to write out her spelling words so many times, I tell her that as she writes the words she learns to spell them. I tell her that when she writes in cursive she is learning to improve her handwriting. Then she realizes the logic behind most of the homework she does.

Laura can be doing something and I will put a tape in the background. Sometimes you don't think a kid listens to that, but if you can't read to your child, parents can get taped stories or get a tape with the same stories that are in books, then let her listen to the tape and read along with the book. You can get the book and read them into the tape when you have time. So, there are many ways you can do things with your kid [to be involved with their schooling].

I take all of her work and display them around the house. I let her know that I am proud of her. Her failure, I try to go over those areas and help her to understand it and see what went wrong and figure she does not want that to happen again. I also let her know that failure is part of life.

SUMMARY

Mrs. Richy meets with her child's teacher and observes her daughter in the classroom. She is aware of her daughter's progress, and they work through any difficulties. Mrs. Richy supports her daughter's academic skills by using educational materials when her busy schedule limits direct involvement. She encourages her daughter to succeed and supports her educational successes.

She is very involved in her daughter's schooling. She is able to spend a lot of time participating at the school site by helping in the classroom and providing assistance to many school programs and activities. She is also active in her home and community.

COMPARATIVE ANALYSIS OF RESULTS

Actual Parent Involvement

Actual involvement by these mothers was also categorized as involvement at home, at the school site, and through some communication with the school.

AT HOME

These mothers are all involved in the education of their children at home. They encourage and support their children's educational success, as well as monitor their progress at school. Mrs. Dunn's and Mrs. Ashly's involvement is mainly at home. At home, Mrs. Dunn helps her children deal with racial issues that arise, and Mrs. Ashly keeps abreast of her son's school experiences to ensure that he feels comfortable at school. These mothers all spend time with their children discussing their roles and responsibilities as students.

AT SCHOOL SITE

These mothers all support their children at the school site, but the degree to which they are physically present at the school differs. Mrs. Richy spends much of her time at the school in the classroom and working on many school projects. Mrs. Ashly's involvement is limited to attending only some parent meetings, and she does not really want to work in the classroom. Although their involvement is limited, racial issues involving her children cause Mrs. Dunn and Mrs. Ashly to spend time at the school site.

COMMUNICATION WITH SCHOOL

Communication with the school is important to these mothers in order to keep track of their children's progress and deal with any problems that arise. Mrs. Dunn feels it is especially important to communicate her feelings regarding racial issues as they arise in order to increase cultural awareness at the school.

OTHER

Mrs. Dunn and Mrs. Richy see their role in involvement to also include carefully selecting the schools their children will attend.

DISCUSSION

This study documents African-American mothers' involvement in the schooling of their children. These mothers describe their individual perceptions of how mothers should be involved in their children's schooling. These mothers want to encourage their children academically by participating in activities at school and in the home. The data presented here highlighted four key points that these mothers perceived as critical for the support of their children's schooling: (1) the importance of home-school communication for collaboration and partnership, (2) the involvement of African-American parents outside schools, (3) a need to incorporate multicultural education into the main curriculum, and (4) involvement of African-American parents in selecting schools that are supportive of their children.

The literature on parent involvement suggests that ethnic minority families are not as involved with schooling as are white families, but reasons for this discrepancy are unclear (Epstein, 1990; Lightfoot, 1978, 1981; Swap, 1993). It is clear, however, that most parents have an interest in their children's academic success (Epstein, 1987; Irvine, 1990; Liontos, 1992).

According to Slaughter and Kuehne (1988), little attention is paid to cultural differences in parent involvement and how minority group membership might affect level of involvement. Recent studies have documented that minority and hard-to-reach families are participating with schools (Chrispeels, 1993; Comer, 1984; Liontos, 1992; Swap, 1993), contrary to earlier findings (Lightfoot, 1981). However, their involvement is very different from the typical involvement expected by the schools. This study provides additional evidence that most African-American parents are concerned and involved with their children's schooling.

Importance of Home-School Communication

The data from this study suggest that our three mothers would like to communicate with the schools more regularly in order to ensure their children's success. (Success and communication have been linked, and much of their children's success has come from this communication.) The mothers in this study appreciate the importance of home-school communication because it helped them to better understand the school environment. They want schools to be sensitive to their children's individual needs, to encourage their children's academic abilities, and to meet with them to discuss and work through any difficulties. They feel that communication with the school fosters a partnership in setting educational goals and expectations. They, in turn, communicate with their children about their responsibilities as students and learners. These mothers are also interested in developing better communication with other parents, feeling that this communication would help disseminate information about teachers and principals. Improved communication might possibly avoid problems for their children in the future. These mothers are concerned that their children may not be getting the best education possible because of miscommunication. Meeting and talking with school officials is one practice that African-American parents feel would help their children's schooling.

These African-American mothers feel that teachers direct and support their involvement simply by being in communication with them on a regular basis. Results found in this study show that past negative experiences with teachers of older children may shape parents' relationship and communication with schools for their younger children.

Our three African-American mothers' attitudes about communication do not differ significantly from what the literature reports on white parents (Epstein, 1987). Both African-American parents and current research on home-school relations acknowledge the need for increased levels of communication between home and school. Through this communication there are fewer chances for families and schools to develop communication misconceptions (Comer, 1980, 1984, 1986, 1988).

In order to increase parents' involvement, parents need to feel empowered, and communication appears to be one way parents feel they can help in the schooling of their children. Schools should increase their attempts to communicate with all parents, but especially African-American parents.

Research on home-school relations should focus on ways to establish effective channels of communication and build a partnership between African-American parents and teachers (Berger, 1987; Hudley-Paul and Barnes, 1994).

Involvement of Parents Outside Schools

The mothers presented here are involved in the schooling process by constantly encouraging and monitoring their children's academic, social, and emotional development. They are willing to be responsible for preparing their children for school and learning. Of the three mothers, Mrs. Dunn and Mrs. Ashly are more likely than Mrs. Richy to be involved with their children's schooling away from the school site. Yet they have been forced to come to schools to deal with racial and academic issues on several occasions.

Many of these mothers cannot come to the school during normal school hours and cannot afford to take time from work to visit the school. However, they regularly discuss school experiences with their children. Mrs. Dunn feels that parents must help children understand school and classroom requirements. One mother was concerned that her children be treated fairly, and she encouraged her children to be cooperative.

Research on African-American parents documents that African-American mothers are involved with their children's schooling in the home (Swap, 1993; Taylor, 1991). Clark's (1983) work, for example, examines the relationship between parents' involvement and school success. Successful students had parents who were actively involved in their child's education in the home (Shade, 1986). They monitored all of their children's education and extracurricular activities. Parent involvement in their childrens' education cannot be limited to the school alone.

Therefore, one focus of further research would be to encourage schools to develop better strategies to reach all parents. For example, schools must utilize parents as teachers in the home. Teachers could take advantage of parent involvement at home by providing parents with the yearly academic plan. Parents could also be provided with schoolwork-related activities that the parent and child could work on at home. These activities would allow parents to be more involved with the child's education.

In this study, African-American mothers expressed concern that schools are not sensitive enough to the cultural backgrounds of their children. They perceive their children's schooling experiences to be tainted with racial and cultural insensitivity. They are concerned that cultural awareness may not be part of the schools' educational plan. Teachers may not be adjusting classroom activities to reflect the culture of African-American children, as evidenced by each mother's expression of desire for a multicultural curriculum.

The mothers profiled in this study feel that schools should teach students to be responsible citizens. These mothers report that schools failed to teach all children to respect different cultural backgrounds of people, which often creates racial conflict for these children. These mothers feel that this would not be the case if school officials would incorporate multicultural education as a part of the general curriculum.

There is also a concern that schools do not feel responsible to children for multicultural education. Mrs. Dunn mentioned that she feels that schools expect African-American mothers to teach black history to their children. Mothers acknowledge that the school attempts to recognize Black History Month, but this appears not to have a long-lasting effect on children.

Prior research indicates that schools must incorporate multicultural curricula in order to encourage positive attitudes toward people of color (Comer, 1980; Edwards, 1993; Irvine, 1990; Ogbu, 1990). Although parents might function as decision makers giving input on curriculum matters, this role is not often practiced by parents or encouraged by schools (Chrispeels, 1993; Comer, 1986; Epstein and Dauber, 1991; Irvine, 1990). African-American parents must take disproportionate responsibility for making students aware of the contributions members of their race have made to society (Comer, 1980, 1988; Hale-Benson, 1986).

Future research and schools need to recognize the importance of multicultural education as part of the general curriculum. Involving parents in the design of programs that teach cultural awareness could lead to a collaboration between parents and schools. Parents could also send suggestions and materials on cultural awareness to school for teachers to use in the classroom. This parent-teacher partnership could go a long way toward reducing conflicts between African-American students and their peers and teachers pertaining to multicultural issues. Such partnerships are essential for building a better connection between homes and schools.

Involvement of Parents in School Selection

This chapter found that mothers attempt to place their children in a safe, nurturing environment. They want their children in schools that consider individual needs, as well as encourage participation in schooling processes for all parents, regardless of race. Mrs. Ashly, in particular, is constantly monitoring her children's school experiences, making sure that the environment is supportive and nurturing. Deciding which schools better serve the needs of African-American children and those that validate the presence of parents was a key role and practice for all mothers in this study.

Parents tended to choose schools that were recommended by another African-American parent, identifying good schools as those that encourage parent participation at any level, consider their children's needs, are safe places to leave their children, and strive to develop a collaboration between home and school. There are repeated reports that African-American children are treated differently by both school officials and their peers. Differential treatment may be the result of the child's behavior or to the limited number of African Americans in the local community. As a result, Mrs. Dunn is very concerned about the schools her children attend and spends time choosing schools that offer a safe environment for her children.

Giving parents choices in selecting schools has proven to be helpful in developing positive interactions between parents and schools (Jackson and Cooper, 1989). There are also reports of positive relationships between parents and schools when schools respect African Americans' cultural background, learning styles, and languages (Brice-Heath, 1989). Research confirms that parent involvement in school selection is increasing and that African-American parents are searching for schools that are safe and nurturing environments for their children (Comer, 1980; Lightfoot, 1981).

African-American parents have become increasingly involved in selecting schools for their children. Schools that provide more opportunities for students to learn about the cultures of all people are likely to be the schools chosen by proactive African-American parents. Administrators could do more to build programs within schools that attract all parents and students regardless of their racial backgrounds, rather than losing potential students to schools that are more responsive to the needs of our diverse society. Research should study how parents' choice in selecting a school affects their children's academic, social, and emotional adjustment in school.

CONCLUSION

This study, like others on African-American parent involvement, tends to confirm that African-American parents care about their children's success in school and are involved both at home and at school to support their children. The in-depth and qualitative nature of this study contributes specific details about African-American parents' perceptions of ideal and actual involvement, and adds insights about how middle-class African-American parents, a group not well represented in the literature, are involved.

There are, however, several limitations to this study that must be considered. First, the small sample size, the geographic confines of the study, and the limited number of interviews of only one group of African-American parents mean that the findings cannot be generalized to other groups of African-American parents or to other parts of this country. The sample represented in this study is unique in that African Americans comprise less than three percent of the school population. The children in this study stand out in their school, a factor that both hinders and contributes to their parents' involvement (Slaughter, 1986). A second feature of this sample is that all of the African-American mothers represented are middle class, either with a college degree or some college education. They all had high regard for education and expected their children to attend college.

A related limitation is the researcher's biases and subjectivity. However, to safeguard accuracy of the interview data, the transcriptions of the interviews were given to the mothers to corroborate the data. The mothers were also given the case studies (the researcher's interpretation of the data), with opportunities to respond to the analyses. These strategies helped to validate the data collected. In addition, the researcher brought to the study experience as a qualitative methodologist, knowledge of the literature on home-school relations, and experience as a parent and educator.

Because of the general limitation of ethnographic research, additional studies about African-American families from different geographic areas and from different economic and educational levels will be needed to corroborate the findings from this study. A collection and comparison of similar studies will compensate for the limits of the individual studies and will provide more generalizable findings and a more complete picture of African-American parent involvement. No single study can capture the multiple voices that are represented in the population of African-American parents. The rich diversity and complexity of this group of parents will best be represented by the accumulation of a substantial body of qualitative data.

When parents and schools come together to make decisions about children's schooling, there are positive results. Parents and schools must learn effective means of collaborating in order to minimize problems and misunderstandings.

Future research might investigate how parents want to be involved with the education of their children. In addition, qualitative research of this nature should be done with African-American families because very little has been done to date. Research should also investigate the effects of socioeconomic status on parent involvement. The dual influences of race and class on African Americans must be made visible to gain a more comprehensive understanding of their lived experiences. In this study, race is a factor that affects parent participation. However, it is possible that socio-economic status may have a greater effect on how parents of all races are involved with their children's schooling.

REFERENCES

Barnes, R. A. (1994). *African-American parents' involvement in their children's schooling.* Unpublished doctorial dissertation, University of California, Santa Barbara.

Becker, H. J. (1982). *Parents' responses to teachers' parent involvement practices.* Paper presented at the annual meeting of the American Educational Research Association, New York.

Berger, E. H. (1987). *Parents as partners in education.* Columbus, OH: Merrill.

Berger, E. H. (1991). Parent involvement: Yesterday and today. *The Elementary School Journal, 91,* 209–219.

Boutte, G. (1992). Frustrations of an African-American parent: A personal and professional account. *Phi Delta Kappan, 74,* 786–788.

Boykin, A. W. (1986). The triple quandary and the schooling of Afro-American children. In U. Neisser (Ed.), *The school achievement of minority children* (pp. 57–92). Hillsdale, NJ: Lawrence Erlbaum.

Brice-Heath, S. (1989). Oral and literate traditions among black Americans living in poverty. *American Psychologist, 44,* 367–373.

Chrispeels, J. (1993). *Using an effective schools framework to build home-school partnership for students' success.* Paper presented at the National Center for Effective Schools, Wisconsin Center for Education Research, Madison.

Clark, K. B. (1977). *Social science and the courts. Educational Forum, 41* (3), 281–288.

Clark, M. (1976). *The effects of teacher practice on student learning and attitude in small group instruction.* Technical Report No. 47.

Clark, R. (1983). *Family life and school achievement: Why poor black children succeed or fail.* Chicago: University of Chicago Press.

Comer, J. P. (1980). *School power.* New York: Free Press.

Comer, J. P. (1984). Home-school relationships as they affect the academic success of children. *Education and Urban Society, 16*(3), 323–337.

Comer, J. P. (1986). Parent participation in the schools. *Phi Delta Kappan 67,* 442–446.

Comer, J. P. (1988). Educating poor minority children. *Scientific American, 259,* 42–48.

Edwards, P. R. (1993). Before and after school desegregation: African-American parents' involvement in schools. *Educational Policy, 7,* 340–369.

Epstein, J. L. (1984). *Effects on parents of teacher practices in parent involvement.* Baltimore, MD: Johns Hopkins University, Center for Social Organization of Schools.

Epstein, J. L. (1986). Parents' reactions to teacher practices of parent involvement. *The Elementary School Journal, 86,* 277–294.

Epstein, J. L. (1987). What principals should know about parent involvement. *Principal, 8,* 4–9.

Epstein, J. L. (1990). School and family connections: Theory, research, and implications for integrating sociologies of education and family. In D. Unger and M.

Sussman (Eds.), *Families in community settings: Interdisciplinary perspectives* (pp. 99–1126). New York: Haworth Press.

Epstein, J. L. and Dauber, S. L. (1991). School programs and teacher practices of parent involvement in inner-city elementary and middle schools. *The Elementary School Journal, 91,* 289–305.

Hale-Benson, J. E. (1986). *Black children: Their roots, culture, and learning styles* (2nd ed.). Baltimore, MD: Johns Hopkins University Press.

Haynes, N., Comer, J., and Hamilton-Lee, M. (1989). School-climate enhancement through parent involvement. *Journal of School Psychology, 27,* 87–90.

Henderson, A. T., Marburger, C. L., and Ooms, T. (1986). *Beyond the bake sale: An educator's guide to working with parents.* Columbia, MD: National Committee for Citizens in Education.

Herman, J. L. and Yeh, J. P. (1983). Some effects of parent involvement in school. *The Urban Review, 15,* 11–17.

Hester, H. (1989). Start at home to improve home-school relations. *NASSP Bulletin, 73,* 23–27.

Hoover-Dempsey, K. V., Bassler, O. C., and Brissie, J. S. (1987). Parent involvement: Contributions of teacher efficacy, school socioeconomic status, and other school characteristics. *American Educational Research Journal, 24,* 417–435.

Hudley-Paul, C. A. and Barnes, R. A. (1994, April). *Home-school partnership through the eyes of parents.* Paper presented at the annual meeting of the American Educational Research Association, New Orleans.

Irvine, J. J. (1990). *Black students and school failure. Policies, practices, and prescriptions.* New York: Greenwood.

Jackson, B. L. and Cooper, B. S. (1989). Parent choice and empowerment: New roles for parents. *Urban Education, 24,* 263–286.

Leler, H. (1983). Parent education and involvement in relation to the schools and to parents of school-aged children. In R. Haskins and D. Adams (Eds.), *Parents' education and public policy* (pp. 144–180). Norwood, NJ: Ablex.

Lightfoot, S. L. (1978). *Worlds apart: Relationships between families and schools.* New York: Basic Books.

Lightfoot, S. L. (1981). Toward conflicts and resolutions: Relationships between families and schools. *Theory into Practice, 20,* 97–104.

Liontos, L. B. (1992). *At-risk families and schools: Becoming partners.* Eugene, OR: ERIC Clearinghouse on Educational Management, College of Education, University of Oregon.

Ogbu, J. (1974). *The next generation: An ethnography of education in an urban neighborhood.* New York: Academic Press.

Ogbu, J. (1990). Overcoming racial barriers to equal access. In J. Goodland (Ed.), *Access to knowledge* (pp. 59–98). New York: College Entrance Examination Board.

Powers, T. J. (1985). Perceptions of competence: How parents and teachers view each other. *Psychology in the School, 22,* 68–78.

Reynolds, A. J. (1989). A structural model of first-grade outcome for an urban, low socioeconomic status, minority population. *Journal of Educational Psychology, 11,* 49–67.

Rich, D. (1988). Bridging the gap in education reform. *Educational Horizons, 66,* 90–92.

Shade, B. J. (1986). Social psychological characteristics of achieving black children. *Negro Educational Review, 29,* 80–86.

Slaughter, D. T. (1986). *Children's peer acceptance and parental involvement in desegregated private elementary schools.* Paper presented at the meeting of the American Educational Researcher Association, San Francisco.

Slaughter, D. T. and Kuehne, V. S. (1988). Improving black children's education: Perspectives on parent involvement. *The Urban League Review, 11,* 59–75.

Strauss, A. and Corbin, J. (1990). *Basic qualitative research: Grounded theory procedures and techniques.* Newbury Park, CA: Sage.

Swap, S. (1993). *Developing home-school partnerships.* New York: Teachers College Press.

Taylor, A. R. (1991). Social competence and the early school transition: Risk and protective factors for African-American children. *Education and Urban Society,* 24(1), 15–26.

Thomas, A. and Chess, S. (1977). *Temperament and development.* New York: Brunner/Mazel.

10 CHESTNUT RIDGE LEARNING CENTER

A THEORY PUT INTO PRACTICE

Katherine Higginbotham

Thirty-one miles southeast of Knoxville, Tennessee, lies the tranquil county of Loudon. It is a small county, 240 square miles comprised of gentle, tree-covered mountains and numerous waterways.

The Tennessee Statistical Abstract 1994/95 indicates that 66.6 percent of the total population of 31,255 live in a rural setting (pp. 32, 39). As of 1990, 19.1 percent of the population 25 years old or older had an education level of less than ninth grade. Only 9.6 percent of the population had attained a bachelor's degree or higher (p. 657).

Information provided by the East Tennessee Development District (1995) indicates that Loudon County enjoys a low unemployment rate. Unemployment for the fourth quarter of 1994 was 3.3 percent. This figure is below the state and national levels for the same period. However, the per capita income for 1992 (most recent data given) was $15,569. This figure is also below the state and national levels. These figures are explained by the fact that over half the population is employed in trade or service positions, the two lowest paying industries.

DeYoung's research on rural school systems shows that high school graduation rates are lower in areas where most employment opportunities are not dependent upon formal education (DeYoung, 1994). Loudon County was no stranger to this fact. In 1990 the county school board was facing a 30 percent drop-out rate. This problem was one of the five areas identified as in critical need of attention when the school board developed their state-mandated five-year plan. The board recognized that the conventional high school curriculum was not working for these students and they needed to do something different.

A committee comprised of teachers, school board members, and faculty and administrators from the University of Tennessee at Knoxville began developing the idea of an alternative high school. Using the latest research, a program was devised that called for team integrated instruction, with two teachers taking one class all the way through their high school academic subjects, a pass/fail method of grading, team learning, the use of technology in the classroom, incorporating vocational classes and on-the-job training, and a mentor program.

Increased scholastic demands from the state had left little time for the county's students to pursue shop class electives, which were taught at an off-site campus. The declining enrollment in the trades programs left a school building virtually empty. The little-used site provided the perfect place to set up this new program, and Chestnut Ridge Learning Center (CRLC) was born.

Public interest in the new program was high. A public forum held to give people information about the school drew several hundred participants.

The new school opened its doors to its first class of 60 ninth grade students in the fall of 1992. These students came to the school on a voluntary basis. Most of the students were referred by their teachers and/or principals. All were selected because they had multiple factors that identified them as being at risk for dropping out of high school. The plan was to add a new ninth grade class in each subsequent year until the full range of grades nine through 12 was achieved. Once the first ninth grade class graduated, the first two teachers would go back and pick up the incoming ninth grade students for the following year, and the cycle would begin again.

In the spring of the second year of the school's existence, when the school was comprised of ninth and tenth grade students, a survey ["the survey"] was completed by 85 students. Also, five of the tenth grade students were interviewed anonymously in groups of two and three. The results of the survey and the interviews will be interspersed throughout the remainder of this chapter. The school principal, Mr. Davis, the assistant principal, Betty Galyon, the guidance counselor, Carol Beilharz, and the supervisor of Special Education for Loudon County, Dr. Gary Dutton, were all interviewed in July, 1995. Each contributed greatly to the content of this work.

THREE SCHOOLS IN ONE

CRLC is really three programs in one school. In addition to the alternative high school, there is a WAVE program and a special education resource program.

WAVE is the acronym for Work, Achievement, Values and Education. It is a program designed for kids who have already dropped out of school or who have made the decision that they are going to leave school. WAVE graduated 22 students its first year, 46 students its second year, and 38 students in the spring of 1995. As of early August, 1995, 29 seniors are registered for the 1995–96 school year, and the staff expects that more will be enrolled by the time school begins.

The Special Education program has more than 60 students. Thirty are integrated into the regular classrooms with minimal modification of the curriculum. Approximately seven are severely disabled and receive special instruction tailored to their individual needs. Thirty are in a resource classroom where their basic instruction consists of being taught life skills.

While the focus of this chapter is on the alternative high school program, it is important that the reader is aware of the existence of these other two programs since the three programs do not function independently of one another. The principal, Mr. Davis, spoke of how the kids in the alternative high school program "are very protective of children that have low ability. They won't allow anyone to mistreat a Special Ed kid." The student interviews confirmed this statement. Following is what two of the students had to say about the kids in the Special Education program:

Student 1: "We involve the special kids in every grade."

Student 2: "Instead of like . . . at the other schools, in their yearbook they would have a couple of them in there, in our yearbook, that we had last year, they were in everything!"

Interviewer: "What have you learned by having this interaction with Special Ed kids?"

Student 1: "When I was at [former school], I always thought that they were just like people that you didn't get around or anything like that. But then when I came here the first thing Tom Black [name changed], he's got Down's syndrome, he tickles me to death, first thing he just came up and put his arm around me and said, ' I love you.' He is the sweetest thing. I'll tell you what, the school wouldn't be the same without him."

Student 2: "First, when I saw them I kinda felt sorry for them cause I know what people do to them and everything. Then you come in here and they're so independent, you know, and they are so proud of themselves. Our first year out here we taught [a Special Education student] how to ride a bicycle."

The survey gives us the following picture of the student population during the 1993–1994 school year. The students ranged in age from 14 to 18, and the modal age was 16. Forty-three of the respondents were in ninth grade and 42 were in tenth grade. The student body is predominantly male. Females comprise only 24.7 percent of the population. 98.8 percent of the students are white and 1.2 percent are African American. (This racial imbalance may seem startling to readers from more urban areas; however, it is consistent with the county statistics provided by the Tennessee Statistical Abstract, wherein one percent of the total population in 1990 was African American and 98.3 percent of the population was white.)

The survey asked about the education level attained by the student's parents. Of the 78 students that responded to the question regarding their father's education, 21.8 percent did not know. That left 61 students that did know their father's education level and they indicated the following: 44.3 percent of their fathers have an 11th grade education or less, 39.3 percent completed 12th grade, and 16.4 percent had at least some formal education beyond high school.

Eighty-one students responded to the question regarding their mother's education level. Of that group 16 percent did not know about their mother's education. Of the 68 students who provided concrete information, 47 percent reported that their mothers have an 11th grade education or less, 34 percent that their mothers completed high school, and 19 percent that their mothers had at least some college education.

The survey did not ask about family income levels. However, the statistics provided earlier would indicate that the county as a whole has a majority of residents in the lower socio-economic level. The school administrators support this assumption and estimate that 75 percent of the students are eligible for the reduced rate or free lunch and fees program. It has not gone unnoticed that on Mondays, regardless of the menu, the cafeteria has few if any leftovers.

All 85 students provided information regarding their parents' marital status: 55.3 percent reported that their parents were married, 38.8 percent that they were divorced; 4.7 percent of parents were widowed, and 1.2 percent were never married. Eighty-four of the students contributed information regarding their living arrangements: 47.6 percent live with both parents; 19 percent live with their mother; four percent live with their father; 17.9 percent are living with one biological parent and step-parent; 3.6 percent are living with both divorced parents through a joint custody arrangement; and 7.1 percent report that they live with "other" people such as friends or extended family members.

The Program

As mentioned earlier, the original plan called for two teachers to teach one class all of the academic requirements from ninth through 12th grade. However, as the first class of ninth grade students prepares to begin their senior year, the program has been modified. The senior year includes on-the-job training, so the administration felt that it was not necessary to provide two teachers to teach the senior academic course requirements. Therefore, the teachers who began the program will be picking up a new class of ninth graders in the fall of 1995, and the seniors will have one new teacher to get them through their remaining course work.

The administration and staff are continually striving to close the gap between vocational education and academic education. They are developing ways to instruct the children in the team concept in response to input from industry. The students enjoy this approach, saying that "if one gets it and another gets something else, then we can put it all together!" This cooperative learning experience seems to impart a sense of belonging and also accomplishment, a theme repeated in many other areas of the school experience.

Social activities are an evolving part of the program. The principal has been known to announce that regular activities will cease in half an hour and they will have a dance in the middle of the day. Students are responsive to the spontaneity and the break from their routine. Davis says, "We are always trying to think of something new and different to engage the children." Social activities are stressed because so many of the students at CRLC have been excluded from such activities in the past. Social skills training is also emphasized because so many students were found to be seriously lacking in this area. A very poignant story was told of a student being taken to lunch by a staff member of the county department of education. The student and a couple of others were taken to a local family-style restaurant. The student told the staff member, "You'll have to order for me, I've never been out to eat." And recognizing that his inexperience could be a source of embarrassment, the student added, "Don't let me mess up."

The use of technology is an important component in CRLC's program. Each grade level has a computer lab equipped with enough computers so that each student has one to use for the class period. Videos, laser discs, and television monitors are also integrated into the classroom instruction. A student explains how the process works:

Like with science, they don't give us a textbook. Like we're watching "Trials of Life" we're actually going to see the animals and what goes on, and [then] write a report about it and type it up on the computer.

A new instructor with a background in radio has agreed to create a program that will allow students to produce the school news. They will get a weather board, and they will include some current events as well as school events and birthdays. The production will be taped and then aired on the televisions in each classroom. Davis and Galyon see this as an opportunity to increase the budding broadcasters' self-esteem and improve their public speaking abilities.

Students at CRLC are allowed to take most of their elective subjects in vocational education. The former vocational school setting provides many opportunities that would not be available to them at conventional high schools. The students can learn machining, welding, auto mechanics, and auto body repair, subjects typical of most vocational programs. They can also take graphic arts, cosmetology, builder's trades, commercial foods, and childcare and guidance.

The graphic arts program operates a full-service print shop. The students learn how to do computer typesetting, burn plates, develop photographs, and run printing presses. The local sheriff's department, area police departments, most of the local government agencies, and other schools are among their regular customers.

The childcare and guidance program provides training in caring for young children in a daycare setting. The on-site nursery has room for five infants. The beds are usually full with children of CRLC students, because of a high teenage pregnancy rate. Toddlers and preschool-age children are also cared for at the site. A government Head Start school is being built adjacent to CRLC's campus. There are plans for the childcare and guidance students to get on-the-job training at that facility when it opens.

The commercial foods program operates the school cafeteria. The students are involved in every aspect of the operation from menu planning, through preparation and serving, right down to cleanup. When Head Start opens, the commercial foods students will also provide meals for the children in that program.

The cosmetology program covers all aspects of that vocation. Students who so desire can get sufficient training at CRLC to be eligible to take the state cosmetology licensing exam when they graduate. Personal hygiene is also taught in this program. While most of us take this type of training for granted, CRLC staff found many students had inadequate information in this area.

The builder's trades program has made the most visible impact on the school. That program is responsible for redesigning existing space, creating new classrooms from old, and building the cafeteria. Plans are in the works for the students to build a modular office, complete with fittings for plumbing, which could be set up on a lot for use as headquarters for a business such as used car sales. The finished office would be displayed at a local commercial area and offered for sale.

Davis feels that the vocational programs are successful because they are hands-on. All of the programs are activity oriented. In the past, being active is what got many of these students in trouble. The command to "shut up, sit down and be still" is not part of the CRLC ideology. In fact, CRLC is not a quiet school. But it is not a place of chaos either. The noise and activity are the result of students being actively engaged in learning. This is a curriculum that works for these students and they recognize the difference. As one student noted, "We're not the traditional form of actual student. We're different. This school is different. It suits us. Everything about this school is made to suit us."

A typical day at CRLC begins with homeroom. From 9:00 a.m. until 11:20 a.m. students attend either vocational or academic classes. Lunch activity is scheduled from 11:20 a.m. until 12:20 p.m. During this time the students are divided into two groups. Each group is allotted thirty minutes for lunch. The remaining half hour is devoted to participation in a number of activities. Subdivided into approximately 15 groups, the students pursue their physical education credits or other activities that are just for fun. The remaining block of time from 12:20 p.m. until 2:50 p.m. is used for academic or vocational instruction.

The academic teachers divide the courses. One teacher focuses on science and math and the other on English and social studies. They work cooperatively to coordinate the use of the block of time. One teacher may need the entire block one day this week and the other may need it the following week.

Extended school is held during the month of June to allow students time to complete assignments that they did not complete during the regular school year. Summer school also provides an opportunity for students to make up missing credits or advance their studies in order to graduate early. Students have until graduation time to complete all the requirements to receive their diplomas.

Grade cards do not contain letter grades. Progress is rated as satisfactory or unsatisfactory. Courses are completed with either pass or fail ratings. This unconventional grading system has caused confusion for some parents, and the staff has devised a method for interpreting the report cards into letter grades when necessary.

Each spring an Awards Day is held. Teachers can give awards for anything they want and they can give as many as they want. Students receive a nicely printed parchment award for being most courteous, most improved, most helpful, or whatever the teacher designates. This is a special event for these children, as most have never received such acknowledgement before. Davis states, "They are not blown out of the water by the ten top honor students. They don't feel threatened by high academic kids. They are all in the boat together."

Davis says that there is very little fighting at the school. He feels there is less at CRLC than at the regular high schools, and he attributes this achievement to the high amount of communication between the staff and students. The school administration has an "open door" policy. Office doors are left open and students know they are welcome to drop in to talk when they have a problem or an issue to discuss, or just to say "hi!"

When it is necessary to discipline students, Davis uses what he calls "discipline with dignity." The school does not use corporal punishment. Davis feels that the students understand that they have done something wrong and that there are consequences for that behavior, but it is past and the offense is not held against them in the future.

The students had the following to say about discipline at CRLC:

Student 1: "Like if you get in a fight here, the teachers would talk to you and, you know, try to calm everything down and make sure it's not going to happen again. [Other high schools] if you get in a fight you are out. You're suspended."

Student 2: "When they come back they're just gonna beat each other up again. Here they try to counsel the people. First one student goes in to Mr. Davis and tells his side of the story, then the other person involved tells his side of the story, then both go into his office together. And he says, 'Well, you all did fight, so do you want in-school?' He will give them a choice, that I know of, I've never been suspended."

Student 1: "In other schools they give you a book of rules and the teachers will have them on the wall. Here we don't see none of them posters. They treat us like we want to be treated, you know. But if we start being like kindergarteners, they treat you like kindergarteners. It's a lot better."

Davis sets a personal goal of trying to contact as many students and/ or their parents as he can throughout the school year and during the summer to tell them good things about the student. He reports that this usually comes as a shock. Most families have experienced being contacted by the school system to be informed about problems with the student. It is a new experience to hear that the student is doing a good job and the staff is enjoying having him or her in their school.

THE STAFF

Of course the success of this school rests squarely on the shoulders of the administrators and teachers and their ability to turn the idea into a reality. This school takes the team teaching and learning concepts it promotes and applies them to their own method of operation. Recognizing the importance of cohesiveness between the teachers that will be teamed, teachers become a part of an interviewing panel that considers all future prospective teachers. There is a strong emphasis on finding teachers that really care about young people. A teaching position at CRLC goes beyond academic or vocational training—these teachers all serve as guidance counselors in one way or another. Davis feels that finding teachers with this special compassion for children has been the biggest asset of the whole program. He states, "The most successful teachers are those that are relentless, they never give up on a kid. Most of our students have already had someone wash their hands of them. Many of their parents have washed their hands of them. The kids are used to that approach. It's really tough for them to manage a teacher that just keeps on coming."

The students are responsive to this intense involvement. The interviews with the students are filled with comments such as, "my teachers are there for me"; "they understand a lot more than at my other school"; and "they take the time to listen." One student expressed his appreciation for his teacher's efforts as follows:

The teachers, they're there for you and more. They show me I can do it. My other teachers said if you didn't do it the first time, then you weren't going to do it at all. [CRLC teachers] always give you a chance to try again. That's another reason I like it.

Another student observed:

Chestnut Ridge teachers are more involved. They can do more one-on-one student/teacher help that the other [school] could not. My other school was totally opposite. The teachers didn't care about you personally. They only cared about getting their money and getting you *out* of their class. Chestnut Ridge is better.

Davis notes that many students identify with one teacher as "my teacher." Once they do connect with a particular teacher, they become very protective of that person.

The school guidance counselor works with agencies such as the Department of Human Services, Omnivision, Overlook Mental Health, juvenile court, and The Children's Plan to assist in providing additional needed services to the student. As the total school enrollment is now approaching 300 students, the counselor is not able to stay involved as easily as when enrollment rates were lower. However, the agency workers check with her regularly and she, in turn, checks with the student's teacher and reports back to the worker.

THE MENTOR PROGRAM

Though not official employees of the Loudon County school system, the mentor program volunteers are an important component of CRLC. The mentor program was created to provide additional one-on-one experience for the students. Mentors serve as tutors, confidants, and friends. The children that participate in the program are referred to the program by their teachers. It is a voluntary process and the selected children are urged to give the program a try if they seem hesitant. Most tutors work exclusively with one student. However, some mentors provide group instruction with up to four students.

The volunteers make a commitment to participate in the program for the entire school year. The mentors come to the school at their convenience. A schedule does exist, but it is not always followed due to the continuing evolution of the larger school program and the private demands of the individual volunteers.

Mentoring sessions usually take place during school hours and on campus. However, some mentors do take their students on special outings off campus. For example, a husband and wife serving as mentors have frequently combined their sessions with their respective students and have taken them on outings to local museums and boating places.

The first pool of 15 mentors was provided by the Tennessee Valley Authority (TVA). As a part of TVA's community outreach programs, the company provided a coordinator to recruit volunteers and organize the program.

Prior to the beginning of the second year of the program, its direction was turned over to CRLC's guidance counselor. The counselor created her own criteria for volunteers, looking for people who have a strong interest in children and the school. The counselor focused on the volunteer's area of interest rather than his or her educational or work background.

This method produced a mentor who is a retired orthopedic surgeon with a passion for machining. This volunteer gives many hours to the metals shop program, sharing an avocation that he loves. Other volunteers have been nurses, teachers, corporate executives, an artist, a newspaper columnist, engineers, and retired military personnel.

Twenty volunteers, most from a nearby upper-middle-class retirement community, were recruited for the second year. An awards/recruiting luncheon at the end of the second year and a kick-off breakfast at the beginning of the third year brought 30 volunteers to the program for the 1994–95 school year. The guidance counselor expects an even larger group of volunteers for the upcoming school year.

A majority of the students view the program positively. The survey of the ninth and tenth grade students showed 73.7 percent of the 78 responding students felt that the mentor program was a good idea.

PUBLIC IMAGE

Faculty and staff feel that the public's negative perception of CRLC is the biggest obstacle they have to overcome. They feel that many people have formed negative opinions about the school without ever having actually visited the campus. There is a perception that it is rowdy, disruptive, and potentially dangerous. Assistant principal Galyon states that she frequently receives criticism that the students are "always outside." She quickly points out that the lack of a gym necessitates conducting physical education activities outside. The school also participates in intramural sports that must be conducted outside.

Davis and Galyon accept all invitations to speak at civic groups and other organizations in an effort to let the community know what they are doing at CRLC. Says Davis, "We'll try almost anything if it will work for our kids."

This negative community perception also touches the students. When asked what they thought was important for people to know about CRLC, one student replied, "That we are not rejects. That this is a high school." Another student wanted people to know "that we're not a bunch of losers."

The first group of students is aware of their role as pioneers in this alternative program. One student said that the scrutiny made her "want to do better."

Is It Working?

Is this alternative program making a difference for these students? The staff says the students entering 12th grade have changed dramatically since the ninth grade. Most arrived at CRLC mad at the world. Many had never had a break anywhere in their lives. CRLC has offered them a sense of belonging and an opportunity to experience success.

The survey asked the students several paired questions comparing Chestnut Ridge with their previous school experience. T-tests for paired samples were then run with a level of significance greater than .05 indicating a statistical significance. Following are the noteworthy results:

Students were asked if they get along well with their teachers at CRLC and if they got along well with their teachers at their former school. Of the 83 students that responded, 42.4 percent reported getting along well with their former teachers most of the time. This figure jumps to 72.6 percent of the students getting along well with their teachers at CRLC most of the time. 72.3 percent felt that their teachers at their former school liked them; however, 95.3 percent believed that the teachers at CRLC like them. Similarly, 68.2 percent felt that the teachers at their former school cared about them, but 90.6 percent said that they felt the teachers at CRLC cared about them.

The students were asked a number of general questions about school. With 83 students responding, 36.5 percent said that they had liked their middle school most of the time; 84.7 percent reported liking CRLC most of the time. While 54.1 percent found their former school boring most of the time, only 4.7 percent found CRLC boring most of the time. When asked if they received help at school for their problems, 64.6 percent reported receiving help at their former school, but 94.0 percent said that they received help at CRLC.

Further evidence of the success of the program is the fact that 40 students out of the first ninth grade class of 60 are on track to graduate on time. Eight of the students have graduated early. Of the 12 remaining students, two dropped out and got their GEDs; two transferred to regular high schools; two moved out of the area; one student quit, married a fellow student that graduated early, had a baby, is working full time, and is now planning on getting into the GED program; one student is in juvenile custody; one student is running from the law; and the last three quit completely. Of the last three, one student attempted to obtain a GED but was not successful, and one of the students is working full time.

When one considers the number of students that are on track to graduate or have graduated, the number that have obtained GEDs, and the number that have gone back to their regular high school, this produces a 13 percent dropout rate for the county. This is a far cry from the 30 percent dropout rate the county was experiencing four years earlier when the program began. This figure takes on greater significance when one considers that this graduation rate has been achieved by students that theoretically were headed to become part of the 30 percent dropout rate.

Perhaps the best source to answer the question regarding the success of the school is the students themselves. The last item on the survey asked the students to identify what they saw as the biggest difference between CRLC and their former schools. Following are some of their comments:

"It is more fun here."

"The teachers here are nicer and help people more."

"Chestnut Ridge Learning Center is a really good school, and to top that we got a good principal."

"Teaches you trades and you get to work on computers."

"This one is better because it helps me more than the other."

"The teachers help us a lot more and they don't go on to another subject until everyone learns that one thing and over at my other school teachers used to assign work and go over it the next day then they would go to the next lesson!"

"At my other school the teachers didn't help me and made fun of me. But here all students are treated the same."

"The people at Chestnut Ridge care about you and try to help you with your problems, and try to help you with your school work too."

"The work is not boring and I understand it better."

"CRLC is more fun and the teachers are more caring."

"I like Chestnut Ridge Learning Center because [there] are a lot of fun things to do and the work is not stressful."

"I think the most important thing about Chestnut Ridge is that we are all like one big family and we all work together in groups, and our teachers care enough to take time to show us what to do."

"Chestnut Ridge is a good place to attend when you are having difficulties in other schools."

"I feel like someone here."

Making school fun, teacher involvement, and learning useful trades are all wonderful achievements for this program. However, some may still question the level of higher learning being attained. Here is what one student has gained from CRLC:

> They help you understand that the stuff we do here is things that we're actually going to use. You know, before I never understood why we needed to learn about history. What's the point? It's past, you know, it's not going to happen again. I didn't care. It was brought up the other day at lunch with a friend of mine. She asked the same thing, she don't understand this. But, what I told her was everything that happened then reflects on now. It dictates what will happen in the future. That is one of the things I learned here.

REFERENCES

DeYoung, D. J. (1994). Schools and students at risk: Context and framework for positive change. In Robert J. Rossi (Ed.), *Children at risk in America's rural schools*, (pp. 229–251). New York: Teachers College Press.

East Tennessee Development District (1995). *Loudon County Economic Statistics— Winter 1995*. Knoxville, TN: Author.

University of Tennessee, Knoxville (1994). *Tennessee Statistical Abstract 1994/95*. Knoxville, TN: University of Tennessee, Knoxville, Center for Business and Economic Research.

11 APPALACHIAN CULTURE AND SCHOOLING

Eva Thaller

INTRODUCTION

Nature provides tremendous variety in the landscape of Appalachia. There are tall mountains, fertile valleys, and long, tenuous lakes. The four seasons provide endless variety as they slumber in winter gray and white, or blossom in dogwood pink and white, or grow green, green, green, and then blaze with brilliant foliage and tourists' brake lights.

There is even a lot of variety in the definitions of Appalachia and much dispute about where the boundaries of the region are, with the definition depending upon who is doing the defining. However, most of the more than 20 million people (Pickard, 1991) who actually live in the region do not define it at all or even call it "Appalachia"—they just call it "home." Generally Appalachia is considered to be the mountain, ridge, and valley region that stretches from Pennsylvania and southern New York state down to northern Georgia, Alabama, and Mississippi (Ergood, 1991).

Appalachia is a region characterized by striking contrasts. There are crowded cities in Appalachia but also vast expanses of wilderness. There is a rich supply of natural resources but widespread poverty. There are many highly educated residents but even more who dropped out without completing high school. There is a rush ahead to technology but a movement back to traditional handicrafts.

Traditions are often strong in Appalachia. Some of these traditions continue because people consciously want to perpetuate them, as in the case of the traditional handicrafts. Other traditions just seem to take on a life of their own and continue whether anyone wants them or not. One such "tradition" is the nature of education in the region. Traditionally the schools are not very effective, and there is still a high number of students who drop out before graduation. Under-education and dropping out seem to continue without anyone being "for" them.

Those who are considered to be Appalachians could have been (1) born and raised in the region, or (2) the children and grandchildren of Appalachians. It is in the second category that I fit. Although I was born in another state and have lived many places, currently I live on the Appalachian farm that first belonged to my great-grandparents. I moved there partly because my parents live there and partly because I have a strong attachment to the place. I love the landscape—the shady wooded cove, the gurgling spring, and the glorious view of distant mountains from the top of our ridge. I like the evidence of family history in the root cellar my grandfather dug under the smokehouse, and the rocks he hauled out of the fields and piled in the fence rows, and the crooked little house he built room by room.

Although this Appalachian neighborhood has changed greatly since I used to visit my grandparents here as a child, one aspect that has not changed is that graduating from high school is the exception rather than the rule. During the early 1900s, my grandfather was one of the few in the neighborhood who was able to attend two years of high school. At that time the only high school in the county was a boarding school at the county seat about eight miles away. During the Depression my mother could not finish her fourth year of high school because the family did not have enough money to buy her a pair of shoes. She dropped out and took a job in a factory to help support the family.

While today's schools are more accessible, transportation is provided, and there are social services to help those in dire financial straits, there is still a high dropout rate and a high rate of residents who are functionally illiterate. According to the 1990 census, about 54 percent of adults over 25 years old in our county have acquired neither a high school diploma nor a GED—the state average is about 42 percent. Of the 54 percent in our county who didn't finish, 34 percent have less than a ninth grade education, while the others entered high school but dropped out before graduation (Tennessee Literacy Coalition, 1992).

And nowadays the low educational level cannot be blamed on the Depression, or poor transportation, or lack of accessible schools. As a firm believer in the potential of education, I think the under-education is a real problem. As a permanent resident of this Appalachian neighborhood, I want to know why this problem still exists and what can be done about it. We are all in this together, and all parts affect the whole. I want some answers and some solutions. From my studies I have come to believe that at least part of the problem lies in the structure of the educational system, and at least part of the solution lies in using a cross-cultural approach to education in this region.

One problem with doing research on Appalachia is that much of the best known literature about the region is very old. Many of the really good studies were conducted decades ago, and since their publication there have been culture-shaking changes in transportation, communications, education, and the economy of Appalachia. Now there is a new generation of Appalachians that is quite different in outlook from the parents and grandparents that the published studies describe (Cox, 1988, p. 250). But in many cases there is really nothing available better than the studies done decades ago. Quite a few research studies about Appalachia have been conducted recently, but they are difficult to locate and to organize since they utilize very diverse approaches and philosophies.

In my Appalachian family the main traditional handicraft was the creation of quilts. Quilting was begun as a practical way of recycling the good fabric left in worn-out garments by using the scraps to create warm quilted bed covers, and then it evolved into a hobby and an art form. My grandmother loved making quilts. One of my earliest memories is napping under a bright quilt with butterfly appliqués she had pieced and quilted. And although she passed away many years ago, many of the quilts she made are still bright and pretty.

But in my family the art form is dying out, since very few in the younger generation of this family are involved in quilting. Although I enjoy sewing, I find that I am personally drawn more to creating quilts of words and ideas rather than fabrics. Of course, a quilt is made by sewing together small bits of fabric into larger units or "blocks." Then the blocks are sewn together into even larger units, eventually creating a large complete whole.

This chapter has been composed in much the same way. I have gathered small bits of information from various sources about concepts related to this topic and gradually pieced those together into larger units or ideas, which I arrange in various patterns to achieve the best design. Both quilters and writers have to be selective since no one creation can contain every possible piece or color. The design "blocks" comprising this verbal creation are: Physical Setting, Education in Appalachia, Cultural Diversity, Appalachian Culture and Dialect, Multicultural Education, and Successes and Suggestions for Reform.

THE PHYSICAL SETTING

Whether one takes a positive or negative view of the physical setting, few people would deny the strong influence it has had on Appalachian history and the life of the Appalachians. Jim Wayne Miller, a well-known Appalachian writer, said that he had no interest in mountains as mere landscape but in "people in their place: how they have coped, what they have come to be as a result of living in that place" (Miller, 1988, p. 85). Miller commented that the Appalachian region has had a "triple history": first, a history shared with the rest of America; second, a history shared with the rest of the South; and third, a relatively unknown history that is all its own.

Reading a book called *A Darkness at Dawn* (1976), I was intrigued by Caudill's startling comparison between the European country of Switzerland and eastern Kentucky, Caudill's home region. Caudill used eastern Kentucky for the comparison because both Switzerland and eastern Kentucky are mountainous and approximately the same size—about 15,000 square miles each—and also because the tourist industry in eastern Kentucky had started referring to the region as an American "Switzerland." Both Switzerland and eastern Kentucky are located on heavily industrialized continents where people are highly competitive. But these are about the only similarities between the two lands.

At first glance, one would not expect Switzerland to be prosperous. The soil there is very poor, with about 21 percent of it permanently covered with ice and snow. The slopes are very steep, and the forests are sparse and limited. Brine beds that are used by the chemical industry are about the only mineral resource. The country is landlocked and has to transport all goods by road or rails. Because of its location, Switzerland has had to maintain a strong military force. Since the country is surrounded by Italy, France, and Germany, school students have to study Italian, French, and German, while many rural people also speak another ancient language.

By contrast, eastern Kentucky has thick forests and rich deposits of coal. In spite of the scars of coal mining, there is still much natural beauty in the landscape. The area has a mild climate and plenty of water. The soil is rich and tillable in the bottom lands.

But there is even more contrast between the "fruits" of the two lands. The Swiss are insurance brokers and bankers on a worldwide scale, with their currency known for its stability. Their prosperity is almost total, with an annual national unemployment rate of about 50 people. There are 22 institutions of higher learning, including five top-quality medical schools. Their schools are effective, with less than one percent of all adults being illiterate. But children are in school each day only from 8 a.m. until 12:30 p.m. and are then sent home to study or to work with their parents. The Swiss armed forces are effective and efficient. Their democratic government is known for its honesty, with officials who are honest, diligent, and frugal. Switzerland has to enforce strict immigration laws because so many want to move into the country.

By contrast, people in Kentucky have been cursed by the riches of their land. Outsiders (or "furriners") bought up land or mineral rights for nearly nothing. Then the people elected officials who sided with the industrial robbers against the mountaineers. "In Kentucky politics it has become a case of the bland leading the bland, with predictably bland results" (Caudill, p. 47). The ones who prospered were the outsiders who had learned to "understand the purposes and functions of government and bend it to their purposes" (Caudill, p. 48). When this comparison was made in the 1970s, one-fifth of the adults in eastern Kentucky were illiterate, with one-third of them on relief. There has always been a constant outflow of people moving away. Caudill adds: "The Swiss mountaineers took a depressingly poor land and, by good judgment and hard work, became rich, powerful, and respected. Kentucky mountaineers took a rich land and became poor" (Caudill, p. 47).

It is probably not necessary to add that most areas of Appalachia could have been used in this comparison instead of eastern Kentucky. So while many may cite "place" as a handicap in Appalachia and encourage Appalachians to move away in order to prosper, the place itself could have been a tremendous asset if used wisely.

EDUCATION IN APPALACHIA

Traditionally, education has not worked very well in Appalachia. According to R. G. Eller (1989), "With high drop-out and illiteracy rates, the educational failure of students in the region is typical of that of other subpopulations in the nation" (p. 1). Although many social commentators have written extensively about the weaknesses of education in Appalachia, ethnographic research on education in this region is rare. A few community studies have included some observations about education, but generally these have been only limited parts of the studies. "The observations that have been made in these studies suggest that schools in Appalachia do have many of the same problems that face other schools serving more familiar ethnic groups" (Reck et al., 1987, p. 15).

Caudill (1976) charged that in spite of the good done by the schools and colleges in the region, in one sense, the Appalachian institutions of education have had calamitous effect because they have educated students only for the outside world and not for building prosperity at home. Generally the graduates have moved to urban areas where there were already large numbers of well trained workers while their homeland continued to suffer from a lack of educated leaders (Caudill, 1976).

Schools at all levels have been guilty of a colossal failure in that they do not teach and have never taught fundamental truths about the Appalachian land: how misuse of the land has led to social and economic decline for most of the inhabitants, how exploitation of the land has built great fortunes for a few, how wise use of the land might make the word "Appalachia" a synonym for progress instead of blight. The hill people probably know as little about their native heath as any folk on earth, and for the dire consequences the schools must shoulder a major share of the responsibility. (Caudill, 1996, p. 38)

Further, Caudill charged that the reason Appalachian teachers had not taught their students about the geology, natural resources, and wonders of the native woodlands was that they knew so little about these things themselves—an indictment of teacher education in the region. During the 1960s "War on Poverty,"

Colleges and universities that serve the region unwittingly did their share to perpetuate the economic distress. None hired a professor to teach a course on the economics of the Appalachian region. All continued to spread the worn myth that Appalachian people are poor because their land is poor and, by implication at least, that the wisest course is to leave. Thus indifference on campuses combined with greed in boardrooms to work the ruin of one of the fairest and most promising parts of the globe. (Caudill, 1996, p. 43)

In 1905 Emma Bell Miles wrote in *The Spirit of the Mountains*: "For although throughout the highlands of Kentucky, Tennessee, and the Carolinas our nature is one, our hopes, our loves, our daily lives the same, we are yet a people asleep, a race without knowledge of its own existence." And in many ways that is still true today. Since area schools have not helped mountain children to understand themselves, those who took "education seriously began the process of severing the organic connection between themselves and their culture" (Best, 1986, p. 49).

According to Holland, "Children in Appalachia have unique problems because teachers and principals held strong attitudes against their culture, especially concerning the children's attitude toward education, their high degree of mobility, persistent absenteeism, high drop-out rate, and cultural language problems" (Holland, 1987, p. 97). This discrimination is particularly evident in regions bordering Appalachia, where there are substantial numbers of Appalachian students mingling with larger numbers of students from other cultural groups. "Rural, poor, and Appalachian students are perceived by others to be culturally and intellectually inferior and are socially isolated in the school system" (Reck et al., 1987, p. 21). Thus we see examples of "blaming the victims" for their own problems.

When statistics on Appalachian education are quoted, they often include the rate of "functional illiteracy" as well as the dropout rate, and some of the literature about Appalachian education concerns literacy. Thus it should be helpful to understand what "literacy" and "illiteracy" mean. The literature yielded varying definitions of literacy. Freeman (1992) defined literacy as "the ability to read and write to some extent; numeracy is sometimes included in it. . . . Being literate means being able to present ideas using the written word, and understanding, storing and analyzing words to react appropriately" (pp. 216–217). Sometimes there is also an element of fluency implied; a literate person is fluent enough in reading and writing to be able to concentrate on the purpose rather than the process itself.

UNESCO (1988) defined a literate person as one "who can with understanding both read and write a short simple statement about his everyday life." UNESCO defined a "functionally literate" person as one "who can engage in all those activities in which literacy is required for effective functioning of his group and community." Thus literacy is set within a context and has a functional purpose within that context. Most of the early Appalachian literacy studies and writings were aimed at adult learners, but recently there is a trend toward referring to "early literacy" in elementary schools.

Some of the published definitions of literacy indicated that its development does not end at the end of a literacy course. For example, Freeman said, "Literacy is probably the most important foundation stone of lifelong learning. Even so, millions of people all over the world leave school never having acquired the ability to read or write" (1992, p. 78).

Freeman also mentioned the need for the content of literacy lessons to be culturally appropriate for the students:

> Good literacy teaching encourages the newly qualified to continue reading, but if the ideas presented to them differ too widely from what they already know, there may be misunderstanding, loss of interest and poor learning. Worse, it may actually widen the gap between the indigenous culture, associated with illiteracy and ignorance on the one hand, and modern society, associated with literacy, knowledge and progress on the other. (Freeman, 1992, p. 219)

One historical study that examined literacy movements in Appalachia during the early 20th century showed that designers of literacy programs need to understand the perceptions of the people who are the target audience for such programs in order to achieve success. For example, promoters of early programs often spoke of illiteracy as a stigma or a disgrace. However, this was not a motive for most of the program participants, who did not view illiteracy in this way. Instead they saw literacy as a means to an end. Literacy would allow them to write their own correspondence, conduct their own business without fear of being cheated, vote by themselves, etc. (Estes et al., 1987).

FROM BLAMING THE VICTIM TO CHANGING THE SYSTEM

The process applied to almost every American social problem, from public health to anti-poverty programs, from social welfare to under-education in Appalachia has traditionally been what Ryan (1976) called "Blaming the Victim." The process happens so smoothly that it seems downright rational, a logical plan of action that appears genuinely altruistic and humanitarian at first glance. Ryan outlined four steps in the formula for Blaming the Victim:

1. Identify a social problem, which is easy since social problems exist in great abundance.

2. Study people affected by the problem and find out how they differ from "typical" people in the population who don't have the problem.

3. Define the differences in the people as the cause of the social problem itself.

4. Assign a government bureaucrat to invent a program to correct the differences in the people. (Ryan, 1976)

Thus many programs which were supposed to "solve" social problems in America were based on the assumption that individuals "have" social problems because of some kind of unusual circumstances; some accident, illness, personal defect or handicap has kept the individuals from using the usual mechanisms for success. The effort was aimed at changing the people to fit within the system. And the process of victim blaming has mainly worked to block any real social change.

The "victims" in this society are not just those who are officially below the poverty level or those who are non-white. At least two-thirds or three-fourths of all Americans could be potential victims. Anyone who depends on salary and wages and does not have a separate source of income through some substantial wealth is potentially a victim in America, since all of us are somewhat vulnerable to inflation, unemployment, unfair taxes, environmental pollution, catastrophic illnesses, traffic accidents, and the greed of large corporations (Ryan, 1976).

For decades Blaming the Victim has been the dominant style in American social welfare. At the same time there has been a competing style of action which springs from a different paradigm or view of the world. Change agents with this view searched for defects in the community or the environment rather than in the individual people. Instead of trying to change people to fit the system, they changed the system to accommodate more kinds of people. The difference between the two paradigms can be illustrated by varying approaches to health problems. For example, victim blamers might deal with smallpox by providing remedial treatment to the afflicted people through an arrangement with a local doctor. The opposite approach was followed by public health agents who "changed the system" by providing preventive smallpox inoculation to the total population (Ryan, 1976).

Of course, Blaming the Victim has also been practiced widely in our educational system. The problem was obvious: thousands of children were dropping out of school and thousands of graduates were still illiterate. But the victims—the mis-educated children—were blamed for their own mis-education. The victim blamers thought that these children contained within themselves the causes of their failure to become literate. In the 1950s educationists devised the term "cultural deprivation," which implied that lower-class children did not bring with them enough intellectual baggage as they entered school. Such "culturally deprived" children had no books or newspapers in the home. If they talked at all, they did not talk correctly; they used some non-standard dialect of English. The expectations of their teachers were low because the students came from culturally deprived backgrounds (Ryan, 1976).

Thus cultural deprivation became a catch-all excuse for the failure of so many schools. It was interesting that one of the few places where I found Appalachian children mentioned specifically in the general education literature was in published proceedings of a national conference on "Education for the Culturally Disadvantaged." The conference dealt with "poverty subcultures" which included "White Anglo-Saxon people, mainly located in the Appalachian and Ozark mountains" (SCREL, 1967).

During the cultural deprivation era, the victim blamers saw that middle-class children were better prepared for school than lower-class children. And so they established programs of "compensatory education" to build up the attitudes and skills of the lower-class children. In fact, programs such as Head Start did help children in the primary years, but their edge on success wore off after a few grades because no basic changes had been made in the structure of the schooling experience. The victim blamers saw that middle-class children were better prepared for school than lower-class children, but they failed to see the reverse view: that schools were better prepared for middle-class children than for lower-class children (Ryan, 1976). Ryan wrote,

> We are dealing, it would seem, not so much with culturally deprived children as with culturally depriving schools. And the task to be accomplished is not to revise, and amend, and repair deficient children but to alter and transform the atmosphere and operations of the schools to which we commit these children. Only by changing the nature of the educational experience can we change its product. (Ryan, 1976, p. 61)

Thus, education in Appalachia can be more effective if the move is completely away from Blaming the Victim toward changing the system. It is encouraging that educators are now beginning attempts to change the nature of the educational experience and assure success for all children. It appears that, for maximum efficiency, all restructuring efforts should take into account the cultural background of the students who will be served by a particular institution. As Cherry Banks (1993) pointed out:

> Changing schools fundamentally requires that we confront harsh reality. We must recognize that, for many low-income and minority students, there is little or no continuity between schooling and the rest of their lives. To be successful in school, they must cross barriers of language, values, cognition, and culture. Restructuring schools for equity challenges schools to establish greater congruence between themselves and students' homes. Children have a better chance of succeeding in school when such congruence exists. (Banks, 1993, pp. 42–43)

CULTURAL DIVERSITY

It seems that the first step in the process of making schools more culturally compatible is to come to understand what culture really is. A number of different definitions for culture can be found in the literature, since almost every author seems to have a different favorite definition. Caudill (1976) defined culture rather poetically:

Every person and society is a product of two factors, genes and culture. The workings of each is still poorly understood if, indeed, it is understood at all. A culture—the subconsciously and deeply ingrained "truths," mores, prejudices, biases, superstitions, and preferences that link a people together—can bind as surely as shackles of steel. But as those bonds are forged slowly over many generations so they outlast steel, enduring until their origins are lost in the shadowy mists of a common beginning. (Caudill, 1976, p. 1)

According to Brown (1963), culture is defined as:

all the accepted and patterned ways of behavior of a given people. It is a body of common understandings. It is the sum total and the organization or arrangement of all the group's ways of thinking, feeling, and acting. It also includes the physical manifestations of the group as exhibited in the objects they make—the clothing, shelter, tools, weapons, implements, utensils, and so on. (Brown, 1963, p. 3)

According to Shade (1989b), culture represents:

a group's preferred way of perceiving, judging, and organizing the ideas, situations, and events they encounter in their daily lives. It represents the rules or guidelines of a set of individuals who share a common history or geographical setting used to mediate their interaction with their environment. As such, culture might involve adherence to a specific religious orientation, use of a certain language or style of communication, as well as preferences for various expressive methods to represent their perceptions of the world, i.e., in art, music, or dance. (Shade, 1989b, p. 9)

Thus cultural groups can be bounded in many ways. It is common to think of different races as cultural groups. But it is possible to think also of religious groups as cultural groups. Additionally people who speak the same language, or dialect, often share a common culture. It is also possible to think of cultures which are groups with common life-styles based upon common experiences and understandings. Such a group could be determined by geographic considerations, such as the 20 million persons who live in Appalachia from New York to Mississippi (Baker, 1983, pp. 5–6). A culture could be the culture of a region, of a community, of a school, and even of a family.

Although there is little agreement on how to define culture, there generally is agreement on the existence of cultural diversity among citizens of the United States. "In the prevailing context of cultural pluralism there is less of a tendency to view regions and the local life of particular places as aberrant, and a greater willingness to see these as evidence of natural diversity" (Miller, 1988, p. 97).

APPALACHIAN CULTURE

Historically there has been a debate between those who saw Appalachia as "an incomplete, perhaps even deformed, version of what the nation should be" (Estes et al., 1987, p. 85) and those who saw Appalachia as a distinct region with a unique culture of its own. Since most Appalachians are in many ways similar to mainstream America—white, Anglo-Saxon, and Protestant—Appalachians have become one of the most neglected of minority groups. Porter (1981) referred to Appalachians as a people "adrift in the mainstream." Although the differences may not be immediately visible, they do differ from mainstream Americans in their history and in value orientations. In fact the value orientations and behavior patterns are often directly in opposition with those of mainstream America. One example is a mainstream emphasis on achievement and competition as opposed to the Appalachian emphasis on equality and cooperation (Porter, 1981, pp. 13–14).

A 1984 study argued that earlier studies incorrectly announced that traditional Appalachian values were dead and that mountain culture had been absorbed into mainstream modernism (Welch, 1984, p. 4). In this qualitative study, Welch concluded that aspects of the traditional highland values remained as a working force in the lives of a majority of rural mountain people. These values served as protective "buffers" against rapid change and against the detrimental aspects of mainstream culture seen as invading Appalachia (Welch, 1984).

Caudill (1976) listed several cultural traits he believed had developed as a result of the early history of the region:

1. Sense of place—a strong attachment to the land.
2. Clannishness—a strong attachment to a small community of close, intermarried families.
3. Childlike trust in others—a factor that allows outsiders to rob and exploit them.
4. Ignorance of the nature of the land itself—a factor that allows highlanders to misuse and abuse the land without realizing how disastrous consequences may be.

5. Deeply rooted mistrust of government.

6. Disregard of education—one of the factors that has kept highlanders naive and vulnerable to the problems of the outside world. (Caudill, 1976, pp. 11–20)

Some authors would probably argue with Caudill about the last trait, citing research showing that Appalachian parents have high educational aspirations for their children. And yet it is obvious that traditionally schooling has not been an extremely high priority and that many Appalachians have had low educational expectations for themselves and their children. Perhaps that is due to a lack of any relevance the highlanders have been able to see between their schooling and their life in the real world.

A 1985 ethnographic study conducted in Cincinnati by John Williams found that an oral tradition continued to play an important role in the lives of Appalachian migrants. In the conversations he recorded, many allusions to mountain traditions revealed an ethnic identity steeped in Appalachian folklore. Socio-economic conflict with other ethnic groups in Cincinnati was mentioned often and seemed to be a strong force in shaping their ethnic identity, along with the "hillbilly" stereotype (Williams, 1985).

SENSE OF PLACE

Several authors have commented about a strong sense of place in Appalachia. As Ron Eller wrote, "Whether one views place as something to be preserved or as something to be overcome, few observers would deny the central role which place has played in Appalachian history and life" (R. D. Eller, 1988, p. 3).

A popular misconception of the idea of place in Appalachia is that people are attached just to a specific parcel of land. Although mountain people may tend to be tied to a specific plot of land (the "homeplace") they are tied also to people (their kinfolks) and to memories (shared experiences). Such a sense of place is part of a larger paradigm or outlook on life that is communal rather than individualistic or self-centered (Eller, 1988, p. 4). Although many earlier writers have said that Appalachians had no sense of community, Eller proposed that a sense of place in Appalachia represents a form of community—a set of long-term relationships that bind people together. From the very beginning the early settlers were able to survive by being part of an extended community of interdependent families that helped each other.

A history professor at a small Appalachian university said the following:

The sense of place is not necessarily a positive experience . . . For more than a decade I have taken a non-binding unofficial survey of my Appalachian history students, and until recently, the number of those who cannot wait to go back to their home county and the number who cannot wait to leave their home county were in every instance, almost equal. My most recent informal poll shows would-be out-migrants to be in a majority. (Sprague, 1988, p. 25)

Right-Brain Orientation of Appalachian Culture

Bill Best (1986) commented that the key to understanding Appalachian culture was to understand the pull inside all people between right brain hemisphere and left brain hemisphere processes. Best asserted that Appalachian culture is primarily right-brain: intuitive, sensuous, and creative. The Appalachian culture "promotes intuition, inductive reasoning, sensuousness, spirituality, sensitivity and creativity in the arts, emotional bonding (especially within families), and the languages of metaphor, simile, and poetry" (Best, 1986, p. 47).

Although people who think are not a rarity in the Appalachian culture, not much time is spent in idle, abstract speculation, but rather the product of thought is usually concretely connected with real life (Best, p. 46). Appalachian people tend to be emotional and to have a feeling for artistic form expressed in such things as singing, quilting, laying out fields for planting, and special family or community rituals. Intuition is important and reasoning is generally inductive. There is a heavy reliance on oral as well as on non-verbal communication, with children being very sensitive to body language (Best, 1986).

Appalachian Dialect

People are often judged by their dialect. A study conducted by Williams (1985) of Appalachian migrants to Cincinnati confirmed the findings of sociolinguists that certain dialects are highly stigmatized and lead to sharp social stratification. A study of 65 employment recruiters showed that 58 percent of the Appalachian English variables presented to them were considered to have a negative effect on job interveiws, with nonstandard grammar judged more negatively than nonstandard pronunciation (Atkins, 1993).

But most of the educational research done on dialects spoken by school children has focused on ethnic groups other than Appalachians. For example, one research study about teachers' knowledge and attitudes toward black English showed that teachers held significantly less positive attitudes toward students who spoke black English (McCullough, 1981).

Recently a woman from a northern state who had settled in an Appalachian county told me about meeting one of her daughter's middle school classmates: "She was beautiful. When you looked at her, you thought she could be 'Miss America.' But as soon as she opened her mouth, you knew that she couldn't make it past 'Miss Ridge County' because of her accent."

CULTURAL STEREOTYPING

Of course it is important to remember that culture is a dynamic, living, ever-changing thing, not something static that has been preserved in a museum. An attachment to one's region or one's traditional culture no longer signifies "provincialism" or even isolation, since we live in a world where monks in India now copy ancient stone tablets on a Xerox copier and where Bedouins riding their camels listen to transistor radios—or perhaps portable CD players by this time (Miller, 1988).

Unfortunately, there has been a tendency to stereotype Appalachian culture, even among those who value it. After the Civil War, two different groups of flatlanders became interested in Appalachia. One group was Protestant missionaries looking for new converts. Another group was local color writers who found that superficial travel sketches about Appalachia were popular with editors. "The two groups gave Appalachia a high profile and by transmuting the atypical into the norm, stereotyped the region" (Sprague, 1988, p. 22). And to a large extent those stereotypes persist until the present day in the characters of Snuffy Smith, the Beverly Hillbillies, the Dukes of Hazard, etc.

Recently there was an interesting incident in a Miss USA pageant on television. During one of the final rounds the master of ceremonies was talking with Miss Louisiana and inquired if she happened to be Cajun. (Recently it seems to have become stylish to be Cajun.) The contestant proudly asserted that she was and demonstrated by reeling off several phrases of Cajun dialect. She was rewarded by enthusiastic applause from the audience.

At this time it is impossible to imagine a beauty contestant from one of the Appalachian states being asked, "Are you really a 'Hillbilly'?" and the contestant's responding by proudly belting out several phrases in mountain dialect. Perhaps we will have to arrive at such a point of cultural pride before much real progress can be made.

MULTICULTURAL EDUCATION

The earliest educational programs that dealt with cultural diversity were outcomes of the civil rights movement in the 1960s and 1970s. But many of the reforms of that era failed to become institutionalized, and multicultural education programs all but disappeared from some areas. Lately there has been increasing recognition of American cultural diversity and a renewed interest in multicultural education. Baker (1983) commented about the need for a multicultural approach to education:

> The public school, because of its nature, is expected to address the educational needs of all learners. Past attempts have failed to provide the type of learning that took into consideration the diverse background of the students. Schools were designed to pay particular attention to the needs of one group of students; these students represented the mainstream of life in the United States and the schools failed to make adjustments for those whose lifestyles differed from the mainstream. (Baker, 1988, p. 8)

The recognition of cultural differences helps determine if an educational program will enable or disable students. Enabling educational programs "work with students and their home communities to build on what they bring; disabling programs ignore and attempt to eradicate knowledge and strengths students bring, and replace them with those of the dominant society" (Sleeter, 1991, p. 5). Baker (1983) outlined three main goals of multicultural education:

1. To become aware of oneself, one's culture and /or cultures, and ways to function within the larger society.
2. To develop an appreciation of other cultures. Since peoples of the world are bound together within the "system," survival depends on how well we can live together. Also understanding the ways of others increases self-knowledge and objectivity.
3. "To encourage individuals to support and to participate in as many cultural groups as they choose. Multicultural education encourages the freedom of individuals to maintain the lifestyles, values, and beliefs of any ethnic and/or cultural groups they choose to be a part of." (Baker, 1983, pp. 4–6)

As Baker (1983) mentioned, one of the important functions of multicultural education is to make students aware of their own culture. Ferguson (1987) explained the importance of such awareness:

> Culture is almost impossible for one to identify or recognize on one's own. Culture has been learned from earliest infancy and most cul-

tural learning is firmly planted even before the first day of school. Culture has become sublimated. It is not something that easily comes to the surface in an individual in a conscious manner. It is almost impossible to learn about (oneself) through pure self-examination. While culture holds the individual prisoner, it is possible for the person to learn of his culture . . . By knowing one's culture, one becomes intellectually and spiritually freed. (Ferguson, 1987, p. 13)

Baker mentioned that one function of multicultural education is to encourage students to be part of more than one cultural group. According to Hunter, "In a truly multicultural classroom, the teacher recognizes, encourages, and values the bicultural development of students. Rather than forcing all students into the majority culture mold, the teacher . . . can help children live in two cultures" (Hunter, 1974).

Thus there is currently a rise in utilizing cross-cultural approaches to educating recognized cultural groups such as African Americans, Native Americans, even smaller groups such as Cajuns. But one of the difficulties in proposing a multicultural approach to education in Appalachia is that often there is still no recognition of Appalachians as a separate cultural or ethnic group.

Successes and Suggestions for Improvement

One step in the right direction for educational reform in Appalachia was seen in the efforts of teachers who were associated with the Eastern Kentucky Teachers' Network. Many of these teachers believed that educational failure was being perpetuated in Appalachia "through the material forms and structures of the school, which tend to maintain relationships of power and domination" (R. G. Eller, 1989, p. 1). Thus many of the Network teachers were attempting to "realize an alternate rationality in their classrooms by implementing a more critical literacy, i.e., a literacy that legitimates their students' culture and language, and that encourages students to confront inequitable relationships in society" (Eller, 1989, p. 2). Teachers of the four classrooms observed by Eller in her study recognized "the inadequacies of current instructional practices for the students they teach, and all are attempting to counteract failure in their classrooms by redefining literacy for their students" (Eller, 1989, p. 2).

One naturalistic study investigated and described home-school communication patterns between special reading teachers and parents of first-grade Appalachian children enrolled in the Reading Recovery Program. This is an early intervention program which takes first-graders "at risk" of failure in literacy and moves them to a level of success within a four- to six-month period. Teachers in the program were found to have two different styles of communication with parents. Those with a passive style used formal printed announcements to invite the parents to come to the school "sometime" and didn't really expect the parents to participate. The teachers who had active styles of communication were able to involve parents in the children's literacy efforts. They phoned the parents, sent notes that were handwritten, and met the parents face-to-face whenever possible. They communicated that they really needed and wanted the parents' help with the program. The active teachers personally invited most of the parents one at a time to observe a Reading Recovery lesson. These observation sessions were the first positive school visit many parents had ever had (Holland, 1987).

One educator pointed out that many children are raised in a cultural environment that is very different from what predominates at school; when that occurs, the children use up so much energy adjusting to the school's expectations of appropriate behavior that there is very little energy left over to devote to learning (Gay, 1975). Researchers studying Appalachian children in northern schools observed that they had problems with non-achievement and that they were discriminated against by automatically being placed in the lowest categories in ability groupings and tracking. Also the teachers had very low expectations of the children's abilities or achievements (Porter, 1981, and Bennett, 1991).

> The problems of their children in urban schools for three decades have contributed to the visibility of Appalachians in the north. First, since these Appalachian learners are not of the middle class, they do not bring with them the experiences, standard English verbal abilities, concepts, or values which are middle class, and they do not share many cultural understandings with the teacher. (Porter, 1981, pp. 14–15)

Best (1986) commented on the need for classrooms in public schools that are responsive to the cultural traits of Appalachian children:

> The combination of shame, emotional sensitivity, and artistic forms of expression makes Appalachian children poor candidates for success in the public schools where almost all such attributes are not valued and where very few of their strengths are perceived as such. It is no wonder that the very bright, the very sensitive, and the very artistic drop out at the earliest opportunity if they can't find ways to

circumvent the school, go in their own directions, and gain their own education despite the system. (Best, 1986, p. 54)

All three of the main goals of multicultural education outlined by Baker seem appropriate in cross-cultural efforts in Appalachian schooling:

1. Appalachians need to become familiar with their own culture and learn to value their roots. This is needed both to increase their self-esteem and to make it acceptable to remain in Appalachia if that is what they choose to do.

2. Appalachians need to learn to appreciate other cultures and people who are different from them. This is particularly important in areas where there are virtually no residents from other ethnic groups. Lack of exposure to diversity often allows extreme racial prejudice to continue. Learning tolerance is important especially if Appalachians decide to live in other areas where they will be dealing with a global world.

3. Many Appalachians experience "marginality"—living in two social worlds. With few jobs available in the rural areas of Appalachia, they often live in one culture and work in another. Thus multicultural education is needed to educate them for both social worlds and then allow them to choose either or both.

Eller proposed that we need more research on Appalachia from the perspectives of those within the region, not just from the perspectives of those who have come from outside, including the federal government and the private sector. "Renewal must begin from within, with the revitalization of communities and of the spirit of self-help and civic virtue" (R. D. Eller, 1988, p. 12).

According to Best (1986), "The best hope for developing an educational system which will allow Appalachian people to grow in ways appropriate for us is to build upon educational philosophies . . . which are congruent with thought and action modes already existing in the mountains" (Best, 1986, p. 52). One of the suggestions that Best made was to have the arts be given more priority at all levels of schooling in order to be more compatible with the right-brain orientation of many Appalachians. A study by McNeal showed that participation in fine arts could significantly reduce a student's likelihood of dropping out of high school (McNeal, 1994).

Both Miller (1977) and Best (1986) recommended a bilingual approach to literacy. Christine Bennett commented that when comparing mainstream Americans, Hispanics, and Native Americans (and Appalachians could be added),

> . . . the existence of different languages makes the coexistence of distinct cultures within our boundaries apparent. The many similarities between Anglo and black culture, though, often prevent the recognition and acceptance of some distinct cultural characteristics. For instance, black English is often perceived as "slang" or poor quality standard English. (Bennett, 1989, p. 79)

> The almost exclusive use of standard English in our nation's schools is a blatant example of mainstream orientation. We are not debating whether or not we accept the position that all school children should develop enough skill in standard English to make its use a functional option. We are examining the cultural conflict many children experience in schools that ignore or repress the language they have lived with since birth. (Bennett, 1989, pp. 82–83)

Bennett goes on to say that educators often realize how much frustration is experienced by first-graders whose native tongue is a language other than English, such as Spanish, Japanese, etc. However, it is less often recognized that the same problems with standard English may exist for children whose native tongue is a nonstandard dialect of English such as black English or Appalachian English (Bennett, 1989, p. 83).

> Attempting to teach children from language or ethnic minorities to use reading in middle-class ways promoted egalitarianism and homogeneity. Simultaneously, it often denied the children's home context and estranged them from their origins. However, to accept and extend the literacy patterns of the home honored and promoted cultural diversity. Success in this vein may decrease the compliance of some children with mainstream ways, but it may also reinforce their identities and preserve pluralism. (Holland, 1987, pp. 96–97)

Some recent educational efforts have been aimed at helping children utilize both their native dialect of English as well as standard English. According to Hunter:

> The teacher who understands children who speak nonstandard English can encourage culturally different youth in creative writing, cre-

ative drama, and other learning activities. If students are allowed and encouraged to utilize their native language, their creative efforts, whether in writing or drama, can be enhanced greatly. (Hunter, 1974, p. 98)

Bill Best told about his third grade son's announcement that he had discovered two "kinds of talk" which he called "school talk and country talk."

He described "school talk" as a particular kind of talk used only at school. It was to be used when teachers and students talked with each other, but it was not good anywhere else—as least as far as he knew at that time. In contrast, "country talk" was what one used at home and in the rural community where we live. He said that "country talk" was the better kind of talk because it allowed one to "tell about feelings." He also said that "country talk" was better because "you can say what you mean using country talk." I told him that "school talk" did have some uses and that he should learn to use "school talk" so that he could use it when necessary. I also told him to hold on to his "country talk" because he might continue to have feelings which he might wish to share. (Best, 1986, p. 56)

A study conducted by Pollock in 1988 found that teachers should learn to accept a young reader's use of Appalachian dialect during oral reading when the meaning of the passage was not adversely affected. It was also found that understanding dialect features used by students was important and that pre-service teachers should be provided with sources of information on Appalachian English (Pollock, 1988).

A study by Cantrell (1991) showed that for young Appalachian dialect speakers, their dialect had a significant influence on spelling when children were first learning to read and spell. A teacher in an Appalachian elementary school told me that I should see her fifth grade students trying to figure out how to spell "you'ins." She also mentioned that some of the native teachers in the school where she taught spoke Appalachian dialect themselves in the classroom, making it even more unlikely that their students would learn standard English. Thus, there appears to be a need for more training in speech for pre-service native teachers, as well as training in English as a second language for teachers from other regions or cultural groups.

It is also important to choose textbooks and materials that are culturally compatible. Sometimes children living in rural areas have trouble relating to the same stories that would be relevant to children in urban areas. It may still be difficult to locate good materials since, to a large extent, the cultural stereotyping of Appalachians continues.

> Reading and language arts should begin where the children are in the literal sense. It is not enough to have Dick and Jane passing through the mountains on their way to Florida from New England. Early readers should contain stories about life as it is lived in the particular areas where the children live. Children should learn and be allowed to appreciate the meanings of words and language patterns they hear at home and not just those they hear at school. (Best, 1986, pp. 55–56)

According to Holland, "The language and literacy of home accompanies the child to school. Vice versa, the language and literacy of the school enters the family literacy context through the child" (Holland, 1987, p. 95). Increasingly it appears important to work with the entire family so that literacy is integrated into the family culture.

Since schools in Appalachia traditionally have not been very effective, many areas still have very high illiteracy and dropout rates. Often Appalachian cultural values are still strong and in opposition with those espoused in a classroom designed for mainstream students. It appears that changes are needed in both the curriculum and the instructional delivery in the classrooms, so that students can be educated both to live in their home region and to function in a global world. Caudill (1976) felt that it was extremely important for students to learn about their home region, not only to improve the efficiency of Appalachian education but also to improve the chances of economic and social progress for the region. It is also likely that students should be empowered by studying the local government, justice system, and economy.

> How might the tragedies of the Appalachians have been avoided? Or, more aptly, how may the present mess be converted into a genuine North American Switzerland? The answer lies in a change of attitude toward government and a willingness to use this prime tool for huge and constructive tasks. As long as . . . mountaineers mistrust government, keep it weak, and elect jovial nonentities to govern them, they have no hope for significant social, moral, or political improvement. (Caudill, 1986, p. 47)

Also reform is needed in teacher education, so that teachers will be knowledgeable about this region and will be able to teach the language arts bilingually, respecting both standard English and the students' home dialect.

Our nation needs *all* citizens to function at the peak of their abilities. Culturally compatible educational programs, which help students to stay in school and to succeed, can do much to achieve the goal of having all 20 million Appalachians learn to live up to their full potential.

REFERENCES

Atkins, C. P. (1993). Do employment recruiters discriminate on the basis of nonstandard dialect? *Journal of Employment Counseling, 30*(3), 108–118.

Baker, G. C. (1983). *Planning and organizing for multicultural instruction.* Reading, MA: Addison-Wesley Publishing Company.

Banks, C. A. M. (1993). Restructuring schools for equity. *Phi Delta Kappan, 75*(1), 42–48.

Bennett, C. (1989). Teaching students as they would be taught the importance of cultural perspective. In Barbara J. Shade (Ed.), *Culture, style, and the educative process* (pp. 71– 84). Springfield, IL: Charles C. Thomas.

Bennett, K. P. (1991). Doing school in an urban Appalachian first grade. In C. E. Sleeter (Ed.), *Empowerment through multicultural education* (pp. 27–47). Albany, NY: State University of New York Press.

Best, B. (1986). *The great Appalachian sperm bank and other writings.* Berea, KY: Kentucky Imprints.

Brown, I. C. (1963). *Understanding other cultures.* Englewood Cliffs, NJ: Prentice Hall.

Cantrell, R. J. (1991). *Dialect and spelling in Appalachian first-grade children.* Doctoral dissertation, University of Virginia, Charlottesville.

Caudill, H. M. (1976). *A darkness at dawn: Appalachian Kentucky and the future.* Lexington, KY: The University Press of Kentucky.

Cox, G. C. (1988). Topophilia and technological change in Appalachia. In S. M. Whitson (Ed.), *Sense of place in Appalachia* (pp. 248–256). Morehead, KY: Office of Regional Development Services, Morehead State University.

Eller, R. D. (1988). Place and the recovery of community in Appalachia. In S. M. Whitson (Ed.), *Sense of place in Appalachia* (pp. 3–19). Morehead, KY: Office of Regional Development Services, Morehead State University.

Eller, R. G. (1989). *Teacher resistance and educational change: Toward a critical theory of literacy in Appalachia.* Doctoral dissertation, University of Kentucky, Lexington.

Ergood, B. (1991). Toward a definition of Appalachia. In B. Ergood and B. E. Kuhre (Eds.), *Appalachia: Social context past and present* (pp. 39–49). Dubuque, IA: Kendall/Hunt Publishing Company.

Estes, F., Neufeldt, H., and Akenson, J. E. (1987). Appalachian and southern literacy campaigns in the early twentieth century: Historical perspectives in two keys. In *Proceedings of the UK Conference on Appalachia.* Lexington, KY: Appalachian Center.

Ferguson, H. (1987). *Manual for multicultural education.* Yarmouth, ME: Intercultural Press.

Freeman, J. (1992). *Quality basic education: The development of competence.* Paris: UNESCO, International Bureau of Education.

Gay, G. (1975). *Cultural conflict in the classroom.* (Videotape). Symposium sponsored by the Alachua County Teacher Center, Gainesville, FL.

Holland, K. E. (1987). Parents and teachers: Can home and school literacy boundaries be broken? In *Proceedings of the UK Conference on Appalachia*. Lexington, KY: Appalachian Center.

Hunter, W. A. (1974). *Multicultural education through competency-based teacher education*. Washington, DC: American Association of Colleges for Teacher Education.

McCullough, M. P. (1981). *Teachers' knowledge of and attitudes toward Black English and correction of dialect-related reading miscues*. Doctoral dissertation, The University of Michigan, Ann Arbor.

McNeal, R. B., Jr. (1994). *Dropping out of high school: Individual and school variation*. Doctoral dissertation, University of North Carolina at Chapel Hill.

Miles, E. B. (1905). *The spirit of the mountains*. New York: J. Pott; reprinted Knoxville, University of Tennessee Press (1975).

Miller, J. W. (1977). Appalachian education: A critique and suggestions for reform. *Appalachian Journal, 5*(1), 13–22.

Pickard, J. (1991). Appalachia's decade of change: A decade of immigration. In B. Ergood and B. E. Kuhre (Eds.), *Appalachia: Social context past and present* (pp. 123–133). Dubuque, IA: Kendall/Hunt Publishing Company.

Pollock, M. A. C. (1988). *Preservice teachers' correction responses to Appalachian English miscues after training in miscue analysis*. Doctoral dissertation, University of Kentucky, Lexington.

Porter, J. D. (1981). Appalachians: Adrift in the mainstream. *Theory into Practice, XX*(1), 13–19.

Reck, G. G., Keefe, S. E., and Reck, M. (1987). Ethnicity and education in Southern Appalachia: Implications for educational equity. In *Proceedings of the UK Conference on Appalachia*. Lexington, KY: Appalachian Center.

Ryan, W. (1976). *Blaming the victim*. New York: Random House.

Shade, B. J. (Ed.). (1989a). *Culture, style, and the educative process*. Springfield, IL: Charles C. Thomas.

———. (1989b). In B. J. Shade (Ed.), *Culture, style, and the educative process* (pp. 9–15). Springfield, IL: Charles C. Thomas.

Sleeter, C. E. (Ed.). (1991). *Empowerment through multicultural education*. Albany, NY: State University of New York Press.

South Central Regional Educational Laboratory (SCREL). (1967). Education for the culturally disadvantaged. *Proceedings of the National Conference on Educational Objectives for the Culturally Disadvantaged*, Little Rock, AR.

Sprague, S. S. (1988). Inside Appalachia: Familiar land and ordinary people. In S. M. Whitson (Ed.), *Sense of place in Appalachia* (pp. 20–26). Morehead, KY: Office of Regional Development Services, Morehead State University.

Tennessee Literacy Coalition. (1992). *Tennessee adult education 1992 status report*. Nashville, TN: Author.

UNESCO. (1988). *Compendium of statistics on literacy*. Paris, France: UNESCO, Office of Statistics.

United States Office of Education. (1965). *Quality education for Appalachia: A prospectus proposing the establishment of a regional educational laboratory*. Washington, D.C.

Welch, J. G. B. (1984). *A study of Appalachian cultural values as evidenced in the political and social attitudes of rural West Virginians*. Doctoral dissertation, University of Maryland, College Park.

Williams, J. R. (1985). *Appalachian migrants in Cincinnati, Ohio: The role of folklore in the reinforcement of ethnic identity*. Doctoral dissertation, Indiana University, Bloomington.

12 THE TRIBALLY CONTROLLED COMMUNITY COLLEGE

NEW DIRECTIONS IN NATIVE AMERICAN EDUCATION

Gabrielle Elliott

"You have no education."
— Capt. Richard Henry Pratt to Spotted Tail (Brule Lakota), 1879

A close friend of mine, an Oglala woman, and I left Bozeman, Montana, in the early Spring of 1995 to visit the Red Crow Tribal College on the Blood Reserve in Alberta, Canada. The air was clean and cold. The sky was as blue as only a Montana sky can be. The nine-hour trip up through the Blackfeet Reservation, along the eastern side of Glacier National Park and across the Canadian border was for business and for pleasure. We wanted to visit with staff, faculty, and students at Red Crow, to learn all we could about how the college was born and how the community viewed its mission for the future.

I was not prepared for the four-story brick structure that rose from seemingly nowhere up out of the plains. It looked like an old hospital or a reform school. I was even less prepared to discover an open field in which someone had built life-size Stations of the Cross out of marble with the tomb of Christ made out of rock and almost as large as the church next to it. I was born into a Catholic family, raised Catholic, sent to Catholic school. Never in my life had I seen life-size Stations of the Cross. I stood still in this field listening, feeling the winter wind blow snow in on this Spring day. I could hear the words of Mary Crow Dog, a woman my age, telling us her experiences in Catholic boarding schools in South Dakota.

It is impossible to explain to a sympathetic white person what a typical Indian boarding school was like, how it affected the Indian child suddenly dumped into it like a small creature from another world, helpless, defenseless, bewildered, trying desperately and instinctively to survive and sometimes not surviving at all. I think such children were like the victims of Nazi concentration camps trying to tell average, middle-class Americans what their experiences had been . . . In traditional Sioux families . . . the child is never left alone. It is always surrounded by relatives, carried around, enveloped in warmth. It is treated with the respect due to any human being, even a small one. It is seldom forced to do anything against its will, seldom screamed at and never beaten . . .

Mary Crow Dog followed her mother and her grandmother to a boarding school where buggy whips, four-inch straps, and boarded-up dark cubicles much like coffins were used to punish children. Many ran away. A few hanged themselves or jumped to their death. Over one hundred stories of boarding school experiences express the fear and the feeling of being in a penal institution. When I compare these experiences to my own, I know I am looking into the heart of racism legitimized by the American legal system.

We had planned to spend several days on this campus but it started to snow, the kind of snow that you know is going to last for several days. The staff became concerned that we might not make it out if we did not leave. They saw to it that we had meal tickets for our lunch and offered their prayers for a safe journey home. As we started down the stairs to the basement where the cafeteria is housed, Alberta began to cry. Stopping on the stairwell, looking down the spiraling staircases into the basement, she told me she could hear and feel the pain of the years of cruelty inflicted on Indian children. It was extremely difficult for her to make her way to the basement. Even though we were surrounded by love and friendship in a place now safe from harm, she could not eat.

This is a simple story, a true story that I shared with one friend. But it is a story told by all Native Americans in one voice to anyone who will listen. American education, as we know it, has always been and is today the "enemy" of the Indian people. It is the battlefield where Indian values have been sorted and shredded into vast empty deculturalized deserts.

I have worked for nearly 20 years in one capacity or another inside Indian communities. I do not pretend to be an expert or to have answers. I am simply positioned as an ambassador, which I do well sometimes. Those are the times when non-Indian people want me to help them work through the stereotypical beliefs they hold about Indians and Indian cultures. If they want to do this work, most often they are afraid to do it with Indian people. That is when I become the bridge on which they will stand to look at their own fears and prejudices. One day, maybe, they will be able to walk over that bridge on their own. It is in that spirit, as an ambassador, that I paint this picture, as I understand it, of why Native American students see American public school education as the "enemy," a fact that has resulted in the highest dropout rate of any population in the nation. It is in that spirit that I share my observations about what Native Americans are doing in their own communities to unlearn education as "the enemy" and to help their children return to their own traditional ways of knowing.

RESEARCHING THE MAZE

Dr. Ardy Sixkiller Clarke concluded a definitive study which she reported to the Office of Educational Research and Development in Washington in 1994. In her report she examined multiple factors that contribute to the decision of the Native American student to stay in school. Recurrent themes that emerged in the interviews focused on teacher expectations, teacher attitudes, abuse by school personnel, tribal self-identity and pride, discrimination and racism, and bilingualism.

A common theme throughout the research addresses the cultural differences and/or "cultural deprivation" of the American Indian child, the racial biases of white teachers, the negative self-image of American Indian children, drug/alcohol abuse, and language barriers. American Indian students have often been the subject of cross-cultural research in which a comparison of American Indian cultural values and the white American cultural values is made. This research suggests that American Indian students fail in school because of a value system which is different than the ideology within the school system (Clarke, p. 12, 1994).

To appreciate fully the complexity of research on Native American dropouts it is necessary to understand both the structural differences in the umbrella of control and regulation over Indian education and the history of ever-changing federal and state policies addressing the purpose of Indian education.

Multiple systems of control over the educational structures and the learning environment itself makes it extremely difficult to produce credible research on Native student populations. This difficulty is compounded by the ever-changing policies of governmental administration towards Native educational issues. Although we are in a historical era now known as the era of self-determination, in which policy professes to encourage Native control of education, interpretation and implementation of this policy has suffered from inconsistent interpretations of the meaning of the legislation. The legislation, enacted in 1975 as the Indian Self-determination and Education Assistance Act (PL 93–638) provided the legal basis for the government to pay local Indian people, through contract agreements, to run their own schools. Tribal members and the BIA viewed this act very differently. Tribal members saw the opportunity to create their own educational programs. The BIA, on the other hand, viewed the Act as giving tribal control to operate BIA facilities under BIA supervision (DeJong, 1993). Guy Senese, a well-known Indian policy analyst, argues that the BIA authority to write rules and regulations that govern the contractual process is a denial of the power of self-determination. According to Senese, "Congress intended to retain certain discretionary authority over contract schools to prevent total tribal control" (DeJong, 1993, p. 230).

POLICIES FOR ASSIMILATION

The history of government efforts to assimilate Indian students through public education is one of abuse. Under the Johnson-O'Malley Act of 1934, federal and state politicians agreed that the government would provide the states with a per diem for each Indian student who went to public school. Just a few short years after the Depression states were more interested in building up their financial coffers than they were in providing an education to Indian students. A common problem that continued throughout the JOM program was the ever-present struggle by both federal and state government for autonomy over the educational process. Present too were the BIA efforts to place a higher value on BIA education as opposed to public education provided by the states. Careful reading of related historical documents leads to one overriding conclusion: all interested parties wanted control of the money the government was obliged by treaties to invest in Indian education. The less talked about, but certainly equally obvious result, is the picture that is painted of the impact of multiple systems of control on the lives of the students. The overall impact of multi-control has not only intimidated students, it has precluded meaningful participation and created hidden curriculums. The 1960s witnessed, through federal policies aimed at assimilation, piece after piece of legislation stating an intent to put Indian children on the same level playing field with non-Indian children in public schools. In fact, public schools routinely put all the federal funds they could get into the generalized budget. The special needs of Indian children and their presence were ignored. The move from federal boarding schools to public schools was supported by the government for a number of political reasons. But the single most important reason was to create the appearance of a new federal policy toward Indian education. This action was a direct response to one of the most damaging documents published in the history of federal control over Indian education: the Merriam Report.

John Collier, a social worker from New York City, Lewis Merriam, a Harvard law graduate, and Henry Roe Cloud, a Yale graduate who was a member of the Winnebago Tribe, spent seven months making some 95 visits to reservations looking at the conditions of Indian boarding schools. The pamphlet, published in 1928, became known as the Merriam Report. It reported that the efforts of the government to assimilate Indian students through the boarding schools process had been a dismal failure. The boarding schools themselves were grossly inadequate. Government policy between 1900 and 1926 had separated almost 70,000 children from their parents. Discipline was harsh. Students were forbidden to speak their own language, practice their own religion, wear their own clothes. Many photographs exist of students who attended the first Indian boarding school founded by Captain Richard Henry Pratt, the Carlisle School. In those photographs the students have short hair and they wear the uniforms of a military cadet. Physical abuse was rampant. Child labor was used to maintain the schools. They were overcrowded, understaffed, and without proper medical care and food. Government reports pride themselves on feeding children for 11 cents a day. The children went for years without seeing their families. Some never saw their families again. Many died. Those who did make it home had no life skills in their own cultures. Government fraud and neglect were clear. Blame was clear. This fact led to the public school movement in which the government negotiated contracts with each state and territory to admit Indian students to public school.

With the failure of policy after policy to "civilize" Indian students and to rip them from their own culture, came the evolution of the complex and convoluted patchwork quilt approach to education that exists today. The bizarre mixture of off-reservation boarding schools, on-reservation boarding schools, tribally contracted schools, and public schools has produced great uncertainty, confusion, and resentment. Federal experiments in Indian education have not only lost their credibility with Indian people, but the failure of these experiments has been the driving force behind the attitudes of local school districts toward Indian students. If the government can't educate and civilize them, how can we expect the public school system to do it? The attitude that Indian students are not to be taken seriously permeates school districts across the nation. One state superintendent wrote, "the teachers simply mirror the attitudes of those who control their professional destinies and so they can be even more difficult to convert than the community itself" (DeJong, 1994. p. 187). By 1969 a budget of 530 million dollars earmarked for Indian students in public schools was being dumped into the general budgets of public schools and, for the most part, these funds were untraceable. The failure of federal aid between 1928 and 1973 to be utilized for Indian students was reflected in poor school attendance, high dropout rates, lack of motivation, and an acceptance of white superiority, all of which led to the general feeling that there was no reason to go to school.

There are more than 500 recognized tribes and many unrecognized tribes in the United States. The blame for the failure of Indian education outside Indian culture is still placed on the Indian student. The general attitude that Indian students are too dumb to be educated pervades the national attitude towards Native Americans, clearly preventing us from learning to appreciate the diversity of Indian culture and the Indian ways of learning and knowing.

In the late 1960s emerging Indian leaders began to demand a voice in the decisionmaking process controlling efforts to educate their children. The failure of public schools to meet the needs of Indian students and the demand by Indian leaders to be involved became the focus of the 1968–69 Senate subcommittee investigation that would become known as the Kennedy Report. Initiated by Senator Robert Kennedy and completed by Senator Edward Kennedy, a report titled "Indian Education: A National Tragedy—A National Challenge" served as a major indictment of both federal and state schools to bring Indian students into the educational process. The failure, according to the report, "stemmed from school curricula, attitudes, values, and dogmas, all of which diminished American Indians and Indian cultures. Lack of Indian control through elected boards of education also prevented Indian communities from influencing the education of their children. As a result many Indians became alienated by a school system that seemed to have little concern for Indian needs and desires" (Kennedy Report). The report held both teachers and administrators responsible for perpetuating a self-fulfilling prophecy by leading Indian students to believe in the Indian stereotypes associated with Indian inferiority. The report concluded that without the participation in and control over their children's education, education would remain the "enemy" of the Indian people.

The Kennedy Report raised many of the same issues raised in the Merriam Report. It talked about Indian control but initiated no mechanism for Indians to take control of their own education. In substance it was a reprimand to non-Indians to open the door to Indian participation. The belief that Indians could still become part of a non-Indian system was alive and well.

Admitting that the government had not lived up to its responsibilities and that the evidence found in the extensive records of the committee represented a major indictment of federal policy and its results in Indian education matters. These initial statistics were printed in the report:

- dropout rates are twice the national average in both public and federal schools. Some school districts have dropout rates approaching 100 percent;
- achievement levels of Indian children are two to three years below those of white children; and the Indian child falls progressively further behind the longer he/she stays in school;
- only one percent of Indian children in elementary schools have Indian teachers or principals;
- one fourth of elementary and secondary teachers—by their own admission—would prefer not to teach Indian children; and
- Indian children, more than any other minority group, believe themselves to be "below average" in intelligence. (Kennedy Report)

The conclusions reached in the Kennedy Report, although reached in 1969, still provide an accurate picture of why Native students today still view educational institutions as the "enemy." Coercive policies to force assimilation have resulted in the destruction of Native communities, a self-perpetuating cycle of poverty, a bureaucracy which requires constant confrontation to exercise self-determination. This same policy has shaped a negative and grossly misinformed attitude toward Native American history and culture. It has been a breeding ground for prejudice, racial intolerance, and widespread discrimination. Inside this climate, the classroom has become a battlefield where Indian children fight to protect their identity and their integrity. School fails to recognize cultural differences or the importance of Native community. The result has been, and is today, a dismal record of absenteeism, dropouts, negative self-image, low achievement, and ultimately, failure for a majority of all Native children. Today, dropout rates are as high as 70 percent on some reservations. With a clear federal policy to continue to exploit and expropriate Native land and resources combined with intolerance of tribal communities and cultural differences, any change, no matter how small, has been initiated by Native Americans, sometimes at great cost.

Following the release of this report, President Nixon, in a speech to the nation on July 8, 1970, advocated "legislation which guarantees the right of Indians to contract for control or operation of federal programs that would directly channel money into Indian communities." He reasoned that Indian control, like an insurance policy, would insure that Indians would hire Indians to administer programs and that in doing so, salaries would remain in the community. More importantly, there would be Indian accountability. Whatever Nixon's true intentions in wanting Indian accountability, they would take a backseat to the forces that were emerging in Indian country with the birth of the American Indian Movement. (AIM) Two hundred years of submission, forgotten promises, broken treaties, and shifting policies had finally brought together a handful of young warriors who were not only willing to go to war with the government, some of them would lay down their lives.

SELF-DETERMINATION: THE IDEOLOGY OF LIFE

In the Winter of 1890 federal troops massacred 300 unarmed Indians, mainly women and children, and buried them in a mass grave. This tragedy, not written up in the history books, is known as the Wounded Knee Massacre in Indian Country. The physical site of Wounded Knee is on the Pine Ridge Reservation in south central South Dakota, home to the Oglala. In the winter of 1973, at the request of traditional leaders, several hundred Oglala and friends, including AIM members, occupied Wounded Knee in an armed confrontation with the United States military. For 71 days the United States military bore down on the occupants with an arsenal of tanks, helicopters, and machine guns. The press was not allowed inside the armed camp. In a diary kept by a member of the underground press who had hiked in, an entry on April 12 shows,

> the government is trying to isolate us from the outside world more than ever. But the isolation is bringing people closer together. All we have is each other to depend on . . . the Oglalas meet often . . . some are the original residents of Wounded Knee and some are from other parts of the Reservation. They're the ones who make the major political decisions. Their meetings are usually in the round church where they sit in a circle and everyone participates; none of this face the front and listen to the speaker at the podium business. I go just to listen, and each time I am more amazed at how much they have it together. (Voices of the Participants, 1974, pp. 171–172)

People died. Promises made in the negotiations to cease fire were never kept by the government. But in those 71 days the era of Self-Determination had been seized by the Indian people. The 1975 Self-Determination and Assistance Act, (PL93–638) that followed appeared to give legitimacy and government support to an action that had already been taken. Guy Senese, in an analysis of the legislation, makes the argument that self-determination and community control were "severely compromised," that "both" the language of the law and its implementation severely limit legitimate self-determination . . . It offers Indian people the opportunity to "show" that Indian people can run their own institutions, yet it does not provide the flexibility or the resource availability for efficient operation of a school. In addition it allows the BIA bureaucracy to maintain indirect control . . . we can see the codification of a series of self-help schemes intended to provide not only the illusion of control but the illusion of competency. Self-help has been reduced to a struggle for survival. (Senese, 1986, pp. 153–164)

To Indians and non-Indians alike the rhetoric of self-determination rang out across the land like church bells on Easter Sunday. Finally, Indian communities would take the reins of control. Their educational destinies would be determined by communities deciding together. Critical analysis of Indian educational policy ground to a halt on all fronts. The realities are known only to those who took up the opportunity to contract with the BIA for control of their schools. If, as Senese argues, it was legislative intent to allow Indian communities to show the BIA that they could successfully operate their own schools, the rhetoric of the language of self-determination, as empty as it may have been, has backfired. Indian Country took the language and raised it like a flag. Language initiated to placate Indian communities has been used by those communities to save tribal culture, language, and custom. Self-determination in Indian Country today is the ideology of life.

IMAGES AND DREAMCATCHERS

Not all confrontations in the 1970s were armed. On a quieter front, community leaders began meeting in homes around the kitchen table, drinking coffee and sharing ideas about how they could build a tribally controlled community college (TCCC) that would become the sanctuary for cultural tradition and the cornerstone for building a future. The birth of the TCCC would alter the course of Indian education forever. How, in isolated pockets already declared economic disaster areas, where illiteracy reigned supreme and education was the "enemy," did a handful of leaders bring to life a force that now holds the hopes and dreams of all future generations? They used what they had, no matter how meager or seemingly incidental. They assessed their needs, reviewed their resources, their circumstances and they defined their goals accordingly. They began with the concept of the movable school and the simple belief that you begin where you are. Traditional Native philosophy does not place learning and education inside a physical structure or even in a place. Although none can say for certain just why these leaders came together at this time in history, many factors are a matter of record.

The importance of the occupation of Wounded Knee cannot be underestimated. The drawing together of many Indian people in 71 days to take a stand against government's failure to protect them from the BIA corruption fused a seemingly long-lost strength to fight together against oppression and abuse of power. During those 71 days they realized that they could depend on each other; they could create strategies, act, and win. The essence of their true spirits was reborn through collective action. They lifted each other out of paralysis to a place where they could refire the creation of each of their souls. Together they did this. One more failure by the government to honor its promises mattered little after those 71 days. The occupants of Wounded Knee had reclaimed their warrior spirits.

Tribal colleges cannot be compared to any other educational institution. They have to be looked at in the historical context of Indian education. In that context they have made it their primary mission to become a place of spiritual renewal for all Indian people. In the last two decades this has been a mission with pervasive consequences. At the spiritual heart of the tribal college mission is the shared commitment to reclaim culture and language. Once on the threshold of annihilation, culture and language are now the foundation of the tribal college curriculum. Indian history speaks of despair and destruction. Images of reservation life depict poverty, hunger, hopelessness, alcoholism, certainly not hope. The tribal colleges have changed all these images by becoming "dreamcatchers" in their communities.

These colleges today serve over 10,000 Indian people in one capacity or another. There is never enough funding. Although they are funded directly from the government under the 1978 Tribally Controlled Community College Act, the government has yet to honor its commitment in dollars. Despite funding issues and rundown physical structures tribal colleges have never been in better shape to serve their students. Their mission as a spiritual center shines like a light in the night in Indian Country. These schools are the hopes and dreams for tomorrow's children and a generation of parents who have taken control of their lives. Although these schools, like all community colleges across America, do provide professional and vocational classes, they also provide an academic foundation for any student wishing to transfer to a four-year school after graduation. In fact there are now two tribal colleges that offer four-year degrees and a master's degree in several fields. An example of just how unlike American universities these tribal colleges are can be seen at the Oglala Lakota College in Kyle, South Dakota, where they offer an intensive master's program for "modern warriors" who want to participate in the business life of the reservation. One requirement of this course of study is the mastering of the native language.

It is necessary to understand that these tribal colleges exist for and plan their future for the people they serve. They do not exist in the abstract for students who may or may not come to study there. They do not exist as a bureaucracy with administrators whose most important goal is to perpetuate their own existence. Tribal colleges exist at the center of the circle of the people. It is in the spirit and the mission of the college that people go to talk there and solve problems they face together. Much has been written about the physical appearance of these schools by reporters who want a cover page of the *New York Times*. In fact, the appearance of these schools is of no significance whatsoever. What they do in these schools is write a new history of Indian education.

Where We Are Now

The mission of the tribal college responds to changing times and changing student needs. They take into consideration where each student comes from and where they are in life now. Janine Pease Pretty-on-Top, President of Little Big Horn College at the Crow Agency, has received numerous honorary degrees as well as the prestigious McArthur Foundation Award for her work at the young age of 44. She tells us,

> . . . the creator gave us many chances to acquire knowledge; not just one, not two, not ten, but as many through our lifetime as we wish . . . we even go so far as to eliminate the F because we felt that no one had to bear the burden of failure. We were close enough to our students to understand negating factors and also the need for compassion. Knowledge can be acquired, and there can be many mitigating factors. We can have the compassion as educators to give our students a number of tries. (Windy-Boy, 1990)

This acceptance of the economic, political, and social conditions under which students have lived is the cornerstone of successful teaching and learning between student and teacher in the tribal college environment. Flexibility in defining goals and teaching strategies combined with a sensitivity to students and to the social and political climate of the times have been fundamental to the success of students in the tribal college setting. Teachers have been allowed to experiment freely with techniques to help students overcome their lack of academic background. They have not limited teaching to the classroom. They have a well-deserved reputation for non-formal teaching, one-on-one instruction and the use of indigenous leaders. Underlying this flex-response model of teaching is the belief that there are leaders and role models in the community outside the classroom; that they can be identified; that they are sensitive to student problems; that they are willing to act as the catalytic agents for change; and that they can be effective disseminators and communicators of information.

This philosophy, executed in a reality-based style, creates a wealth of free knowledge on which any student can draw on at any time. These colleges have succeeded in developing an extraordinary mentoring system within the whole community by simply calling on that community to help. Job opportunities are important but not nearly as important as a sense of command over our future or a new perception of our own ability to improve our perceptions of our prospects. Likewise, President Carol Murray from the Blackfeet Community College tells us:

> Our mission here at Blackfeet Community College is to teach our students how to succeed in today's world without neglecting their heritage. Both our worlds will be strengthened if we accomplish our mission. We need to share our heritage, knowledge and strengths. (Interview, 1994)

Richard Pratt, head of the Carlisle school, was convinced that Indian controlled education would work against assimilation. The last two decades tells us clearly that Indian controlled schools are not trying to retreat from the outside world. To the contrary, they are trying to prepare their students to have the confidence and competence to take on the outside world as an equal. Many universities have simply ignored the tribal colleges but those same colleges were unconcerned about the 90 percent dropout rate of Indian students who managed to make it to their campuses. A handful of universities have taken a hard look at their history of neglect and are reaching out to negotiate articulation agreements and to support tribal colleges through legal hoops. These friendships have been slow in the making but they are budding. One such effort can be seen in Lawrence, Kansas, where Haskell Indian University has over 1000 students from 139 tribes. Talks between Haskell and the University of Kansas are now ongoing in an effort to find ways to relate to one another and to utilize each other's talents and resources (Mercer, 1992).

STUDIES IN DIVERSITY: EMPOWERMENT AND RESPECT

Tribally controlled colleges, at first glance, have many outward similarities. They are in fact, a genuine study in diversity. They do share an underlying commonality in their mission and that is empowerment and respect for cultural heritage. They want to create links with the outside world, social and economic opportunities for their students. Each school, due to its distinctive cultural history, economic needs, and geographical location, will approach these goals in different ways. This reality of responsiveness is what makes these schools so unique. Despite the lack of physical facilities, low pay, and isolated conditions, non-Indian students and non-Indian faculty are drawn to these schools. Here we see a rededication to student-centered learning. I believe the very presence and the strength of the tribal colleges in the community will ultimately force a review of the failure of reservation schools to nurture and educate their students.

Tribal colleges are now positioned to empower students to take control of their educational future. In time this fact will lead to social and economic changes in reservation communities. If the tribal colleges can influence this generation of students, life as it has been portrayed on reservations, will finally come to an end, concluding the most abysmal chapter of government neglect and broken promises in American history. And this chapter of history will not be closed by the government for the Indian people but by the Indian people themselves.

The Ecology of the Inner and Outer World

The tribal college, in providing teacher education programs and continuing educational programs for teachers in practice, is posited to bring about the beginning of an authentic dialogue between two philosophically opposed systems of education. Teaching methods for Indians and non-Indians are based on polar opposite philosophical beliefs. Traditional non-Indian education is rooted in learning in the abstract. Native learning is rooted in the belief that we have an intimate relationship with all living things. Moving between the two models is no easy task for most students and teachers. The near impossibility of moving between these two models is well documented historically in the continued failure of Indian students to achieve academic success in the abstract tradition. The tribal college as a role model is breaking the back of abstract learning by returning to traditional ways of learning.

> Gregory Cajete, a highly regarded theorist of traditional Indian education tells us, . . . objectivist research has contributed a dimension of insight, but it has substantial limitations in the multidimensional, holistic, and relational reality of the education of Indian people. It is the affective elements—the subjective experience and observations, the communal relationships, the artistic and mythical dimensions, the

ritual and ceremony, the sacred ecology, the psychological and spiritual orientations—that have characterized and formed Indigenous education since time immemorial. These dimensions and their inherent meanings are not readily quantifiable, observable or easily verbalized, and as a result, have been given little credence in mainstream approaches to education and research. Yet it is these aspects of indigenous orientation that form a profound context for learning through exploring the multidimensional relationships between humans and their inner and outer world (Cajete, 1994, p. 20).

Traditional philosophies of Indian education represent ways of knowing and doing through a nature-centered, or an ecological systems, approach. Efforts to force assimilation into the mainstream in the past have focused on teaching trades and skills alien to most Native cultures. The Puritan work ethic laden with values such as productivity was intended to educate Indian people out of their cultural histories and into the American dream. Traditional tribal education focuses on a circle of relationships that mirror the seven orientation processes of preparing, asking, seeking, making, understanding, sharing, and celebrating. Environmental relationship, myth, visionary tradition, traditional arts, tribal community, and nature-centered spirituality have formed the foundation for discovering one's true face (character, identity, potential), one's heart (soul, creative self, true passion), one's foundation (true work), all of which lead to the expression of a complete life (Hampton, 1988).

Mitakuye Oyasin is a Lakota phrase that means we are all related. In tribal education, knowledge gained from first-hand experience in the world is transmitted and shared through ritual, art, ceremony, and today, even technology. Knowledge gained is used in everyday living. Education in this context is education for the sake of life. The essence then is learning about life through participation and relationship within the natural community. This orientation is in direct contrast to a system that emphasizes objectivity and detachment, marginal participation, and perpetual observation. A new paradigm that would bring the two orientations together in a new curriculum would move from a focus on specialization to a focus on holistic knowledge, from a focus on structures to a focus on processes, from objective science to systemic science, and from trying to create knowledge individually and competitively to networking and collaborating (Capra, 1982). Non-Indians in positions of authority need to understand, to accept the validity of that body of knowledge that is the Indian way of knowing. A new circle of education must begin, rooted in tribal tradition and reflecting the needs, values, and socio-political issues as Indians perceive them. The basis of contemporary American education is the transfer of academic skills and content that prepare students to compete in society as it is defined by the prevailing economic, political, and social order. Traditional Indian education represents an anomaly for the prevailing objectivist theory and practice. This reality is a fundamental obstacle to cross-cultural communication. American Indian philosophies of education contain the seeds to new models of education, models that can address the multicultural realities of education in the 21st century. The tribal college mission and its curriculum stand as a blueprint for educators who truly want to provide multicultural learning environments.

The emerging consensus in Indian Country is that you can be a lawyer and dance in a pow-wow too. "Cultural adaptation can take place if it is not forced and there is free inter-play of ideas between the cultures," according to researcher Jon Reyhner (1992). Indian education must be a synthesis of the congruent strengths of the non-Indian and Indian culture, not a process of destruction of a culture and the assimilation into another culture. If we allow this interplay we liberate the learner and the educator to participate together in a creative and transforming dialogue based on equality and mutual respect. We free the learner from that feeling of being needy and the teacher from that feeling of having to be in control. Both become learner and teacher. Together they create a learning experience that takes them to a new level of self-knowledge. They enter each other's cultural universe as learners, not outside figures of authority. By creating a learning experience together they empower one another, altering past negative relationships through the learning process. They become the transforming agents of their own social realities through authentic dialogue.

All educators who have worked in Indian education have the opportunity, even the responsibility to take what they have learned to other non-Indian educators and to begin a cross-cultural dialogue about what it takes to provide an informed learning environment with a culturally relevant curriculum that truly addresses the community needs and breaks down cultural stereotyping. It is this stereotyping that inhibits learning. This is no small role for the non-Indian educator who has worked in Indian education.

Bringing non-Indian teachers who teach in elementary and secondary schools into this dialogue is essential if we really want to change drop-out statistics into well-lived lives. Tribal colleges have a variety of ways of initiating such dialogue between Indian and non-Indian teachers, especially through the presence of satellite graduate programs on their campuses. Major universities who have graduate programs in teacher education preparation should be working with tribal colleges to formulate curricula that will bring Indian and non-Indian teachers together. Montana State University has initiated such a program under the leadership of Dr. Robert Fellenz and Dr. Gary Conti. This program has met with great success in Indian Country. For the first time in Montana history an entire generation of teachers, Indian and non-Indian, are talking with one another, a fact that bodes well for all the students they teach.

So That Our People May Live

Many reasons can be cited for students dropping out of school. Recent studies have shown beyond a shadow of a doubt that the primary reason for Indian students dropping out of school is connected to cultural insensitivity. Native language is an important dimension of cultural identity. Although cultures are always in a state of change there are certain customs and beliefs that help sustain a people's identity. These beliefs are best expressed in their own language. "Indian Nations at Risk: An Educational Strategy for Action" (1991) and the "Final Report of the White House Conference on Education" (1992) recognized the need to retain Native languages as a national priority. They also found that learning more than one language does not retard English language development. In short, children who are more comfortable with their own culture and the place of their culture in a larger society will demonstrate a stronger performance in school. The Task Force recommended that by the year 2000 " . . . schools serving Native children be restructured to effectively meet the academic, cultural, spiritual and social needs of students for developing strong, healthy and self sufficient communities" (Task Force Report, 1991, p. 22). The Task Force had ten recommendations for change. Those ten recommendations were used as the organizational structure of the 1992 White House Conference on Indian Education (WHCIE).

The White House Conference took an act of Congress and four years of grassroots political work before it actually took place. The year prior to the conference states developed steering committees to meet and develop a review of what, for them, were the critical issues in Indian education. Thirty reports were submitted. Twenty-two of those reports concluded that their Native language was in danger of being lost and that cultural priorities were inconsistent with what children were learning in school. The schooling community has made little or no effort to form partnerships with Indian parents in addressing their concerns about the education of their children.

From January 22–24, 1992, delegates from around Indian Country met at the White House bringing to the president recommendations they believed should guide future legislation. The Conference Committee responsible for language and cultural issues was chaired by Chief Wilma Mankiller of the Cherokee and William Demmert, an Oglala and teacher at Western Washington University. They submitted eight recommendations addressing the need for long-term assessment and evaluation of language and cultural programs (WHCIE, 1992).

Both the Task Force and the White House Conference addressed the need for systemic reforms to improve education for Indian students attending public schools. Those recommendations focused on developing intercultural harmony, teacher preparation, relevant curricula, strategies to support diverse cultural needs and learning styles, including parents, finding new methods for evaluating the success of students, increasing intergroup activities at an earlier age, replacing inaccurate information, negative attitudes and discriminatory behavior. They also advised that non-Indian teachers have extensive training in teaching in a multicultural environment, developing appropriate curricula and using authentic indicators of learning (White House Conference, 1992).

Change in the attitudes towards and recognition of the needs of Indian students has been slow in coming. Achievement in the last two decades has had little to do with any change in government attitudes towards Indian students. Change has come when and where it has come because parents are fighting for the lives of their children. That self-determination that was rekindled through the events of Wounded Knee and the birth of the Tribal College is burning brightly. Ask anyone in Indian Country today if this is a passing battle that will fade away into the annals of history and you will hear an emphatic No! Many of these changes that Indian parents and educators are fighting for are changes that all educators and parents, Indian or not, should be fighting for if we expect our children to be happy and well adjusted in school in the 21st century.

Mary Crow Dog, reflecting on the impact of the occupation of Wounded Knee, tells us:

> Once we put down our guns and the news and the television reporters went home, the arrests began. They could say anything they wanted. Whatever we said was gone on a cold Pine Ridge wind. Here where I found my life, my center, my people, where I found my first born, nearly everything is gone now. The government tried to extinguish all signs that Indians once made their stand here. It will do them no good because the world saw. The world heard . . . our leaders murdered by goons . . . Even though once again the government lied

and betrayed us. Even though some of our leaders are still in jail. In the end it will do them no good at all to try and hide it. Because it happened. Today is still not ours. But tomorrow might be because of that long moment those short years ago at Wounded Knee where we reached out and touched our history. I was there. I saw it. It happened to me.

So that our people may live. So that our people may live. (Crow Dog, 1994)

REFERENCES

Bowker, A. (1993). *Sisters in the blood: The education of women in Native America*. Newton, MA: WEEA.

Cajete, G. (1994). *Look to the mountain: An ecology of indigenous education*. Durango, CO: Kivaki Press.

Capra, F. (1982). *Turning Point*. New York: Simon and Schuster.

Clark, Ardy Sixkiller (1994). Native American youth at-risk study, OERI. Montana State University, Bozeman, Montana (ERIC Document Reproduction Service No. ED 373 951).

Conti, G. and Fellenz, R. (1988). Teaching and learning styles and the Native American learner. *Proceedings of the 29th Annual Adult Education Research Conference* (pp. 67–72). Calgary, Alberta: University of Calgary.

Conti, G. and Fellenz, R. (1991). Teaching adults: Tribal colleges must respond to the unique needs and talents of adult students. *Journal of American Indian Higher Education, 2*, 18–23.

Crow Dog, Mary (1994). *Lakota Woman*. Turner Pictures; Fonda Productions.

DeJong, D. H. (1993). *Promises of the past: A history of Indian education in the past*. Golden, CO: North American Press.

Hampton, E. (1988). *Toward a redefinition of American Indian Native/Alaska education*. Analytic paper presented at the Harvard Graduate School of Education, Cambridge, MA.

Kennedy Report. Senate Subcommittee on Indian Education. (1969). *Indian education: A national tragedy-a national challenge*. 91st Congress, 1st Session. (S. Report No. 501 [serial 12836]: IX-XIII, 21–136).

Mercer, J. (1992). Haskell Indian College and the University of Kansas. *Black Issues in Higher Education, 2*, 15.

Merriam, L. and Cloud, H. R. (1928). *The problem of Indian administration*. Baltimore: Johns Hopkins Press.

O'Brien, E. M. (1992). American Indians in higher education. The division of policy analysis and research. *American Council on Education, 3*(3).

Oppelt, N. (1990). *The tribally controlled Indian college: The beginning of self-determination in American Indian education*. Tsaile, AZ: Navajo Community College Press.

Performance of Bureau of Indian Affairs Off-Reservation Boarding Schools. Oversight Hearing To Review the Performance of Bureau of Indian Affairs Off-Reservation Boarding Schools. Hearing Before the Committee on Indian Affairs. United States Senate, One Hundred Third Congress, Second Session (June 10, 1994). U.S. Government Printing Office.

Pretty-on-Top, J. P. (1995). [Speech to the graduating class in education]. Bozeman: Montana State University.

Reynher, J. (1992). American Indian cultures and school success. *Journal of American Indian Education, 32*(1), 30–39.

Reyhner, J. (1993). New directions in Untied States native education. *Canadian Journal of Native Education, 20*(1), 63–76.

Reyhner, J. (1994). *American Indian/Alaska native education.* Bloomington, IL: Phi Delta Kappa Foundation.

Reyhner, J, et al. (1995, Winter). Inservice needs of rural reservation teachers. *Rural Educator, 16*(2), 10–15.

Senese, G. (1986). Self-determination and American Indian education: An illusion of control. *Educational Theory, 36*(2), 153–164.

Senese, G. (1991). *Self-determination and the social education of native Americans.* New York: Praeger.

Stein, W. (1992). *Tribally controlled college: Making good medicine.* New York: Peter Lange.

———. (1994). The survival of American Indian faculty. *Journal of Thought and Action, 10*(1), 101–113.

The Tribally Controlled Community College Act of 1978.

White House Conference on Indian Education. (1992). Washington, DC: Author. Final Report, Volumes 1 and 2. (ERIC Document Reproduction Service No. ED 353 123).

Windy-Boy, J. P. (1994). *The tribally controlled college act of 1978: An expansion of federal Indian trust responsibility.* Unpublished doctoral dissertation, Montana State University, Montana.

———. (1990). *Learning in the social environment: A Crow perspective. Social environment and adult learning.* Bozeman, MT: Kellogg Center for Adult Learning Research.

PART VI
NEEDED AND NECESSARY CHANGES

13 EARLY INTERVENTION PREVENTS AT-RISK STUDENTS

Lawrence M. DeRidder

The school principal is the major facilitator of school reform, the person responsible for getting things right for the kids who need help to make it through. Every school has some students who are unprepared to live successfully within the school's instructional practices and demands and/or its regulations. To accomplish the National Education Goal of graduating 90 percent of all students and reduce the current national dropout rate of 25 percent, we must prevent educational failure at all school levels (National Education Goals Panel, 1993, p. 2).

Children in crisis are at risk to themselves, their families, and to society generally. Most dropouts, without a diploma or the GED certificate, suffer from limited employment opportunities, poverty, criminal involvement, and substance abuse, and are at risk in achieving productive lives. Society pays six times more to maintain an uneducated adult than it pays to keep a student in school to graduation. Prevention, therefore, is the most cost-effective and humane way to help students succeed rather than incurring the social costs of drug abuse, school dropout, or delinquency and the financial costs of welfare, intensive treatment, or incarceration. Albee and Ryan-Finn (1993) concluded that prevention is proactive and reduces the crisis problems of at-risk students by assisting them to change their high-risk behaviors.

A number of recent research studies have concluded that students at risk for dropping out, drug abuse, teenage pregnancy, and/or delinquency share similar social, psychological, and familial backgrounds (Amaro et al., 1989; American Public Welfare Association, 1986; Brooks-Gunn and Furstenberg, 1989; Dryfoos, 1988; Finn, 1989; Jessor and Jessor, 1978; Jessor, 1982; McLaughlin and Vacha, 1993; Mills et al., 1988; Zigler et al., 1992). Whichever problem behavior appears first predicts the likelihood that the other problem behaviors will follow (Jessor, 1982).

The risk factors that predict problem behavior include: poor family management techniques, limited parental/family encouragement to achieve, low parental support and control, history of family conflicts, antisocial behavior of family members, child abuse or neglect, racial or ethnic background, non-intact homes, separation from parents, low socio-economic status, low educational attainment of parents, and chronic poverty (Entwisle and Hayduck, 1988; Hawkins et al., 1985; Jesness, 1987; Jessor and Jessor, 1978; Loeber and Dishion, 1986). Poverty alone causes powerlessness, alienation, educational hopelessness and a sense of incompetence (Albee and Ryan-Finn, 1993; Chilman, 1980). Children who live through these life conditions become poor school performers. They make halting progress, are often retained in grade, become truant, and have minimal participation in and identification with school (O'Connor, 1985). These students, in addition, demonstrate many interrelated problem behaviors such as depression, substance abuse, violence, and low self-esteem (Veasy, 1989). The school's response to what these students bring to school in turn determines their success in school.

Many dysfunctional behaviors are already evident at kindergarten and become more evident each year, culminating in more serious antisocial behaviors during high school (Funk et al., 1986; Simner and Barnes, 1991). Since the root causes of vulnerability for these groups are similar, early identification and subsequent intervention would prevent many dysfunctional behaviors from developing.

To reduce the student behavioral problems administrators face, a comprehensive and consistent K–12 program that facilitates the development of social and academic skills for all students is required. This program must examine the school climate, classroom instructional practices, school policies, and organizational structure to which the students respond. To reduce behavioral problems, Goplerud (1991) recommended that the plan should include the following elements: good program management, adequate use of program resources, a response to basic student needs, multi-faceted plans to meet the complex problems of youth, flexibility, limited red tape, an outreach to the at-risk student, equitable response to different ethnic/racial groups, early intervention, the use of adults as models and as mentors, parent involvement, and an expectation of different effects on different students (pp. 4–7).

Because social skill development contributes heavily to academic achievement and conduct, much research consistently recommends the need to improve students' social skills. Consequently, schools must encourage student-student communication. Small task-oriented classroom groups and more activity programs of interest to the at-risk will help them to achieve feelings of self-adequacy, to interact positively, and to develop the ability to cooperate. In addition, the extensive involvement of others—the peer groups, the home, and the school's social community—is critically important.

To prevent later behavior problems such as alcohol and drug use, teenage pregnancy, and school dropouts, interventions must *first* be available at the preschool and early elementary levels. For many children their initial entry into the school is a major transition to values and social norms quite different from what they have experienced in the family. Unless each child makes this transition comfortably and successfully, as evidenced by meeting the expectations of the teacher and school, the school is setting the stage for later problems. Enhancing a feeling of self-adequacy and of competence is the best way to prevent many kinds of problems.

Children who are less ready for school than their peers need immediate assistance and caring interaction with the school's teachers and counselor. If they do not begin to be academically successful, they will more likely be either among those retained (failed), or, the longer they remain in school, lag increasingly behind their peers in basic skill development. Therefore each child must be successful socially and academically in kindergarten and at least through the third grade in order to bond with the school and its purposes. Thereafter success in each grade will be more likely. As a result of identifying at-risk children early and providing each of them with appropriate interventions, the later behavioral crises of drug abuse, teen pregnancy, and dropping out will be greatly reduced. In turn the school more effectively serves society.

What can the school principal do? Principals at all levels can assist their teachers in making an early identification of at-risk students, preferably completed within the first month of school. School counselors can help teachers select or develop a valid instrument, each incorporating some of the family variables that are most influential in creating problem behaviors. Several approaches are already available.

Spivak (1983) found that adolescent conduct and behavioral problems could have been predicted in kindergarten or first grade when teachers observed acting out, overinvolvement in socially disturbing behaviors, impatience, impulsivity, defiance, and negativism. One possible scale that teachers can use, developed by Spivack and Swift (1973), is the *Devereaux Elementary School Behavior Rating Scale* (K–6). This scale rates such behaviors as disrespect or defiance, impatience, classroom disturbance, irrelevant responsive behaviors, and external blaming. Research using this scale confirmed that it was highly capable of identifying children at grade levels

K–6 who were at high risk for later delinquent behavior. Other indicators that would identify at-risk children at the kindergarten through third grade levels include: number of parents in the home; father's education; family income; gender; and membership in a black or other ethnic group.

At middle-school grade levels research has found teachers' comments in reading and arithmetic and/or the number of absences to be useful (Barrington and Hendricks, 1989; Simner and Barnes, 1991). To identify potential dropouts at subsequent grade levels, Weber (1988) concluded that the following four variables were the most useful: days absent last full year; grade point average; years repeated or age relative to classmates; and reading level (pp. 36, 40, 44, 45). Because the family backgrounds of at-risk groups have much in common, these four variables would likely identify students who would eventually demonstrate the at-risk behaviors of drug abuse and/or teenage pregnancy. Students with the largest number of risk factors leave school the earliest.

PARENTS

If our American children are important, serious effort must be given to support and strengthen their families. The adequacy of parental care and involvement with the children affects their growth in language, social competence, and curiosity and, in turn, their school readiness and their future attachment to school (Liska and Reed, 1985; Spivack and Cianci, 1987). The family is the social system within which optimum development can occur and the mediating agent for transmitting the values and attitudes of the culture. If children do not have a nurturant and supportive caregiver at home, they become vulnerable. The extent to which children bond with their parents and feel that they are important members of their family reduces later at-risk behaviors (Finn, 1989) and in turn affects their readiness to attach to the school.

Research data have demonstrated that parents of at-risk children will spend time to assist their children to improve their school readiness when they are provided with simple-to-use publications and easy-to-read interesting materials such as *Family Connections* (Appalachia Educational Laboratory, 1993). The child carries this family-nurtured self-esteem into life (California Task Force to Promote Self-esteem and Personal and Social Responsibility, 1990).

A number of techniques that schools might adopt or adapt to form a genuine school-family partnership and to increase communication between the school and home are available. Suggested options include phone calls or, if no phone, early morning or evening parent-teacher conferences; sending homework instructions to parents; individualizing teacher-parent notes; and class newsletters. In addition, parents need to be encouraged to listen to their children read, to help them with their math, to check their homework, and to reinforce appropriate behaviors. Research data suggest that the involvement of parents in schools, at all grade levels, improves the attitudes of their children toward school and, in turn, increases their academic achievement (Coleman, 1991; Liontos, 1992).

Teachers could consult with parents and their children concerning family situations that affect performance and attitude. When possible, a home visit frequently helps in understanding how the family interacts in coping with its strains, tensions and problems, the several roles each family member plays, and what may be causing or contributing to problem behavior. Teachers who involve parents are successful because they work at it, but it requires commitment, patience, time, and creativity. As a result the parents are more involved in their children's schools and give higher ratings to the teachers who are trying to involve them. Their children are more successful in school and are less likely to drop out (Epstein, 1992).

Many at-risk parents feel insecure about their parenting skills and would like to develop more adequate parent-child communication, set reasonable limits for their children, provide consistent discipline and support, encourage preschool behavioral and skill development, and reinforce appropriate behaviors rather than focusing on defects. Many families respond to their children with anger, neglect, or messages that they are stupid or lazy. Improved parenting skills will help parents to cope with the demands of raising children in today's world and, at the same time, assist them in understanding the developmental changes their child is experiencing.

Support groups for parents can provide information and assistance, preferably at times and in places that are convenient to busy work and family schedules and held in non-threatening and convenient settings away from the school. Some schools have used *Active Parenting, Systematic Training for Effective Parenting*, or similar approaches with groups of parents, step or blended families, single parents, etc. to improve family interaction and communication. Individual conferences on specific problems are also likely. These approaches address changing family responsibilities and patterns and the role of families as teachers (Council of Chief State School Officers, 1990).

The Wisconsin report *Children At Risk* (1986) concluded that low cost and simple intervention activities can be effective, but only if all of the communities' educational and service resources and efforts are used. Within the community the school is the catalyst to equip all of its younger generation to learn and perform the adult roles required for entrance into society, but all of the community's groups must share responsibility for the education of its children.

School

The school principal has the responsibility, on behalf of its students, to create a successful school experience at all school levels and to change whatever it is in the school's environment that promotes failure for many. Beginning in kindergarten and first grade the at-risk children need a successful introduction to reading and arithmetic, one-to-one tutoring if necessary, and home support and assistance. Early intervention can prevent school failure for nearly every child (Slavin et al., 1994).

Students become at-risk because they have not had a reasonable number of school successes; are not involved in any meaningful school activity; and, as a result, have not bonded with the school and its purposes. Being blamed for social and academic problems when they are really the victims is common. Students at risk need the school to help them develop the positive self-concept and esteem that results from positive academic experiences and useful coping skills. They need an in-school support group and an atmosphere characterized by much challenge and little threat (Albee and Ryan-Finn, 1993).

Principals are in a leadership role to confront the barriers to success that the school creates and to suggest/recommend ways to resolve them. To accomplish needed changes the principal must necessarily understand and work with the school's parents, the community, and those others whose prestige, personal characteristics, reputations, special skills, or conservative values exercise considerable influence on the making and implementing of crucial decisions. The immediate critical task is to identify at-risk K–12 students, track them at every grade level, communicate with and involve their parents, and develop a comprehensive program of long duration. The result will likely be fewer retained and at-risk students, happier and more successful students, and fewer administrative headaches. The suggestions that follow include many that effective schools use to reduce student crises. Some practices may already be in place and not all may be necessary.

Possible Intervention to Improve School Retention

1. Many research studies conclude that retention does *not* improve academic achievement but instead lowers the child's self-esteem, makes him or her over-age for the peer group, and sets the stage for dropping out. Most students do not benefit from an additional year to mature or another year in the same grade (McGill-Franzen and Allington, 1993; Shepard and

Smith, 1989). Therefore the school's principal's first approach would be to assist each teacher to eliminate failure at all levels and especially in the K–3 grades. Providing family support services together with tutoring, "hands on" activities, and/or the use of computer-managed learning may be all that is needed. To prevent additional school expense and future administrative problems, a marked reduction in retention should be the goal (Slavin et al., 1994).

2. Insist that the family is the channel through which all the school's efforts are focused. Encourage teachers to find ways to make parent contacts, to make telephone contacts in the evening, and to know the family of each at-risk student.

3. Survey the interests of parents, involve them at all school levels, and help parents feel they are partners in a collaborative process, a two-way communication.

4. Engage both parents and children in school decision making, curricular changes, and activities capitalizing on their abilities and skills and allowing them to be heard and respected. A strong link exists between parents' involvement in the school and their students' success.

5. Provide parents, especially of preschool children, the opportunity to improve their parenting skills.

6. Develop parent workshops in the evening on parent/child communication skills for parents of at-risk children. Some parents may also need literacy and job readiness skills. Children whose parents are learning are more eager to learn.

7. Encourage efforts to provide developmentally appropriate pre-kindergarten learning opportunities and an ungraded K–3 program to allow children to develop and learn at their own speed.

8. Encourage the school superintendent and board to make serious dollar commitments at grades K–5 to achieve: (a) lower pupil/teacher ratios; (b) full-time school counselors for each school; (c) full-time system-wide human service workers; (d) after-school daycare and enrichment for latchkey kids (with an evening meal if possible); (e) health care for kids; and (f) an extended or year-round school to provide more on-task and continual learning.

9. Place the best teachers in the kindergarten and first grade and provide additional resources in order to accomplish learning success for each child.

10. Encourage teachers to be developmentally focused and child centered—flexible, positive, caring, creative, and interactive with their students.

11. Provide students who continue to be at risk of academic failure

because of limited reading and/or math skills with remedial assistance at all grade levels.

12. Encourage teachers to use "hands-on" application of what is taught as well as to relate learning to actual job functions. At-risk students especially need to see *themselves* as participants in the daily lessons (the tech-prep approach) and to see the relationships or connections between their subjects and real-life learning, emphasizing thinking rather than rote memorization.

13. Help school personnel to understand and accept the cultures, the histories, and the communities from which ethnic and racial children come and find ways to bridge the communication gap. These children tend to be among the most likely to become at-risk.

14. In order to improve attendance of at-risk students, as well as to demonstrate that the school cares, on the day of absence check directly with all parents of absent students, preferably by phone, and communicate the school's attendance policy to the parent.

15. Assess student interest in a broad array of possible activities in order to make the school's activity program more responsive to the social interests of all students. Research has consistently demonstrated that assisting social skill development helps reduce problem behavior. Social skill deficits predict long-term relationship problems with others at school, at home, and at work. On the other hand, social skill development improves self-esteem, problem and decision making skills, academic achievement, and the ability to resist inappropriate peer influence.

16. To improve social skills, encourage teachers to place students at work in small, four- to-five-member units that include top, middle, and low performing students in order to reduce social isolation and encourage social skill development. This approach enables students to assist, know, and accept one another, and encourages cooperation. Where appropriate, each participant could be evaluated on the results of the group's academic performance.

17. Because many at-risk students are essentially lost to schools at the transition points, especially to high school, provide school tours for the incoming student group and their parents and monthly orientation activities and a "buddy" system for the students.

18. Because grouping students into tracks assists only the most capable and segregates and limits what the other groups are expected to learn, use heterogeneous grouping at all levels except for reading and mathematics (Robinson, 1992; Slavin, 1987).

19. Encourage school counselors at the middle and secondary school

levels to assist the at-risk students in identifying tentative career interests and in examining relevant job literature (NOICC, 1992). A tentative career choice, once made, improves school attendance, makes retention less likely, and causes more students to graduate (Miller and Imel, 1987).

20. Assist students to develop employability skills and teach them as how to find and keep a job. Help them to obtain part-time work, preferably school supervised and time-controlled. For the at-risk, develop flexible programs and schedules that make part-time work possible.

21. Give leaves of absence for a limited time to students who must interrupt their schooling for circumstances beyond their control, inform them about access to independent study options, and encourage them to re-enroll to complete their graduation requirements.

22. Invite students who have dropped out to re-enroll either in school or in an evening program that leads to graduation. Adjust their programs to their academic and personal needs, including tutoring and a morning or afternoon schedule.

23. Establish a student-run mediation procedure to reduce the need for punishment and suspension of students, most of whom are already at-risk.

24. Develop an in-school alternative program for all truant, suspended, expelled, and other at-risk students in order that their legal right to an education and eventual graduation may continue. At-risk students, preferably, need to be in the learning community to which they have been assigned. Each school then continues to be responsible for the education of all of its students, which in turn reduces the potential loss of state reimbursement.

25. Because the nutrition available to at-risk children is frequently inadequate, eliminate the availability of junk foods and, in the school's cafeteria, the use of lard and hydrogenated vegetable oil. If children lack a nourishing iron-rich diet, and most low-income children do, their bodies respond apathetically and with limited attention span and memory.

26. Initiate a school-based or school-linked health service to provide at-risk youth, their families, and the larger community with preventive education, health clinics, and family planning.

27. Serve as a catalyst to link the school to the community's social agencies, businesses, and industry, and, with them, develop work/study experiences and programs especially for the at-risk.

28. Emphasize equity, the right of all students to achieve. Unfortunately too many schools and too many teachers are using external tests to create school rejects (a "de-schooling" process) in order to accomplish the

current emphasis on high and rigorous standards (Clark and Astuto, 1994). Challenge teachers to help students who are rarely successful to become academically competent and to help the school become a hospitable place for learning. Student evaluations or assessments are of little or no value unless they serve to assist their teachers to make learning more effective.

29. Give teachers a sense of individual empowerment by creating a cooperative work environment characterized by shared ideas and shared efforts, by taking risks, and by implementing new and meaningful learning activities. This approach eliminates teacher competition, dependence, and lack of self-control.

30. Change the school's grading practices. The at-risk are made more vulnerable by some teachers who average the student's initial attempts to learn the subject's content into the student's periodic and final grade. Because of their environmental deficits, some students must take longer to demonstrate the desired accomplishment. The time constraint for grading places undue pressure on achieving adequate performance. It should ignore all process failures and reflect only final demonstrated achievement.

31. Consider a more "authentic" evaluation, an approach that reflects the actual accomplishment of real learning, motivation, and perseverance. The portfolio, the physical and cumulative evidence of accomplishment, may be useful. The typically low-performing student is helped because the portfolio reflects what these students actually know and are able to do.

32. In order to provide for any proposed changes, provide release time for teachers to communicate and to collaborate with others. Additional staff development and pay for work or training beyond the school day would be helpful.

CONCLUSION

Some changes in practice must occur to reduce the number of students who do not make it to high school graduation. Research results clearly demonstrate that these students can be easily identified at their first school entrance and thereafter. Early and direct interventions together with some school reforms that would encourage school success, particularly for those at-risk, should result in many fewer adolescent crises. A major contribution to such an outcome would be a high level of involvement between the schools and parents, prior to kindergarten and thereafter, to develop a team approach characterized by communication and collaboration. Problems begin in the home. Children who come to school healthy, who have bonded with their family, who have participated in early childhood programs, and have had parents read to them are ready to learn and bond with the school. Children who do not have this school readiness and/or who exhibit unacceptable behavior need early assistance and early school success if the school's goals of eventual graduation are to occur. The costs of preventive programs are minimal compared to the social costs of drug abuse, teenage pregnancy, delinquency, and school dropout.

REFERENCES

Albee, G. W. and Ryan-Finn, K. D. (1993). An overview of primary prevention. *Journal of Counseling and Development, 72,* 115–123.

Amaro, H., Zuckerman, B., and Cabral, H. (1989). Drug use among adolescent mothers: Profile of risk. *Pediatrics, 84,* 144–151.

American Public Welfare Association. (1986). *Issues and factors: Dialogue from Wingspread.* Washington, DC: Author.

Appalachia Educational Laboratory. (1993). *Families count.* Charleston, WV: Author.

Barrington, B. L. and Hendricks, B. (1989). Differentiating characteristics of high school graduates, dropouts, and nongraduates. *Journal of Educational Research, 82,* 309–319.

Brooks-Gunn, J. B. and Furstenberg, E. F., Jr. (1989). Adolescent sexual behavior. *American Psychologist, 44,* 249–257.

California Task Force to Promote Self-Esteem and Personal and Social Responsibility. (1990). *Toward a state of esteem.* Sacramento: California State Department of Education.

Chilman, S. C. (1980). Social and psychological research concerning adolescent childbearing: 1970–1980. *Journal of Marriage and Family, 42,* 793–805.

Clark, D. L. and Astuto, T. A. (1994). Redirecting reform. *Phi Delta Kappan, 75*(7), 513–520.

Coleman, J. (1991). *Policy perspectives: Parental involvement in education.* Washington, DC: U.S. Government Printing Office.

Council of Chief State School Officers (1990). A concern about preparing students for employment. *Concerns, 37,* 1–8.

Dryfoos, J. G. (1988). School-based health clinics: Three years of experience. *Family Planning Perspectives, 20,* 193–200.

Entwisle, D. and Hayduk, L. A. (1988). Lasting effects of elementary school. *Sociology of Education, 61,* 147–159.

Epstein, J. (1992). *School and family partnerships* (Report No. 6). Baltimore: The Johns Hopkins University, Center on Families, Communities, School and Children's Learning.

Finn, J. D. (1989). Withdrawing from school. *Review of Educational Research, 59*(2), 117–142.

Funk, S. G., Sturner, R. A., and Green, I. A. (1986). Preschool prediction of early school performance. *Journal of School Psychology, 24,* 181–194.

Goplerud, E. N. (Ed.). (1991). *Preventing adolescent drug use—from theory to practice* (OSAP Prevention Monograph 8). Rockville, MD: Office of Substance Abuse Prevention.

Hawkins, J. D., Lishner, D. M., Catalano, R. F., and Howard, M. O. (1985). Childhood predictors of adolescent substance abuse. *Journal of Children in Contemporary Society, 18*(1–2), 11–48.

Jesness, C. F. (1987). Early identification of delinquent-prone children. In J. D. Burchard and S. N. Burchard (Eds.), *Prevention of delinquent behaviors* (pp. 140–158). Newbury Park, CA: Sage Publications.

Jessor, R. (1982). Critical issues in research on adolescent health promotion. In T. Coates, A. Pedersen, and C. Perry (Eds.), *Promoting adolescent health: A dialogue on research and practice* (pp. 447–465). New York: Academic Press.

Jessor, R. and Jessor, S. L. (1978). Theory testing in longitudinal research on marijuana use. In D. B. Kandel (Ed.), *Longitudinal research on drug use* (pp. 41–71). New York: John Wiley and Sons.

Liontos, L. B. (1992). *At-risk families and schools: Becoming partners*. Eugene, OR: ERIC Clearinghouse on Educational Management.

Liska, A. E. and Reed, M. D. (1985). Ties to conventional institutions and delinquency: Estimating reciprocal effects. *American Sociological Review, 50*, 547–560.

Loeber, R. and Dishion, T. J. (1986). Antisocial and delinquent youths: Methods for their early identification. In J. D. Burchard and S. N. Burchard (Eds.), *Prevention of delinquent behavior* (pp. 75–89). Newbury Park, CA: Sage Publications.

McGill-Franzen, A. and Allington, R. L. (1993). Flunk 'em or get them classified. *Education Research, 22*(1), 19–22.

McLaughlin, T. F. and Vacha, E. F. (1993). Substance abuse prevention in the schools: Roles for the school counselor. *Elementary School Guidance and Counseling, 28*(2), 124–132.

Miller, J. V. and Imel, S. (1987). Some current issues in adult, career vocational education. In E. Flaxman (Ed.), *Trends and issues in education* (pp. 11–21). Washington, DC: Council of ERIC Directors.

Mills, R. C., Dunham, R. G., and Alpert, G. P. (1988). Working with high-risk youth in prevention and early intervention programs: Toward a comprehensive wellness model. *Adolescence, 23*(91), 643–660.

National Education Goals Panel. (1993). *Handbook for local goals reports*. Washington, DC: National Education Goals Panel.

National Occupational Information Coordinating Committee. (1993). *National Career Development Guidelines*. Washington, DC: Author.

O'Connor, P. (1985). *Dropout prevention programs that work*. Eugene, OR: Oregon School Study Council.

Robinson, T. (1992). Transforming at-risk educational practices by understanding and appreciating differences. *Elementary School Guidance and Counseling, 27*(2), 84–95.

Shepard, L. A. and Smith, M. L. (1989). *Flunking grades: Research and policies on retention*. Philadelphia: Falmer.

Simner, M. L. and Barnes, M. J. (1991). Relationship between first-grade marks and the high school dropout problem. *Journal of School Psychology, 29*, 331–335.

Slavin, R. E. (1987). Ability grouping and student achievement in elementary schools: A best evidence synthesis. *Review of Educational Research, 57*, 293–336.

Slavin, R.E., Karweit, N.L., and Wasik, B.A. (1994). *Preventing early school failure*. Boston: Allyn and Bacon.

Spivack, G. (1983). *High risk early behaviors indicating vulnerability to delinquency in the community and school*. Report given to the Office of Juvenile Justice and Delinquency Prevention. Philadelphia: Hahnemann University.

Spivack, G. and Cianci, N. (1987). High-risk early behavior patterns and later delinquency. In J. D. Burchard and S. N. Burchard (Eds.), *Prevention of delinquent behavior* (pp. 44–74). Newbury Park, CA: Sage Publications.

Spivack, G. and Swift, M. (1973). The classroom behavior of children: A critical review of teacher administered rating scales. *Journal of Special Education, 7*(1), 55–89.

Veasy, J. (1989). State awards grants to replicate teen pregnancy programs. *Spectrum, 16*, 31.

Weber, J. M. (1988). *An evaluation of selected procedures for identifying potential high school dropouts*. Columbus: Ohio State University, National Center for Research in Vocational Education.

Wisconsin Department of Public Instruction. (1986). *Children at risk*. Madison, WI: Author.

Zigler, E., Taussig, C., and Black, K. (1992). Early childhood intervention: A promising preventative for juvenile delinquency. *American Psychologist, 47*(8), 997–1006.

14 GRADING AND ASSESSMENT PRACTICES THAT PLACE STUDENTS AT RISK

Charles H. Hargis

We have come to believe that poor grades and poor test scores are symptoms of the problems faced by students at risk of dropping out of school. We have been misled. Low test scores and certainly low grades are not merely symptoms; they themselves are very much a cause of the problems. If they are symptomatic of anything, it is of the wrong-headed approaches we take to grading and testing our children.

In this chapter I will attempt to illustrate the destructive ways we grade and test our students, not only with letters and numbers but in lockstep calendar sequences that have assigned specific doses of curricular items and textual material to each step. I will try to describe our counterproductive assessment procedures, both standardized and informal. I will itemize a number of the most prominent ills that our grading and assessment procedures create. Along the way, I will suggest the reforms that I believe are necessary to change these abhorrent, institutionalized practices. These reforms include the breaking down of our lockstep curricular organization and making it one which assigns curricular sequences to students, not calendar units, honoring variability in learning rates. These reforms also require the adoption of substantive rather than normative assessment procedures and success-based systems of assessment and teaching.

THE WAYS WE GRADE

As if they were agricultural products, we grade our children when they enter and as long as they remain in our schools. First they are graded by chronological age. If they have attained a certain age by a specific date, they are permitted to start kindergarten or first grade with a group of other children within a 12-month age grouping. We even use the word "grade" to indicate each one of the graded levels that constitute the organizational pattern of our schools. We use the term K–12 as a given, as if this were the natural order of things, above suspicion, a part of the given paradigm, so firmly in our minds that there is no reason to question its validity. This is so even though our graded school organization is a relatively new addition to the educational scene (Hargis, 1990).

Within each school grade we further grade our students relative to each other or relative to their performance on the curricular items assigned to each grade. Though we group children by 12-month age units, we have in no way eliminated individual differences in readiness and learning rates (let alone variation induced by social, health, and environmental factors). The curriculum content and sequence provide much of the standard by which the students are graded.

Curricular content is sequenced and distributed over each of the grades. At each grade that segment of the curriculum is again sequentially placed over the 180 days that constitute the school year. All students entering a particular grade are theoretically supposed to engage in learning the content in a lockstep order with their age mates in that grade. In fact, however, all students do not engage in learning to the same extent or with the same efficiency. Every year, in virtually every classroom, some students are not able to engage at all. On the other hand, some students do very well, and some of those are actually confined by the curricular content limited to their grades. This inevitable variation in performance is the dependent variable. The independent variable is the one curricular level supplied by our lockstep curricular organization. Thus one instructional level produces variable performance in the students who are quite variable in readiness and learning efficiency.

Letter grades are assigned to this normal array of variable performance. Those children who are unable to engage, or engage only poorly, are given Fs and Ds. The average learners (those who fit the lockstep structure) get Bs and Cs. Those students who easily engage or who have already mastered the content get the As. For the most part, the distribution of grades assigned in a classroom simply reflects the normal variability of the students in them. I should add that this is the usual case, except for those unfortunate students who end up in classrooms with teachers who have "high" standards. More will be said about this later.

Evidence of this normal variability can be obtained by examining the normative (standardization) data from any popularly used achievement test. These data are collected during the construction of these tests. They express the range of performance of children at each grade level by means of several numerical indexes. In terms of grade equivalent indexes, we find that one can expect more than three years range in performance in reading achievement at the end of the school year in the typical first grade. In other words, it is normal for some children to be reading at the third grade level or more, but it is also normal for some children to be still struggling at the reading readiness level.

If we were to track the reading achievement of this same group of children at the end of each subsequent year in school, we would find that the range of achievement would increase by about a year at the end of each school year. In other words, at the end of the second grade the range would be about four years and at the end of third grade about five.

Figure 14.1 illustrates the widening reading achievement performance that occurs through the grades. Notice also that the top and bottom five percentile ranks of achievement have been omitted. This is done in order to eliminate those children who might be considered "exceptional" by some definition (Hargis, 1995). Even with the highest and lowest achievers being eliminated from the normative data, one can witness the normal diversity in achievement that should, and I emphasize should, be expected in each elementary grade.

Grades simply reflect this quite normal variation in performance. However, normally lower and slower performance is dealt with harshly while higher performance is honored with high grades. One level of curricular difficulty produces a range of achievement when engaging or attempting to engage in the learning of it. When teachers give a normal distribution of grades to these students it means several things: the teachers are giving the same curriculum-based assignments, lectures, activities, tests, etc. to all the students; their students vary in ability; the teacher is not dealing in any effective way with the individual differences of the students. As point of fact, a wide distribution of grades is concrete evidence that the teacher is attending to only the curricular level that is assigned to that classroom and that no individualization of instruction is occurring.

The reader's immediate reaction to the above may well be, "Should not all students in a specific grade or class be doing exactly the same work?" Certainly the question seems almost absurd given our habitual mode of thought on how our schools are organized. The notions expressed here require the reader to escape from this habitual mode of thought and begin to deal with the obvious problems we and our children face daily.

Normal Variability

Notice that though the range in achievement grows dramatically as children move through our lockstep system, the average achievement at each grade remains only a year apart from each adjacent grade. Herein resides

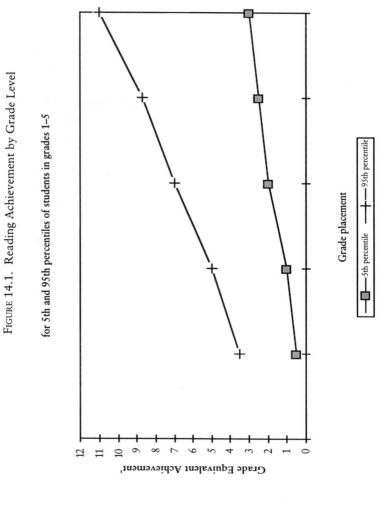

FIGURE 14.1. Reading Achievement by Grade Level for 5th and 95th percentiles of students in grades 1–5

Range, yrs.	.5–3.4	1.1–5.3	1.9–7.1	2.5–8.7	3.2–11.0
Difference, yrs.	2.9	4.2	5.2	6.2	7.8

Source: Dunn, Lloyd M. & Markwardt, Frederic (1970) *Peabody Individualized Achievement Test.* Circle Pines, Minnesota: American Guidance Service.
Note: Figure was prepared from the national norms of this test. Currency can be established by comparing this data with norms from PIAT Revised (1989) by Frederick C. Markwardt, or the norms from any national standardized reading test.

part of our problem in accepting the actual variability that will always exist in any given grade. We confuse average with normal. We forget that it is normal for a wide variation in every human trait to occur in any group of 25–35 children. Parents notice wide variation in these traits even between two siblings. Little variation is expected only between identical twins.

Grouping children by 12-month chronological age ranges does little to reduce normal variation in readiness and learning rate. It is odd that we recognize and accept variability in height, motor skill, artistic and musical talent but are reluctant to accept similarly wide variation in academic readiness and achievement in basic curricular areas. When it comes to school, we attempt to fit all children to rigidly formed lockstep curriculum order.

This lockstep order reminds me very much of the bed of Procrustes, that mythical figure from Greek antiquity. He was the fellow who offered his iron bed to travelers who stopped for rest. However, if the traveler did not fit the bed to Procrustes' liking he would alter the traveler to fit. If the traveler were too short, he would be stretched on a rack; if too tall, then shortened with an ax.

Our lockstep curricular organization is very much like the bed of Procrustes. We try to make every child fit his or her grade. If they do not fit we use our red pens instead of axes and racks. It is indeed fortunate that most children in each grade do fit the tolerance limits of their iron curricular beds. Still, every year, in virtually every grade, three or four children do not fit and are subjected to some excruciatingly painful failure experiences. This has been a problem long noted by a few educators. The late Emmett Betts, a notable authority on reading instruction and reading problems, stated in 1936 that our lockstep curriculum was causing the greatest portion of learning problems. He estimated then that about 15 percent of reading problems were due to children being out of the tolerance limits and so out-of-step and failing (Betts, 1936).

We need to remember that normal variation in ability extends well below and well above actual grade placement. When children are failing and when they are required to repeat grades, it is usually only evidence of the fact that those children are out of the tolerance limits for that grade. We should try to keep in mind that individual differences are not curable maladies and that our lockstep organization cannot provide the standard for normality or wellness. The graded lockstep curriculum and the system of grading students within it cause most of the risk at which we place a great many of our students.

The grading systems based on the normal curve were originally intended to protect students from unreasonably harsh grading by teachers and to add more science to grading practice (Hargis, 1990). A number of different distributions for grades have been used but the most popular distribution of grades based on the normal curve was presented by Florian Cajori in 1914 (Cureton, 1971). Cajori advocated the 7-24-38-24-7 distribution, the top and bottom seven percent being As and Fs respectively, next-to-the-top and next-to-the bottom 24 percent Bs and Ds respectively, and the center 38 percent Cs.

Though the normal curve became a popular concept, relatively few teachers use it. Most teachers use percentage scales or point scales, something on the order of: 93–100 for A, 85–92 for B, 77–84 for C, 70–76 for D, and 0–69 for F. The ranges and cutoff points vary somewhat, but all systems are keyed to levels of failure.

We often hear criticism of "grade inflation," or the increasing skewness toward higher grades. This criticism encompasses the entire history of grading (Hargis, 1990). Unfortunately, however, there always have been children unable to do the work in their assigned grade and so get failing grades. Since there are poor grades to give, there is the tacit assumption that poor grades must be given. Many teachers feel an obligation to give them. There may even be pressure to give more poor grades from school administrators and school boards in the guise of upholding "standards."

Within the framework of the lockstep curriculum, by its very nature, one level of curricular difficulty is provided. Consequently a quarter or more of the students in each lockstep grade will not be able to do their work well enough to reach cutoff scores or percentages sufficient to receive passing or acceptable grades.

Having grades does two evil things. It provides a rationale and a means of approval for having one level of instruction so that we can have poor performance to which we assign poor grades. Then it makes it OK, even honorable, to give poor grades. We have come to the mistaken assumption that being a "hard grader" is the equivalent of having high standards.

We should, indeed, have high standards. However, successful learning should be a major constituent of the standard. This means our standard should be that we want each and every student to engage in learning at the highest performance level at which he/she can do well.

The evil in permitting, even requiring, some students to do poor and failing work is that they cannot learn well, if at all, at that level. Stated in simple terms, one learns right answers by getting right answers and then practicing them, again, correctly. The only thing learned by getting wrong answers is wrong answers. Working at failing levels ultimately requires remedial work to unlearn the wrongs learned.

When students who are doing well get things wrong and need correction, the number of things needing correction is quite limited. The corrective help they receive is helpful. However, when students require too much correction because of large numbers of errors, they cannot benefit because the sheer number of corrections overwhelms their memory limits and intimidates and demoralizes them. Corrective feedback is helpful and efficient only when the students receiving it are doing well and the requisite correction is manageable.

Grades require failure, and failure compounds the risk. Children don't willingly and voluntarily fail, but grading in the lockstep requires some children to fail. For these students learning ceases.

GRADE RETENTION

Grade retention is often a treatment for failure. Some believe it to be a cause of making students drop out of school. Actually, it is not much of either of these; it is another symptom. Since the lockstep has no provision for students to make continuous progress along the curriculum at a pace that varies from that assigned to their grade, the students who can't progress are placed back a step. The lockstep goes on relentlessly. Every teacher repeats the 180-day order of the curriculum assigned to her or his grade or courses. The repetition of the 180-day cycle is the rhythm of the lockstep. It is very difficult to find an appropriate entry point in this system for students who are out of the cycle and failing. The way it is typically done is that an out-of-step and failing student is made to repeat a grade or course. In other words, after failing for an entire year, a student is to start again at the beginning of the 180-day cycle. This is a very inefficient and destructive system. No action is taken to stop failure when failure occurs. If students can't succeed in the curriculum cycle, then they will be recycled entirely; but that typically means 180 wasted days. Even after the recycling has occurred, there is no assurance whatsoever that the students have been placed at an appropriate position in the curricular sequence at a place where they can succeed and make continuous progress.

Grade retention is one of the common items in the educational record of dropouts. It is for this reason that grade retention is occasionally mistaken as a contributing factor in making students drop out. However, it is not a cause; it is only a symptom of the deficiency in the lockstep system. The cause of grade retention and the deficiency in our system is failure. The lockstep produces failure. Failure comes first and is the cause. Grade retention is merely the way we attempt, most often futilely, to deal with failure. The weakness in the system is that it permits children to fail if they do not fit.

Grade retention is what occurs when children are still at an age when they must stay in school. When children reach the age at which they may legally leave school or have to leave school, the recycling stops. They are then dropouts or are dropped out without benefit of diploma or much, if any, learning.

Grade retention is common in the lockstep. What else does one do with a child who can't keep up with the pace set by the lockstep cadence? On the other hand, what does one do with those precocious students who are bored and troublesome when they are squelched to fit the lockstep pace? Teachers with the lockstep mind-set feel no responsibility for providing instruction at any other level than the one assigned to their particular step.

GRADES AND THE QUALITY OF TEACHING AND LEARNING

It would seem that high grades would be evidence of good learning. Students doing well, it would seem, should be getting good grades.

Effective teachers, it would seem, should make all their students do well so as to learn well. It is obvious, it would seem, that students of truly effective teachers should all be doing quite well. In other words, the achievement gains of the students of effective teachers should all be positive.

These seemingly obvious notions are not, however, part of the prevailing view of the characteristics of an effective teacher. In fact, quite the contrary view is often held. Some teachers even feel that some students should not do well. These teachers are content centered rather than student and learning centered. They feel that if the students are unable to learn the content that is presented in their classrooms, the resulting poor performance is a normal and expected outcome. These teachers feel that they must maintain "standards," and the way to uphold standards is to make sure that only those students who are able to learn or master the specific curricular content in their class can be given a passing grade. Poor performance is to be expected. To them, all children should not be doing well. This would contribute to grade inflation.

These teachers equate hard grading with good teaching. They withhold high grades from all but those few students who perform at a standard that is purposefully set out of reach of most children. If all children did well and therefore got good grades, then grades wouldn't mean anything, would they?

Grades have meaning, but grades certainly cannot indicate whether or not teaching is good. In fact, if a teacher gives a wide distribution of grades, it is primary evidence that that teacher is not doing a good job of teaching. Consider what a wide distribution of grades means. First, it means that only one level of instruction is occurring with those students. Students with variable academic skills will invariably demonstrate variable performance on the tasks and on the tests measuring their mastery of it. Second, it means that little or no attention is given to the individual differences of the students. If the students were given learning tasks that more nearly matched their current instructional ability levels, then, by definition of the instructional level, their performances would be acceptable and very similar.

If good teaching is occurring, it is not possible to give a wide distribution of grades. Granted, the instructional activities may vary considerably in their curricular level, but the performance levels should be very similar, indicating a good match between ability and instructional level has been made. The basic measure of good teaching is seen in the evidence that this match has been made. It tells how well teachers are dealing with the individual differences of the students in their charge. Providing appropriate, engaging instructional level activities for every student is the fundamental job of a teacher, and it should be used as the main evidence of good teaching. Our grades and grading procedures misdirect our attention from this fundamental truth. We have acquired the twisted perspective that a distribution of grades is necessary, even good. It is a major obstacle to educational reform in the United States.

Wasted Energy

Educational assessment should be a far more useful activity. It should be used to identify a student's current skill level in each subject area so that instruction can proceed from a developmentally appropriate starting point. Further, it should be used to monitor the appropriateness of the fit of instructional materials and activities to students. It should also reveal explicitly and substantively what students have learned. Stated slightly differently, it should show specifically what students can do, not merely report normative rankings with indexes such as percentiles and grade equivalents. It should show how accurately the teacher has matched instruction and materials to students, not merely show how variably students have done on grade-level instruction and material. It should guide instruction in order for each student to succeed.

Far too much assessment effort is devoted to none of these ends. Most assessment is done in order to grade students. Teachers are required to grade routinely and frequently. Assignments are graded and tests are given and graded. The school year is divided into "grading" periods of various lengths and even the year itself may be a larger grading period. Each school year is itself called a grade.

Teachers keep record or grade books in which to note the scores and grades accumulated through each grading period. The marks in the book are totaled and/or averaged so that final grades can be given on report cards. The point of all this activity in the end is a mark, a letter grade, or a number. It may reflect more than just how well a student has done relative to lockstep, grade-level work. It may also include a suggestion of attendance, behavior, attitude, personality, even dress. What grades do not reflect is specifically what a student has learned or what a teacher should do next in order for the student to engage successfully in learning.

PREVENTING INDIVIDUALIZATION

Assessment should guide the individualization of instruction. Specific information on what a student can do is necessary for individualizing instruction. This information permits the teacher to match instructional activities and materials to individual students.

Our current grading practices are passive activities that simply reflect how groups of students do in their lockstep, group instructional settings. They are passive in the sense that they require no action to match instructional level and activities to students. In a dynamic system, assessment would require that the match be made. Evidence of this match would be uniform high performance. Uniform high performance with variable instructional levels is evidence of individualized instruction. Variable test performance with a wide range of grades results from one level of instruction with little or no individualization.

Some argue that individualization does go on in lockstep systems. However, the form that individualization takes within the lockstep must preserve it. Individualized instruction in the lockstep system attempts strategies to assist individual students to work up to grade level. Different modes of teaching/learning are attempted. Visual, auditory, or tactual modes of learning are explored. New commercial materials, various media, and different lecture and discussion methods are tried. When the resources are available, one-to-one or small group tutoring activities are employed. Here again the attempt will be to help the student with grade-level or course-level work.

These forms of individualization generally have questionable or equivocal results. The reason is that instead of identifying the appropriate instructional level placement for each student and beginning work there, work is done at grade-level placement, which is too frequently at the frustration level.

True individualization itself is frustrated because the lockstep must be served and the grading system preserved. I might illustrate this with an experience that occurred many years ago. I was visiting a teacher in a rural school. Her class was comprised of all the intermediate grades, roughly 30 students in grades four, five, and six. The classroom was alive with activities. The children were engaged in many different things: board work, seat work, small groups reading to each other. I off-handedly asked the teacher how she managed so much individualized instruction. She gave me an astonished look and replied that she didn't do much individualized instruction; she didn't have time for it.

In turn, I said that every one of the children was busily engaged in some activity that was clearly at an appropriate instructional level.

Her response was that of course she had to provide work that was an appropriate level for all her children. They were at many levels, and if she didn't, she would have many frustrated children.

It became clear to me then that we had two very different views of what individualized instruction was. She had the notion that it meant individual attention, much one-to-one instruction.

At one point this teacher raised the issue of grading. She said it was very difficult for her to give poor grades to any of her students. Even when some children were working at levels below their age peers she had to engage them at those levels so they could do well and learn. She could not figure out how to give a "C" or worse to any one of these children when they were doing very well on what they were able to do.

I had no answer. She was required to give grades. We concurred that Fs and Ds were totally inappropriate in this classroom. Incidentally, this teacher had never referred any of her students for special education services—this after a teaching career spanning many years. When asked why she had not, she seemed apologetic and simply said that she had always managed somehow to find a place for and time to work with those of her children who seemed a little "off."

My encounter with this teacher occurred some years before the term "mainstreaming" had been coined and much before the word "inclusion" was ever used with regard to handicapped children.

Shifts Blame

Our notion of good teaching, as was previously noted, is seldom associated with good learning. However, should not good teaching be associated with much learning? Why is it that achievement is not used as a measure of good teaching? Part of the answer to these questions is in illogical perspectives we have on the relationship between grades and good teaching.

When students perform poorly and receive poor grades, they are admonished to work harder, study more, apply themselves with diligence. When teachers give many mediocre and poor grades, are they admonished to perform better? No, teachers are more likely to be honored than admonished for giving poor grades. In my opinion this perspective and this practice should change. Blame for poor performance is readily shifted to children in this malignant paradigm. Poor grades in our lockstep curriculum system are blamed on students. If not put on students, the blame is readily shifted to parents or lack thereof, or to the supposed inadequacies of previous teachers, or to poverty. Grades permit endless finger-pointing. The net effect is that at-risk students don't get a fair shake in our system.

Conclusion

As I write this chapter, I prepare to be an in-service consultant at a high school where tough grading is equated with high standards. The school has a 70 percent or higher class failing rate each semester. Many students are placed at risk and many, without hope for passing, drop out. The concerned principal who has attempted to confront the teachers over this problem was accused of trying to lower the standards.

How will I approach teachers with this mind-set? The ideas that I express here and will express at the in-service meetings are extremely simple and should be obvious. The difficulty lies not in the new ideas but in shaking free from the old ones which, for those brought up like most of us, occupy every corner of our minds.

References

Betts, E. A. (1936). *Prevention and correction of reading difficulties.* Evanston: Row Peterson.

Cureton, W. L. (1971). The history of grading practices. *NCME, 2,* 1–8.

Hargis, C. H. (1990). *Grades and grading practices: Obstacles to improving education and to helping at-risk students.* Springfield, IL: Charles C. Thomas.

Hargis, C. H. (1995). *Curriculum based assessment: A primer* (2nd ed.). Springfield, IL: Charles C. Thomas.

15 EPILOGUE

A CALL TO HIGHER EDUCATION TO KEEP PACE
WITH REACHING AT-RISK STUDENTS

Robert F. Kronick

After reading these 15 chapters, the question arises what roles do teacher training programs play in all of this? It is evident from the material presented in this book that there are many concrete possibilities that could and should be tried with at-risk youth. It is of critical importance that colleges of education, and other pertinent aspects of the university, make substantial changes in some, if not all, of the programs outlined in this chapter. These possibilities are both curricular and noncurricular. I would like to address the curricular first, beginning with teacher preparation in colleges of education.

CURRICULAR CHANGES

I informally interviewed some educators and asked them what they would recommend for teacher preparation and change in colleges of education. An elementary school principal with 25 years of experience made the following four points:

1. Students model what they see in their professors; hence, colleges of education faculty need to diversify their teaching styles, add experiential components to their classes, and keep current with what is ongoing in the field.

2. The principal emphasized the importance of micro-teaching. She said that it was interesting to see the number of student teachers who came into her school whom she could see fairly quickly were not going to be good teachers. "They just don't have the technique." For her, micro-teaching was defined as the breaking down of teaching skills into small workable bits and explaining them to the teacher-learner. This process involved audio- as well as videotaping and involved the concept of reflective practice.

3.   There needs to be an emphasis on multiculturalism. This principle states that colleges of education need very badly to expose students to multicultural issues, because the students they will teach in the future will come from a variety of social, economic, cultural, racial, and ethnic backgrounds. By the year 2010 the non-white child will be the majority child in America's public schools.

4.   A need for teacher education students is to get more involvement with the human services curriculum. Teacher education students need more experience with human service theory and a greater awareness of human service agencies within their community.

The emphasis on a need for greater understanding of multiculturalism runs throughout this book and is a central force in the literature today. Students drawn to teaching and human services work tend to be overwhelmingly white and female. Their students or clients will be children and people of color as well as male.

Multicultural education is certainly not a part of the contract with America, but it appears imminently clear that it must be if we are to see a decease in dropouts, violence, illiteracy, and other social ills that can be tied to America's public schools.

An associate dean of the College of Education at the University of Tennessee, Knoxville, said that by definition teachers are conservative and need to be shaken up. They need to be educated where they come to see themselves as change agents. He said that this would require a move away from tradition. This would certainly require colleges of education to take a long look at themselves. This dean also made the point that it would be of great importance for colleges of education to look at the courses that they offer. Are they merely a collection of courses or are they a true curriculum?

It's apparent that if other parts of the educational system are going to make changes colleges of education must also. It would be nice if colleges of education were the engine rather than the caboose in this change process.

Other themes that continue to appear regarding necessary changes at colleges of education are:

1.   Conflict resolution can be taught to faculty and students while in college. A conflict resolution center might even be established within the college of education. Conflict resolution may be used to settle disputes between students and teachers, between students and students, between teachers and administrators and even students and admin-

istrators. In some areas conflict resolution has been found to be the most effective program to prevent dropouts.

2. The use of curriculum-based assessments where the curriculum is tailored to the child rather than where the child is forced into following a lockstep curriculum. With a lockstep curriculum student failure is inevitable. This recommendation is reminiscent of the one-room schoolhouse. It may well be that small is better and that a return to the past is a great step forward.

3. Another suggestion was to look at curriculum as mentioned above. In many instances there appears to be no rhyme or reason to the courses that pre-service teachers take. At the same time the most highly rated course will often be the practicum or student teaching. This is all well and good, but as Kurt Lewin once said, there is nothing so useful as a good theory. In other words, the field-based learning must have some useful and valuable information preceding it to give it its maximum value.

A Case in Point

To get an *in vivo* look at necessary changes for colleges of education, the following material from the University of Tennessee is offered. The New College, if you will, came about because of perceived shortcomings for the next century. Financial support for this endeavor came from Phillip Morris and the Rockefeller Foundation.

The vision of the New College is that of a dynamic college that is in the forefront to improve education, health, and human services (The New College Document, 1994). Its mission is to promote critical inquiry, reflection, and social actions through multidisciplinary studies. The key component of all this is planning. The planning process, if it is to be successful, must be ongoing. As unexpected events occur the plan will change but the planning process will be continuous.

The social context of the college will play a strong role in how the New College evolves. Being keenly aware of certain social factors will impact the curriculum and its delivery of courses. As reported in several chapters in this book, multiculturalism is a key factor here. This college is committed to multiculturalism. An awareness of the following factors will drive much that must go on in a changed college of education.

Noncurricular Factors

Social factors that are a key to the new curriculum include the changing ethnic composition of our nation and the specifics of the region, that is, Hispanic,

Native American, migrant, and others. A changing age distribution where more people are living longer requires a commitment to life-long learning. An awareness of the older student returning to school will have an impact on how courses are taught and delivered. These students bring new challenges to the field of education, albeit exciting ones. Changing family structure—an increasing number of families where both parents work outside the home—must be taken into consideration when scheduling family conferences at school. There is an increasing number of single-parent families. It must be remembered that sometimes when there is just one parent at home, getting to a meeting may not be possible. The number of children living in poverty is growing faster than any other segment of the poverty population. Schools, teachers, and colleges of education within the university setting must make moves forward to address these horrific facts. The changing nature of the work force—the fact that it takes so many more workers to support a person on Social Security than it did 60 years ago—must be remembered. The need for higher level skills for workers, even for changing an automobile battery, is critical. The importance of technology in the work place cannot be ignored.

Viewing health as more than the absence of disease with an emphasis on human potential is a must. We must see that people have the right to thrive. We can no longer operate on a deficit model but must work on a potential model.

We must work to eliminate stereotypes of people with disabilities. Where else but in the college of education can we hope to see that people with disabilities are not limited by the perception of what they are or are not capable of. Teachers who will be working in collaboration with special education teachers must know how to do this kind of work, hence an emphasis on both the disability and collaboration.

The college will move away from top-down bureaucracy and will help departments spend more time on teaching, research, and service. This new administrative structure will place administrative matters in a central office that will handle these necessary activities. This new administrative structure within the college of education could become a model for schools as well as human service agencies.

Collaboration should be the hallmark of teacher-student learning. There is no question that one of the major findings of this book is that there is a need for collaborative skills to be learned by teacher education and human services students. This collaboration will be with other teachers as well as human service professionals as well as parents and families. What will evolve from this is learning communities where sharing and cooperation and a sense of community will evolve.

What is presented here is designed to impact directly on higher education with subsequent effects on other parts of the education and human service system.

This quote from the National Commission on Children is telling both in its cogency and that it is now five years old. "All schools and communities (should) reevaluate the services that they currently offer and design creative multidisciplinary initiatives to help children with serious and multiple needs reach their academic potential" (Lawson and Anderson, 1996). How many children have suffered because this call has not been answered?

Universities must prepare people who can do this type of work by teaching and utilizing collaborative skills in their classes. Colleges of education must move away from extreme specialization and teach across intellectual and disciplinary boundaries.

The Renaissance Group (1992), a group of deans of education, assert that college and university programs have not kept pace with changes in American society. This group recommends that community agencies work cooperatively with schools.

To this end the following seven steps to collaboration are presented as ways to begin the necessary teaching-learning process to meet the needs of at-risk children (Lawson and Anderson, 1996).

Steps to Collaboration:
1. Communication
2. Clear agreements
3. Decision making
4. Monitoring and evaluation
5. Recognition
6. Trust
7. Leadership

This following glossary of terms (Lawson and Anderson, 1996, p. 164) is at the heart of the collaborative mode.

1. At risk—those children, youth, and families who because of multiple challenges are likely to experience academic, economic, and life skills difficulties.
2. Coeligibility—common criteria. Procedure and application forms for use by multiple agencies and institutions.
3. Colocation—a number of services sharing physical space.
4. Collaboration—a process of joining together education and human

services with the intent to change the way in which services are currently delivered. A collaborative effort must share a common goal as well as share decision making and evaluation duties.

5. Cooperation—agreement made between schools and human service agencies to provide services to students and families; information shared but no common goals are developed in cooperative models.

6. Family service worker—also known as a project coordinator this is a profession that facilitates the collaborative process by assessing needs, coordinating services, assisting children and families, securing services and establishing follow-up and assessment procedures

7. Pre-service—education at undergraduate and graduate levels that address the collaborative process and cross training between disciplines.

8. Resiliency—resilient children possess the following attributes: social competency, problem solving skills, a sense of his or her own identity, and a sense of purpose and future.

9. School-linked services—partnership formed by schools helping human service agencies to provide services to students.

10. Service learning—a process where students learn by actively participating in community volunteer efforts. This process is integrated into students' academic curricula and strives to help them develop a sense of civic responsibility and care for others.

We close with this comment taken from Robert Lawson and Peggy Anderson (1996, p. 168): *"The most important institution for children whose families are not able to provide the support they need, is the school."*

REFERENCES

Lawson, R. and Anderson, P. (1996). Community-based schools: Collaboration between human services and schools as radical educational reform. In H. Harris and D. Maloney (Eds.), *Human services: contemporary issues and trends* (pp. 161–180). Boston: Allyn and Bacon.

The New College of Education Document. (1994). Knoxville, TN: Author.

Contributors

Rhoda Barnes, a specialist in parent involvement and home/school relations, is director of Field Placement for Human Service Education Interns at the University of Tennessee, Knoxville. Dr. Barnes serves as a consultant with local agencies seeking to develop partnerships among schools, homes, and communities.

W. Thomas Beckner, associate professor of English at Taylor University, Ft. Wayne, Indiana, is engaged in developing courses for distance education programming. He has been a television producer and teaches courses in script writing.

Robert Cunningham, professor of Political Science, at the University of Tennessee, Knoxville, has designed and conducted an intensive management development program for the Tennessee Department of Correction and served on the research advisory board for the Tennessee Department of Youth Development.

Lawrence M. DeRidder, an emeritus professor, and former head of the Department of Educational and Counseling Psychology at the University of Tennessee, Knoxville, is now affiliated with the Counselor Education and Counseling Psychology Unit of the university's College of Education.

Jean E. Dumas is associate professor in Child Clinical Psychology at Purdue University, West Lafayette, Indiana. In collaboration with Dr. Peter J. LaFreniere (University of Maine), he developed a widely used psychological test to evaluate the social competence and behavior difficulties of young children.

GABRIELLE ELLIOTT is a legal consultant specializing in Native American educational issues. She is doing research on the legal history of Native American education for use on the Internet in distance learning programs.

CHARLES H. HARGIS has, since 1971, been teaching methods of diagnosis and correction of reading problems at the University of Tennessee, Knoxville; he also teaches in the special education teacher training program. He is the author of several books on educational assessment, reading, and teaching at-risk students.

KATHERINE HIGGINBOTHAM, currently studying law at the University of Tennessee, Knoxville, has worked as education advocate at a shelter for battered women and is a member of the Board of Directors of Families First, an organization in Brooklyn, New York, that assists families with young children.

GRAHAM E. HIGGS has spent the past 20 years in the southern Appalachian region as a counselor and teacher working with at-risk populations. He is currently assistant professor in the Department of Education and Psychology at Columbia College, Columbia, Missouri.

CYNTHIA HUDLEY is an associate professor in the Graduate School of Education, University of California, Santa Barbara. Her research interests include achievement motivation among minority youth as well as peer relations and students' social behavior in the school context.

ROSA KENNEDY's work at the Alternative Center for Learning, Knoxville, Tennessee, as a professional artist teaching at-risk students, supported her doctoral research at the University of Tennessee. She continues to do educational research at the university and is writing a book on teaching strategies for at-risk students.

ROBERT F. KRONICK, is professor of Human Service Education at the University of Tennessee, Knoxville. He serves as a consultant to the Children and Youth Section of the Tennessee Department of Corrections and Mental Health, and he continues to be an advocate for children.

SUNG ROE LEE is a doctoral candidate at the University of Tennessee, Knoxville. His research interests center on policy formation and implementation in education and energy.

JAMES E. MALIA, a sociologist, has directed programs that provide educational services to disadvantaged high school students and rural communities, and has done telephone counseling and substance abuse education. He teaches and conducts workshops in community development, communication skills, and management effectiveness.

SANDRA L. PUTNAM is director of the Community Health Research Group in the Graduate School of Planning at the University of Tennessee, Knoxville. A medical sociologist and demographer, Dr. Putnam has 18 years of experience in health services research, health program planning, and needs assessment.

SUZANNE F. STREAGLE is senior research assistant and survey director with the Community Health Research Group at the University of Tennessee, Knoxville. She has been involved in studies of high school students in Tennessee, with an emphasis on health issues such as alcohol, tobacco, or other drug use and problems.

NANCY TARSI is completing her doctorate in Education and Counseling Psychology at the University of Tennessee, Knoxville. Her specialization is in working with disenfranchised populations in diverse settings that include prisons, residential treatment centers, and alternative schools.

EVA A. THALLER, landscape painter, has been an artist-in-resident at community colleges and public schools in North Carolina and Tennessee. In 1993 she completed a doctorate in education with emphases in Instructional Technology and Adult Education, She now lives and teaches art in an Appalachian community.

INDEX

violent behavior, 198
visual
    bias toward, 181
    information processing, 165, 181
    literacy, 185

Wallis, C., 32
Walsh, R. and Ducharme, E., 14
Watson, James, 135
WAVE, 46, 228
Waxman, H., 143
Weedon, C., 136
Weiner, B., 129
Weiner, M. and Quaranta, M., 6, 16

Welch, J. G. B., 254
West, Cornel, 122, 128
Wheelwright, P., 1966, 126, 128
White House Conference on Indian Education, 282
White, R., 129
Williams, J. R., 255–256
Wilson, E., 123
Wisbet, R. & Ross, L., 5
Wounded Knee, 274, 276, 283–284

Yourgrau, T., 123
Youth Build USA, 46
Youth Development Block Grant (YDBG), 45

SOURCE BOOKS ON EDUCATION